Women Communicating:
Studies of Women's Talk

COMMUNICATION AND INFORMATION SCIENCE

Edited by
BRENDA DERVIN
The Ohio State University

Recent Titles

Women Communicating:
Studies of Women's Talk

edited by

Barbara Bate
Drew University

Anita Taylor
George Mason University

ABLEX PUBLISHING CORPORATION
NORWOOD, NEW JERSEY

Library of Congress Cataloging-in-Publication Data

Women communicating : studies of women's talk / [edited] by Barbara Bate and Anita Taylor.
    p.   cm. — (Communication and information science)
    Includes bibliographies and index.
    ISBN 0–89391–475–4. ISBN 0–89391–476–2 (pbk.)
    1. Women—Communication. 2. Women—Language. 3. Feminism. I. Bate, Barbara, 1943– . II. Taylor, Anita, 1935– . III. Series.
P94.5.W65W66 1988
305.4–dc19   88–1582
                                                      CIP

Ablex Publishing Corporation
355 Chestnut Street
Norwood, New Jersey 07648

Table of Contents

Preface

Rarely will books be created without major contributions by many people. In the case of this book, several groups of people, in effect several communities, deserve credit for the birth of this single volume.

First, the editors of this book* owe a great debt to Julia Wood and Gerald Phillips and their colleagues who organized and chaired the 1984 Pennsylvania State University Conference on Gender and Communication Research. At this gathering the absence of valid and useful knowledge about women as communicators became obvious. We left that conference convinced as never before that this gap in the knowledge about a majority of the human species had to be addressed.

A second community, partly overlapping the first, also contributed to this book. Members of our editorial board were compensated only by our repeated "thank you's" and the chance to add to the store of knowledge about women as authors and editors. The quality of this book is due in large part to the selfless work of these people. While we made the final choices about what to include in the book, the help of these wise and generous people made our work much easier.

The editors and publishers at Ablex Publishing Co. are the third community essential to the existence of the book. They showed confidence in this project from the time they first read a prospectus and brief outline, and have encouraged us through both the normal and not so normal trials that attend this kind of "multiple birth of ideas."

We wish to acknowledge as well perhaps the most important community of all, the marvelously varied and lively women whose intelligence, courage and humor are documented in the chapters that follow. We are proud of having taken the opportunity in this book to contribute to an important feminist goal, letting women's voices be heard. We trust that our work will provide an incentive for others, both inside and outside the academic community, to do more of the same.

Anita Taylor   Barbara Bate
Fairfax, VA   Madison, NJ

---

* Our names appear on the title page in alphabetical order, adhering to a widespread convention. Our work throughout this project has been a happily equal collaboration.

Editorial Board

1

Introduction: Women's Realities and Women's Talk

Barbara Bate

Anita Taylor

Drew University

George Mason University

In 1973, linguist Robin Lakoff's ground-breaking essay "Language and Woman's Place" argued that women's talk is less powerful, and thus less effective, than the talk of men. Lakoff's essay generated a significant amount of both controversy and research. Hundreds of studies aimed at testing Lakoff's thesis have been conducted in the 15 years since her essay appeared. In addition, many researchers have attempted to examine the nonverbal as well as linguistic dimensions of women's talk. Even now, however, Lakoff's thesis remains unproved but not dismissed. What is sometimes called "women's language" attracts responses ranging from celebration to defense to ridicule.

A research conference at Penn State University in April 1984 convened to examine the question "What do we know about gender role in communication?" The several dozen scholars in attendance concluded that if one emphasized the word *know* in the question—"What do we (really) *know* about gender role in communication?"—the answer had to be, "Not much" (Phillips & Wood, 1984). Since a major barrier to answering questions about gender was the lack of knowledge of women's actual talk with other women, the editors began plans for this book.

This book provides original inquiries into the communication of women with other women, a type of research striking in its absence from the hundreds of recent studies of gender and communication. Communication of women with each other has rarely been treated as a serious research subject. Scholarship in rhetoric and communication has focused traditionally upon the study of public communication, and women have rarely appeared as public speakers or visible leaders of organizations or rhetorical movements. Though scholars interested in

1

communication have increased the scope of communication studies during the past three decades—examining interpersonal, organizational, and nonverbal communication—male speakers have often remained the sole subjects of research, or male speech has been considered the normative standard for all human communication. Further, research subjects have been predominantly college students in laboratory or paper-and-pencil research conditions, both quite different from the actual life situations in which both sexes communicate. Little attention has been paid to communication of women as they mature beyond adolescence, or to the ways that gender and communication style vary for a given woman across same-sex and cross-sex communication situations. This book exists to remedy some of these deficits.

The timing of this volume is apt. As more women move into a wider array of public and private roles, knowledge about how they adapt to situations and how others react to their communicative choices becomes critical. Since reliable knowledge about women's talk is limited, there is widespread dependence even in the scholarly community on preconceived notions and gender stereotypes. Citing several reviewers of research who have drawn essentially the same conclusion, Mary-Jeannette Smythe (in press) concludes that "the vigor of gender-based stereotypes is almost as striking as the absence of empirically documented differences in the communication of the sexes." Because researchers have tended to find what they expected to find concerning women's as well as men's communication, it is essential that both scholars and lay readers of research recognize the prevalence of unexamined assumptions in the literature on gender and communication.

Cheris Kramarae (1981) has argued that women's communication should be viewed as that of a "muted group." She and others have noted that it is just as important to know what are the social expectations and receiver perceptions of women speakers as it is to know how women themselves speak. Researchers have only begun to examine how the "male dominant-female submissive" pattern has served as an unproved and untested paradigm for testing the communication of both women and men. When many people of both sexes believe that only men are "natural" public speakers, leaders, and organizers, and when women have rarely been seen as competent, decision-making adults in public or mediated communication, little can be known about speech effectiveness as a human phenomenon.

A point of clarification about use of the terms "sex" and "gender" in this book: many writers have used both "sex" and "gender" to refer to the biological features that distinguish the two sexes from birth. Yet biological *sex* and the psychological and sociocultural features called *gender* easily become confounded when scholars employ sex and gender as undefined, overlapping terms. It is both clearer and conceptually more valid to use the term "sex" to denote the two categories of physical features that distinguish men from women, and to use the term "gender" to refer to the learned and socially evaluated behaviors and attitudes people associate with the words "feminine" and "masculine." The distinction is significant: communication is the means by which most children learn to connect their physical selves with actions that are expected for one sex more than the other. They are born with a label as to sex; they are taught how to relate to a gender ideal (Bate, 1988). Communication continues to affect individuals' views of themselves in relation to these gender ideals throughout life. Women's talk with other women thus bears on the basic symbols by which individuals think of themselves—not only explicit gender labels such as "feminine" or "masculine," but also the implicit gender expectations that are conveyed by words such as "assertive," "cooperative," "dominant," or "caring." What women say to other women, individually or in groups, often alters personal gender identifications, judgments, and values. This volume addresses this issue by illustrating women's styles of talk and women's opportunities to influence one another in joint endeavors.

Some of the studies in this volume directly test the paradigm of dominant men and muted women. Others demonstrate that paradigm as it continues to work in women's lives. These studies bring to light some of the elements of choice that operate when women talk with other women. Since women now interact with other women in a large and increasing number of settings, a major goal in choosing essays for this volume has been to tap as many as possible of the kinds of circumstances in which women talk with other women. Rather than being compared with the other sex, the women emerge in terms of their struggles to articulate their own issues, find their own symbols, and choose their own responses to particular human situations. As a result, the diversity of experience and outlook among women becomes clearer. At the same time, certain values and themes weave through the different accounts of women communicating—a respect for the communication process, a search for identification with others, an effort to take account of multiple perspectives, and a delight in human creativity. These themes will be examined more fully in the last chapter of this book, along with four perspectives that help to illustrate the varying, often contradictory, beliefs and values held about the talk and lives of women.

In terms of approach, the research studies reported here are characterized by qualitative methods—with interviews, participant-observation, discourse analysis, and rhetorical criticism the prominent methods used. The studies share an emphasis on people in natural settings, talking about continuing interests and concerns, and making decisions about matters of importance to them. Our goal in choosing essays to include has been to convey the flavor and variety of particular women's lives as they are lived, rather than to argue that these thirteen studies exhaust the range of women's talk.

The Studies

In the first study in this volume, Sonja K. Foss analyzes Judy Chicago's "The Dinner Party," an extremely large traveling piece involving an array of porcelain plates, needlework, and a display of hundreds of names of individual women in history. Foss argues that a complex visual phenomenon such as this can serve as visual rhetoric, affirming women's bodies, social history, and artistic talents. By shifting the basis for discourse, "The Dinner Party" allows women's voices to be heard instead of muted, and thus offers the opportunity to generate new theory about our own lives and our means of communicating with each other.

A. Susan Owen examines an organization, the Emma Goldman Clinic for Women, which exists to empower women to gain control of their bodies, instead of depending on a hierarchical and paternalistic medical community. The health workers' communicative strategies center on the need to provide women with reliable knowledge about their bodies and means to promote health. As Owen demonstrates, mystification about the body deprives women of the chance to make reasonable decisions, whereas matter-of-fact knowledge about sexuality and reproduction liberates each of us into a more complete and affirmative being.

Carole J. Spitzack in "Body Talk" examines symbols about the body from the standpoint of individuals concerned about their weight and physical appearance. Using a phenomenological approach to analyzing interview discourse, she reveals that the emphasis on beautiful bodies in American popular culture makes it both imperative and impossible for individual women to become comfortable with their bodies and their identities as they currently exist.

Cindy L. White demonstrates conclusively in "Liberating Laughter" that feminists are not without a sense of humor. She shows that feminist humor tends to operate differently from customary joke telling among males, for it relies on situational humor rather than outgroup stereotypes, and it asserts a shared resistance to oppression. White makes a case for the power of shared feminist humor to create and nourish a feminist culture.

Dorothy K. Williamson-Ige addresses the question, How can a black female candidate for president of the United States adapt her public rhetoric to deal with separate black and white female audiences? Williamson-Ige discovers that Shirley Chisholm in speaking to women is consistent in portraying sexism as the root cause of social and political evils in the nation. Chisholm changes her emphasis between speeches, however, choosing different examples of the personal frustrations that can lead middle-class white women or urban black women to identify with Chisholm's vision of a nation free of sex bias.

Deanna L. Hall and Kristin M. Langellier examine "Storytelling Strategies" of mothers and daughters with shared experiences regarding food during family events. The authors develop a series of 10 strategies, ranging from the least to the most collaborative, to demonstrate that—while storytelling can be an isolated individual act in some circumstances—many of these women tell a story in such a way that they define and develop their own mother-daughter relationship at the same time they are conveying information to a listener.

In the single essay in this volume that concerns the talk of fictional women, Barbara A. Larson illuminates the varied means of "Coping with Victimization" of five different women in two plays by Lillian Hellman. Using the theories of Kenneth Burke and Gordon Allport, Larson reveals a wide range in how the five women react to prejudice, from Machiavellianism to religious escape to a display of personal courage and initiative.

Nancy Wyatt focuses on leadership in her participant-observation study of an ongoing group of weavers. By interviewing other members of the Weavers Guild she discovers that the group has more than one kind of leader, with personal qualities of expertise, cooperativeness, and long-term reliability—each having importance for various members. The leaders themselves express a desire to offset their own power and influence in the group with efforts to develop others' talents and leadership.

Melanie Booth-Butterfield and Steve Booth-Butterfield contribute new knowledge about female "Jock Talk" through their interview-survey study of the Jennies, a nationally-ranked women's college basketball team. They find a high level of cohesion among the players, who combine individual competitiveness in the sport and an expressed commitment to avoid interpersonal conflict. The authors note the team's mixture of a "feminine" communication style and their aggressive play on the field, concluding that the development of a team subculture has aided the team in living with the apparent contradictions in its behavior.

Marie Nelson analyzes in "Women's Ways" the interaction patterns and implied rules of five teacher-researcher teams that she has supervised in a university tutorial center. While the teams do not exclude men, the large majority of members have been women. The teams' patterns of collaboration, collegiality, and interpersonal support have been noticed by some male members as being strikingly different from their own experiences in hierarchical organizations. Nelson reports that such differences can make it difficult to switch from a "feminine" style of teamwork to a more competitive style expected in other settings.

Cynthia M. Lont follows the fortunes of Redwood Records from its founding in 1973 as a production company for singer-activist Holly Near to its present existence as an alternative institution, one which seeks to maintain feminist goals, to form coalitions with ecological and antiwar groups, and to make enough money selling records to support its social change agenda. Lont claims that Redwood Records has found a workable middle ground between the structurelessness of completely open communication and the strict hierarchy characteristic of traditional businesses.

Lynette Secombe-Eastland analyzes the communication of the collective of women who ran a feminist bookstore-coffeehouse, as the women attempt to deal with a mixture of "Ideology, Contradiction, and Change." The group's expressed goal, to provide a safe haven for Salt Lake City lesbians, conflicted with their need to sell books and food to a wider community to support their meeting place. A participant-observer in the situation, Eastland shows some of the ways that the organization's communication processes both addressed and denied their basic conflict.

Anita Taylor examines another feminist organization in the arts, Studio D of the National Film Board of Canada. This unit, created in 1974 to join the other English production units within the Film Board, has evolved from the production of films by, for, and about women toward the goal of producing feminist films in an atmosphere of collaboration and mutual support. Taylor discusses the tensions brought about by the mixture of feminist philosophy, a structure with central leadership by the executive producer, and an environment where feminist insights and situational constraints frequently come into conflict.

References

Bate, B. (1988). *Communication and the sexes*. New York: Harper and Row.

Kramarae, C. (1981). *Women and men speaking: Frameworks for analysis*. Rowley, MA: Newbury House.

Lakoff, R. (1973). Language and woman's place. *Language in Society, 2*, 45–80.

Phillips, G., & Wood, J. (1984). Report of the conference on gender and communication research. *Communication Quarterly, 32*, 175–76.

Smythe, M. J. (in press). Sex differences in communication: An analysis. In B. Dervin (Ed.), *Progress in communication sciences*, Vol. 10. Norwood, NJ: Ablex.

2

Judy Chicago's *The Dinner Party:* Empowering of Women's Voice in Visual Art

Sonja K. Foss

University of Oregon

With his notion of the discursive formation, Michel Foucault has focused attention on the lack of input into mainstream discourse by subordinate groups on the periphery of society. A discursive formation is the code of a culture that governs "its language, its schemas of perception, its exchanges, its techniques, its values, the hierarchy of its practices" (Foucault, 1970, p. *xx*). It is the characteristic system, structure, or network that defines the conditions for the possibility of knowledge or for the world view of an age. Various rules govern who is allowed to speak and be heard in a discursive formation, the conditions under which they are allowed to speak, and the content and form their discourse must assume (Foucault, 1972, pp. 41–44, 56–67, 68, 224–225). Knowledge is generated by the discursive practices of a discursive formation so that those individuals who are not "heard" or allowed to participate in the dominant discourse do not have their knowledge incorporated into the common cultural knowledge.

Kramarae (1981) arrives at similar conclusions about the role of a submerged group's discourse in a culture in her discussion of the minority perspective on language. Minority groups in a culture, she asserts, tend to have little power because they have little control over their economic fortunes or social status. Consequently, they find that their speech is not evaluated highly by those in the predominant culture, they generally are not represented in decision-making or policy-making processes of that culture, and they thus are denied a voice in it. Samuel Beckett (1958) explained this inability to be heard particularly well: "I

9

am walled round with their vociferations, none will ever know what I am, none will ever hear me say it, I won't say it, I can't say it, I have no language but theirs, . . ." (p. 52).

A prerequisite to having their voices heard in a discursive formation or the dominant culture is that members of a submerged group must develop their own authentic voice. They must develop knowledge and discourse out of their own experiences and interpret and label these experiences in their own terms. Perhaps even more important, they must come to see their experiences and discourse as legitimate and valuable. Developing this authenticity and attributing power to it are difficult for a submerged group, however, because their experience has been interpreted for them for so long by others and devalued by those others. The submerged group has been trained to see itself as represented in the dominant discourse of the culture and has come to subordinate even its authentic and potentially powerful voice to that culture (Schulz, 1984). Certainly, the submerged group faces difficulties following development and empowerment of its authentic voice—it must secure acknowledgment of its authority to speak by the dominant group. But empowerment cannot happen without a strong sense of identity within the submerged group apart from the dominant culture. Group members first must possess the "courage to be and to speak. . . . the Courage to Blaspheme" (Daly, 1978, p. 264) the definitions of themselves as powerless that have been established by the dominant discourse.

My purpose in this essay is to identify some of the strategies that submerged groups use to empower their own perspective or to develop legitimacy for the knowledge and discourse that are available to them. I have chosen to examine the discourse of women as a case study of this process. In a male-dominated culture where "[p]atriarchy is itself the prevailing religion" (Daly, 1978, p. 39), women constitute a marginal group. They have been excluded in many ways from public life, and they occupy largely peripheral and powerless positions when they do enter that realm. Because of their different positions from men, women have experience that "is institutionally and linguistically structured in a way that is different from that of men" (Ferguson, 1984, p. 23). Yet, this experience, along with the knowledge and discourse it generates, is submerged, devalued, and generally not heard in the male-dominated culture. As Daly (1978) explains, "It is when women speak our own truth that incredulity comes from all sides" (p. 91). Women's words, because they do not conform to the rules of the dominant discursive formation, are treated as "officially worthless" (Daly, p. 92).

While numerous scholars have attempted to identify the characteristic qualities of women's perspective or voice as a result of their different experiences in the culture, I do not want to make a case either for or against particular qualities as representative of the female voice. Instead, my focus in this essay is on the process by which women come to see their symbols, rituals, and regular practices—the *content* of their experiences that tends to be overlooked in the male world view—as legitimate.

I have selected for the study of strategies used to empower women's voice a work of visual art, Judy Chicago's *The Dinner Party* (a detailed description and photographs of the work can be found in Chicago, 1979). I chose this work for my object of study because of its richness of data. Because it incorporates both discursive and nondiscursive data—words, colors, lines, textures, and images—it may reveal strategies that would not be apparent in a work of discursive rhetoric alone. In addition, if, in fact, women's perspective is submerged in our culture, a work that is free to go beyond the bounds of the conventional language system, which gives voice largely to men, might demonstrate more clearly strategies used to empower that alternative perspective.

In selecting *The Dinner Party* as the data for my study, I am aware of a number of assumptions I require the reader to accept if this study is to be seen as capable of contributing to theory development in communication. First, of course, I am assuming that visual images are included in the scope of rhetoric or communication. As the conscious production or arrangement of colors, forms, images, textures, and other elements in a manner that affects or evokes a response, I see visual images as forms of rhetoric that attempt, as does discursive rhetoric, to influence others' "thinking and behavior through the strategic use of symbols" (Ehninger, 1972, p. 3).

I also recognize that works of art contain both rhetorical and aesthetic qualities. Experience of a work at an aesthetic level is the apprehension or perception of the sensory elements of the object—enjoyment of its colors or the valuing of its texture, for example. But when a viewer attributes meaning to those sensory elements and they begin to refer to images, emotions, and ideas beyond themselves, the response has become a rhetorical one—that with which I will be concerned here.

No one true meaning or interpretation can be made of an art object's function as a rhetorical symbol. To say that an art object has meaning for a viewer does not suggest that it signifies some fixed referent. Rather, meaning results from and requires a viewer's creation of an interpretation of the visual object. Different meanings are attributed to a work of art, then, by different viewers as a result of the differing endowments and experiences brought to the work.

The predominant role of the viewer in the establishment of the meaning for a work of art, however, does not mean that a viewer has total freedom to attribute any meaning at all to the work. A viewer's interpretation is limited by the actual object itself. Although that meaning is not an inherent part of the object, the solid physical presence of a work of art makes possible the work's aesthetic and rhetorical effects. More important, the physical characteristics render one rhetorical interpretation more likely to occur than another.

In my analysis of *The Dinner Party*, I will identify the physical or material properties of the work that a viewer is likely to use as the basis for attribution of meanings to it. While my description may seem anthropomorphic in that I will use phrases such as, "*The Dinner Party* provides" or "the work generates," this style was selected simply as a matter of convenience. I do not intend to suggest that the meaning of the work lies in these physical attributes or that *The Dinner Party* itself is a rhetor capable of producing purposive communication. Rather, I am suggesting that as the physical embodiment of its creator's intention, the work can be examined as containing particular characteristics that are likely to guide the viewer's interpretation in particular directions. The viewer is free to interpret *The Dinner Party* or create meaning for it according to her own experiences, as long as the meaning attributed is grounded somehow in the material form of the art object.

The Dinner Party

The Dinner Party opened on March 14, 1979, at the San Francisco Museum of Modern Art. The show next traveled to the University of Houston in Clear Lake City, Texas, opening there on March 9, 1980. It was shown at the Boston Center for the Arts in July and August of 1980 and at the Brooklyn Museum in New York from October, 1980, through January, 1981. In July and August of 1981, *The Dinner Party* was on display in Cleveland Heights, Ohio, followed by its exhibition in Chicago from September, 1981, through February, 1982. It now is in storage until a permanent gallery space can be located for it.

The work itself is a room-size installation piece whose primary element is an open-centered, triangular table approximately 48 feet long on each side and 26 inches wide. Resting on the table are 39 sculptured plates, each representing a woman from history—from the mythical past through the present. The first wing of the table represents women from prehistory to the decline of Greco-Roman culture and includes plates representing women such as the Primordial Goddess; Kali, an ancient Indian goddess; Hatshepsut, an Egyptian pharoah of the eighteenth dynasty; and Sappho, a Greek poet of about 600 B.C. The second wing of the table represents women from the period of Christianity to the Reformation and includes plates for such figures as Saint Bridget,

Figure 1

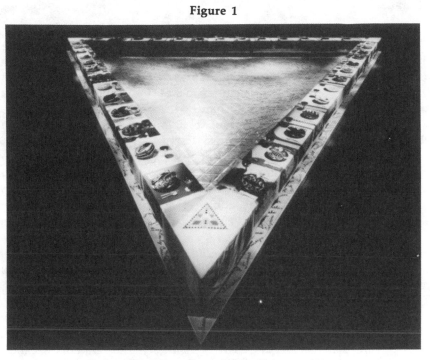

Source: The Dinner Party © Judy Chicago, 1979.

Figure 1b

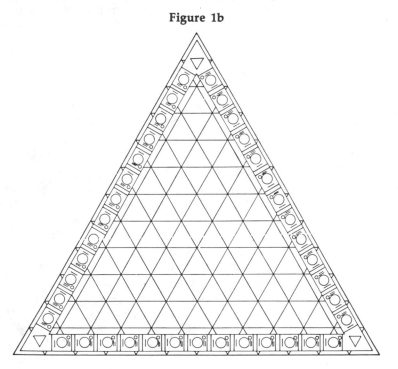

a sixth-century Irish saint; Eleanor of Aquitaine, a French queen of the thirteenth century; and Petronilla de Meath, a woman who was burned as a witch in Ireland. The third wing represents the seventeenth through the twentieth centuries and includes plates for Anne Hutchinson, a seventeenth-century American Puritan and reformer; Caroline Herschel, a nineteenth-century German scientist; Sojourner Truth, an American abolitionist and feminist; and English writer Virginia Woolf.

Each place setting includes a ceramic or painted china plate, a gold-lined ceramic goblet, lustre flatware, a gold-edged napkin, and an elaborate needlework runner that contains the name of the woman represented in gold script. The goblets, napkins, and flatware are the same for all the place settings, but each of the plates and runners is different.

The place setting representing Emily Dickinson, for example, contains a very feminine, pink plate with a vulva-like center surrounded by six rows of real lace that were dipped in liquid ceramic and then fired. The plate rests on a round pink-and-white lace "collar" or placemat, and the gold runner beneath it is edged in the same pink lace of the plate.

The plate that represents Susan B. Anthony also contains a center vaginal form—this time in a deep red color, edged by a fold of lighter red. Four molded, draped "wings" spread out from this center and curl up at the edges of the plate, suggesting a butterfly rising from the plate. The butterfly form is a luminescent red, which seems to vibrate against a beige background. The plate rests on a bright red triangle of sturdy woven fabric edged with fringe. Streaming out from behind this triangle are strips of white and black fabric, representing a "Memory Quilt" for Anthony. Embroidered on each white strip is the name of a suffragist from Anthony's period, including Anna Howard Shaw, Harriot Stanton Blatch, and Paulina Wright Davis.

In the plate of Theodora, a Byzantine empress of the sixth century, the illusion of separate mosaic tiles in green, pink, and gold is created through a series of lines etched into the plate. While this plate is flat, in contrast to Dickinson's and Anthony's, it again features a butterfly form. The butterfly image is composed of circles, diamonds, and other forms that suggest traditional designs of stained-glass windows. Theodora's plate rests on a round, braided gold placemat on top of a gold satin runner. At the front of the runner, below Theodora's name, is a strip of purple satin edged with purple and gold lace and ribbon.

The table, containing 39 such place settings, rests on a raised triangular platform called the Heritage Floor. It is composed of more than 2,300 hand-cast white pearlescent triangular tiles. Written across the tiles in gold script are the names of 999 women, grouped by historical

Figure 2

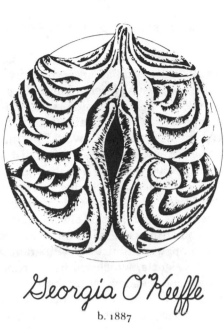

Georgia O'Keeffe

b. 1887

Elizabeth Blackwell

1821–1910

period around the woman's place at the table who represents that particular period.

The Dinner Party was the creation of artist Judy Chicago, born Judy Cohen in Chicago in 1939. She studied art at the University of California at Los Angeles, where the sexually feminine images she employed in her work were ridiculed by her male professors. She began to realize the need for more support for women artists and for recognition that the images produced by women artists would be different from those produced by men. She became known as a feminist artist and in 1969 renounced "all names imposed upon her through male social dominance" (Chicago, 1977, p. 63) and chose her own name: Judy Chicago.

While teaching at Fresno State, Chicago organized an art class for women. With the members of the class, she founded Womanspace, an exhibition space for women housed in an old mansion in Los Angeles. She went on to develop a Feminist Art Program at the California Institute of the Arts in Valencia, which led her to conclude that women artists need an entirely independent structure in which to work. She then organized the Feminist Studio Workshop in Los Angeles. In 1973, the Workshop, Womanspace, and other feminist galleries and organizations were incorporated into the Woman's Building in Los Angeles, which was designed to provide a feminist context for women artists.

Chicago worked on the execution of *The Dinner Party* by herself for three years, studying ceramics and china painting in order to learn the techniques necessary for the execution of the piece. In October, 1975, faced with the growing awareness that she could not complete a work of this magnitude alone, Chicago began taking on help. She obtained the assistance of a graduate student with experience in porcelain to work on the execution of the plates, an assistant to supervise the needlework on the runners, researchers to compile the biographies of the 3,000 women from which the names for the floor tiles were selected, and an assistant to supervise the casting and sanding of the floor tiles. Diane Gelon, an art historian, was added to coordinate the entire project and to serve as second-in-command to Chicago.

In addition to the five or six individuals who fully participated during the three-year cooperative period of the project, about 125 individuals were considered "members of the project," and another 300 assisted with smaller contributions of both work and ideas to the execution of the piece. The work was carried out in Chicago's Santa Monica studio, which had been remodeled with the assistance of a grant from the National Endowment for the Arts to include a ceramics studio, an electric kiln, a needlework loft, and a dust-free china painting room. Thus, although the piece was conceived and directed by Chicago, it incorporated the work and ideas of many others as well.

Strategies of Empowerment

Analysis of *The Dinner Party* reveals three primary strategies used in the work as means to empower and legitimize women's authentic voice: (a) The work is independent from male-created reality; (b) it creates new standards for evaluation of its own rhetoric; and (c) women are clearly labeled as agents.

Independence from Male-Created Reality

In *The Dinner Party*, the presentation of women's culture occurs entirely apart from the male-dominated world outside the setting of the exhibition. It is a separatist piece not only because it deals exclusively with women's culture but also because it lacks reference to anything male. Women's achievements are the sole focus of the work, and men are not referred to in any way in it. The work is formed entirely from women's traditional arts such as china painting and needlework, art forms not recognized as having value in the male-dominated art world. Further, female imagery predominates. The triangular shape of the table is a primitive symbol of the feminine; vaginal images appear in the centers of many plates; and the dinner-table setting suggests women's traditional concerns. *The Dinner Party*, then, encourages the viewer to focus only on women, a stance that has two consequences.

First, the work's independence from male culture defines women's culture as derived from women's positive experiences rather than in opposition to men's culture. It presents the creation or formation of a new, separate symbolic order for women that "does not essentially depend upon an enemy for its existence/becoming" (Daly, 1978, p. 320). Refusal to create in opposition to a male enemy allows the formulation of positive, affirming discourse in contrast to that created from a sense of inferiority.

The danger of focusing on an enemy as the basis for creation and empowerment of an authentic voice, explains Daly (1978), is that it does not allow that voice to grow and develop. It remains at the level of attacking the enemy. The individual who defines herself and her voice only in opposition "may become fixated upon the atrocities of androcracy, 'spinning her wheels' instead of spinning on her heel and facing in Other directions" (p. 320). Betty Friedan (1981) makes the same point, asserting that there is value in a fight "within, and against, and defined by that old structure of unequal, polarized male and female sex roles. But to continue reacting against that structure is still to be defined and limited by its terms" (p. 40). In contrast, in *The Dinner Party*, women's culture by itself is portrayed as rich, abundant, self-sufficient, and positive, with energy and worth arising from its own special qualities. It is seen as having authentic qualities that constitute a significant and valuable perspective in and of themselves.

Definition of women's culture totally apart from men's also enables *The Dinner Party* to present an alternative to the male-dominated view of the world more effectively. It creates this view not by comparing the female perspective to that of men but through presentation of an alternative vision on its own terms. Ferguson (1984) makes a strong case as to why empowerment of a dissenting voice will not result from the integration of the subordinate group into the existing structure. When members of a submerged group attack the system from within by integrating themselves into the system, climbing to the top, and then attempting to change it, they are doomed to fail. As Ferguson asks, after "internalizing and acting on the rules of [the dominant system] for most of their adult lives, how many . . . will be *able* to change? After succeeding in the sytem by using those rules, how many would be *willing* to change?" (p. 192). She continues: "It is hard to be a 'closet radical' when an inspection of the closets is part of the organization's daily routine" (p. 193). The dominant system, then, cannot be resisted on its own terms, since they are terms that render opposition invisible.

Ferguson (1984) explains how discourses of opposition must function in order to be effective: they must present their visions in terms other than those of the dominant structure. This task is accomplished by "unearthing/creating the specific language of women, and comprehending women's experience in terms of that linguistic framework rather than in terms of the dominant discourse" (p. 154). By creating a rhetoric in terms other than those of the dominant discourse, Ferguson explains, experiences are changed:

> Just as our experience is defined by the intuitive and reflective awareness that our language makes available, our language in turn is circumscribed by our experience; to alter the terms of public discourse one must change the experiences people have, and to restructure experiences one must change the language available for making sense of those experiences. (p. 154)

The Dinner Party, then, frames a world and uses images and forms rooted in the female experience. Thus, it poses an alternative to the dominant discourse, the "old molds/models . . . by being itself an Other way of thinking/speaking" (Daly, 1978, p. xiii). *The Dinner Party*, through its presentation of women alone and lack of reference to men, suggests that women "eject, banish, depose the possessing language—

spoken and written words, body language, architectural language, technological language, the language of symbols and of institutional structures" (Daly, 1978, p. 345), inspiriting and empowering their own vision of the world.

Creation of New Standards for Evaluation of Rhetoric

A second strategy used in *The Dinner Party* to authenticate the female experience is the development of new standards for judging women's rhetoric. Just as viewers are led, in *The Dinner Party*, to reject the male-dominated perspective as the only reality, so they are encouraged to develop new means of evaluating women's discourse. Rejection of male domination and focus on the creation of an independent women's reality frees participants from dependence on, as Daly (1978) names it, "Male Approval Desire" (p. 69)—male standards of evaluation. Thus, participants are able to construct their own expectations and criteria for evaluation derived from the authentic experiences of women's culture: "Depending less and less upon male approval, recognizing that such approval is more often than not a reward for weakness, we approve of our Selves. We prove our Selves" (Daly, 1978, pp. 341–342).

The evaluation typically accorded the discourse of a submerged group such as women tends to be negative. One of the earliest to express this view formally was Otto Jespersen in 1922, who described women's speech as an aberration of men's. He said women use less complex sentences, talk faster and with less thought, and have less extensive vocabularies than men. Studies that revealed that women's speech contained more hedges and qualifiers frequently were interpreted as suggesting women's lack of certainty and confidence, while nonverbal gestures sometimes described as characteristic of women, such as more frequent smiling and eye contact, were seen as suggesting powerlessness and submissiveness. These kinds of conclusions illustrate a view of women's speech as a deviation from "real speech." It is "non-standard" because it is different from the speech of men and does not conform to the norms of male speech; consequently, it is inferior. When women's rhetoric is judged negatively according to the standard of conformity to male rhetoric, it is accorded little status and is unable to affect, in any significant way, the dominant discourse (Kramarae, 1981, pp. 95–97).

In *The Dinner Party*, viewers are able to see a number of possibilities for new standards for judgment of women's discourse. They center not around the impact of women's rhetoric on the dominant discourse but rather around the effects of women's rhetoric on themselves. One standard that emerges is the degree to which the rhetoric corresponds to women's experiences, suggested from the focus in *The Dinner Party* on the dinner-table setting. The dinner-party setting is a traditional one for women. It points to the domestic role usually assumed by women, which includes setting tables, preparing meals, and giving dinner parties. The traditional art forms of needlework and china painting used in the work—traditional art forms for women—also are derived from women's experiences, as are the vaginally suggestive images of many of the plates, corresponding to women's biological and physical experiences.

A second standard suggested by *The Dinner Party* to use in assessing women's rhetoric is whether female imagery is presented as positive and valuable. Application of this standard suggests that images unique to or at least typical of the submerged group must not be demeaned, as they might be outside of the culture. In *The Dinner Party*, Chicago almost makes the feminine holy by elevating and celebrating female imagery and traditionally female arts to provide affirmative symbols for women. Because each woman represented at the table stands for one or more aspects of women's experiences and achievements, the viewer is led to see that women have achieved in many areas throughout history, which also points to the notion that the feminine is valuable. The idea is repeated in the sophistication and excellent craftsmanship of the plates and runners, suggesting that women's creations and women as creators are outstanding and certainly deserving of positive evaluations. The 13 place settings on each side of the table, which suggest the 13 individuals seated at the Last Supper, encourage the conclusion that this is a gathering of particular worth and significance, again suggesting the value of the female.

The Dinner Party has the potential capacity to evoke a number of strong emotions in its viewers, suggesting yet another standard by which to judge women's rhetoric—its capacity to evoke emotions. A submerged group develops authenticity and legitimacy only when its users are excited by that discourse and thus have strong desires to use and maintain it. One emotion evoked by *The Dinner Party* is hope or optimism, which is generated by the work's presentation of steady progress in women's status and condition. This progress is suggested by the gradual rising of the butterfly images of the plates as they move from historical to contemporary times. The plates representing the contemporary women appear as though they may fly off the plates, suggesting continued growth and movement for women in their accomplishments and achievements. Viewers also are encouraged to feel the emotion of pride in the accomplishments of women through the numerous women represented in the work as well as anger that the many achievements of women presented in the piece have been ignored for so long. The variety and the brightness of the colors used in *The*

Dinner Party also function to induce qualities of joy, celebration, and excitement in the female experience.

A fourth criterion offered in *The Dinner Party* by which women's rhetoric might be judged is whether or not the rhetoric provides a context in which it should be viewed. When rhetoric is presented apart from the dominant culture, it may appear disconnected, irrelevant, and perhaps even a bit absurd simply because it does not conform to the standards established in the dominant discourse. To avoid these negative perceptions, a new context is needed so that the users of the rhetoric understand it in a context in which it is significant and legitimate.

The provision of context can assume many forms. In *The Dinner Party*, context is provided for women's voice through a presentation of the history of that voice. Of particular importance to a submerged group is the need for knowledge of its history—usually a history that has been forgotten or suppressed by the dominant group. The recapturing of that history provides a basis for constructing current culture and generates a sense of pride in it. In *The Dinner Party*, women's history is re-created for viewers through the traditional women's art forms of needlework and china painting. It is also shown in the presentation of women's accomplishments from the past, both in the plates representing women and in the names of women on the Heritage Floor.

A second way in which context can be provided for a submerged group's discourse and knowledge is through presentation of a vision for that group in the future. Such a vision suggests to members of the group that their rhetoric will survive and that it will continue to create a version of reality that is authentic and strong. *The Dinner Party* helps viewers envision the future of women's culture, discourse, and knowledge in a number of ways. The butterfly image of many of the plates is a conventional symbol of flight and growth. As the butterflies lift farther off the plates as they progress through time, they indicate that women currently are capable of flying much farther than they have in numerous realms of endeavor. The table setting itself creates expectancy and anticipation in the viewer that women will continue to achieve and make valuable contributions. The table is ready, and food presumably has been prepared; the hosts now await the arrival of the guests, just as the viewer awaits further contributions by women.

The rhetoric of *The Dinner Party*, then, standing apart from the dominant discourse and the usual context it provides, creates its own context with a past and a future. Thus, the female voice gains greater authenticity as a legitimate alternative to that dominant discourse.

A final criterion for evaluation that emerges from *The Dinner Party* concerns a work's accessibility. If discourse is to have sufficient impact on its users to be given legitimacy as an authentic and powerful voice, it must be accessible to them. This requirement does not mean that all symbols used must be conventional and concrete and that nothing abstract or ambiguous can be included in the rhetoric of a submerged group. But major aspects of the rhetoric must be available to all participants—regardless of their stage of development as participants in their own culture. *The Dinner Party* exemplifies this accessibility in that it is a work of art that almost any viewer can understand. It relies heavily on conventional form—an everyday, familiar dinner-table setting—that is easily understood and accessible in its meaning. This form evokes expectations that have been learned from past experience with the dinner-table form and that the viewer brings with her to the work of art. Experience with the form, then, makes the image and thus the voice represented comfortable and familiar; the reactions of bewilderment and puzzlement that many viewers may have to contemporary art are not those accorded *The Dinner Party*.

Just as *The Dinner Party* rejects the view that male culture is normative by creating a culture apart from it and refusing interaction with it, so are male standards of the dominant discourse rejected for judging women's discourse. Instead, *The Dinner Party* suggests a new set of standards by which to judge rhetoric derived from the culture of a submerged group: The goodness of fit with the experiences of the submerged group; the degree to which the images of the submerged group are presented as positive; the rhetoric's capacity to evoke emotions; the capacity of the rhetoric to provide a context in which it is seen as appropriate and significant; and the degree to which the rhetoric is accessible to members of the submerged group.

Labeling of Agents

A prominent feature of *The Dinner Party* is that it specifically and clearly names who the agents are in the rhetoric it presents—who has the power and authority to act in the world presented. In contrast to rhetoric in which the agent who is communicating is not revealed, subjects of the rhetoric are clearly named in *The Dinner Party*. The women represented at the table and those whose names appear on the Heritage Floor are described in biographies available to viewers and in the images used to depict them in the plates and the runners. Viewers can learn a great deal about the women who serve as the subjects of *The Dinner Party*.

Simply viewing the place setting of Theodora, for example, tells a great deal about who she was. The tiny squares on her plate that create the illusion of mosaic work suggest her connection with churches. The placemat of gold embroidery that surrounds her plate suggests a gold halo and thus rule in the religious realm. The runner of gold and purple satin suggests royalty, as does the illuminated capital letter of her name on the runner. Thus, viewers of *The Dinner Party* leave the work with a sense of the individuality of these distinctive women's experiences and qualities.

Two consequences arise from this specific labeling of agents in *The Dinner Party*. First, it shows women how they can create and control the discourse and knowledge of their world. Total lack of control and responsibility is the result of rhetoric that mystifies, deletes, or hides the agents involved (Daly, 1978, pp. 120, 123–124). In such rhetoric, women are not able to control the world because that control belongs to some unknown authority that cannot be questioned and challenged simply because it is unknown.

In contrast, when agents are specifically named and described, as they are in *The Dinner Party*, women are able to question old authority and control structures. They are allowed to see that women have been and are active agents who have the capacity to control their lives; this control is not exerted by some unknown source. Thus, clear labeling of who the agents are and the nature of their qualities enables the viewers of *The Dinner Party* to begin to conceptualize about themselves as controllers in relation to one another and to the world.

A second consequence of the labeling of agents in *The Dinner Party* is that it allows and encourages a relationship to develop between the viewers and the subjects of the work. It suggests a reciprocity between the viewers and the women who are the subjects of the work by providing points of identification between the two parties. The agents, because they are made known in such detail, then, may begin to have an impact on the viewers and affect their existence so that viewers' and agents' lives become related. As the viewers investigate and analyze why the subjects made the decisions they did to follow particular paths, the women who are the subjects of *The Dinner Party* may perform the role of guides.

Viewers thus may find in the lives of these women qualities and models to make their own lives whole or more meaningful. A viewer of a place setting representing a woman who clearly was the architect of her own choices, for example, might experience confidence or uncertainty about her own choices or lack of them. Personal identifications may develop between subjects and viewers of *The Dinner Party* as the subjects offer their stories, encourage, and suggest new options for the viewers in their own lives. By understanding better the sources of their respective positions in the world and gaining a clearer sense of themselves from the subjects of *The Dinner Party*, viewers may become better able to see the legitimacy and value of their own discourse and knowledge.

The Dinner Party avoids naming the enemy in order that undue attention is not given to responding and reacting to that enemy. Instead, the focus of the work is on women themselves as subjects. These agents are specific women with concrete stories and personal qualities much like those of the work's viewers. *The Dinner Party* thus creates a strong sense of who women are and of their potential to control that definition, meeting a criterion essential to the development of a powerful and legitimate voice for women.

Implications for Generative Theory

Investigation of the strategies used by submerged groups to develop an authentic voice and legitimize that voice in the face of a dominant discourse yields findings relevant to a number of research areas. One is the possibility it raises for the development of generative theory. A generative theory "is one that unsettles common assumptions within the culture and thereby opens new vistas for action" (Gergen, 1982, p. 133). It is a theory that has *"the capacity to challenge the guiding assumptions of the culture, to raise fundamental questions regarding contemporary social life, to foster reconsideration of that which is 'taken for granted,' and thereby to generate fresh alternatives for social action"* (Gergen, p. 109). A generative theory may accomplish these tasks by instigating doubt, generating doubt and implying alternative courses of action, or fully articulating alternatives to current investments (Gergen, p. 169). Certainly, some research in gender and communication already is contributing to the development of generative theory, but other research is done within the framework of the dominant discourse. What I am advocating is the development of theories about gender and communication that challenge that framework systematically, comprehensively, and consistently.

An investigation of the efforts of a submerged group to develop its own authentic discourse encourages the construction of generative theory in two ways. First, it provides a new set of data or "facts" from which to develop theory. While most researchers generally hold that theory should be premised on sound facts, what counts as a fact is determined by the theoretical framework in which the researcher is operating. When an investigator begins with the facts of how rhetoric operates in the dominant discourse, he or she already has incorporated the consensus of that framework, and "the potential for a generative outcome is thereby reduced" (Gergen, 1982, p. 135). But when an investigator views and collects as data the rhetoric of a submerged group that is not valued by or given input into the dominant discourse, a new theory of communication or implications for current theories may be discovered that encourage us to invent and study "new modes of Be-ing/Speaking" (Daly, 1978, p. 33).

A second way in which this type of investigation may result in generative theory is through an examination of theory in its linguistic aspects. The chief products of research and inquiry are essentially word systems, and the theoretical language selected determines the function the language and thus the inquiry plays in the culture (Gergen, 1982, p. 95, 98). Every theory or form of interpretation can be viewed as a potential form of social control, legitimizing and victimizing various groups by the conceptions expressed in the language of that theory. By formulating theory in the language of a submerged group, the linguistic context of research can be critically examined, suggesting new theoretical conceptions as a result.

When we develop generative theory, as the study of submerged rhetoric encourages, we will have the satisfaction of knowing that we have not necessarily or unjustly constricted our inquiry by neglecting alternative views of understanding, and we will not "place a range of significant restrictions over the kinds of theories that are likely to be developed and sustained" (Gergen, 1982, p. 133). Our central product of research, then, will not be simply an elaboration and extension of a singular world view. Instead, we will have a clearer picture of the production and maintenance of the dominant order from which some of our biases about women's communication and their associated ideologies are derived and clear the air of "the conventions of the powerful solidified into universal truths" (Ascher, 1984, p. 101).

References

Ascher, C. (1984). On "clearing the air": My letter to Simone de Beauvoir. In C. Ascher, L. DeSalvo, & S. Ruddick, (Eds.), *Between women* (pp. 84–103). Boston: Beacon.

Beckett, S. (1958). *The unnamable.* New York: Grove.

Chicago, J. (1977). *Through the flower: My struggle as a woman artist.* Garden City, NY: Anchor/Doubleday.

Chicago, J. (1979). *The Dinner Party: A symbol of our heritage.* Garden City, NY: Anchor/Doubleday.

Daly, M. (1978). *Gyn/ecology: The metaethics of radical feminism.* Boston: Beacon.

Ehninger, D. (Ed.). (1972). *Contemporary rhetoric: A reader's coursebook.* Glenview, IL: Scott, Foresman.

Ferguson, K. E. (1984). *The feminist case against bureaucracy.* Philadelphia: Temple University Press.

Foucault, M. (1970). *The order of things: An archaeology of the human sciences.* New York: Pantheon.

Foucault, M. (1972). *The archaeology of knowledge* (A. M. S. Smith, Trans.). New York: Pantheon.

Friedan, B. (1981). *The second stage.* New York: Summit.

Gergen, K. J. (1982). *Toward transformation in social knowledge.* New York: Springer-Verlag.

Jespersen, O. (1922). *Language: Its nature, development and origin.* London: George Allen & Unwin.

Kramarae, C. (1981). *Women and men speaking: Frameworks for analysis.* Rowley, MA: Newbury House.

Schulz, M. (1984). Minority writers: The struggle for authenticity and authority. In C. Kramarae, M. Schulz, & W. M. O'Barr, (Eds.), *Language and power* (pp. 206–217). Beverly Hills, CA: Sage.

3

Speaking the Politics of Reproduction: Discursive Practices at the Emma Goldman Clinic for Women*

A. Susan Owen

University of Puget Sound

Emma Goldman's likeness, captured and framed in a large, imposing lithograph, dominates the waiting room of the feminist women's health clinic in Iowa City, Iowa. Emma's uncompromising gaze and the deeply etched lines of determination in her face signify well the politics and practices of her namesake, the Emma Goldman Clinic for Women. The clinic, established in 1973 after the Roe vs. Wade Supreme Court decision, seeks to provide general health care and safe, affordable abortion procedures for women in the surrounding areas (Chiavetta, 1980; *Emma Goldman Clinic for Women: A Feminist Approach,* n.d.). The original founders of the clinic chose the name carefully, wishing to signify to the community at large that the practical philosophy of the Emma Goldman clinic would be predicated upon two political commitments: feminism and patients' rights. Emma Goldman, as the clinic is commonly referred to in the community, is so named because of the original Emma Goldman's unyielding belief that all women have the right to determine and to control how many children they will have, and that they thus require easy access to adequate birth control information and methods (Drinnow, 1961; Shulman, 1983; Barki, 1982; Falk, 1984).

---

*Research for this project was carried out while I was a doctoral student at the Department of Communication Studies, University of Iowa, Iowa City, IA 52242. I wish to thank Rebecca Arbogast, former public relations director at the Emma Goldman Clinic for Women, for reading and responding to an earlier draft of this essay.

27

Emma Goldman's commitment to a political philosophy of anarchism almost certainly informed her views on the liberation of women. But it was her practical and often bitter experience as midwife to the poorest classes of foreign-born women that propelled her into the streets and that sustained her revolutionary fervor as she faced frequent imprisonment. The historical Emma Goldman believed that access to the vote and to economic stability were necessary but not sufficient conditions for the ultimate liberation of women from the constraining institutions of church, state, and family (Goldman, 1917/1969). She understood freedom as a quality of consciousness, constituting a perspective on self-in-the-world through which women can perceive of themselves as human beings with political and social potential, rather than as sexual commodities. In an important essay entitled "Woman Suffrage," Goldman wrote that woman's "development, her freedom, her independence must come from and through herself . . . by trying to learn the meaning and substance of life in all its complexities, by freeing herself from the fear of public opinion and public condemnation." Only that, Goldman believed, not the ballot, "will set woman free, will make her a force hitherto unknown in the world, a force for real love, for peace, for harmony; a force of divine fire, of life-giving; a creator of free men and women" (Goldman, 1917/1969, p. 11).

Viewed from Emma Goldman's perspective, a necessary condition for women's freedom *had* to be the ability to choose whether, when, and how often they would give birth. It followed, therefore, that entailments of female freedom consisted both of: (a) the ability to negotiate the constraining forces of the ideology of motherhood, and (b) easy access to birth control methods and education about reproduction. In short, Emma Goldman believed that freedom from the tyranny of reproductive practices was a practical necessity for the economic, political, and social empowerment of women.

For women living in Emma's historical context, such possibilities were out of reach, but 45 years after her death, post-pill generations of women have met at least the second of the two criteria set forth by Emma Goldman for reproductive emancipation. One imagines that Emma would be disappointed—but not altogether surprised—to learn that the technological and discursive possibilities for reproductive freedom have not developed equally. Hi-tech management of human birth loosens some of the constraints on the professional and political development of women, but stands mute in the face of the subsequent politics and moral argumentation about sexuality, abortion, and the "normalizing" cultural standards of mothering. Michael McGee (1985, p. 33) aptly pointed out that modern birth control technology virtually repealed a fundamental law of nature. He observes that "through [recorded] time, we have practiced birth control. But it was not until 1960 that we discovered *sure* means of birth control." Now that women are no longer "prisoners of the reproductive cycle," he argues, both women and men are "liberated in principle from what had seemed for millenia to be as inevitable as death."

Scientifically and biologically speaking, we have successfully duped gametes into avoiding one another: Under the influence of synthetically produced hormones, gametes do not become zygotes. Culturally, we have not worked out with any satisfaction what this scientifically engendered possibility means. Successful delineation of the ethical dimensions of gender relationships, medicine, and law has not occurred. That we can, with little physical trauma to a woman's body, remove a stubborn zygote, predicts with little reliability how we will make sense of that possibility.

Technological possibilities are absorbed into the daily practices of a cultural community by and through talk about the relative merit of these technologies-in-practice. Accordingly, competing discourses have sprung up in the public domain that argue the ethical, political, moral, and legal dimensions of reproductive technologies. In this essay I address in particular the discourse of the feminist women's health movement as exemplified by the Emma Goldman Clinic for Women. Set within the broader context of more general public conversations about sexual mores, abortion legislation, illegitimate birth rates, and so forth, study of the Emma Goldman clinic enables us to focus on a group of communicators whose interests in these matters are avowedly women-centered. I will describe some aspects of the clinic's services for women and analyze some communication strategies used in this health organization where services are doctrinally feminist and holistic and where woman-to-woman interaction is highly valued.

I focus here upon the rhetorical strategies manifest in the spoken discourse of feminist health practices, working from a rhetorical framework to examine critically the perspectives governing the communication practices at the Emma Goldman clinic and the ways in which the practitioners of the clinic position themselves in relation to institutionally powerful discourse communities. Because the clinic struggles to offer an alternative health care for its patients by advocating self-help health care, lay health workers, and patients' rights, it is often at odds with institutionalized sources of medical, ethical, and cultural knowledge. I assess the ways in which the discourse practices of this particular feminist health clinic intersect with, challenge, and evolve within the more conventional communities of standard medical, legal, and educational practices.

Working from published texts furnished to the public by the clinic, interviews and conversations with former and current practitioners at the clinic, published accounts of controversies surrounding the clinic, and personal observations made as a client of the clinic, I identified four primary strategies of rhetorical invention used by feminist health practitioners at the Emma Goldman clinic: historicizing, politicizing, translating, and demystifying. The chief goal of the feminist women's health movement in general is to promote a developing consciousness among women of their right to exercise control over their bodies. The inventional strategies at the Emma Goldman clinic aim to produce for women a new knowledge about health and reproductive practices through which such a control is possible. Consequently, the goals of the clinic are to promote open talk among women, to produce alternatives and choices through affordable services and woman-centered information, and to provide women with experiences that will equip them as competent interactants in the conventional medical community.

Power/Knowledge:[1] The Politics of Health and History

The philosophy and practices of the Emma Goldman Clinic for Women invoke an historical memory of the urgency that propelled its namesake into the streets and back alleys to speak the politics of reproduction. Historicizing women's health care functions to illuminate past abuses or neglect of women in conventional medical practices. Emma Goldman is thus a rhetorically powerful namesake for the clinic, since she dramatized women's historical plight in the area of reproductive and sexual health care. It is significant, therefore, that the discourse and clinical practices of this particular feminist health organization embody the voice of the historic Emma. Further, the practitioners of the clinic deliberately have problematized the control of the body, making the capacity for control a political issue, central to an understanding of fundamental human rights. Politicizing women's health care is a rhetorical strategy calculated to make the problems therein more visible and compelling. In addition, it is a strategy which flows naturally from the political character of feminism.

The politicizing of women's health care is accomplished, in keeping with Goldman's historical commitments, through two different but related efforts. First, the clinic works to insure that the women with whom they interact have access to affordable and safe birth control

---

[1] My criticism borrows from Foucault's (1972; 1980) assumption that all knowledge is inextricably bound to the will to power; that is, all knowledge is power-coded. Foucault's discursive theory of power accounts for the ways in which the production of signifying practices textualize and dominate an environment.

methods. Second, the clinic produces written and oral discourse that relates technological possibilities productively to women's practical experience. That is to say, in addition to dispensing contraceptives and providing abortion services, health care workers at the clinic involve themselves and their clients in the public discourse of political and ethical valuations of human sexuality and reproduction. The clinic's commitment to philosophies of feminism and holistic health frame both of these efforts. The commitments are manifest in the range and quality of services offered to women and their partners. Since a primary source of talk at the Emma Goldman clinic stems from its political commitment to institutional feminism, it is useful here to examine the character and role of feminism in the practices of this particular woman-centered clinic.

Feminism and Health Care

One keystone of the American feminist movement has been a commitment to an understanding of the life world from the perspective of womens' practical lived experiences (Sarachild, 1973). From this feminist point of view, most of the conventional ethical, political, legal, and social claims to "reality" constitute debilitating constraints on the lives of women, denying them a full range of choices with regard to lifestyles, employment possibilities, sexual expression, reproduction, professional development and so forth. In an attempt to identify and overcome these constraints, feminist activists turned to their own experiences, insights, and feelings to make sense of the world (Ehrenreich, 1980; Editorial Statement, 1974, 1975, 1977, 1980; Morgan, 1970; Tanner, 1970). As the feminist movement advanced upon and within the academy, its proponents claimed that no prior accumulations of knowledge about women were above suspicion or reproach (Spender, 1983). Operating from the simple but foundation-fracturing proposition that there is no such thing as disinterested knowledge, feminist scholars set as their task a deconstruction of institutional discourses that had determined the horizons of what was "knowable" about women (Bowles & Klein, 1983).

Scholars and activists developed arguments, methodologies, theories, and case studies whereby the experiences of women were to be taken as legitimate and vital sources of data for the production of academic knowledge (Bowles & Klein, 1983). In addition, feminists took as a fundamental assumption the notion that sex or gender roles have been enforced, perpetuated, and challenged largely through discursive practices. Feminist historians, for example, argue that gender roles and behavior are not based on logical criteria or physiological characteristics, but require social indoctrination. (Kelly-Gadol, 1976; Bridenthal & Koonz, 1976; Norton, 1979; Hartman & Banner, 1974; Carroll, 1976; Lerner, 1969). Gender roles are symbolic constructions that reflect, in any given historical epoch, a consciousness of what is believed to be "true" or "natural" about men and women, their relationships, and their presumed capabilities and inclinations. Feminist scholars and activists argue that any practice predicated upon traditional or unexamined conceptualizations about women and their presumably "inherent" qualities is potentially harmful to women. Subsequently, feminist activists have *argued* into existence legislation which identifies and upholds the rights and privileges of women. They have discouraged the usage of constraining signifiers to the extent that gender discriminatory language not only is prohibited by law in some contexts, but has come to represent intellectual and cultural naiveté as well. In sum, feminist activists have identified, challenged, and to some extent modified a cultural consciousness of what it means to be woman. They have done so largely by creating—through argument, conversation, and polemic—alternative stocks of knowledge about what gender can mean in any context in the human community.

In turning our attention to a feminist health clinic for women, then, we can expect to find a set of discursive practices which (a) assume that gender roles are constructed and potentially constraining; (b) constitute an ongoing conversation about womens' health that seeks to place women in full control of their bodies and all social practices associated with the female body; and (c) create and sustain a practical consciousness of the privileges and responsibilities that accompany a full range of sexual, reproductive, and health care choices. At the Emma Goldman clinic, that is, indeed, what we find. All of these practices are stated in a clearly articulated policy of patients' rights. An explanatory and descriptive pamphlet about the clinic states that "patients' rights include being informed of medical diagnoses, the benefits and possible complications from treatment procedures and medications, the right to read and copy medical records, . . . confidentiality, and access to a patient advocate." The clinic notes that a client is expected, "in short, to become an active participant in [her] own health care (*Emma Goldman Clinic for Women: A Feminist Approach*, n.d.)."

Clients of the Emma Goldman clinic not only have access to adequate information but are encouraged to actively participate in their health care. One of the goals at this clinic is to place clients in control of their interactions with members of the medical and health community. Consequently, it is presumed that clients must be educated and empowered in at least three ways. First, practitioners at the clinic believe that consumers of health care services must be *knowledgeable* about medical practices to the extent that they grasp what is happening during consultation sessions or treatments. As a result, all examinations at the clinic are "talked through" with the client. Women are told in advance what is to be expected in any sort of treatment or examination situation.

Second, practitioners seek to inform clients sufficiently to make competent *choices* about alternative plans for treatment or services (Brooks & Niemand, 1980; Emma Goldman Clinic, 1982; Health Organizing Collective, n.d.; McDonald, n.d.; *Infections of the Vagina*, 1976; *Prenatal Fitness*, n.d.). For example, women who come to Emma Goldman to choose a birth control device or practice will be carefully informed of all available methods. They will be told of the known advantages, disadvantages, effectiveness ratios, and potential risks of each approach. They will be encouraged to examine themselves and to work with more than one device. They will be urged to make their choice based on a consideration of sexual practices, general state of health, and the attitudes of their partner or partners toward birth control responsibility. Final decisions will be the culmination of conversation, thought, and educational instruction.

The third means of empowering clients through knowledge is to help the clients know how to translate specialized medical knowledge into common or practical experience so that they may care for themselves in the best possible way. Because the clinic is staffed primarily by lay health workers, health problems requiring medical treatment must be referred to other professionals in the conventional medical community. However, women referred by the clinic are informed of the alternatives and choices available. This is accomplished through extensive conversations with practitioners at the clinic and through reading material made available by the clinic on a variety of women's health issues and problems. Understanding the side effects and limitations that inhere in prescribed antibiotics, for example, often encourages women to practice preventive health care and to explore natural remedies for early symptoms of minor problems. In sum, the feminist assumption that knowledge empowers is fundamental to clinic practices that function to heighten understanding, clarify and illuminate a range of alternatives, and transform medical terminology into lay conversation.

Translation: Female Experience as the Center of Health Care

A pivotal concern in feminist scholarship in general ensues from the struggle to assess the translatability of gender experiences (Kelly-Gadol, 1976). That is, feminist scholars are concerned with the extent to which male and female life experiences differ radically and whether those "differences" are culturally defined determinants or the inevitable entailments of biology (Boston Women's Health Book Collective, 1984). In the case of reproductive health care, feminist health workers have been concerned with educated self-determination and the development of a wide range of choices. For example, the pioneer health workers of the Boston Women's Health Book Collective argued as early as 1969 that biology need not be destiny for women. Rather, they stressed the importance of enlightened self-help "body education" so that Emma Goldman's vision of reproductive choice might become a feasible and practical reality for as many women as possible. To that end, feminist health care workers stress the importance of creating a critical base from which women may evaluate "expert" information, recognize the constraining power of cultural myths and stereotypes, and overcome ignorance, perhaps the chief obstacle to reproductive freedom.

If we are to understand the ways in which the feminist perspective seeks to reshape or translate conventional health care for women, then we must also understand the rhetorical entailments of translation itself. In other words, how can we say that a feminist translation of medicine and culture creates the critical base from which feminist health care workers evaluate and educate? The translator *acts* on external stimuli by claiming, personalizing, and thereby textualizing the surrounding environment. Feminist health care workers *act* on the perceived authority of institutional medicine and on the lay ignorance of sexual and reproductive health practices through *discourse* that interprets conventional medicine, critiques cultural myths, and popularizes holistic health practices. These textualizing strategies function to personalize health care by promoting open talk among women in general about sexual and reproductive health problems and by involving women directly in their own health maintenance. Not only are women encouraged to turn to other women for input, advice, and reassurance, but they are stimulated as well to value their own experiences-as-women as sources of information for maintaining health.

Translation understood as a rhetorical strategy entails two related maneuvers, each of which may act upon sets of circumstances in order to manage them to the greater benefit of the translator. In some instances, human agents may claim and reshape what is alien or foreign, placing primary emphasis upon exclusivity from other points of view (Gadamer, 1982). Or, human agents may attempt to mesh vastly different cultural experiences, placing primary emphasis upon expansion and enrichment of each of the perspectives involved (Benjamin, 1969). At the Emma Goldman clinic, both strategies are employed by practitioners. However, the emphasis upon exclusivity generally overshadows enthusiastic movement toward interfacing the goals of the clinic with the standard practices of the conventional medical community. This is the case, in part, because of the role that institutional feminism plays in the health practices at the clinic. As emphasized previously, their feminist view of the world grounds itself in conscious opposition to conventional knowledge about women. This is true simply because conventional knowledge about women seldom has been informed by the practical experiences of women. Thus, the acts of claiming and reshaping the alien territory of conventional health care are pivotal functions in feminist health politics.

Both approaches to translation used at the clinic can be seen in the efforts by clinic practitioners to integrate their work into the conventional medical community. Despite the aggressive practices and critical perspectives of lay health workers toward professional medical practitioners, there exists between the two communities an aura of mutual respect and moderate cooperation. Institutional approval of the quality of health care services at Emma Goldman came in 1983 from the vice chair of the Department of Obstetrics and Gynecology at the University of Iowa College of Medicine. In a statement to the *Des Moines Register*, (Santiago, 1983), Dr. Zlatnik commented that he believes "the clinic, in general, provides a good service to [its clients] at a high quality and at a reasonable cost." In like manner, lay health workers at the clinic demonstrate their approval of various physicians in the community through an informal referral system. When clients requiring medical attention bring back good reports of services rendered by specific physicians, workers at the clinic make a note of it, and the name is circulated as "someone good to see."[2] In short, the clinic staff enrich and expand services for their clients through cooperative interaction with select members of the conventional medical community.

For the most part, however, a consciousness of the power of gender stereotypes that pervade the conventional medical community and of the suasory appeals sustaining the political economy have motivated the practitioners at Emma Goldman to translate conventional health care services and products in an uncompromising fashion. These translations constitute a discourse of critical assessment that seeks to enable female listeners and readers to make their own judgments about the potential usefulness and safety of the products and services. This consciousness of the power of gender myths and commercial appeals manifests itself in common communicative practices at the clinic: oral

---

[2] "Because we have close contact with many pregnant women, we often get feedback on local doctors and hospitals. We would be happy to share this information with you. We would also like you to share your experiences with us so that we can pass on this knowledge to others." This paragraph is titled as "Referrals" in a pamphlet printed by the Emma Goldman Clinic (*Positive experience pregnancy* n.d.).

and published critiques of marketed hygiene products and birth control methods.

"Textualizing" as a Rhetorical Strategy

Clinic critique of hygiene products and birth control methods functions rhetorically to "textualize" the cultural environs affecting sexual expression and reproduction practices. Such strategies entail a redefinition of the alien (conventional medicine) and the inexplicable (cultural myths about sexuality and reproduction) in terms of feminist perspectives on manageability, usefulness, and safety. The practitioners at the Emma Goldman clinic recognize that while science and technology often enable people to live longer and more satisfying lives, the results of scientific research and technological innovation are not always well-integrated into the practical lives of lay persons. In the many pamphlets available through the clinic, special care is taken to translate into easily understood prose the specialized discourse of medical terminology, anatomical designations, and the uses, contents, and probable side effects of commonly prescribed drugs (e.g., Brooks & Niemand, 1980). In addition, many booklets address specific health problems that seem to plague a majority of women. Each booklet explains a problem—for example, bladder infections—in full detail, incorporating medical knowledge, a female experience of the problem, and a strong emphasis on preventive practices (Brooks & Niemand, 1980). In other words, the discursive practice renders complex medical knowledge comprehensible, commonsensical, and manageable. Above all, the booklets and pamphlets strive to explain common female health problems so readers will know why and how to manage day-to-day sexual and hygiene practices to ensure the necessary conditions for good health.

Clinical practices at Emma Goldman seek to establish an understanding of health care in the context of women's experiences rather than in the context of professional medicine. Lay health workers at the clinic believe that medical knowledge is often poorly adapted to the practical needs of women because of the power of gender myths and because of the realities of the political economy. Scientific research and related medical practices often are insensitive to the safety, specific demands, and special problems connected with the health of women. In other words, because the experiences of women do not inform the doing of science and medicine, the latter do not provide products and services well-suited to female health care. Cases in point are birth control devices which fail, create health hazards, or are simply unsuited to the sexual needs and practices of the women using them. The serious health hazards of the Dalkon Shield (Perry & Dawson, 1985) and the tragic history of the consequences to female children of DES users illustrate the medical community's willingness to take substantial risks with the lives and health of women. Along the same lines, industrial and pharmaceutical companies that manufacture and market health care products for women often make unreasonable and unsubstantiated claims about the safety, potency, effectiveness, or *usefulness* of their products, thus creating markets for products which have little or nothing to do with health. The "feminine hygiene products" industry, for example, appeals to cultural stereotypes of feminine daintiness by insisting that natural odors are offensive, and paradoxically, unnatural—thereby selling dangerous or medically unjustified products to women. A standard line of conversation between and among women at the Emma Goldman clinic reviews and critiques these realities in the political economy.

Because counselors and practitioners at the Emma Goldman clinic believe in holistic health practices that emphasize preventive activities, they are skeptical of marketed hygiene products. In addition, they criticize the unthinking use of prescription drugs and the misleading information that often accompanies nonprescription contraceptive devices. The informational booklet prepared by the clinic on the subject of vaginal infections argues that "feminine hygiene" products are "often overpriced and probably not worth trying unless other methods have failed" (*Infections of the Vagina*, 1976). The booklet clarifies other methods of avoiding such infections. It cites standard practices of cleanliness, which do *not* include the use of commercial products; gives general guidelines for avoiding the transmission of infections from one individual to another; and describes a collection of home remedies which relieve symptoms and, if used properly and consistently, offset the likelihood of continuing infection. In like manner, the information booklet on bladder infections states flatly that "vaginal deodorants should never be used," because they "contain harmful chemicals which could irritate the skin and cause infection" (Brooks & Niemand, 1980, p. 11). Clinic practitioners argue that the sprays do more harm than good because, in addition to their potentially hazardous chemical composition, they mask natural odors that constitute pivotal cues about conditions of health. These lines of discourse seek to provide sound information for female consumers of health care products and to overcome the constraints of culturally defined "appropriateness" that constrain discussions of "female complaints" to narrowly prescribed contexts. In other words, these efforts are made in the hope of stimulating talk among women about the shortcomings of commercial remedies.

Almost all pamphlets and booklets prepared by the clinic recommend natural herbs and vitamins to prevent and treat minor infections. Extensive description and advice are offered on how to best utilize these natural products. This advice is offered against a background of evaluative discourses on the potential advantages and disadvantages of prescription drugs. While acknowledging the necessity of drugs in treating many painful or potentially dangerous conditions, clinic practitioners also offer thoroughly researched explanations of the chemical composition, positive effects, shortcomings, and potential side-effects of each drug. Since most drugs take a toll on some part of the body, even as they rid other parts of infection, the Emma Goldman clinic advises clients to practice principles of holistic health that might diminish the likelihood of problems requiring treatment by drugs (Brooks & Niemand, 1980).

In addition, feminist health workers at the clinic rebuke sharply the manufacturers of some nonprescription birth control methods. Of the popularly marketed Oval Encare birth control suppository, the *Emma Goldman . . . Newsletter* (n.d. No. 3) argues that the printed instructions on the package are "poorly written, easily misinterpreted, and misleading." Obviously, the potential for unwanted pregnancies is increased drastically by products that are not accompanied by easily read and understood instructions. The health workers at Emma Goldman counsel their clients that birth control suppositories should be used along with some other method of contraception. Clinic staff consider the margin for error that accompanies a 60 to 70 percent effectiveness ratio much too great a risk. Such marketing criticism is common practice at the clinic and contributes significantly to the discourse directed to women about their health care.

The foregoing illustrates the subtle transformation enacted through clinic practices, all of which entail the translation of institutionalized knowledge into the fabric of everyday experience. Health care is represented as a way of life, rather than as a one-down power relationship within which women often feel intimidated by conventional physicians. Explanatory pamphlets are written by women who have mastered technical information and who have experienced the health problem first-hand as well. Having incorporated research and experience to produce a clear explanation of the problem, the writers encourage other women to look to themselves to recognize early symptoms and to treat them sensibly so that the need for prescribed drugs and other forms of conventional treatment will not be necessary. The emphasis on holistic health care encourages women to inform themselves about common, minor health problems, and to rely on their competency of informed "good sense" about health to prevent or treat these minor problems.

Rhetorically, these strategies discursively remove conventional medical knowledge from its traditionally privileged location as the most credible discourse about health-related issues. Conventional knowledge is re-placed, symbolically, at the periphery of women's experience. Choices for prevention and cure are illuminated, but not determined, through access to medical knowledge. Feminist health workers do not deny the value of institutionalized medical knowledge to the health of women. But from their perspective on health, a woman should look to the medical community only as a way to clarify her health problems and to add to the possible range of solutions available. At the Emma Goldman clinic, both choice and the responsibility to act consistently on choices made are said to constitute good health and good politics.

Demystification of the Female Body and the Semiology of the Gyn/Exam

For centuries, women have been denied the ability to exercise full control over their bodies in terms of reproduction, health care, and sexual activity (e.g., Degler, 1975). One of the more powerful means of denying women the right to self-determination has been the denial of access to adequate knowledge about their bodies. As the preceding section makes clear, a familiarity with the body and the various ways in which health can be maintained have been the mainstay of the feminist politics of health care.[3] As the practitioners at Emma Goldman point out, women typically have learned more about their bodies, their sexuality, and reproduction from women's magazines and private conversations with other women than from doctors and clinics. Unfortunately, much of the talk between and among women is marred by misinformation. The Emma Goldman clinic believes that women must regain control of their bodies through creating, possessing, and acting on sound knowledge about them ("Women's clinic," 1982). To help them do so entails inventing discourse and manipulating conventional medical semiology. Both strategies remove disabling mystification from female physiology and from the practical applications of medical science.

A common experience for many women is to be uneasy and grossly un- or misinformed about their reproductive systems, a condition manifest in everyday talk about their own bodies. Many women rely upon euphemisms, veiled references, and slang to make sense of the menses, sexuality, and birth experiences. Such signifiers are problematic because they bring with them cultural and historical baggage which reinforces, at the very least, the mythically "dark and mysterious" qualities of

---

[3] The exemplar of feminist health politics originates within the Boston Women's Health Book Collective (1984).

female sexuality. The practitioners at Emma Goldman have found, for example, that many women do not consider using certain forms of birth control because the devices would require that the women touch themselves and become familiar with their own sexual anatomy. For example, many clients dislike or avoid using diaphragms or cervical caps simply because the women are mystified by or uncomfortable with their own sexual anatomy ("Women's clinic," 1982). The avoidance is unfortunate, both because manual forms of birth control are less hazardous to health than oral contraceptives, and because these women are, in effect, alienated from themselves in the most fundamental way.

To offset anxiety and ignorance, gynecological examinations at the Emma Goldman clinic are designed to be as educational and nonthreatening as possible. In addition to involving clients in their own examinations, practitioners at the clinic have considered carefully the semiology of typical examination settings. The design and utilization of the typical aresenal of ob/gyn examination equipment reflect such thought. Examination rooms, for example, are furnished as comfortable sitting rooms, in pointed contrast to the typically sterile conventional medical settings. Examination table designs permit women to sit up and take an active part in their examinations, thus avoiding passive, prone posture typically assumed in conventional medical settings that inhibits positive interaction between patient and practitioner. The stirrups on the examining table are covered with tube socks, a homey touch which also meets the practical need of blunting the shock of cold metal on bare flesh. Speculums are plastic rather than metal for the same reason—comfort of the client. In addition, because plastic speculums are inexpensive, the clinic provides each client with her own. This particular instrument is potent with cultural meaning, at least among women. For women to be able to control an instrument that has come to constitute *the* phallic symbol of gynecology is not only demystifying, it may be the ultimate empowerment. But perhaps most important, women learn to see that self-examinations are an important part of ordinary, personal health maintenance. Acquiring the ability to distinguish between healthy and unhealthy signs in the cervical area, for example, can help women seek early medical attention for indications of cervical cancer.

Part of the service that clients receive at Emma Goldman is firsthand experience in a health partnership wherein patient and practitioner have an equal relationship. The client-practitioner relationship is designed to train women for effective interaction in the conventional medical community. Primarily for this reason the clinic asks clients to assume an active role in their gynecological examinations. Through extensive conversations about what is entailed in such a procedure, and by an examination of their own bodies under the supervision of a trained lay health worker, women become more familiar with their own bodies, increasing the likelihood that they will assume more responsibility for their overall health maintenance. By actually experiencing active participation in routine examinations, women are encouraged to take some measures of control when they receive services and treatment from within conventional medical practices. Feminist health workers consider the courage and inclination to ask questions of professionals, to request information or clarification, and to challenge treatment choices politically powerful actions. (Downing, 1985).

Meaningful interaction between practitioner and client requires time. During a typical screening examination at the Emma Goldman clinic for the purpose of selecting birth control methods, for example, each client is assigned a patient advocate. The advocate spends time getting to know the client, asking questions to clarify the client's needs, anxieties, and assumptions with regard to sexuality and reproduction. The advocate encourages client questions and talk of doubts or difficulties about her health. Much effort is expended in creating an atmosphere in which the client can feel as comfortable as possible talking about and examining her body. For this reason, the advocate typically does not go through the conventional ritual of leaving the room while the client undresses. Rather, the advocate continues the pre-examination conversation, setting a precedent of normalcy about partial nudity and the examination itself. Nor are clients swathed in sheets, another potent signifier that tends to associate gynecology with secrecy and passiveness.

All of these patterns of interaction are strategically designed to promote a straightforward and unembarrassed dialogue between women about female health. The rationale behind such interaction patterns is that women will become less alienated from their bodies and more familiar with at least the functional aspects of their sexuality and reproductive capacities. As women learn to recognize and respond to symptoms of illness or pregnancy and as they incorporate experience with a vocabulary that allows them to reference sexual and reproductive activities with less of the cultural mystique which reproduces repressive practices, they develop a new harmony with body. From a feminist perspective, the new harmony is enabling because it places the individual woman in charge of her body and the choices to be made about it. In much the same fashion that trained professionals help children protect themselves from sexual molestation, practitioners at the Emma Goldman clinic help women develop the linguistic competencies with which to *say* how they will involve themselves in the sexual and reproductive practices of this culture.

Politicizing Reproductive Choices: The Feminization of
Sexual Expression and Control

Unless they are constrained to defend themselves from public attack, practitioners at the Emma Goldman clinic refuse to speak the discourse of moral and ethical judgment endemic to the discursive spectacle commonly termed the abortion controversy. Though most of the media attention to the clinic during its 14-year tenure has focused on the abortion services offered, the practitioners themselves do not think of Emma Goldman as an abortion clinic. Rather, they see it as a health clinic that in addition to many other services and activities provides safe, affordable abortion procedures. Along with gynecological and pregnancy screening services, the clinic offers "positive experience" pregnancy counseling classes, artificial insemination programs, massage for women, and a fairly extensive library on a broad range of issues influencing women's lives. In addition, the clinic is involved in community service activities which position the practices of the clinic positively and effectively within medical and educational institutional networks. For example, the clinic donates birth control kits to the Iowa City Public Schools and other human services organizations. Practitioners at the clinic staff a speaker's bureau "dedicated to the cause of public education about feminist health issues and sexuality" ("Clinic celebrates," 1983). Two years ago, the clinic began a fund drive to donate scholarship money to the University of Iowa College of Medicine, with the goal of encouraging and supporting women in professional medicine. The clinic creates and presents health care and counseling workshops for residents of the Iowa Women's Correctional Institute ("Clinic celebrates," 1983). In light of the variety of services offered by the clinic, it is reasonable to conclude that the legal and ethical discourses which reference the clinic as "the abortion mecca of the midwest" belittle the holistic health practices of the clinic, and misrepresent the clinic's political position on choice and on abortion (Dutton, 1985; Heth, 1982, "Iowa City U.S.," 1982; Kilman, 1982; "Pro-life Protestors," 1984; Ogintz, 1982; "Some Talk," 1985).

Practitioners at Emma Goldman argue that any woman has the right to choose whether or not she will undergo the physical, emotional, economic, and perhaps professional demands that will be required of her during a pregnancy (e.g., Downing, 1985). Further, they believe that anti-abortion legislation is anti-empowering in endorsing the notion that it is appropriate for sexual and maternal practices to be monitored by and through the state (Petchesky, 1985). The women and men who staff the Emma Goldman clinic believe that a woman's sexuality must be understood in the context of her own life. Thus, any patient seeking an abortion at the clinic will become part of a holistic effort to guarantee that the patient's sexuality is given back to her, as part of her health and general well-being. Consequently, the responsibility for sexuality, reproduction, and body health is given to her, providing control in her own life. In addition, the counselors at Emma Goldman believe that the technology of birth control is, in many ways, unsuited to the maintenance of one's health, body function, and the nature of sexuality itself. Many unplanned pregnancies are the result of fumbled, misunderstood, or simply missed attempts at protection (e.g., Nye, 1978, 1983). When a patient comes to the clinic for abortion services, every attempt is made to understand how the unplanned pregnancy occurred. This entails lengthy conversations with a patient advocate to determine if the birth control method used is suited to the sexual needs and practices of the client, or whether the client lacks sufficient understanding of both the female and male body, the nature of sexuality, or the proper procedure for using a particular birth control device. These conversations take place in an atmosphere that actively discourages guilt on the part of the client. Client staff seek for women to replace guilt with an understanding of the complexity of human sexuality and reproduction.

The staunch dedication to feminism at Emma Goldman generates a broad political perspective within which practitioners make sense of abortion as symptomatic of self- and culturally imposed powerlessness. Contrary to popular opinions about the clinic, manifest in several articles spread across 12 years of newspaper reporting, many of the lay health workers at Emma Goldman believe that abortion rates are too high and that abortion presents itself as a problem (Downing, 1985; Nye, 1978; Baker, 1981). But the warranting structures that produce such conclusions are radically different from those of conventional moral and ethical discourses about abortion: Practitioners at Emma Goldman do not frame abortion in terms of right and wrong, but in terms of power and control (Baker, 1982; Reproductive Rights National Network, n.d. *Women United*, n.d.). As patient advocate, Downing (1985) said: "Women still, in 1985, refuse to take responsibility for engaging in sexual activity which can lead to pregnancy."

The "why" of unprotected intercourse is clear and disturbing to health workers at Emma Goldman. Downing (1985) remarks that even though women know how babies are made, many cannot face their own sexuality. Therefore, the women do not make careful planning and consistent protection part of their normal, everyday routine. The collective experiences of the health workers at the clinic lead to the conclusion that most unplanned pregnancies result from one or more of the following problems: (a) Women do not have, and have not been encouraged to have, respect for their bodies or themselves; (b) Women are not able yet to acknowledge and thus possess their own sexual feelings; (c) Women are less likely to talk about their sexuality to other women or to their sexual partners; (d) Women are uncomfortable with their sexuality because the double standard of sexual morality that structures sexual expression in relation to married monogamy is still potent. (e) Consequently, protection is not yet a part of the *common* sense about sexuality because sexuality itself cannot be acknowledged outside rigidly prescribed contexts. Downing (1985) also points out that unplanned pregnancies may constitute high drama for women deprived of other meaningful life experiences.

Opponents of legalized abortion claim that sanctioned abortion signifies moral and ethical corruption, particularly on the part of women. For feminist health workers, abortion is thought of as a necessary component of reproductive freedom. A former director of public relations at the Emma Goldman clinic believes that the odds of experiencing at least one unplanned pregnancy in a lifetime are very high, considering how many times one woman ovulates (Arbogast, personal communication, Nov. 3, 1985). From the perspective of feminist health politics, then, abortion signifies the failure of cultural practices to embue women *and* men with the linguistic resources of sexual and reproductive competency. They believe that competent talk about sexuality can no longer rely upon the assumptions of the "good girl/bad girl" dichotomies of conventional morality, and that competent talk must acknowledge how our culture's penchant for spontaneous romance ignores the most fundamental principles of biology. Furthermore, the Emma Goldman clinic attempts to provide for as many women as possible the necessary technical information required to make responsible decisions about sexuality and reproduction. But they add to the technical information talk about the precarious gap between the chemically technologized birth control methods available to us and the nature of sexuality itself, because being armed with an array of birth control devices does not mean that women will be able successfully to integrate technology with cultural fictions of love and romance.

Final Reflections

Rhetorically speaking, the practitioners at Emma Goldman are *talking* their way through what they call a "quiet revolution," one that repudiates conventional reproductive practices and generates a competing way of understanding those practices.[4] How is this done? As we have seen, the practitioners at the clinic subjectify the specialized discourse of medicine, translating it into a perspective shaped by feminist commitments. This translation in turn informs the *common* sense of sexual practices. Similarly, practitioners objectify gender myths and common talk about women's bodies and sexuality. In so doing, they compete with cultural discourses about women and sexuality that feed pornography, encourage rape, and devalue the female human. Believing that the control of one's body is the most fundamentally material aspect of human existence, feminist health workers create and disseminate a knowledge which, by engendering new possibilities for understanding, empowers its audience of women.

The original Emma Goldman found the private spaces allocated to women intolerably confining, limiting, and dehumanizing. Most of what she saw in the private spaces of the lives of poor and immigrant women consisted of poverty, despair, and the distress consequent to new births which created unmanageable strains on already inadequate resources. In addition, Emma Goldman expressed even less tolerance with the private spaces of the middle-class: She was bitterly amused by what she perceived to be the irony of genteel prostitution in conventional marriages. For Emma Goldman, the potential for freedom, which she understood to be a quality of consciousness, lay in the political power of the public spaces. Accordingly, Emma Goldman spoke the politics of reproduction to any and everyone who would listen. The Emma Goldman clinic for women creates an alternative public *and* private space for women, at least in regard to their sexual and reproductive health concerns. The clinic publicizes by politicizing the heretofore secret, unspoken, and unspeakable details of gynecology, sexuality, and reproduction. At the same time, however, the clinic creates a closed, noninstitutional private space within which women can talk with other women about sexuality and reproduction. In turn, the private space becomes a cultural pulpit from which practitioners historicize, politicize, translate, and demystify conventional norms.

Health workers at the clinic express some anxiety about the extent to which they reach sufficient numbers of women (D. Nye, personal communication, October 2, 1985). As Downing (1985) pointed out, most of the clients coming into the clinic are self-selecting in that they actively seek feminist, holistic care. In my interview with Downing (1985), I probed her sense of greatest success and failure at the clinic.

---

[4] Dr. Adele Franks, who joined the staff of the clinic in 1980, remarked that "women [haven't known] that they [have] a right to be treated as adults by doctors. We have a quieter revolution going on now. We're just beginning to feel comfortable with being powerful human beings" (Chiavetta, 1980).

As Downing spoke of her disappointment with what the clinic has been able to accomplish, I was struck by the historical parallel with what the original Emma might have said if asked a similar question: "My greatest disappointment is that I don't see the growth that I would have expected in women respecting their bodies, in women being [empowered] to say 'no,' and in women valuing the ability to plan their lives." Downing continued, in words that echoed the historical Goldman's political sentiments, "somehow, we early feminists have not done a very good job in educating or helping younger women in large enough numbers . . . see the importance of controlling their bodies [in order to] control their lives."

In spite of Downing's practical and seasoned assessment, I am convinced that feminism in general and feminist health practices in specific have not altogether failed. Still, it is true that feminist health workers have not as yet persuaded a sufficient number of men and women that as surely as the scientific community has been able to repeal a fundamental law of nature, the potential also exists for enlightened persons to repeal the reproduction of *discourses* that perpetuate repressive and destructive sexual and reproductive practices. An important task for communication scholars interested in persuasion, argument, women's studies, and health communication is to reflect upon the barriers blocking a functional discourse of human sexuality and reproduction from developing with greater ease and speed in this culture.

The development of a feminist consciousness in American culture has illustrated that among the more powerful ties that bind human agents are the various knowledge claims that constrict and direct their behavior. Conventional biological and medical knowledge of the female reproductive system have supported powerful claims about the alleged capacity of women to think clearly and well, to enter the mainstream of the public work force, and to endure physical hardship. Further, feminist-engendered perspectives about women's health have been met with considerable resistance, both in the forthright violence of clinic bombings and in the more subtle hegemony of idealized womanliness. Yet, the quality of conversation created and sustained by women, for women, at the Emma Goldman Clinic testifies to the liberating *potential* of feminist health politics. The practitioners at the clinic have illustrated the necessity and value of restructuring patient-practitioner relationships, primarily in terms of communicative effectiveness. Further, they have illustrated the role that health practitioners might play as consumer safety advocates. What remains to be studied in detail are the barriers that impede sound health communication. This is an important area of inquiry due to the forcefulness of ideology, which constitutes itself as the only way in which something can be said, and which, over time, assumes the normalizing posture of inevitability (S. Hall, personal communication, October 5, 1985). In the case of the Emma Goldman Clinic for Women, feminist health workers are speaking the politics of reproduction, calling into being an importantly different way of talking and thinking about human sexuality. By refusing to reproduce the discourse of repressive practices, their *talk* de-centers the position of women as spoken by conventional medical practices and conventional standards of moral conduct. The difficulty of their task demonstrates the pervasiveness and persuasiveness of the constraints with which a feminist perspective on sexuality and reproduction must negotiate.

References

Baker, A. (1981). *After her abortion*. (Available from The Hope Clinic for Women, Ltd., 1602 21st Street, Granite City, IL 62040).

Baker, A. (1982). *How to cope with guilt*. (Available from The Hope Clinic for Women, Ltd. 1602 21st Street, Granite City, IL 62040).

Barki, N. (1982, March 27). The Emma Goldman you'll never see in the movies. *Ms.*, pp. 27–31.

Benjamin, W. (1969). *Illuminations* (H. Zohn, Trans.). (H. Arendt, Ed.). New York: Schocken Books.

Boston Women's Health Book Collective. (1984). *The new our bodies, ourselves: A book by and for women*. New York: Simon and Schuster.

Bowles, G., & Klein, R. D. (Eds.). (1983). *Theories of women's studies*. London: Routledge & Kegan Paul.

Bridenthal, R. & Koonz, C. (Eds.). (1976). *Becoming visible: Women in European history*. Boston: Houghton Mifflin.

Brooks, B., & Niemand, J. (1980). *A woman's guide to bladder infections*. Iowa City, IA: Iowa City Women's Press.

Carroll, B. (Ed.). (1976). *Liberating women's history*. Chicago: University of Illinois Press.

Chiavetta, L. (1980, August 29). Doctor joins Goldman clinic . . . helping it reach two goals. *Daily Iowan*, p. 6.

Clinic celebrates by giving grants to city. (1983, September 8). *Daily Iowan*, p. 1.

Degler, C. (1976). *Is there a history of women?* Oxford: Clarendon Press.

Downing, B. (1985, August 7). Taped interview. (Available from A. S. Owen, Communcation and Theatre Arts, University of Puget Sound, Tacoma, WA 98416).

Drinnow, R. (1961). *Rebel in paradise: A biography of Emma Goldman*. New York: Harper Colophon Books.

Dutton, J. (1985, May 8). Goldman Clinic wants retraction of anti-abortionists's statement. *Iowa City Press Citizen*, p. 1.

Editorial statement. (1980, Spring). *Frontiers, 5* (1), n.p.

Editorial statement. (1975, January). *Hecate, 1* (1), 4.

Editorial Statement. (1977, May). *Heresies, 1* (2).

Editorial statement. (1974, Summer).*Quest, 1* (1), n.p.

Editorial statement. (1981, Winter). *Signs, 1* (1), p. *v–viii.*

Ehrenreich, B. (1980). A funny thing happened on the way to socialist feminism. *Heresies, 3* (1), 4–6.

Emma Goldman clinic for women: A feminist approach to women's health care. (n.d.) (Available from Emma Goldman Clinic for Women, 227 N. Dubuque, Iowa City, IA 52240).

Emma Goldman Clinic for Women. (1982). *Fertility awareness: Natural birth control for women.* Iowa City, IA: Iowa City Women's Press.

Emma Goldman Clinic. (n.d., No. 3). Encare-oval: How effective? *Emma Goldman clinic for women newsletter,* p. 5. (Available from Emma Goldman Clinic for Women, 227 N. Dubuque, Iowa City, IA 52240).

Falk, C. (1984, September). Amorous anarchist: The lost love letters of Emma Goldman. *Mother Jones,* pp. 14–18.

Foucault, M. (1972). *The archaeology of knowledge* (A. M. S. Smith, Trans.). New York: Harper Colophon.

Foucault, M. (1980). *Power/knowledge: Selected interviews and other writings* (C. Gordon, Trans. and ed.). New York: Pantheon Books.

Gadamer, H. G. (1982). *Truth and method.* (G. Barden & J. Cumming, Trans. and Eds.). New York: Crossroad.

Goldman, E. (1969). *Anarchism and other essays.* Mother Earth Publishing Association; Dover Publications, Inc. (Original work published in 1917.)

Hartman, M. S., and Banner, L. W. (Eds.). (1974). *Clio's consciousness raised: New perspectives on the history of women.* New York: Harper and Row.

Health Organizing Collective. (n.d.) *The gynecological check-up.* New York: Health-Right Inc. (Available from Women's Health Forum, 175 Fifth Ave., New York, N.Y. 10010).

Heth, J. (1982, April 2). Iowa City abortion-rate publicity 'misleading.' *Des Moines Register,* p. 8c.

Infections of the vagina. (1976). New York: Health-Right Inc. (Available from Women's Health Forum, 175 Fifth Ave., New York, N.Y. 10010).

Iowa City U.S. 'abortion mecca.' " (1982, March 28). *Omaha World Herald,* p. 1.

Kelly-Gadol, J. (1976). The social relation of the sexes: Methodological implications of women's history. *Signs, 1* (4), 809–823.

Kilman, S. (1982, March 12). Area abortion statistics reflect migration to use local facility. *Daily Iowan,* p. 1, 7.

Lerner, G. (1969, Fall). New approaches to the study of women in American history. *Journal of Social History, 4* (4), 333–356.

McDonald, T. L. (n.d.) *Bloodpressure.* (Available from Emma Goldman Clinic for Women, 227 N. Dubuque, Iowa City, IA 52240).

McGee, M. C. (1985, May 30). *On feminized power.* The Van Zelst Lecture in Communication. Evanston, IL: Northwestern University, School of Speech Communication.

Morgan, R. (Ed.). (1970). *Sisterhood is powerful*. New York: Random House.

Norton, M. B. (1979). American history: A review essay. *Signs, 5* (2), 324–227.

Nye, D. (1978). *Vacuum aspiration abortion services at the Emma Goldman clinic for women*. (Available from Emma Goldman Clinic for Women, 227 N. Dubuque, Iowa City, IA 52240).

Nye, D. (1983). *Vacuum aspiration abortion services at the Emma Goldman clinic for women*. (R. Arbogast, Ed.). (Available from D. Nye, Clinic Director, Emma Goldman Clinic for Women, 227 N. Dubuque, Iowa City, IA 52240).

Ogintz, E. (1982, Sunday, March 28). Iowa City 'liberally' the abortion capitol of America. *Chicago Tribune*, p. 6.

Perry, S. & Dawson, K. (1985). *Nightmare: Women and the Dalkon shield*. New York: MacMillian.

Petchesky, R. P. (1985). *Abortion and women's choice: The state, sexuality, and reproductive freedom*. Boston: Northeastern University Press.

Positive experience pregnancy. (n.d.) (Available from Emma Goldman Clinic for Women, 227 N. Dubuque, Iowa City, IA 52240).

Prenatal fitness exercises. (n.d.) (Available from Emma Goldman Clinic for Women, 227 N. Dubuque, Iowa City, IA 52240).

Pro-life protestors picket Emma Goldman clinic. (1984, January 19). *Daily Iowan*, p. 1, 6.

Reproductive Rights National Network. *Abortion: Legal but inaccessible*. (n.d.). New York: Author.

Santiago, F. Emma Goldman clinic marks 10th anniversary. (1983, September 4). *Des Moines Register*, p. 56.

Sarachild, K. (1973). Consciousness-raising: A radical weapon. In Redstockings of the Women's Liberation Movement (Eds.), *Feminist revolution* (pp. 144–150). New York: Random House.

Shulman, A. K. (Ed.). (1983). *Red Emma speaks*. New York: Schocken Books.

Some talk of fear as vigil begins. (1985, January 19). *Iowa City Press Citizen*, p. 1a, 10a.

Spender, D. (1983). Theorising about theorising. In G. Bowles & R. D. Klein (Eds.)., *Theories of women's studies* (pp. 27–31). London: Routledge and Kegan Paul.

Tanner, L. B. (Ed.). (1970). *Voices from women's liberation*. New York: New American Library.

Women's clinic just like home. (1982, March 7). *The Sunday Dispatch* (Moline, Illinois), pp. 31, 32.

Women united to defend abortion rights and end sterilization abuse. (n.d.). (Available from Reproductive Rights National Network, 17 Murray Street, New York, N.Y. 10007).

4

Body Talk: The Politics of Weight Loss and Female Identity

Carole J. Spitzack

Tulane University

> A diet mobilizes an acute sense of wrongdoing, something which threatens, which is there every minute of the day. It is only when you sleep that you are sure of not doing something wrong. (Barthes, 1985)

The business of beautifying bodies thrives in American culture. In recent years, texts designed to reduce and tone flesh have exceeded the *Bible* in sales (Watson, 1985). Promised in contemporary texts is a body sanctioned by societal norms, which in turn brings personal rewards including visibility, independence, success, and liberation (e.g., Linn, 1980, Fonda, 1981, Stuart, 1983). The strong and slender body signifies an ability to govern existence. Evidence suggests, however, that the transformation from fat to thin, powerless to powerful, does not occur. This realization acquires particular significance when we note that women more often than men are perceived to have weight problems. For many women, as suggested by the skyrocketing sales records of "body" books, an *unending* battle with the body characterizes their experience (Chernin, 1981). Contrary to popular belief, the discourse on weight loss is successful not because it speaks to the "abnormal" or atypical woman, but insofar as its cultural presence incorporates and draws from a more generalized picture of women; one in which *all* women are potentially abnormal.[1] The weight-conscious woman em-

---

[1] Many parallels can be found between the histories of mental and physical diseases. Chesler's (1972) account of the diagnostic approaches in American psychiatry reveal that women more often than men are labeled neurotic. Additionally, many psychiatrists (implicitly) presume that the root cause is insufficient femininity. Here, it is also relevant to note Sontag's (1979) observations regarding the medical community and its attribution

barks on a task in which her success is contingent on an ability to view her body objectively, to transcend her body while still living in her body. Here, the body becomes an enemy which the mind must conquer. Dieting slogans such as "mind over matter," "you are what you eat," and "will-power" capture the mind/body dichotomy underlying the struggle. Divisions between mind and body, I argue, are constructed culturally and function as metaphors for male-female differences. Zimmerman (1987) remarks, "Man's conception of himself as essentially cultural, non-female, non-natural, immortal, and transcendent, as opposed to the essentially natural, non-cultural, mortal woman, has continued in various guises for several thousand years" (p. 6). The demands of body beautification discourse, then, stand in direct contrast to the sociocultural place assigned to women. This chapter examines the battleground: the female body struggling against itself in an attempt to triumph.

For the past several years I have participated in women's body talk, both as a speaker and a listener. The single most recurring topic has been body size, and in particular, body weight. Indeed, Tucker (1985) finds that women "often perceive themselves to be too fat or too large," and correlates this perception with a "difficulty in maintaining the slim and trim figure held in high esteem by our culture" (p. 936). Women hold images of their bodies and know how those images compare with cultural standards. So strong are the sanctions for violation in educational settings, relational contexts (Cash & Derlega, 1978), and career environments (Widgery, 1974), that women frequently claim a willingness to "do anything" in attempting physical conformity. At the same time, the women who seem to fully grasp the importance of slenderness, and work diligently to resolve body problems, are the same women who speak of failure; the body's resistance to will strength. A high level of body awareness, the very state required to repair the body, appears to be correlated with an *inability* to control the body.

I wanted to understand the processes by which body control— governing the body through will strength—becomes an unending and futile battle in the face of numerous rewards and sanctions. How, in an age where women have sophisticated means by which to evaluate and correct a defective appearance (weight loss methods, surgery, organizations, role models), that is, guaranteed methods for the accomplishment of body transcendence, does the struggle itself lead to a lack of resolve? Orbach (1978) finds that an attempt to master body proportions

---

of diagnostic causality, particularly when considering the extent to which obesity, as a disease, is perceived to be caused by the individual: "Theories that diseases are caused by mental states and can be cured by will power are always an index of how much is not understood about the physical terrain of a disease" (p. 54).

is painful and filled with "an enormous amount of self-disgust, loathing and shame" (p. 29). In fact, disdain for her current body is essential for the woman who is determined to achieve a new appearance. Chernin (1981) observes that "[f]ew women who diet realize that they are confessing a dislike for the body when they weigh and measure the flesh, subject it to rigorous fasts or strenuous regimens of exercise" (p. 25). The future rewards of dieting serve as motivation and consequently add legitimacy to temporary unhappiness and sacrifice, but for many women the future point never materializes; disgust for the body is ever-present. In a decade of female strength and liberation, where women are demanding more rights concerning their bodies, the current obsession to beautify the female body through reduction is worthy of investigation.

During the spring of 1985 I spoke to numerous women, both individually and in groups (e.g., seminars, lectures) about my interest in female body experience, and in particular the struggle to control body size. At the close of each discussion, I expressed an interest in conducting audiotaped interviews to learn more about this experience. The indirectness of approach was intentional. If as Orbach (1978) suggests, the experience of body self-consciousness is filled with pain, I did not want to select individual women who in turn may have viewed my request as an acknowledgment of deficiencies. In addition to Chernin's claim that weight-consciousness is not limited to noticeably large women,[2] Watson (1985) reveals that most women who engage in ongoing weight loss attempts are marginally overweight or "normal" according to medical weight charts; thus I did not presume a necessary correlation between obesity and body self-consciousness. Moreover, anorexic and/or bulimic women often appear to embody the cultural ideals established for female appearance but suffer tremendously from body dissatisfaction and self-consciousness.[3] Finally, my aim was not to determine the type of woman most likely to fail or succeed, nor was it to link outward appearance to internal personality conflicts, but rather to describe the experience of everyday women engaged in a struggle to control the body. I presumed that all women, living in a culture which calls much attention to female appearance, have at some point lived the struggle.

Thirty women contacted me and volunteered for interviews. Volunteers were fairly diverse in age (15–36 years), education level (high-school to post-graduate), and economic class (lower-middle to upper-middle). Twenty women indicated variability in responding to requests

---

[2] Another index of the weight obsession experienced by everyday women, including those who appear to have mastered an admirable body, can be found in Chernin's (1981) analysis of beauty queen regimens (pp. 20–28).

[3] For thorough analyses of bulimarexia and anorexia, see White and Boskind-White (1983), and Palmer (1980).

for demographic information: "I'm 32, but right now I feel 60;" "I'm a senior, or supposed to be. I act like a freshman a lot of the time;" "Economic class is a weird thing. Honestly, sometimes I'm one and sometimes I'm another—it sort of depends." Occupationally, women were students, housewives, teachers, researchers, corporate employees, executives, and legal professionals. Occupation is only provisionally linked to participants because volunteers did not do so: occupation in all cases included more than one category. Women addressed questions regarding occupation with statements such as, "right now I'm a student, but sometimes I'm a teacher," "a lawyer at my office, a housewife after 5:00," and "I guess I'm a housewife, which means I'm also a financial wizzard and a teacher with years of experience." During initial contact, volunteers expressed a strong interest in understanding their concern with weight and appearance, which I presumed to indicate current and immediate struggles with the body.

Interviews were conducted in an open-ended topical fashion, following initial guidelines suggested by Patton (1980, pp. 200–205). In the course of a 40-minute audio-taped interview each woman was asked to address three topic areas: cultural standards for appearance; relationships with others (both male and female); and self-conscious body alteration activities. Particular questions relating to these areas were posed in interviews on an individual basis. I avoided a pre-established protocol because I did not presume to fully understand the body experience of respondents prior to conducting the interviews; nor did I want to frame their experience in a restrictive manner. Moreover, as Oakley (1981) observes, traditional interviewing procedures establish clear differences between respondent and researcher, where the former is presumed to be powerless (and hence *submits* herself to questioning), while the latter is powerful and thus able to demand disclosure from a respondent (pp. 30–41). When asking women to describe their body experience, which as Brownmiller (1984) notes is often grounded socially in a "competitive edge" with regard to other females, I attempted to minimize hierarchical divisions between these women and myself.

As suggested by Oakley (1981), I viewed interviews as *conversations* where talk is purposive and thematic but not entirely predetermined or hierarchical. I did not assume that an absence of interviewer response or a clear division between interviewer and respondent granted objectivity, particularly given the topic and the woman-to-woman communicative setting. Women's interaction, Bell (1982) finds, is based in reciprocol sharing. A refusal to reciprocate sends a strong message. I spent considerable time talking with each woman prior to the actual taping, scheduling 30–45 minutes of interview time for this purpose. Before proceeding with the taping, I wanted each woman to understand that she was not simply an exploitable information source, but someone I wished to talk *with* about body experience, a person with whom I would choose to spend time outside the context of academic research. Throughout the interviews, women periodically asked and received answers to questions about my experience. I laughed with them as they relayed humorous stories, I offered support as they described painful experiences, and I honored their requests to stop the recorder. In view of the interview procedures adopted, the analysis to follow is best conceptualized as a description of several topically focused conversations, in which each interaction partner has allowed me to serve as spokesperson.

Method of Analysis

A phenomenological method was used to analyze the experience of body self-consciousness. My analysis proceeds in three parts. I first *describe* body experience as expressed, which makes a "catalogue of momentary experience, trying to note as much as possible of what occurs within a short span of experience" (Ihde, 1979, p. 55). In the context of the present study, description consists of noting occurences both within and outside the boundaries of recorded interviews. Initial telephone conversations, interaction taking place prior to and following the recording, post-interview discussions, for example, were recorded in a journal. Such occurences help to inform the experience described by respondents and make conscious a range of possible interpretive threads which impinge on the descriptions offered by respondents.

The initial description is followed by a *reduction* or possibilizing of "all phenomena in seeking their structures" (p. 69). A phenomenological reduction requires a "suspension of judgment . . . in order to examine the full range of different dimensions of experience" (Stewart & Mickunas, 1974, p. 26). This methodological step does not seek to distinguish real experience from surface or reported experience, but *brackets* taken-for-granted experience in an effort to describe the meaning structures which ground the relationship of body and world. Female experience, particularly within the confines of so-called weight remedies, is often presented stereotypically, inflexibly, and judgmentally. In Linn's (1980) popular book, *Staying Thin*, the overweight woman is portrayed as a lethargic, sexually paranoid, socially irresponsible person. Generally, weight conscious individuals are viewed in negative terms. In order to listen carefully to respondents, allowing them to critique the social presumptions which exclude and judge them, a suspension of commonly held perceptions regarding weight-conscious women is necessary. Here, the meaning structures emergent in individual and collective respondent experience are richly and comprehensively understood.

Finally, the *interpretation* provides a novel reading of body consciousness. Here, the themes or meaning structures (obtained in the reduction) are interpreted within the context of historical conditions. In methodological terms, the task is to ask how the reported experience of respondents makes sense within the context of sociohistorical practices. In other words, how are women viewed culturally such that they come to view their bodies in the manner described by respondents? In combination, the three empirical procedures permit an understanding of female body experience as expressed and lived.

Description of Body Consciousness

Consciousness of the body is an ordinary occurrence in the lives of respondents. Arguably, the interview situation, particularly the content focus, generates a degree of body awareness; yet feminist scholars note that such awareness is an ordinary occurrence in the lives of women (Chernin, 1981, 1985; Brownmiller, 1984). Berger (1972) describes female existence as a perpetual and reflective process of *appearing* to self and others. A woman must be able to see herself as others see her; to view herself from a position outside the body:

> A woman must continually watch herself. She is almost continually accompanied by her own image of herself. Whilst she is walking across a room or whilst she is weeping at the death of her father, she can scarcely avoid envisaging herself walking or weeping. From earliest childhood she has been taught and persuaded to survey herself continually (p. 46).

Upon encountering others, then, women frequently expect judgments of physical appearance, and often provide a self-evaluation to the other:

> I forgot about this appointment until half an hour ago. I usually don't look like such a slob.

> I know what you're thinking. She's a fine one to talk about looks, right? I'm sorry, I just couldn't get my iron to work this morning.

> I do make an effort to look presentable most of the time. You've caught me on a bad day.

Calling attention to appearance is typically done in negative terms.

Moreover, a failure to "look presentable" must be explained ("I couldn't get my iron to work") and forgiven ("I'm sorry").

Evaluations of personal appearance are tied directly to comparisons with others. Culturally visible *ideal* bodies become the measure against which women judge their own bodies. Mass media present consumers with countless images of women and by excluding socially unattractive women (except for shock or humor value), give women flawless role models (Downs & Harrison, 1985). When describing standards for appearance, respondents speak of media images in the context of their own experience:

> The lady on Tab commercials. Or is it Diet Sprite? Anyway, that's how we're supposed to be I guess. God knows I'll never be asked to wear a white bikini on national T.V.

> These days you have to be tall, blond, and muscular, but not too muscular, not like a man I mean. It's like those women who can just have everything, the Dynasty ladies, Linda Evans. If you reverse everything about me you'd have a good idea.

> I'm embarassed to admit it but I compare myself to those women all the time. I bought a magazine where you could see how your measurements compared to Christie Brinkley's and I did it. Don't ask what the results were. Jesus, I'd give anything to be like that.

Comparisons with cultural appearance standards, like attention to personal appearance, suggest body deficiencies. Respondents are sensitive to valued societal imagery in highly concrete terms (e.g., Linda Evans, Christie Brinkley), yet at an intuitive level they comprehend the premise of beauty ideals; that is, "models," serving to promote consumerism, must embody characteristics which the average woman does not currently have.

Women are often compelled to justify physical inadequacies. Linn (1980) finds that weight-conscious persons (which we can presume are women through his use of roles, e.g., PTA participants, Girl Scout leaders, homemakers) are obliged to provide excuses for their appearance, and frequently avoid social situations altogether (pp. 78–82). Respondents display tendencies toward justification and avoidance when viewing their bodies in relation to *ideal* bodies:

> Last year I gained a lot of weight. I wouldn't go out of my house except just for classes. Even so, I watched T.V. so I still got depressed.

> I haven't always been this heavy. I know I can lose weight if I want to, and I look better when I'm thin. I almost didn't come to talk to you today because of it.

I went to the beach last weekend and was just floored by how all these other girls looked in bathing suits. Big thighs run in my family so I can't help it. Anyway, I pretty much stayed under my towel the whole time.

A desire to *hide* from others, to prevent the body from being seen by others, is tied to perceptions of physical inadequacy. Millman's (1980) investigation of obesity in America reveals that overweight women are expected to conceal excess flesh, often in a manner which causes a heightened awareness of deviance for (and of) the individual. For example, the respondent who "stayed under her towel" at the beach, looking and feeling conspicuous given the context, or the woman who wears oppressively hot clothing on a summer day. Regardless of measures taken to hide excess, the overweight woman is seen for what she is and judged accordingly, both by herself and others. Indeed, Chernin (1981) states, "[w]e loathe the swelling in our breasts, the increase in our thighs, we are terrified by the fullness in our flesh" (p. 54).

Consciousness of physical appearance occurs in relation to other women, but the degree of self-consciousness is often heightened in the presence of men. In the everyday experience of most women, spontaneous attention to physical appearance in the form of whistles or stares comes from men; women are often taught to value male evaluations more than those offered by females.[4] Positive attention from men is likely if the woman in question appears to exhibit feminine characteristics, which is to say she must recognize and present her *difference* from men. Indeed, Brownmiller (1984) claims, feminine beauty accomplishes a "willing demonstration of difference" (p. 15). In Millman's study, "largeness equals masculinity" in cultural perceptions of women (p. 106). An overweight female body, then, fails to signify gender difference and is consequently viewed pejoratively. In sociohistorical terms, especially when considering the extent to which heterosexuality is culturally mandated, undesirable sexual partners from a masculine vantage point are those who mirror, rather than contrast, masculine gender identity. Male socialization equates a strong sex drive with masculinity. As Phillips and Wood (1983) reveal in an investigation designed to study male perceptions of women and sex, "when they (men) first met a woman they speculated on her sexual possibilities

---

[4] Firestone's (1970) definition of "sex privitization" is instructive: "The sex privitization of women is the process whereby women are blinded to their generality as a class which renders them invisible as individuals to the male eye" (p. 149). The practical effect, argues Firestone, is that "women become more and more look-alike. But at the same time they are expected to express their individuality through their physical appearance. Thus they are kept coming and going, at one and the same time trying to express their similarity and their uniqueness" (p. 152).

before anything else" (p. 223). The lack of femininity suggested by large-bodied women, coupled with cultural messages which tell women their sexual possibilities increase through a presentation of difference, produce heightened body consciousness for women.

> I always notice the way I look more when I'm around men. Maybe I just think they notice it more, bodies I mean, because, well, Playboy and stuff like that.

> A guy told me once that guys know right away how much girls weigh, like they can just know that somehow. I always weigh myself before I go out on a date now. Stupid, huh?

> I dated a boy in early college years who was about the same size as me. It didn't bother him but it drove me crazy. I always wore flat shoes and loose fitting clothes to make myself look smaller by comparison, but it just didn't work. I think deep down it bothered him too.

Relationships with family members contribute to a woman's experience of her body. While both male and female relatives play a part in shaping a woman's body image, Friday (1974) argues that the mother figures in families are apt to more directly socialize daughters into feminine roles. Mothers teach daughters about fashion, diet, manners, relationships, to name only a few. Also, mothers are more often present in the home than fathers, functioning as feminine role models. Messages given to daughters regarding diet are often ambiguous and anxiety-producing. While a primary task of motherhood is feeding—in the literal sense of food preparation and distribution—mother must also teach female children the importance of a well-kept, socially acceptable appearance. Orbach (1978) defines a mother as one who "must make sure her daughter is not overfed in case she becomes greedy and overweight—a terrible fate for a girl" (p. 19). The subsequent bind produced for a mother may lead to interaction riddled simultaneously with negative comments about her daughter's body and a focus on eating. Overt pressures to stay thin, women report, more often come from mothers than fathers.

> My dad was really great about it. He never talked about it when I gained weight. My mother hounded me like being skinny was the end all and be all in life. Being nice to look at is really important and I'd pay just about anything to get rid of 20-25 pounds, but you can't do it that way. My mother never understood that. Then she'd keep all my favorite foods in the house.

> Mom's nagging is pretty much a constant in my life. She's always on

diets and thinks I ought to be. Dad, well, I really appreciate it because he only says things when I lose weight; then he compliments me.

When I was little I remember it seemed no one paid attention to how my brothers looked, but boy did my mother ever get in a state if my sisters and I looked out of place. I never remember my father saying anything, he removed himself from those arguments.

Not only do mothers pay attention to the appearance of daughters, but as respondents report, maternal attention is likely to be continuous.

The part played by the father in socializing the daughter's appearance appears initially to be one of support: "My dad was really great about it;" "I really appreciate it because he only says things when I lose weight." Many women report that their fathers either compliment appearance or say nothing. Arguably, compliments can be pleasant, but they can also imply prescription. Through positive remarks the daughter learns her father's conception of attractiveness, which is in turn influenced by social definitions of beauty. The price paid for her lack of conformity is often silence on the part of father. She quickly learns that attention from father is contingent on her ability to present a culturally acceptable picture of femininity. As one woman reports, "He said nothing when I won a sailing award, but praised me like crazy when I lost 17 lbs. during my junior year."

Women often feel more bodily at ease when interacting with female friends than with men or family members. If, as Pearson (1985) suggests, "women need more social approval than do men," (p. 267) and men and family members are tied to potentially negative evaluations of appearance, female friendships may provide an escape from judgment. Women friends are commonly defined as "those with whom one could relax, receive support from, and share things with" (Bell, 1981, p. 66). In the lives of respondents, close friends are accepting and understanding, and do not base relational quality in outward appearance:

[My friend] has listened to me talk about every diet in the book, some of the most hideous plans you can imagine, without ever saying or implying anything bad.

It's really silly how when girls are around other girls, they don't get all fired up about looks. Oh, don't get me wrong, I mean some girls can be real catty about how other girls look, but if they're really friends of mine they don't do that.

I think women have a better grasp of what it feels like to think and worry about their bodies. And even if they thought I was 100 pounds overweight they wouldn't call attention to it in a mean way. Maybe it's sad that we're all in this paranoia together, don't we have anything better to worry about?

Female friends provide support based in "shared experiences, interests, and values," (Bell, 1981, p. 66) and refrain from directly commenting on negative aspects of appearance because, as one respondent points out, "women have a better grasp of what it feels like to worry about their bodies."

Associations between women friends are based on mutual support, yet reciprocity is often strained when a woman loses an appreciable amount of weight. Linn (1980) warns that friends regularly impede progress in weight loss efforts by encouraging eating behavior. An improved body calls forth feelings of jealousy in the other; cycles of competition are set in motion. While female competition is often characterized as a petty, superficial, vicious enterprise in which women claw and scratch until one victor emerges, respondents describe competition negatively not because the battle is difficult, but because it severs an intimate connection. In female experience, competition is filled with concern regarding "the great emotional costs at which success achieved through competition is often gained" (Sassen, 1980, p. 15). Respondents associate positive changes in appearance with a painful reevaluation of existing female friendships:

> We'd been friends ever since grade school. I came home one summer and lost 27 pounds and it made a big difference in the way I look. [My friend] couldn't handle it at all. First of all she didn't recognize me, then when she did we had a lot of trouble talking. I don't know what it was but we haven't been very close since then.

> As long as we were both fighting to get skinny we got on really well. It was like we were on the same side or something. But when I lost a lot or she lost a lot, the whole thing got really tense, awkward I mean.

> I remember [my friend] was a size 9 and I was an 11 for years, all through high-school. Then in college I lost 19 pounds and we were roommates. I came home one day with a pair of size 7 jeans and she hardly spoke to me. I couldn't fathom it. Could an entire relationship be based on blue jean sizes? We didn't live with each other the next year.

Relationships between women are strained not only by changes in physical appearance, but as the experience of respondents indicates, the changes commonly *end* female friendships.

Enacting improvements in the body's exterior requires discipline and perseverance. Relationships with others, predominantly women, are often (perceived to be) at least partially responsible for failed weight reduction attempts; thus success is dependent on an ability to rise above pressures from others. Beyond the threat of female competition, popular dieting literature presents women as cohorts, persons who encourage deviance in one another. As one respondent says, "Sometimes we're our own worst enemies—we just bring out the worst in each other because it's sort of okay to pig out if she's doing it too." Together they validate mutual indulgence through the invention of rationalization schemes (e.g., "We'll begin a diet tomorrow"). Weight loss books encourage women to "stop making excuses" for their bodies and provide formulas for body satisfaction. Outside influences prevent the dieter from a realistic assessment of herself. In Linn's (1980) *Staying Thin*, for example, the reader comes to understand why she is fat and why she wants to be thin (pp. 69–97). Similarly, Fonda's (1981) fitness manual begins with a chapter entitled, "A Body Abused," and moves to "Being Strong" (pp. 13–64). Before a problem with the body can be remedied a woman must become aware of contributing factors in past failures, negative influences which prevented a capacity to think independently; vowing not to repeat mistakes.

Respondents suggest an inextricable link between self-evaluation and a separation from women who complicate such evaluation:

> It's pretty hard to discipline yourself if you don't know why you're eating. I read once that women eat when they're emotional and that's pretty irrational. You can overcome those handicaps but it takes a lot of work. A key is to stay away from friends who bring out the worst in you.

> When I've lost weight in the past I've done it by really watching myself. I mean, what I eat, calories and carbohydrates. I weigh myself every day and know what I can eat that day by what the scale says. I get mad at my mother because she can be looking right at me and say, "you look great," knowing I've just gained 10 lbs. I have to drown out those comments.

> I think it's true that you have to get a heightened sense of awareness when you try and lose weight. Women especially because for them the body, how it looks I mean, is such a big thing. And once you know what affects you, you can do it.

The act of coming to awareness, as responses suggest, in itself often inspires motivation. Watson (1985) defines weight loss texts as "inspirational reading" which "assures you that somebody cares, that there is a way, and that you can be saved" (p. 15). In the case of women, inspiration or salvation often comes through a severing of connections with other women. One woman's testimony captures this point effectively: "It's true that when you lose weight you develop new friends, guys and girls, because your old girlfriends get jealous—they'd like it better if you looked like them—and cuter guys ask you out. You have a better chance of staying thin if the people around you, especially girls, are too because they know how important it is. You realize your old friends just made you feel okay because they didn't want you to change, to be better."

New found inspiration commonly fails to produce sustained weight loss. In spite of problem diagnosis, elimination of negative influences, and new friends, women are apt to lapse into old habits. Bayrd (1978) suggests that more women than men are "seriously overweight" (p. 12) and defines the problem of obesity as "preventative medicine's greatest failure" (p. 26). While "fatness is certainly a personal catastrophe" in the lives of women, "some 95 percent of all diets ultimately fail to produce permanent weight loss" (p. 26). Respondent experience highlights the sense of defeat following periods of vigilance:

> I can be going along, what is it the British say, *swimmingly*, and then I start to sink (laugh). I'm laughing now, but most of the time when it happens I cry.

> When I'm serious about losing weight nothing could stop me from accomplishing my mission. A real *Rocky* approach to getting there. But then something snaps and I just can't do it anymore. I won't even look in the mirror because I don't like what's staring back at me. And I'm right back where I started. I cheat too much.

> I've tried everything. I mean, literally, I could write a book on all my attempts. Only I don't think many people would buy it because, as you can see, I'm not exactly a perfect '10'..

Failure to accomplish the "mission" of weight loss is often ongoing ("I could write a book on all my attempts"), inexplicable ("something snaps"), and painful ("most of the time when it happens I cry"). All the good advice offered by diet books and products, in the end, complicates rather than clarifies the problem and, significantly, contributes to *repeated* failure.

Respondents express hope and hopelessness when envisioning ultimate resolution to body problems and place responsibility for altering appearance with themselves:

> Nobody can tell you to do it, nobody can show you how. You just have to decide to stick with a serious plan. Sometimes this body of mine won't cooperate.

> If I lost just 15 pounds I think my life would improve a lot. I'd be more

sure of myself and not take as much shit from people. That's my problem now, I listen to other people too much. It's hard to get over that.

Yes, I know in my head I can lose weight and I know in my head I'd feel better about myself. I can't seem to convince the rest of me though. Maybe someday it'll snap into line.

Weight loss is possible and decidedly advantageous ("I'd be more sure of myself and not take as much shit from people"), but the body often refuses to "cooperate." Perhaps "someday" both "head" and "body" will stop fighting against one another.

An initial description of the experience of weight consciousness reveals that women typically fail to resolve body problems in spite of recognized rewards. Awareness regarding cultural standards, relationships which promote and minimize body insecurity, and successfully employed past remedies does not facilitate resolution. Respondents associate failure with the positive and/or negative influences of other persons, but ultimately blame themselves when efforts go unfulfilled. A struggle between mind and body, what women "rationally" know versus what they in fact "do," is both possible and impossible, winnable and unwinnable.

Reduction of Initial Description

The phenomenological reduction is a "narrowing of attention" which "involves the suspension of certain commonly held beliefs" (Stewart & Mickunas, 1974, p. 26). Thus far, respondent experience is validated in numerous research studies. The description offers a picture of weight consciousness as an experience; the reduction puts the picture "out of play" in order to look at "what makes that experience possible" (Merleau-Ponty, 1962, p. xvi). What, in other words, grounds the experience of body consciousness? The "chance happenings" in respondent expression, highlighting some experiences and by implication hiding others, can be found to "coalesce and show up a certain way of taking a stand in relation to the human situation, reveal in fact an *event* which has its definite outline and about which we can talk" (Merleau-Ponty, 1962, pp. xviii–xix). By describing the *prereflective* experience of respondents, that is, the structural thematics which make possible the experience of weight consciousness, we begin to understand what it *means* to exist in a body struggling against itself.

Three interrelated themes can be said to coalesce in the prereflective experience of weight consciousness: body as object; body as other; body as person. Merleau-Ponty cautions, "The most important lesson which the reduction teaches us is the impossibility of a complete reduction" (p. xiv). This is to say that no position completely outside of the experience in question is possible; I as researcher, like the women with whom I speak, am prereflectively situated in and by the experiences I seek to understand. It is only with this awareness that I am able to thematize respondent experience: I understand women's experience only insofar as I have experience; insofar as I too am bodily. I proceed, in other words, with the realization that my own speaking carries perspective.

Consciousness of the body, an ability to see the body as object, informs the experience of weight consciousness. The body receives evaluation from its inhabitant: "I came home one summer and lost 27 pounds and it made a big difference in the way I look," "I do make an effort to look presentable," "I've done it in the past by really watching myself." Making oneself "presentable" as an object requires an ability to note alterations in form and bulk ("lost 27 pounds"), which in turn is contingent on "watching" and monitoring the body. Baudrillard (1981) posits a relation of mutual signification between object and owner: "[I]n the objects, one identifies a social category which has, in the final analysis, already been described on the basis of these objects (among other criteria)" (p. 35). Consciousness of the body as object, and molding the body to cultural specifications, require then an ability to see oneself as an object in relation to other objects. In women's experience, the *other objects* are women. The body is valued as an asset, as some *thing* which can be seen only when in appropriate form: "I wouldn't go out of my house except just for classes," "I almost didn't come to talk to you today because of it," "I pretty much stayed under my towel the whole time."

By definition an object is something which can be removed from my visual field, "Its presence is such that it entails a possible absence" (Merleau-Ponty, 1962, p. 90). Millman's (1980) study reveals that obese women experience the body as an "unwanted appendage," something distanced and dissociated from the person (p. 180). In respondent experience the body is often described in object-like terms: "I won't even look in the mirror because I don't like *what's* staring back at me," "women especially because for them the body, how *it* looks, I mean, is such a big *thing*," "men notice *it* more, bodies I mean" (emphasis mine). Removal from the body, seeing it from a distance, insures safekeeping and preservation. The body, like a piece of furniture, is painted, polished, dusted, veneered, lacquered, and refurbished (such as in the infamous *make-over* or *well-preserved* woman); only through such monitoring is its value retained.[5] Indeed, as one respondent notes, "you just can't let it slide."

Weight consciousness, in conjunction with body as object, is thematized experientially by body as other. Only through a prereflective understanding of others as distinct from me, from my body, can I see myself in relation to them. Awareness of the body entails a possibility of perceiving self as other; imagining how I look in the eyes of an outside observer. The popular "before" and "after" photographs used to sell reducing formulas provide the duality of identity confronting the weight-conscious individual. Here, the unpleasant reality of current existence is juxtaposed with an existence resolved. Similarly, dieting manuals give the presumedly unsightly reader the means to an *other* identity (e.g., Stuart & Davis, 1972, Principal, 1983, Sorenson & Bruns, 1983). Within the same body emerges the voice of person and the voice of other: " *I* think its true that *you* have to get a heightened sense of awareness," "I bought a magazine where *you* could see how *your* measurements compared to Christie Brinkley's," "*You* just have to decide to stick with a serious plan" (emphasis mine).

The *other* in the lives of weight conscious women is highly critical and judgmental: "God knows I'll never be asked to wear a white bikini on national T.V.," "If you reverse everything about me you'd have a good idea," "as you can see, I'm not a perfect '10'." The *other* thinks in either/or terms and settles for nothing less than a perfect union between body and mind. At the same time, Merleau-Ponty (1962) reminds us, "in so far as I have a body, I may be reduced to the status of an object beneath the gaze of another person" (p. 167). When we see the perfect other moving about in daily life, "when we gaze with envy at her as she passes us in the theater, proudly swishing her narrow hips, it is the triumph of her will we are admiring" (Chernin, 1981, p. 48). At that moment she is reduced to the status of an object; disembodied and triumphant. She is the goal of weight-conscious women in search of *wholeness:* "It's like those women who just have everything," "Jesus, I'd give anything to be like that," "Being nice to look at is really important and I'd pay just about anything to get rid of 20–25 pounds, but you can't do it that way."

Despite efforts to objectify the body and view it from an other's perspective, a prereflective familarity with the body situates human action. The body, as *person*, moves through the world with a history of habits, predispositions, and perspectives. Ultimately, the body is not

[5] The analogy between *woman* and furniture is based in Baudrillard's (1981) discussion of object functions in contemporary culture. Here, morality is tied to a *ritual hygiene* of "the triumph of varnish, polish, veneer, plating, wax, encausitic, lacquer, glaze, glass, plastic" (p. 44).

reducible to mere object status because, "To say that it is always near me, always there for me, is to say that it is never really in front of me, that I cannot array it before my eyes, that it remains marginal to all my perceptions, that it is *with* me" (Merleau-Ponty, 1962, p. 90). Conquering the body through mental strength is fundamentally a bodily task; the body situates and informs action, its habits ground behavior: "Sometimes this body of mine won't cooperate," "I know in my head I can lose weight and I know in my head I'd feel better about myself. I can't seem to convince the rest of me though. Maybe someday it'll snap into line." Drawing from Merleau-Ponty's discussion of the phantom limb, Collaizi (1978) finds that in body alterations such as weight loss, primordial familarity with the body remains; thus the newly trim body continues to *behave* as a large body (pp. 48–71). Because she has learned to move in certain ways and is accustomed to spatial inhabitance, the formerly obese woman continues to lift her legs into the car and moves the seat back to accomodate her body even though she *knows* such actions are unnecessary. Knowing something "in my head" does not erase the body's history of expression and motility.

Dieting failure is linked to the body, an inability to silence the body's history. Hatred of the flesh for its lack of cooperation is hatred of the body for its refusal to be an object, its unwillingness to undergo seasonal changes in the name of current fashions and shifting norms for *ideal* figures. Chernin (1981) describes the mind-body relation, and the mental *failure* called forth by a body engaged in even the most mundane tasks:

> Thus the body, stubborn or slow, requiring endless practice and repetition before it can even begin to approach the accomplishment of the simplest task, frustrates thought, calls into question the mind's sense of its own power, enrages the mind that cannot, for all its understanding, accomplish the tying of a shoe without the body. The body awakens in us a knowledge of our impotence, our inability to master the external world (p. 59).

Weight consciousness, as experienced, is irresolvable not because women lack determination or discipline, but because the final splitting of mind from body is impossible. When seeking to understand the current obsession with body size, the willingness to "do anything" for slenderness and wholeness, Chernin (1981) asks of the motivation: "Love or hatred?" (p. 24).

Interpretation

Interpreting the experience of weight consciousness entails a description of the intertwining of body and world. By placing women's experience in historical conditions and practices, an understanding of the coconstitution of female body and world is possible. In this section I return to my original question: How, in a decade of female strength and liberation, does a simultaneous sense of love for and hatred of the body come to pervade women's experience? I begin with observations made by Levin (1985):

> In the Western discourse of cultural symbols, the body has always been associated with the feminine, and especially the matriarchal principle, while the mind (reason, law, intelligence, brainpower) has been traditionally tied to the masculine and the patriarchal (p. 56).

And Janeway (1980):

> Western society has long offered two pictures of woman as sexual being. They are not simply contradictory; they have existed in a balanced polarity of good and bad, sacred and•profane . . . Eve is always at work to undermine Mary's dedication to good. Mary is never going to let Eve enjoy herself without waking up to a guilty morning after (pp. 5–7).

The weight-conscious woman embodies both sides of the dichotomy described by Janeway. An active struggle between good and evil is manifest in the lives of women who are socialized to mistrust their own perceptions and behaviors, their own bodies. The struggle exists and gains legitimacy in Western culture as depicted by Levin because the body is represented as a threat by virtue of its opposition to reason. The body is doubly threatening, and hence devalued, then, not only because it is associated with women, but is further linked to a feminine capacity to undermine male power. Morgan (1984) argues that female anatomy "is a destructively imagined difference, *because* it is sensed as a dangerously intuited sameness" (p. 46). Not surprisingly, one of the most devastating insults to masculinity is the accusation of homosexuality; insulting not because the recipient identifies with men, but because he signifies femininity. To *choose* affinity with women is incomprehensible within patriarchal cultures, which perhaps explains the male homosexual tendency to view sexual preference as imposed or mysterious, rather than a product of choice. The woman who worries about her weight, consuming minute quantities of food in public, speaking about the body in pejorative terms, welcoming smaller clothing sizes, comforts the audience that fears affinity with her.

The wholeness offered by contemporary weight loss discourse is mythology in a deadly form. White and Boskind-White's (1983) analysis of bulimarexia presents the life of a woman on the verge of collapse due to binge-purge behavior. Death, the woman maintains, is preferable to an overweight body. But, the astute reader will reply, she is abnormal; extreme. Yet evaluative references to the body among women, for example, "I hate you for being so slim," "I'd kill for her figure," suggests otherwise. Not only do normalizing messages divide and dissect the female body, but as Daly's (1978) chronicle of gynecological practices demonstrates, divides women from each other. It was women who bound the feet of young girls, it is women who encourage daughters to diet, and it is women who torture themselves in the name of beauty. When gangrene infests the tiny foot or when the diet goes too far, women are thought to have only themselves to blame.

The historical development of beauty as business in American culture provides a context for female body struggle. In *American Beauty*, Banner (1983) argues that three recurring themes have characterized female existence since the 1920s. The first, described by Friedan as the "feminine mystique," combines woman's maternal role with sexual seductiveness. Second is "the reality of women's continued discrimination" (p. 275). In apparent contradiction to the first two themes, Banner observes that

> Women have consistently protested against their situation, and this rebellion has led contemporaries in every decade since the 1920s to proclaim that women have attained equality and that feminist goals have been reached (p. 275).

With every struggle for liberation comes a response which *appears* to address the concerns of women, but in fact provides another set of restraints. For example, Banner (1983) notes, when suffragettes protested the class oppression of tight-lacing, which required assistance by servants, they were *rewarded* with an assistance-free corset. No longer dependent on an other, or so the story goes, they had become more independent; more *liberated*. Similarly, as women's lives and habits become part of public records, promoters of female beauty are in a better position to diagnose and "cure" defective appearance; yet the toll taken on the body and human relationships is substantial.

The strong woman in the 1980s has the power to consume and be consumed. She values economic independence, physical attractiveness (for herself rather than others), and control. Jane Fonda is a case in point. The *Workout* has generated multimillion dollar sales in books, video-cassettes, record albums, and clothing. Fonda is a consumer (she devotes a large portion of the book to her own exploitation by advertisers), and is consumed by women in pursuit of desirable bodies. The way out of exploitation, ironically, is to identify with a youthful-looking woman in her forties, clad in a leotard, and positioned lying on the floor (engaged in exercise) for the book's cover photograph. Fonda appeals to and embodies female strength; staggering profits are earned not by constraining female behavior, but by appearing to *enable* female choice and independence.

The experience of women calls into question the strong (and slender) female identity. The uncontrollable body, the consuming body, must be continuously monitored by mental strength; brought back into line by rational powers. Barthes (1985) describes dieting as a religious phenomenon: "Going on a diet has all the characteristics of a conversion. With all the same problems of lapsing, and then returning to the conversion. With certain books that are like gospels" (p. 33). The *fallen* woman in the economy of dieting must amend her ways, confess to the sin of eating, and reinstate vigilance. She does not *resolve* body problems, but rather engages in a perpetual demonstration of a difference which is culturally understood as threatening in its sheer bodiliness. Her distinction is inscribed on the body, in her movements, and in her expression. Foucault (1980) maintains that in contemporary power strategies "we find a new mode of investment which presents itself no longer in the form of control by repression but that of control by stimulation" (p. 57). The very form of power which is used to make the body strong "finds itself exposed to a counter-attack in the same body" (Foucault, 1980, p. 56). Through stimulation, that is, desiring her own body, the weight-conscious woman, like women who appear to have resolved body problems, comes to guard and preserve female identity. Yet, the cultural identity offered to women is one which implicitly castigates the bodies of women; thus there is always more to be done, further action by women which presents the body in a safe, nonthreatening form. What better way to keep women in a state of subordination than to convince them, through their own actions, that they are failures even in managing their bodies.

Consciousness of the body, particularly the crippling awareness experienced by many women, is socially grounded in an "Eve" vs. "Mary" view of woman's body. Either side of the dichotomy has at its base a denial of female experience; the former reduces woman to sexual pleasure while the latter views pleasure as a strictly male commodity. The woman who diets incessantly and hence encounters "before" and "after" characterizations of herself, who speaks of "bad" and "good" foods, and who punishes herself when the regimen is violated, views *herself* as a "failure." A curious paradox pervades the quest for bodily perfection: at one level the individual is responsible for her transformation; yet, purchasing diet books and products, in addition to the strict regulations of weight loss plans, reminds the female consumer that she is incapable of individual responsibility. A perception of personal failure motivates weight loss and the diet functions as penance. As a respondent states, "It's weird, really, setting up things so you'll stay on a diet. You weigh yourself, count calories, keep food in uniform containers, avoid going out to eat—all the things that got you into trouble to begin with—you punish yourself for being a bad girl. It just makes you feel inadequate; maybe that's why you give up in the end."

While the history of body beautification devices for women gives the appearance of self-knowledge, offering greater coherence and wholeness for female existence, such improvement programs work to advance the continuous fragmentation of women. A woman is taught to survey and dissect her body, becoming preoccupied with imperfect parts. She mistakes the eyes in the mirror as her own, failing to realize that through a polarized construction of female existence she judges herself according to the criteria of dominant culture, which fears her body. Perceptively, a respondent observes, "Sometimes I wonder about all this dieting stuff. I'm supposed to be doing it for me, but when I step on the scale and see I've lost weight my first thought is, I wonder if my husband will notice—then it'll be worthwhile." "Female a priori knowledge," argues Janeway, "cannot be taken as valid by the female self who is required by the laws of otherness to live as a displaced person not only in man's world but also within herself. As a result, her primary impulses to action are always caught and held on a frustrating brink" (p. 6). Divided also against other women, with whom experience could be shared, women are left with self-exclusionary standards of judgment.

By encouraging women to fabricate a socially acceptable appearance, without a critical assessment of the views of women inherent in cultural imagery, we teach women to dislike themselves. Each new season's beauty prescriptions announce deficiency, call for alteration, only to repeat the cycle in a few months. Moreover, one so-called improvement in appearance typically sets in motion the need for additional labor. Popular dieting literature, for example, tells women they can "reward" themselves by purchasing a new wardrobe after the transformation from fat to thin, serving as an added implicit reminder that beauty is an ongoing chore, always just beyond reach. More insidiously, the means by which a defective appearance is cured (e.g., fashion, make-up, cosmetic surgery) reveal women as imposters; the "real" woman, underneath the embellishments, is most likely plain and ordinary, indistinct. Yet, the reasoning of beauty arguments promises that added fabrication brings a woman closer to her true individual identity. By making herself *less* distinguishable from other women, working to achieve attractiveness as defined by external, generalized criteria, ironically, she is told she can become unique.

My aim in this chapter has been to question cultural constructions of women by exposing the lack of fit between women's experience and the identities offered to women in current body-shaping discourse. I have done so by describing the extent to which constructions of women invade female expression. When addressing the cultural dualism of body vs. mind, Levin (1985) argues, "We must actually *let go* of our dualistic, propositional way of 'thinking' " (p. 56). In the scheme of body-shaping discourse, women are destined to failure because, culturally, the female body is a metaphor for all that is opposed to reason, transcendence, and ultimately salvation. With each feminine failure, each weight reduction program unfulfilled, women are reinstantiated in their position of inferiority. We might well ask, whose interests are served in the perpetuation of "beauty" programs which are based in a presumption of female deficiency? Indeed, Morgan (1984) observes:

> I think, therefore I am. But men are thinking me; therefore I am not. I exist for them as the metaphor for rape and conquest, for luring them to hell or inspiring them to salvation . . . This has an effect on me (p. 46).

My conversations with women make such effects visible. Critical investigations which expose and deconstruct cultural constructions of women give credence and understanding to the experiences of everyday women, experiences which are often discounted or marginalized within androcentric frameworks. By learning to live with rather than against the body, women are encouraged to validate their own body experience in their own terms.

References

Banner, L. (1983). *American beauty*. Chicago: University of Chicago Press.

Barthes, R. (1985). The shape I'm in: Interview with French *Playboy*. In M. Blonsky (Ed.), *On signs*, (pp. 33–34). Baltimore: John's Hopkins University Press.

Baudrillard, J. (1981). *For a critique of the political economy of the sign*. (C. Levin, Trans.). St. Louis: Teleos Press.

Bayrd, E. (1978). *The thin game*. New York: Avon Press.

Bell, R. (1981). *Worlds of friendship*. Beverly Hills, CA: Sage Publications.

Berger, J. (1972). *Ways of seeing*. New York: BBC and Penguin Books.

Brownmiller, S. (1984). *Femininity*. New York: Fawcett Columbine Books.

Cash, T., & Derlega, V. (1978). The matching hypothesis: Physical attractiveness among same-sex friends. *Personality and Social Psychology Bulletin, 4*, 240–243.

Chernin, K. (1981). *The obsession: Reflections on the tyranny of slenderness.* New York: Harper-Colophon Books.

Chernin, K. (1985). *The hungry self: Women, eating and identity.* New York: Harper and Row.

Chesler, P. (1972). *Women and madness.* New York: Avon Books.

Collaizi, P. (1978). Psychological research as the phenomenologist views it. In R. Valle and M. King, (Eds.), *Existential-phenomenological alternatives for psychology.* (pp. 48–71). New York: Oxford University Press.

Daly, M. (1978). *Gyn-ecology: The meta-ethnics of radical feminism.* Boston: Beacon Press.

Downs, A. C., & Harrison, S. (1985). Embarassing age spots or just plain ugly? Physical attractiveness stereotyping as an instrument of sexism on American television commercials. *Sex Roles, 13,* 1–2.

Firestone, S. (1970). *The dialectic of sex: The case for the feminist revolution.* New York: Bantam Books.

Fonda, J. (1981). *Jane Fonda's workout book.* New York: Simon and Schuster.

Foucault, M. (1980). Body/power. In C. Gordon, Trans. *Power/knowledge: Selected interviews and other writings.* (C. Gordon, L. Marshall, J. Mepham, and K. Soper. (Ed.), New York: Pantheon Books. (pp. 55–62).

Friday, N. (1974). *My mother/my self: The daughter's search for identity.* New York: Dell Books.

Friedan, B. (1983). *The feminine mystique.* New York: Laurel Books.

Idhe, D. (1979). *Experimental phenomenology: An introduction.* New York: Paragon Books.

Janeway, E. (1980). Who's Sylvia? On the loss of sexual paradigms. In C. R. Stimpson and E. S. Person (Eds.), *Women: Sex and sexuality.* (pp. 4–20). Chicago: University of Chicago Press.

Levin, D. (1985). *The body's recollection of being: Phenomenological psychology and the deconstruction of nihlism.* London: Routledge and Kegan Paul.

Linn, R. (1980). *Staying thin.* New York: Zebra Books.

Merleau-Ponty, M. (1962). (C. Smith, Trans.) *Phenomenology of perception.* (C. Smith, Trans.) London: Routledge and Kegan Paul.

Millman, M. (1980). *Such a pretty face: Being fat in America.* New York: Berkley Books.

Morgan, R. (1984). *The anatomy of freedom: Feminism, physics, and global politics.* Garden City, NY: Anchor Books/Doubleday.

Oakley, A. (1981). Interviewing women: A contradiction in terms. In H. Roberts (Ed.), *Doing feminist research* (pp. 30–61). London: Routledge and Kegan Paul.

Orbach, S. (1978). *Fat is a feminist issue: A self-help guide for compulsive eaters.* New York: Berkley Books.

Palmer, R. (1980). *Anorexia nervosa: A guide for sufferers and their families.* New York: Penguin Books.

Patton, M. (1980). *Qualitative evaluation methods.* Beverly Hills, CA: Sage Publications.

Pearson, J. (1985). *Gender and communication.* Dubuque, IA: Wm. C. Brown Publisher.

Phillips, G., & Wood, J. (1983). *Communication and human relationships: The study of interpersonal communication.* New York: Macmillan Publishing.

Principal, V. (1983). *The body Principal: The exercise program for life.* New York: Simon and Schuster.

Sassen, G. (1980). Success anxiety in women: A constructivist interpretation of its sources and its significance. *Harvard Educational Review, 50,* 13–25.

Sontag, S. (1979). *Illness as metaphor.* New York: Vintage Books.

Sorenson, J., & Bruns, B. (1983). *Jacki Sorenson's aerobic lifestyle book.* New York: Poseidon Press.

Stewart, D., & Mickunas, A. (1974). *Exploring phenomenology: A guide to the field and its literature.* Chicago: American Library Association.

Stuart, R. (1983). *Act thin, stay thin.* New York: Jove Books.

Stuart, R., & Davis, B. (1972). *Slim chance in a fat world.* Champaign, IL: Research Press.

Tucker, L. (1985). Dimensionality and factor satisfaction of the body image construct: A gender comparison. *Sex Roles, 12* (9–10), 929–937.

Watson, R. (1985). *The philosopher's diet: How to lose weight and change the world.* Boston: Atlantic Monthly Press.

White, W., & Boskind-White, M. (1983). *Bulimarexia: The binge/purge cycle.* New York: W. W. Norton Publishers.

Widgery, R. (1974). Sex of receiver and physical attractiveness as source determinants of initial credibility perception. *Western Speech, 38,* 13.

Zimmerman, M. (1987). Feminism, deep ecology, and environmental ethics. *Environmental Ethics, 9,* 21–44.

5

Liberating Laughter: An Inquiry Into the Nature, Content, and Functions of Feminist Humor

Cindy L. White

San Francisco State University

Among the more popular stereotypes that purport to explain the differences between men and women is the one that women have no sense of humor. Ingrained in this bit of popular wisdom is the notion that women are incapable of understanding and appreciating jokes, and that they are equally unable to remember and/or retell jokes. Kramarae (1981) highlights the prevalence of this assumption when she notes that "male beliefs about gender differences in humor, or at least their *statements* about women's lack of a sense of humor, appear to be one of the firmest, more constant of the 'accusations' made by men about women's speech behavior" (p. 53). The popular acceptance of the stereotype that women, particularly feminists, are not funny (as in the joke, Q: How many feminists does it take to screw in a lightbulb? A: That's not funny) sparked feminist discussions of the nature of women's humor and inspired attempts to uncover, recover, discover, and create a distinctive women's humor. The purpose of this study is to provide a preliminary empirical investigation and analysis of this emerging feminist humor.

Review of the Literature

The most striking similarity among contemporary analyses of women's humor is the common assumption that women do indeed possess a sense of humor that differs from the male sense of humor and that

75

these differences are largely attributable to cultural differences between the sexes. Kramarae (1981) indicates that in general "humor is largely culture-specific [and] that much joking is based on ingroup/outgroup relationships" (p. 52). As a result, much male humor targets women as the butt of jokes since women are the outgroup among the sexes. Neitz' (1980) research and observations indicate the recent emergence of a feminist culture that does not tolerate or laugh at deprecatory humor aimed at women and that sanctions only that humor which affirms the values of feminist culture. After collecting examples of feminist humor into a single book (Kaufman & Blakely, 1980), Kaufman (1980) posits that "if it is true that people are revealed through their humor" then this collection of feminist humor "testifies to a difference, if not between female and male, at least between female and mainstream male" (p. 15). She further argues that "feminist humor and satire demonstrate that *culturally* we have not been doing what the male does" (p. 15). Kaufman intimates that differing cultures bear direct responsibility for the disparities between feminist and male humor.

Many discussions of feminist humor reflect the position that women are socialized to fit a mainstream male culture which promulgates the notion that women are not and should not be funny (Beatts, 1975; Coser, 1960; Weisstein, 1973). The pronouncements of male culture dictate that women are passive and men are aggressive. Accordingly, women who are perceived to have a good sense of humor are not those who produce humor but those who display appreciation for the male sense of humor (Beatts, 1975; Coser, 1960). In essence, women are socialized to provide an audience for male risibility (Beatts, 1975). Coser's (1960) study of humor and laughter at staff meetings in a mental hospital demonstrated the force and result of such socialization. She reports that while many of the female staff members displayed a great capacity for humor, they deferred in humor production to the male staff, who were responsible for 99 out of 103 witticisms at the meetings. Coser notes that while men made most of the jokes, "women often laughed harder" (p. 85).

Beyond discouraging the display of humor in women, cultural forces also deny the existence of female humor by misnaming it and failing to record it. Beatts (1975) notes that while men are encouraged to joke about one another, the same type of humor, when it occurs among women, is labeled "cattiness" and "cattiness is not encouraged" (p. 184). Hence, what passes for playful jocularity among men is culturally defined as an example of female bitchiness among women. A practice that is perhaps more prevalent and pernicious than misnaming women's humor is ignoring it by failing to include it in general anthologies of humor. LaJoy (1977) notes that while women were historically denied the same opportunities to prove themselves humorous that men enjoyed, there are nonetheless humorous writings dating from 1600 that flowed from the pens of both English and American women. Most anthologies of humor include, however, only a paucity of examples of women's wit. Green (1977) attributes the lack of knowledge of a rich tradition of bawdy lore among Southern women to the fact that most scholars of such tales are men who receive the lore mainly from other men. Mitchell (1977) notes the recent increase in the number of jokes that include a female protagonist and a male butt. She suggests that while newness might account for the increase of such jokes, it is equally possible that these kinds of jokes were omitted by the males who collected jokes or that the same male compilers never heard them. Historically, cultural forces discouraged women from producing humor and disregarded those female humorists who somehow overcame the obstacles of their cultural predicament and displayed a flair for humor.

Feminist explanations of the historical dearth of female humorists blame male cultural forces for quelling the humorous initiative in women and for precluding the collection of available humor. Cultural changes, inspired mainly by the contemporary women's movement, are cited as the reason for the recent change in the posture of women's humor. Essentially, the women's movement has begun to redefine "what is funny to whom." With the emergence of the contemporary women's movement, the stereotypic image of the humorless female assumes a new twist. Rather than seeing the broad category of all women as lacking a sense of humor, the new humorless woman is in a specific category—feminists. Moreover, the allegation does not single out feminists in particular for a notorious lack of humor but suggests that feminists have *lost* their sense of humor, a feature they, as women, purportedly never possessed. Many feminists suggest that their refusal to continue to laugh at jokes which denigrate women has prompted the allegation that they have lost their sense of humor (Beatts, 1975; Clinton, 1982; Neitz, 1980; Weisstein, 1973). Feminist refusal to continue to serve as the butt of the joke threatens the cultural and political superiority of men (Beatts, 1975; Kaufman, 1980; Weisstein, 1973). Male awareness of the political uses of humor, especially as a mechanism for social change and for cultural expression and survival, is responsible for their fear of a distinctive women's humor (Beatts, 1975; Weisstein, 1973). Kaufman (1980) adds that men mistakenly believe that feminist humor will seek to retaliate against the misogynist nature of male humor and hence will be largely anti-male. Thus, according to feminist explanations, the change in women's humor is largely attributable to the recent articulation of the need for cultural changes inspired by the contemporary women's movement.

Specific discussions and studies of the nature and function of feminist humor are relatively scarce. Walker (1981) reviews examples of feminist humor that targets women's rights advocates and their ideals and concludes that feminists have a great capacity for self-mockery which ultimately functions to attack stereotypic images of women. By taking note of what feminist humor deplores, Walker suggests that "the ideal woman who emerges by implication is gutsy, self-determined, clear-eyed" (p. 8).

A self-identified fumerist (a word apparently of her own coinage that combines feminist and humorist), Clinton (1982) stresses that feminist humor "is about exposure" (p. 39). While male humor strives to maintain a culturally imbalanced status quo, feminist humor exposes the sources of imbalance and attempts to eradicate them. Thus, the nature of feminist humor is active rather than passive. According to Clinton, because feminist humor sheds light on women's oppression and points out the need for its elimination, it functions as a source for cultural and political change. Moreover, feminist humor impels women to laugh together, thereby bridging differences among individuals and creating a sense of community. Clinton argues that the combined nature and function of feminist humor cannot and should not be understood as a string of feminist jokes or anecdotes. Rather, feminist humor can and should only be understood as the following:

> It is a deeply radical analysis of the world and our [women's] being in the world because it, like the erotic, demands a commitment to joy. Feminist humor is a radical analysis because we are saying that we have the right to be happy, that we will not settle for less. (p. 4)

Kaufman (1980) utilizes a collection of examples of feminist humor (Kaufman & Blakely, 1980) as the basis for her remarks about the nature and functions of feminist humor. Although she draws on a compendium of examples of feminist humor, a method Clinton warns against, Kaufman reaches the same basic conclusions concerning the nature and function of feminist humor that Clinton articulates. Kaufman suggests that feminist humor is visionary inasmuch as it recognizes the oppression of women and works toward its elimination. Unlike misogynist male humor, feminist humor does not elevate the value of women at the expense of men. Rather than beginning from the assumption that men are the enemy, feminist humor adopts the view that all oppression and exploitation is harmful, unnecessary, and must be repudiated. Kaufman suggests that feminist humor, "since it arises from a subculture that has no patience with stereotyping, especially in relation to sex roles . . . avoids stereotypic characters" (p. 14). Feminist humor is not based on a need for retaliation but rather on a desire for equity. Hence, the major functions served by feminist humor, according to Kaufman, are the obliteration of pernicious myths and stereotypes that solidify and perpetuate oppression and the bonding of people that arises from a humor that cultivates equity. It is important to note that while much of the literature does not distinguish between feminist humor and women's humor, Kaufman draws a distinction between feminist humor and *female* humor. Kaufman argues that female humor, while it may recognize cultural inequities, does not seek to change them. Feminist humor, on the other hand, functions to obliterate those inequities. Thus, according to Kaufman, the difference between the two is that "feminist humor tends to be a humor of hope, female humor of hopelessness" (pp. 13–14). Further, Kaufman suggests that female humor often parallels male humor inasmuch as both perpetuate harmful myths and stereotypes of and about women.

Finally, Blakely (1980), drawing on the same collection as Kaufman & Blakely (1980), suggests that feminist humor is "honest" (p. 12). Its honesty arises from its keen awareness of women's unfair predicament and its attempts to express and protest that predicament. For Blakely, feminist humor serves two major functions. First, it points out the feminist dissatisfaction with the status quo. Second, it functions as a source of comic relief to the war-weary combatants in the struggle for equality. It is used by feminists as a "cure for burnout" (p. 12). There seem to be three basic assumptions that are common to the literature on feminist humor. First, many discussions reviewed here assume that humor is culture-specific. Second, these writers imply that humor relies for its effects on shared knowledge of the assumptions, values, and meanings common to a particular community or culture. Third, the literature suggests that humor reaffirms the values of a culture. These basic theoretical assumptions shaped my orientation to this inquiry which assumes that feminist humor is specific to feminist culture and is an artifact of that culture.

Unfortunately, most of the discussions of feminist humor are largely theoretical and therefore reflect only a theoretical description of feminist culture. Empirical investigations of feminist humor have focused primarily on the collection of examples of humor used by feminists. While collections of feminist humor are indeed valuable, they do not illustrate the nature of feminist culture in the same way a naturalistic study of feminist humor might. The former is constrained by a method of collection that not only assumes that feminists enjoy a common brand of humor (i.e., that all feminists will find a particular story or joke funny), but also assumes that certain jokes and anecdotes represent feminist humor. That is, the method of collection forces the assumption that a particular anecdote exemplifies feminist humor and that therefore feminists would find the anecdote humorous. The most serious deficiency of anthologies of feminist humor, however, is that they do not adequately describe how feminist humor functions in actual situations. In other words, standardized examples of feminist humor rarely provide insight into the more subtle expressions of feminist values and beliefs simply because they do not project the audience into the situation from which those expressions arose. Although I suspect that such examples and collections as reviewed here accurately reflect the nature of feminist humor, there is nonetheless a need to supplement these standardized and formal examples with examples of feminist humor that occur in natural settings among feminist participants.

Thus far, only one study (Neitz, 1980) has attempted to research feminist humor in a natural setting. Neitz found that feminists do not laugh at jokes which denigrate women. She further found that feminists seem to enjoy two specific kinds of humor. First, they enjoyed a brand of self-denigration humor that reaffirmed the values of the group by playing on sexist assumptions about women. Second, feminists enjoyed jokes that depicted hostility toward men (especially castration jokes). Neitz attributed the popularity of castration jokes to the notion that they allow women to display aggression and sexuality, traits that are societally taboo for women, and that they glorify the strength of women.

In contrast to collections of feminist humor that largely present standardized examples of feminist humor (e.g., formal jokes, stories, essays, etc.), Neitz found that much of the feminist humor that occurred among the group she studied "took the form of informal witticisms: particular statements or situations were responded to with one-liners that others chose to interpret as funny" (p. 220). Unfortunately, Neitz reports only one example of such humor. Neitz' findings suggest that much feminist humor is largely contextual and therefore may not be amenable to standardization. If such is the case, then much feminist humor may slip through the fingers of feminist anthologists and remain unrecorded and unexamined.

While Neitz' study did occur in a natural setting, it fails to adequately describe the nature of feminist humor as an indicator of feminist culture. Neitz focuses more on what the humor she observed says about women's resistance to assimilation into male culture than on what that humor says about a feminist culture. Although Neitz argues that the feminists she studied "were consciously attempting to subvert the sexual hierarchy and this is reflected in their humor" (p. 220), she does not correlate her argument to the existence of a distinctive feminist culture that possibly motivated the conscious attempts at subversion she observed. Moreover, since Neitz did not frame her study from the perspective that feminists enjoy a peculiar brand of humor because they identify as feminists, she did not delineate her findings on the basis of feminist values or ideals. Thus, while Nietz' study provides valuable insight into feminist humor, it does not seek to explain that humor as a factor of and in feminist culture. In an attempt to extend Neitz' findings and more fully explore the nature of feminist humor, this study posits the following research questions: (a) What values are expressed in feminist humor? (b) How do feminists differentiate themselves as feminists in and through their humor? (c) What function does humor, as a form of communication, serve in the creation of feminist culture?

Method

The method used in this study is participant-observation. Five self-identified feminists maintained logs of examples of feminist humor that occurred in various natural settings and situations over an eight-week period. Informants varied in terms of geographic location, age, sexual orientation, and group membership.

In order to devise the log format, I maintained a log for a period of two weeks. On the basis of that test, I developed the following log format for the recording of examples of feminist humor. Informants recorded the date on which they collected the humor, indicated the number of persons present in the situation, their sex, and sexual orientation. Informants were also asked to indicate the nature of the setting in which the humor occurred (e.g., professional, social, etc.). The log also includes a notation of the context in which the humor occurred. Finally, informants were asked to summarize the humorous example and record the response it incurred from the participants.

The analysis of feminist humor presented in this study is based solely on my own examination of the logs I received. Three logs, which collectively included approximately 50 examples of feminist humor, were returned to me. Initially I compared the logs with an eye toward determining the similarities and dissimilarities among them. On the basis of this comparison, I noted those features of the humor content that recurred in all of the logs. These features are reported below in the section on humor content. Following my analysis of humor content, I examined the humor in terms of the functions it served in a particular situation on the basis of the content of the humor, the context it arose from, and the response it received. Finally, I surveyed both the content and functions of the humor in an effort to answer the three questions I posed about feminist humor.

Findings and Discussion

Although the content and functions of feminist humor presented below are divided into separate sections, they should not be viewed as detached from one another. The content of the examples of humor that were recorded in the logs and the settings and contexts the humor arose from suggests a deep connection between humor content and function. Often, the function a particular example of feminist humor serves can only be understood in terms of its content. Accordingly, the content of the humor is often enhanced by the way it functions in a particular situation.

Humor Content

Seven broad categories of humor content emerged from my analysis of the logs. A brief outline of these categories with examples follows. It is important to keep in mind that the categories were not predetermined but emerged from a comparison of the logs. Further, it is important to understand that these categories are not mutually exclusive and may not be exhaustive. Many of the examples provided below illustrate two or more categories. I have, however, tried to use examples where they best illustrate a specific category. Where possible, I have reproduced the samples of humor content exactly as they appeared in the logs.

(1)   Much of the humor that appeared in the logs reverses main-stream cultural beliefs, values, and roles. For example, one informant recorded the following scene in a Chinese restaurant:

Two women and one man were sitting in the restaurant when a police*man* (emphasis appeared in the log) walked in to pick up a take-out order. After surveying the physical appearance of the policeman, the man said, "Do you suppose I should tell him that his panty line is showing?"

In this example, the mainstream cultural notion that only women have and should be concerned with panty lines is reversed by applying that cultural dictate to a man.

The following example of this same category appeared in the log of a different informant:

At a staff meeting at a college health center, the clinic director told a story about Harvard University's struggle with their health fee. Men objected to paying the same fee as women, since they couldn't get a Pap smear. So Harvard went through all this rigmarole to figure out what part of the health fee was attributable to the pap smear. Finally, they notified the men that they could come pick up their 50-cent checks. K (who is identified in the log as), a feminist and a therapist, says quietly, " 'Pap smear envy.' " This example, through a clear use of word play, reverses the mainstream cultural belief that women are victims of penis envy.

(2) The second category that emerged from the logs consists of examples of humor that ridicule mainstream cultural expectations. The following description of a conversation that took place at a dinner party illustrates the nature of humor that falls into this category:

The women are discussing breast size, "specifically, how we never feel like our breasts are the 'right' size, because of conflicting cultural expectations of how we're supposed to be flat-chested or voluptuous. One woman says, 'I guess we're expected to have one kind of breast on one side and one kind on the other.' " The conflictual nature of the demands made upon women by mainstream cultural expectations led this woman to ridicule those expectations by her observation.

(3) Mainstream cultural expectations are not the only values that feminist humor ridicules. Often, feminist expectations are exposed as ridiculous as well. For example, a woman who was presenting a paper on lesbian sexuality at a conference reportedly made the following observation:

"Politically correct sex lasts at least three hours, since everyone knows we're process-oriented and not goal-oriented. If we do have orgasms, those orgasms must be simultaneous. And we must lie side by side. Now I know that some people think that orgasms are patriarchal. But I've given up many things for feminism, and this isn't going to be one of them." The objects of ridicule in this example are the feminist-defined expectations of what is politically correct. The woman who produced this humor ridiculed some notions of political correctness by taking them to the extreme and pointing out the absurd proportions they sometimes attain.

(4) Much of the humor collected in the logs is about common female experience and how that experience is viewed from the perspective of mainstream culture. A pregnant woman, for example, had this to say about her experience with pregnancy and how people treat that condition:

"It's like being handicapped. People I don't know come up and ask about the baby and they're always really quiet. And people open doors and try to carry my books. And I've started saying things, like, 'Don't worry, it's not terminal.' " The treatment this woman received as a pregnant woman in a culture that does not always understand the peculiarities of female experience forced her to draw an analogy between pregnancy and being handicapped. Much of the humor that falls into this category suggests that within the confines of mainstream culture women *are* handicapped.

(5) The fifth category of feminist humor consists of humor that stresses the affirmation of women's strength. In the following example, three women are discussing how men deal with women professionally:

" 'One says, they really don't know how to deal with you. They either pretend you're not there or they go through all this pseudo-liberated crap about how terrible it is that some men treat women so badly. They act like they're so threatened if you express even an ounce of sense. And I just want to say, you better be threatened 'cuz I'm smarter than you are, and the game is no secret anymore, and, besides, you can be replaced by a test tube.' " The content of this humor is about women's intellectual and physical strength. In this example, as in others that fall into this category, women are portrayed as strong, capable people who are threatening to break through the male power structure and expose the falsity of the assumption that men are necessary to women's existence, or, for that matter, at all.

(6) A number of examples of feminist humor that appeared in the logs are based on in-group/out-group relationships. Often the distinction between the two groups is made on the basis of shared meanings of words and experiences. Those who understand the meanings are placed in the in-group, those who don't, in the out-group. For example, one of the logs relates the following conversation that occurred among three women:

"A says (in reference to a . . . professor . . .): 'I wouldn't take another class with him. He may be an expert in [a specific area] but he's a racist, a misogynist, and a general asshole.' B enters at this point. C says, 'What's that?' A: 'What's what?' C: 'A misogynist.' A: pause, 'A woman hater.' C: 'Oh (laugh, says to B), are you one of those?' B: 'Oh, no! I love women.' " After recording the example, the informant made the following note: "The joke was intended on C since she would not know how to react if someone announced she was a lesbian." The example and the explanation of it provided by the informant clearly suggest that the content of the humor emerged on the basis that two of the women understood the implicit meaning of the exclamation, "Oh, no! I love women," as an expression of lesbianism while the third did not. Whether or not the woman who uttered the explanation is actually a lesbian is not important. What is important is that the content of the humor yielded an in-group and an out-group and placed two women in the in-group and the third in the out-group.

A second example of this category illustrates the point differently. At a dinner party, one woman made reference to her lover's stepmother in the following manner:

" 'She's a witch in the patriarchal sense of the word.' " In this example, the success of the joke relied on the assumption that the audience would understand that there are two senses of the word *witch*. Using the patriarchal sense of the word to describe the lover's stepmother places the unfortunate woman in the out-group.

(7) The last category of humor that emerged from the logs can be termed anti-male humor. This categorization, however, is not intended to suggest that feminist humor parallels anti-woman humor. While the latter denigrates women on a universal level as women, the former is generally limited to attacks on specific men and/or the abstract cultural notion that men are superior. The following example illustrated feminist anti-male humor:

Two males and two females are "talking about a very successful woman they all know. One male starts talking about how badly she is treated and says they (the men who compromise her) really can't deal with her style and polish, they want her fat and ugly and drooling. Maybe we could get them some fat, ugly glasses and everytime they had trouble with a woman they could put them on and she'd be fat and ugly. One woman says, And we could have reverse ones for women so that they could put them on and not have to look at all those ugly men." As is clear from the example, this kind of anti-male joke is targeted at specific men. Moreover, the humor points out that while men need to see women as fat and ugly in order to deal with them, women are continually forced to deal with ugly men whom they are tired of looking at. The humor, however, does not necessarily attack all men, nor posit that all men are naturally ugly. Male anti-woman humor, on the other hand, seems to attack women on the basis of the assumption that women are "naturally" inferior, ugly, gross, abnormal, and so on.

Functions of Feminist Humor

While it is impossible to determine exactly what function(s) each or all of the examples of feminist humor served in the situations they emerged in and from, it is possible, on the basis of humor content and context, to draw some general conclusions about the functions of the humor.

As was the case in Neitz' (1980) study, many of the examples of feminist humor collected for this study are spontaneous and contextual expressions of humor. Often, situations that were deemed ridiculous by feminists became the subject of humorous observations, as in the case of the Pap smear envy comment. Further, these examples of humor often expose and scoff at ludicrous cultural expectations, as in the observation that women should have two different-sized breasts.

The interplay of context and function seems to serve three general purposes. First, it allows feminists to identify and differentiate themselves as feminists on the basis of knowledge of shared meaning. This purpose was best illustrated in the example that addressed misogyny and lesbianism. In that case, the two feminists identified themselves as such by demonstrating an understanding of the meanings implicit in the humor, and they differentiated themselves from the nonfeminist who failed to grasp those meanings.

Second, it provides both an outlet and a method for responding to the cultural oppression of women. By ridiculing and reversing those cultural forces and expectations that seek to deprive women of the autonomy that is necessary to self-definition, self-fulfillment, and a sense of self-worth, contextual and spontaneous expressions of feminist humor not only return that autonomy to women but allow them to exercise it and define themselves. Thus, the example about Pap smear envy allowed the feminists in that group (who were identified as the only ones who laughed in that situation) to expose the oppressiveness of the notion of penis envy and to reverse that oppression to their own advantage.

Third, the interplay of context and function allows women to bond on the basis of shared meanings and experiences. Thus, for example, the experience alluded to by the pregnant woman addresses problems that only women are forced to face. The articulation of those problems enabled the two women involved to mock common responses to female experience and to bond together, through their laughter, against those responses.[1]

---

[1] In addition to spontaneous examples of feminist humor, I also received examples of standardized feminist humor. One informant, for example, recorded a number of instances of humor from a professional feminist humorist, Kate Clinton. The performance took place at a women's concert and the nature of that setting, in addition to the political

In general, the interplay between the context and content of feminist humor, and the responses the humor received, yield several broad conclusions about the functions of feminist humor. First, feminist humor functions in such a way that allows for identification and self-differentiation by its users; second, it exposes cultural inequities; third, it serves a bonding function; fourth, it stresses the shared experiences (professional, personal, and natural) of women as women; and fifth, it positively values women and their experiences.

Conclusions

The first question this study addressed was: What values are expressed in feminist humor? Both the discussions of feminist humor content and functions point out that this brand of humor stresses the oppressive nature of dominant male culture and demonstrates feminist resistance to the acceptance of patriarchal cultural dictates. We can begin by saying, therefore, that feminist humor does *not* value oppression. It especially does not value rigidly defined cultural roles that function to oppress women. Feminist humor does value women, a point that can initially be made on the basis of the notable absence of anti-women jokes in the logs. Further, the small amount of anti-male jokes seems to indicate that feminist humor values men but not their culture. While there were examples of humor that attacked specific men and women, those attacks were generally made in the larger context of ridiculing dominant culture and did not suggest universal attacks on either women or men. Beyond expressing a general positive valuation of women,

---

attitudes of the comic herself, seems to have influenced Clinton's material. For example, the log indicates that Clinton jokes about the descriptions of differences between heterosexuals and homosexuals: " 'There's life and then there's lifestyle. Heterosexuals have a life; I have a lifestyle.' " This comment functions to identify Clinton as a lesbian and lets her audience share in poking fun at those descriptions on the basis of their common understanding of Clinton's point. Clinton also jokes about the cultural oppression of all women, as is exemplified in the following one-liner: " 'As near as I can figure it, the only woman who has never been oppressed is a man.' "

Clinton's material, while it is standardized rather than spontaneous, seems to serve the same three purposes as spontaneous feminist humor. It elucidates the meanings and experiences feminists share and allows them to differentiate themselves from others on the basis of those meanings, it ridicules cultural oppression, and it enables feminists to bond on the basis of their shared meanings, experiences, and nonacceptance of oppressive cultural dictates. It is important to note that Clinton's material is standardized only in the sense that it is a comic routine. As such, the parallels between the functions of her material and spontaneous feminist humor might be explained by Clinton's efforts to create the illusion of spontaneity in her routine. Unfortunately, absent an interview with Clinton herself, it is impossible to determine the validity of that explanation.

feminist humor stresses women's experiences as women from a perspective that celebrates and applauds those experiences. For example, Pap smears become enviable experiences in feminist humor and pregnancy is treated as a "normal" condition rather than a handicap.

Feminist humor also values the affirmation of women's strengths and capabilities. In that humor, the strong and capable woman is not depicted as maladjusted but rather those who need to see that woman as fat and ugly are the ones who seem to need glasses in order to keep their maladjusted and archaic cultural view intact.

Finally, feminist humor values autonomy and self-definition for women. Just as feminist humor does not tolerate the rigidity of male culture, neither does it tolerate inflexibility in feminism. Hence, a feminist can jest about the disproportional influence the notion of political correctness can exercise in a feminist's life, if she lets it. Because it tolerates jokes about strict feminist interpretations of certain concepts, feminist humor allows feminists the autonomy to define and delimit the boundaries of feminist doctrine in their lives. In this way, feminist humor positively accentuates autonomy and self-definition. The values that are most often expressed in feminist humor, then, are flexibility of cultural roles, acceptance and affirmation of women's strength, and autonomy. The notion of equality seems to underlie all of these values.

The second question this study aimed to answer was: How do feminists differentiate themselves as feminists in and through their humor? Again, we can start by approaching the question from the point of view of the negative. Feminist humor indicates that feminists do *not* differentiate themselves as feminists by referring to some monolithic notion of feminism. Once again, the feminist who joked about not giving up orgasms for feminism illustrated the point. Her humor revealed the fact that feminism, whatever else it may be, is not monolithic in nature. Her refusal to give up orgasms for feminism does not suggest that she no longer defines herself as a feminist but only that she has placed limits on the extent to which she feels she must go in order to retain her feminism.

The analysis of feminist humor in this study suggests that most of the time feminists are self-differentiated in and through their humor on the basis of a shared understanding of meaning and in-group/out-group relationships. Reference to shared meaning allows feminists to identify themselves as such to other feminists and to distinguish themselves from nonfeminists. Thus, identifying someone as "a witch in the patriarchal sense of the word" demonstrates that the producer of the joke distinguishes between that sense of the word and another, more positive, sense of the word. In doing so, she expects a particular response from her audience based on her assumption that they too understand the distinction and will find the joke funny because of that understanding. Moreover, this same example illustrates that knowledge of shared meaning can create in-group/out-group relationships and that self-differentiation can also be achieved by being able to identify with the correct group in terms of the humor.

The final question this study addressed was: What function does humor, as a form of communication, serve in the creation of feminist culture? The most vital role feminist humor seems to play in the creation of feminist culture is in the articulation of common meanings. First, by stressing common feminist-identified meanings, feminist humor can create a sense of community among its admirers on the basis of identification and bonding around those meanings. Second, common meanings that express in-group/out-group relationships in feminist humor function to establish the boundaries of feminist culture. Third, and finally, the use of common meanings and in-group/out-group relationships in feminist humor allows for self-identification as a feminist. In other words, by laughing at a particular example of feminist humor, a participant can identify with the feminist assumptions inherent in the humor and thereby recognize her own feminism. While I do not want to suggest that finding a particular instance of feminist humor funny automatically functions to impel the participant to embrace feminism, I do want to suggest that such an instance may lead to a moment wherein feminist principles are recognized as such and accepted for what they are—expressions of an alternative cultural view. Humor, like other forms of communication, can function to introduce and identify the culture it represents and, by doing so, in turn shapes the expression and ultimately the nature of that culture.

Although it is true that many forms of communication can function to create culture through an expression and reproduction of common meanings, that observation does not decrease the significance of the role humor plays in that function. Indeed, because humor is often a very cathartic process, its power as a creative force in culture production may be greater than other forms of communication. For humor, and the laughter it produces, often lets us bond with people in ways that no other form of communication can.

The results of this study indicate that feminists have a rich and varied humorous tradition that merits further research. However, because of the exploratory nature of the study, many of the conclusions drawn about feminist humor, and especially its relationship to feminist culture, are tentative. Those scholars who wish to proceed in the area of naturally occurring feminist humor should pay special attention to the limitations of this study. First, the current analysis is based on data drawn from a small number of informants. Sampling a greater number of subjects would provide a broader array of examples on which to base conclusions about the nature and functions of feminist humor. Second, other than examining the context of the humor, this researcher made no attempt to discover how and why informants distinguished feminist humor from other brands of humor. Interviewing informants with respect to this issue would provide valuable insight into how feminists themselves define feminist humor. Finally, future researchers should more fully explore the nature of the connection between feminist humor and feminist culture. This study represents only a beginning at uncovering and understanding this connection. Further scholarship might focus on examinations of the role of feminist humor in other cultural forms such as music and theatre. The deep connection between feminist humor and feminist culture and the fabric of both will only be revealed through further analyses. Interested scholars should mine all aspects of that connection so that we may continue laughing—together.

References

Beatts, A. (1975, November). Can a woman get a laugh and a man too? *Mademoiselle*, pp. 140, 182–186.

Blakely, M. K. (1980). Dear Gloria. In G. Kaufman & M. K. Blakely (Eds.), *Pulling our own strings* (pp. 9–13). Bloomington, IN: Indiana University.

Clinton, K. (1982). Making light: Another dimension—some notes on feminist humor. *Trivia, 1*, 37–42.

Coser, R. L. (1960). Laughter among colleagues: A study of the social functions of humor among the staff of a mental hospital. *Psychiatry, 23*(1), 81–95.

Green, R. (1977). Magnolias grow in dirt: The bawdy lore of Southern women. *Southern exposure, 4*(4), 29–33.

Kaufman, G. (1980). Introduction. In G. Kaufman & M. K. Blakely (Eds.), *Pulling our own strings* (pp. 13–16). Bloomington, IN: Indiana University.

Kaufman, G., & Blakely, M. K. (Eds.). (1980). *Pulling our own strings*. Bloomington, IN: Indiana University.

Kramarae, C. (1981). *Women and men speaking: Frameworks for analysis*. Rowley, MA: Newbury House.

LaJoy, M. (1977). No laughing matter: Women and humor. *Women, 5*(1), 6–9.

Mitchell, C. (1977). Hostility and aggression toward males in female joke telling. *Western Folklore, 3*(3), 19–23.

Neitz, M. J. (1980). Humor, hierarchy, and the changing status of women. *Psychiatry, 43*(3), 211–223.

Walker, N. (1981). Do feminists ever laugh? Women's humor and women's rights. *International Journal of Women's Studies, 4*, 1–9.

Weisstein, N. (1973, November). Why we aren't laughing . . . any more. *Ms.*, pp. 49–51, 88–90.

6

Shirley Chisholm With Black and White Women's Audiences

Dorothy K. Williamson-Ige

Indiana University Northwest

Shirley Chisholm, black and female, is one of the few public figures who has expressed ideology rooted in both the black movement and the women's movement. While serving as United States Representative from 1968 through 1984, Chisholm focused many of her speeches toward American females, regardless of color, toward obtaining women's rights. How, why, and with what effect Chisholm has relayed her messages to females about women's issues can shed light on how women talk with other women in public settings.

My purpose is to analyze the communication or rhetorical strategies used by Chisholm in her discourse directed to black and white females on women's rights. Here I examine four of her messages to women on sexism and note the impact of Chisholm's character as well. The essay focuses on the rhetorical vision in Chisholm's public addresses, similarities and differences in Chisholm's rhetoric to black and white female audiences, and draws general implications for female public speakers targeting women's audiences.

Four categories of research literature are relevant to this analysis. First, general background studies have been conducted on Chisholm's life and works. Brownmiller (1975), Haskins (1975), and Hicks (1971) present biographical sketches in which Chisholm is portrayed as a dynamic and sincere politician who struggles to fight sexism in society. Chisholm's (1973; 1970a) two autobiographical works provide the same basic portrayal.

The second category of literature involves communication research on Chisholm. To my knowledge, the only past communication study completed on the Congresswoman is an essay in which I (Williamson-

Ige, 1984) assess two persuasive speeches of Chisholm using Asante's Afrocentric methodology and conclude that the speaker's rhetorical efforts are appropriate in both messages.

Third, communication studies have been conducted on other contemporary women as public speakers on women's rights. Brake and Neulieb's (1983) survey on women orators as well as Brake's (1967) separate bibliography covers various other females as public speakers; including some who focused on women's issues. Both sources provide valuable references for scholars interested in research about female public speakers. Pinola and Briggs (1979) analyze the rhetorical strategies used by Congresswoman Martha Wright Griffiths and determine that Griffiths' use of Burkeian techniques of good, evil, and scapegoating make her successful in persuading other Congress members to support equal rights for women.

A fourth group of studies includes those dealing with female public speakers who face constraints similar to those of Chisholm, including audience adaptation and overcoming the stereotype of being female. Thompson (1979a & 1979b) treats Barbara Jordan's keynote address to the 1976 Democratic National Convention. He indicates that Jordan's adaptation to meet the seemingly contradictory expectations of party loyalty in her immediate delegate audience and high values of patriotism in the general television audience account for her success. Whalen (1976) assesses Ella Grasso's verbal and nonverbal communication and claims that she is a successful politician because of her image as an admirable wife and mother as well as a decisive leader who can wear sneakers and pants on the job when necessary.

These past studies have added insight to my assessment of Chisholm's life and works, as well as clarifying the qualities of discourse employed by other contemporary female public speakers. This essay adds to the extant literature in two ways. It provides additional information on Chisholm's public communication. It also focuses on how a female politician talks to women about themselves while taking into account the various groups' ethnic subcultural boundaries.

The analysis covers four oral messages presented by Chisholm on women's issues since the revival of the women's movement that began in the 1960s. The first speech, "The 51% Minority," (1970b) was delivered in Washington, DC. For easy reference, this message will be referred to as the Washington address or speech. The second speech, "Women in Politics: Why Not?" (1972) was delivered at Mills College in Oakland, California and photocassette tape recorded by the Pacifica Tape Library. It will be referred to as the Oakland address. The third speech "The Contemporary Black Woman," (1980a) was delivered in Cincinnati, Ohio and will be referred to as the Cincinnati address. The fourth message "The Black Woman's Response to Women's Liberation: An Interview," (1980b) was delivered in Columbus, Ohio and will be referred to as the Columbus address.

Although Congresswoman Chisholm probably delivered numerous other messages in which gender concerns are mentioned, I limit my focus to those of Chisholm's messages now in print or verifiably tape-recorded which primarily targeted females. With one exception, the messages under study were all presented as public speeches. The one exception is an interview between Chisholm and myself which she permitted me to tape record.

The first two presentations, the Washington and Oakland speeches, focus on all women—particularly white females of the dominant American culture—while the later Cincinnati and Columbus messages target black females. I am broadly defining audiences as target groups who are affected by and are encouraged to act upon the ideas presented rather than in a narrower sense of the immediate audience physically present for each presentation. Thus the analysis is idea-centered rather than being concerned primarily with the specific time, place, and non-verbal delivery.

Two qualifications are needed at this point. First, one may notice that a well-published address "Equal Rights for Women" (1969), delivered by Chisholm to Congress, is absent from the analysis. The omission is purposeful. While the speech deals with women's issues and many ideas Chisholm presents are present in other messages studied here, the Congressional speech is largely structured for and aimed at a predominantly male legislative audience rather than representing Chisholm's talk to women.

Second, I want to note that Chisholm often mentions other ethnic groups of women in her public communication (1970b, p. 910; 1970a, p. 116; 1969; p. 13380). While issues concerning Asian, Native, and Spanish-Speaking American females are certainly important, this study focuses specifically on the interplay between the concerns of race and sex in Chisholm's discourse with black and white American women's audiences.

Rhetorical Vision Theme in Chisholm's Messages

As the contemporary women's movement grew, so did a counter movement in response to women's liberation rhetoric (Solomon, 1978). It is important to understand the major claims of the counter movement in order to comprehend Chisholm's response to the traditional ideology of the counter women's movement. Solomon (1978) terms the counter movement as the "rhetoric of stop ERA (Equal Rights Amendment)" and identifies Phyllis Schlafly as the major spokesperson of the movement. The counter women's movement makes several contentions, including the following: (a) The traditional roles women play in society are appropriate, should be preserved, and result in less frequent divorce and better maintenance of the family system; (b) Women are different from men and should behave differently; (c) Women should be thankful for privileges and their uniquely favored status in receiving alimony, child custody, protection, affection, and a sense of love and belonging; (d) Having children increases family position, emotional fulfillment, and societal approval and support; (e) Finally, the women's liberation movement is closely tied to gay and lesbian rights, abortion, and paranoia about natural limitations (Solomon, 1978, pp. 45–51). Solomon concludes that even though the counter movement "is implicitly fatalistic and manipulative, its reaffirmation of traditional perspectives and its appeal to the need for personal security make it extremely effective rhetorically" (1978, p. 42).

In contrast to counter women's movement rhetoric, Chisholm rhetorically creates a vision of a future society free from discrimination based on sex. The speaker's vision applies to all women, regardless of color, and the major theme is philosophical and social revolution. Rather than supporting armed rebellion, Chisholm calls for women to think of themselves as equals and to behave as equals in society. Chisholm makes several key claims which include: (a) The social order is male-dominated. A society that discriminates against its members because of sex is unjust; (b) Potential is not a matter of gender. Both females and males have leadership abilities; (c) The qualities of gentleness and sensitivity are good but are viewed stereotypically as feminine weaknesses; (d) Women should stop contributing to their own oppression by willingly cooperating with discrimination that limits their human potential. Females should think and behave in revolutionary ways to eradicate sexism from society; (e) Women should have choices as to whether to become homemakers or seek fulfillment though contributing to society in other ways; (f) Finally, sexism crosses racial boundaries and is more prevalent than racism (1970b, 1972, 1980a, 1980b).

The claims in Chisholm's public speeches guide receivers from a past and present unjust social order to an enlightened future vision of gender equality. Related to this theme of the future, Bormann (1982) and Mohrmann (1982) indicate that the fantasy theme approach is particularly effective for understanding persuasive communication. Bormann states that "fantasies always provide an organized artistic explanation of happenings and thus create a social reality" (1982, p. 134).

Chisholm presents a rhetorical vision of sex equality as a possibility for women and as a goal worth their struggle.

Chisholm—The Person As Speaker

Through her life experiences, Chisholm demonstrates how the vision of egalitarianism through revolutionary thought and deed can operate. Chisholm's own experiences make statements about women's equality that are as powerful as what the speaker says in the four messages under study. She continually defies traditional gender norms and behaves as an equal.

Chisholm was born in 1924 in Brooklyn, New York as Shirley St. Hill. She possesses a near genius I.Q. Chisholm received early education in Barbados and earned a master's degree from Columbia University. Chisholm was married to Conrad Chisholm from 1949 to 1977. After divorcing, she married Arthur Hardwick, Jr., in 1977. Having been married during most of her career, Chisholm's life refutes possible claims that she is anti-male.

The speaker's professional experiences have strengthened her credibility. Chisholm served as a nursery school teacher and director, as New York State Assemblywoman in 1964, and—in 1968—she became the first black woman to be elected to the United States House of Representatives. Chisholm has also written several books and articles (1973, 1971, 1970a, 1970c). In contrast to popular belief that Geraldine Ferraro was the first woman and Jesse Jackson was the first black United States presidential candidate, Chisholm campaigned for president in 1972 (Chisholm, 1973).

Chisholm stresses her commitment to women's rights. In her book, *The Good Fight* (1973), the Congresswoman indicates that she is a woman first, a black woman second, and a politician third. In *Unbought and Unbossed*—after acknowledging that minority groups have too long been under-represented—Chisholm states "I hope if I am remembered it . . . can be some kind of inspiration, particulary to women" (1970a, p. xii).

Chisholm openly admits she has been accused of being more loyal to the women's movement than to the black movement. In denying this charge, Chisholm's adamant response skips over black and white women to blame some black men. Chisholm indicates that the very men she asked to join in supporting the acquittal of Angela Davis on a murder charge would not stand with her because it was not politically expedient (1973, pp. 33–34). Having thus refused to support a black woman (Davis), these men, Chisholm charges, are illegitimate in questioning her own (Chisholm's) commitment to black causes that conflict with those of women.

In addition to Chisholm's stand on women's rights being controversial, so is her verbal and nonverbal manner of speaking in general. In a heated meeting in New York, when a listener in the audience screamed to Chisholm, "Get off that stage!" the Congresswoman retorted, "You come up here and get me off!" (Hicks, 1971, p. 114). Chisholm's nonverbal communication is just as striking. When I heard Chisholm speak at The Ohio State University in 1980, her voice and gestures were a combination of fiery preaching and heated argument. She used a variety of hand and arm gestures and, at times, jerked her entire small frame in one sweeping, meaningful gesture. In the words of Hicks, there is little wonder that Chisholm's speaking style has earned her the description of "the skinny little school-teacher with the fearless mouth who turned out to be a political dynamo" (1971, p. 111).

Given her experiences, Chisholm can speak to women about practicing gender equality first-hand. Chisholm is what her speeches are about. She demands equality through word and deed outside the traditional limitations of race and sex.

Chisholm's Public Messages to Women on Sexism

This analysis proceeds chronologically, beginning with the earliest speech delivered to a predominantly white female audience. Chisholm's vision of a change to a society free from sex bias was already clearly formed in 1970.

Speeches to White Women

The Washington Address. Chisholm's Washington speech (1970b, pp. 909–915) primarily targets white females. In this 1970 address, Chisholm creates a human drama by establishing a dichotomy of victim and devil characters in the minds of listeners. At the same time, to avoid being mistaken for an evil character herself, Chisholm indicates that she is concerned about sexism because it not only hurts women but men as well. Chisholm states "My sisters all, . . . anti-feminism, like every form of discrimination is destructive both to those who perpetuate it and to their victims—that males with their anti-feminism, hurt both themselves and their women."

Chisholm acknowledges that women often contribute to their own oppression through thinking of themselves in stereotypical ways. She notes that "women cannot, for the most part operate independently of men," because "their education and training is programmed and planned for them from the moment the doctor says 'Mrs. Jones, it's a beautiful baby girl'." It is Mrs. Jones, herself, who "begins deleting mentally the things that [the baby] might have been and adds the things that society says that she must be." It is Mrs. Jones who wraps her daughter "in a pink blanket—pink, because that's the color of her caste; and the unequal segregation of the sexes will have begun."

Chisholm suggests that women re-evaluate the stereotypes commonly assigned to females—"It is not feminine egoism to say that the future of mankind may very well be ours to determine. It is simply a plain fact that the softness, the warmth, and the gentleness that are often used to stereotype us are positive human values." Chisholm cautions that "we must move outside the walls of our stereotypes, but we must retain the values on which they were built."

As a black female conscious of both racism and sexism, Chisholm creates an interesting paradoxical phrase that relates to the docile slave character in *Uncle Tom's Cabin* (Stowe, 1852) who gladly cooperated with his slave masters. Chisholm draws a parallel to women who cooperate with and defend their subservient gender role in society, stating that "the harshest discrimination that I have encountered in the political arena is anti-feminism, both from males and brain-washed, Uncle-Tom females."

Later in the same address, Chisholm offers examples to prove that society is unjust. She notes that "although more women are working, their salaries keep falling behind men's. Some occupations are still closed by law to women." Chisholm comments further that "property laws still favor men."

Chisholm continues to support her claim that our unfair society should be replaced by women changing their own perceptions and behaviors. Only through revolution, according to the speaker, will the vision of a nonsexist society become a reality:

> The true question is not whether or not woman dares. Women have always dared. The question which now faces us is—Will women dare in numbers sufficient to have an effect on their own attitudes towards themselves, and thus change the basic attitudes of males and general society? . . . . Your time is now, my sisters . . . . Susan B. Anthony, Carrie Nation, and Sojourner Truth were not evolutionaries. They were revolutionaries. . . . More and more women must join their ranks (1970b, pp. 913–914).

Chisholm's final statements in the Washington address present an interesting pattern of reasoning. Through instructing listeners to concentrate on fighting sexism over racism, Chisholm implies that both types of discrimination derived from the evil white male-dominated power structure. Chisholm subtly suggests to listeners that if sexism is eradicated, racism will eventually begin to fade, too. The leadership of women, who have developed humanitarian characteristics during their oppression, should be encouraged toward minimizing any kind of discrimination against humans—"I don't want you to go home and talk about integrated schools, churches, or marriages if the kind of integration you're talking about is black and white. I want you to go home and work for, fight for, the integration of male and female—human and human . . . . Thank you"

The Oakland Address. Chisholm's Oakland speech (1972) also addresses white women of the majority American culture. Delivered in 1972, close to the time of her presidential candidacy, the address centers on women's roles in politics. Chisholm's ideas about removing sexism from society are stated much more candidly in the Oakland address than in the previous speech. The women's movement is a bit more advanced and the Oakland speech is delivered at a women's college to young females. These factors possibly account for Chisholm's stronger tone.

Again, Chisholm claims that women need to revolt to achieve a positive future society are evident. The speaker's opening statement recognizes injustice—"All is not well in the republic." She asserts that input and sensitivity of women are needed in politics to improve society "if, indeed, this country is going to be turned around in terms of man's humanity to man; in terms of focusing on the things that are of vital concern to people. . . ." Chisholm reaffirms that females should be allowed equal participation in the future vision of America when she states "people look at me merely because I am a woman and say 'step back.' I will not step out of the political arena until these problems are dealth with!"

Chisholm restates other key claims. She assert that women should organize politically. "Nobody is going to give you anything . . . . Minorities and women are hopelessly divided. We must really understand power in this country." Chisholm explains that "even if we don't like each other; we must still form coalitions; come together in order to get things that will benefit all of us. . . ."

Chisholm also claims that sex discrimination cuts across all races. She discloses "I have met more discrimination as a woman than being black. Men in America, I don't care what color they are, cannot accept women in the political arena. . . ." The speaker further implies that we need more females in leadership roles when she reasons that "we need the best brain power the nation can muster."

Finally in the Oakland speech, Chisholm makes logical suggestions for revolutionary action as well as emotional appeals to change America's direction for our future children. She again uses the revolutionary theme as a vehicle for changing her rhetorical vision of a nonsexist society from fantasy to fact: "Women, get it together! The children of Kentucky, Alabama, and the Carolinas need women. The children of America are her future."

Speeches to Black Women

The Cincinnati Address. Chisholm's Cincinnati address (1980a, pp. 1–10) targets black females as a primary audience. Chisholm's rhetoric in this 1980 speech to Midwestern black women is more cautious than in her messages to white women during the more liberated 1970s. However, Chisholm's central themes of revolution and a future vision of a nonsexist society remain in clear focus.

Chisholm asserts that because of their blackness and gender, black females are doubly oppressed by America's male-oriented culture. She finds that "the black woman cannot be discussed in the same context as her Caucasian counterpart because of the twin jeopardy of race and sex which operates against her and the psychological and political consequences which attend them."

The speaker notes that black women were forced to take on family leadership roles because of education and jobs denied black men. These same black women according to Chisholm, were accused of emasculating black men—"Since time immemorial, the black man's emasculation resulted in the need of the black woman to assert herself in order to maintain some semblance of a family unit." As a result of this historical circumstance, according to Chisholm, "the black woman has developed perseverance, strength, tenacity, and other attributes that today quite often are being looked upon negatively." Chisholm charges that a double standard based on gender is the main reason for concern over black women's assertion of necessary family leadership.

Chisholm indicates that the segregation of male/female roles has not only limited black women but has hurt the black race through judging leadership based on gender rather than ability. Chisholm says, "such statements as 'The black woman has to step back while her man steps forward' and 'The black woman has kept back the black man' are grossly, historically, incorrect and serve as scapegoating techniques to prevent us from coming together as human beings."

On one hand, Chisholm recognizes that some issues for white females have not attracted black women. She indicates that "black women, in the majority, are not interested in walking and picketing a cocktail lounge which historically has refused to open its doors a certain two hours a day when men who have just returned from Wall Street gather in said lounge." This is a "middle class white woman's issue. So is the Ms. versus the Mrs. label," acknowledges Chisholm.

On the other hand, coping and survival issues of the women's movement do interest black women. Chisholm notes that "an aspect of the movement that will and does interest many black women is the potential nationalization of day care centers in this country." Chisholm points out that it is particularly important for black females to derive any benefits they can from the women's movement because the black woman is "trapped between the walls of the dominant white culture and her own subculture—both of which encourage deference to men."

According to Chisholm, all women are plagued by sex discrimination. She makes it clear to listeners that their rights as women are as important as their rights as blacks since both racism and sexism limit their choices and potential. Using the civil rights movement to illustrate her point, Chisholm states that "with few exceptions, black women have not had active roles in the forefront . . . Coretta King, Katherine Cleaver, and Betty Shabazz have come to their positions in the shadow of their husbands."

Finally, in the Cincinnati speech, similar to other messages under study, Chisholm indicates that the issues that divide black and white females are less basic than those which unite all women: "It is important first to become free as women in order to contribute more fully to the task of black liberation." She acknowledges that some "black men, like all men, have placed women in the stereotypes of domestics whose duty it is to stay in the background, cook, clean, have babies—leaving all the glory to men.."

The Columbus Interview. Chisholm's Columbus message (1980b) also focuses on black women. This 1980 dialogue represents the most recent of the four messages included in this study. The contents are the results of an interview I personally conducted with Chisholm and recorded with her permission. Chisholm's theme of revolution toward a society free of sex bias remains as steadfast in the 1980s as it did in the 1970s.

I asked the speaker whether or not black women should join the women's movement. Chisholm emphatically agreed that "it is very important for black women to join the bigger movement because we are in the minority in this country." Chisholm notes that "we need not have any permanent friends nor any permanent enemies; but just permanent interests."

Remaining consistent with her earlier messages, Chisholm depicts black women as victims and males as perpetrators:

> I think what caused the shift of opinion [of black females to the women's movement] was that a number of black women began to realize as they moved up and out into the so-called middle-class society and business world . . . . the black man felt a kind of veiled threat or competition from the black woman and sometimes lashed out at her in a subconscious way . . . . (1980b).

Chisholm identifies the problem of sexism across races as a reason to justify black females joining the women's movement and demanding a future social order that is fair to all. The speaker's personal examples reiterate her claim of male dominance and sex discrimination in the present system—"I met more discrimination on the basis of sex than my race in the field of politics."

Finally, in the Columbus message, Chisholm asserts that sex inequality is as pervasive in black America as it is in white America. Consistent with past addresses, Chisholm provides evidence that revolutionary change in thought and deed are necessary to make her vision of gender equality a reality. Chisholm does this through drawing again from personal experience—"When I ran for President, I can't tell you what black men did to me in some parts of the country . . . . They perceived me as some kind of threat." Chisholm continues, "In this society there are certain values that have been inculcated which have said that the man is dominant."

Chisholm's Treatment of Black and White Female Audiences

Balancing black interests of African American females with the interests of Caucasian females is obviously a challenge for Chisholm since the two groups emphasize different goals. How does Chisholm behave as a public speaker while discussing women's rights with predominantly black or white female listeners? As Chisholm openly admits, her speeches are "freely adapted to suit the occasion" (1973, p. 187). This adaptation necessitates Chisholm using both similar and different rhetorical strategies with black and white female audiences.

Identification strategies offer one way for a speaker to appeal to both black and white females on women's issues. Cheney describes the rhetoric of identification as functioning to promote commitment and unity within a group (1983, pp. 143–158). Chisholm establishes identification in at least two ways. First she attempts to increase cohesion through claiming that race and sex bias make minority and white females common victims. Frequent references to sex discrimination during her political career reinforce this identification claim. Throughout her four messages on women's rights, Chisholm uses the technique of identification to refer to black and white women as inherently united.

Second, Chisholm uses what Campbell (1973, p. 82) labels "attack metaphors" to make unusual comparisons and establish identification. Campbell (1973, pp. 74–86), Hancock (1972, pp. 269–271), and Hope (1975, p. 19) contend that emotionally disturbing metaphors in women's rhetoric are attention-getting enough to possibly transcend alienation of female listeners and awaken them to a personal level of identification. The use of metaphors toward a conscious-raising level to which receivers can identify can lead to a feeling of group unity and persuasion. Several examples of striking metaphors that refer to women and men in unusual ways appear throughout Chisholm's messages. The Washington speech serves as a prime example. In this address, Chisholm refers to baby girls being wrapped in pink blankets because this is the color of women's caste (1970b, p. 911). Chisholm also metaphorically draws attention to the irony of females who fight against their own rights as women, through her mention of the brainwashed Uncle Tom label (1970b, p. 913).

Thus Chisholm uses rhetoric of identification to appeal to both black and white women. Establishment of a common group bond which transcends race and the use of striking metaphors are similar strategies the speaker uses to draw black and white females together toward revolutionary thinking and social action to end sexism.

Chisholm also uses different strategies when talking to black and white females about women's rights. The difference is a matter of content rather than form. In earlier speeches to predominantly white females, the speaker focuses more on middle- and upper-class interests. Several brief examples can be cited. In the Washington speech, Chisholm refers to heroines such as Susan B. Anthony whose names should be more familiar to the dominant culture (1970b, p. 914). In the same address, Chisholm alludes to sex bias in property laws (1970b, p. 913). In the Oakland speech, Chisholm (1972) expresses her consternation that before the 1970s white males exclusively had sought the presidency of United States. These examples reflect Chisholm's emphasis on middle- and upper-class interests when talking to white women. Thus Chisholm's supporting examples with white female target audiences uniquely highlight middle- and upper-class concerns. Yet, the speaker's basic theme of revolutionary thought and action to remove sex discrimination remains clear.

Chisholm faces a different set of circumstances in dealing with black

female listeners. Black women have been exposed to both black movement and women's movement ideology. Chisholm's messages reflect
cognizance of possible divided loyalties between the two movements.
The speaker adapts her material in at least three different ways which
have the potential of creating an even closer rhetoric of identification
while speaking to black women in the 1980s.

First Chisholm recalls African American history. In the Cincinnati
speech, for example, Chisholm cites black heroines such as Coretta King
(1980a, p. 3) with which listeners can readily identify. In the same
address, Chisholm points to the double jeopardy these women have
had to face being black and female during their history in the United
States (1980a, pp. 4–10).

Second, Chisholm refers to contemporary issues of primary concern
to women of color. In the Cincinnati speech, for instance, Chisholm
comments on black women's stifled leadership during the black civil
rights movement (1980a, p. 3). In the Columbus address, the speaker
points to black male chauvinism faced by professional black women
(1980b). As a third adaptation, Chisholm uses pronouns to refer to
herself and the black race as one in order to win support from black
female target audiences. Symbols such as "we," "the black woman,"
and "We are a minority in this country," are sprinkled liberally throughout both of her discourses targeting black women.

Therefore, in referring to black history, citing social issues of interest
to black females, and using symbols that connote intragroup unity,
Chisholm attempts to establish strong identification with black women
separate from men, as a way of minimizing the black interests vs.
women's interests controversy in the minds of black female receivers.
The speaker's recognition that sexism is as much of a problem as racism
for the black community is unmistakable.

It is apparent that Chisholm uses somewhat different content with
predominantly black and white females audiences. It is equally clear
that Chisholm's basic theme remains consistent throughout the years.
With both groups of receivers, the speaker advocates gender equality
through revolutionary thinking and social action.

Discussion

Chisholm has been a popular politician and women's rights advocate
throughout her political career. She remained in public office until she
chose to retire in the mid-1980s. What contribution do her person and
her key messages on women's rights make toward giving guidance to

other women public speakers talking to diverse groups of women? Five points should be considered.

First, Chisholm makes the ethical choice of dealing seriously with sexism instead of playing safe, conflict-free politics. In her view, prejudice based on sex is wrong, regardless of race. She calls for females to practice women's rights, but not at the expense of men's rights. If other females using public discourse follow Chisholm's example of making ethical judgments that benefit all humanity, they stand a chance of increasing their rhetorical appeal as Chisholm did.

Second, Chisholm has remained consistent over the years in talking to audiences of all races about women's rights. In the four messages studied, Chisholm exposes sexism as ugly discrimination against humans, illogically based on gender. The speaker calls for revolutionary change. Chisholm consistently attempts to change reality though creating a vision of a better society in which all humans will be judged on individual merit rather than physical characteristics of their group. This rhetorical vision is a part of the American Dream that is yet to be fulfilled. Other public speakers could learn from Chisholm's example of long-term commitment in dealing with basic human issues such as sexism versus short-term or shallow concerns.

Third, rhetorically speaking, Chisholm's ability to adapt her message for varying audience types of women can be considered an asset rather than a liability. To use Thompson's (1979b) analogy "one would not question the ethics of an arbitrator who persuaded both strikers and management that they should accept the arbitrator's proposed settlement." (p. 231). Female public speakers talking to women about sexism need to be especially cognizant of audience adaptation. Some women cling to traditional gender-prescribed behavior as tenaciously as men. As Campbell (1973, p. 86) implies, this is most likely due to the fact that women are often not isolated from men as a homogeneous group. Thus the traditional thoughts of some women about their gender roles are similar to the perceptions of men. This factor should be considered when adapting messages to women's audiences. The problem of audience adaptation appears to be doubly taxing to female public speakers when other variables such as culture and race are present. Chisholm shows that appropriate adaptability is possible.

Fourth, the use of striking metaphors to serve conscious-raising purposes works well for Chisholm in addressing both black and white females. Other women speaking to female audiences in one-to-many settings could benefit from making unique comparisons which cause women listeners to identify with the speaker and to think in new ways.

Finally, not only has Chisholm advocated women's rights ideology; she has lived it. She is a black woman practicing equality against all odds of traditionally imposed race and sex limitations. There is little contradiction between Chisholm's public messages and her life experiences. The consistency between word and deed is especially important with female target audiences. Henley's (1977, p. 13) research shows that women are more sensitive to nonverbal cues in their lives than men. Thus it stands to reason that women listeners would be more likely to note contradictions between a public speaker's verbal messages and her nonverbal actions. Other public speakers may want to analyze the consistency or contradiction between what they say publicly and what they do when they leave the platform.

Summary

I have analyzed four of Shirley Chisholm's messages about women's equality delivered to predominantly black and white female target audiences. Chisholm's life experiences and the four messages studied support the theme of a philosophical and social revolution by black and white women to achieve a future vision of gender equality. Faced with an ethical choice, Chisholm does not take the easy route. The speaker raises the issue of sexism with both women's audiences. While Chisholm adapts her rhetoric to appeal somewhat differently to black and white women's experiences, she consistently calls for both groups to rise up and claim their rights as women.

References

Bormann, E.G. (1982, May). A fantasy theme analysis of the television coverage of the hostage release and the Reagan inaugural. *The Quarterly Journal of Speech, 68,* 133–145.

Brake, R.J. (1967). Women orators: More research? *Communication Quarterly, 15,* (November), 20–22.

Brake, R.J. & Neulieb, R.D. (1983). Famous women orators: An opinion survey. *Communication Quarterly, 21* (Fall), 33–37.

Brownmiller, S. (1975). *Against our will: Men, women, and rape.* New York: Simon and Schuster.

Campbell, K.K. (1973). The rhetoric of women's liberation: An oxymoron. *The Quarterly Journal of Speech, 59* (February), 74–86.

Cheney, G. (1983). The rhetoric of identification and the study of organizational communication. *The Quarterly Journal of Speech, 69* (May), 143–158.

Chisholm, S. (1969, May). Equal Rights for women. *The Congressional Record 115,* May 21, 13380–13381.

Chisholm, S. (1970a). *Unbought and unbossed.* Boston: Houghton Mifflin.

Chisholm, S. (1970b, July). The 51% Minority. Speech delivered at the Conference on Women's Employment. Printed for use of the Committee on Education & Labor, House of Representatives, 91st Congress, 2nd Section, Washington, DC: Government Printing Office, 909–915.

Chisholm, S. (1970c). Racism and anti-feminism. *The Black Scholar, 1,* (January-February) 40–45.

Chisholm, S. (1971). Race, revolution, and women. *The Black Scholar, 3,* (December), 17–21.

Chisholm, S. (1972). Women in politics: Why not? Speech delivered at Mills College, Oakland, CA. Phono-Cassette Tape Recorded by Pacifica Tape Library, Los Angeles.

Chisholm, S. (1973). *The good fight.* New York: Harper and Row.

Chisholm, S. (1980a). The contemporary black woman. Speech delivered at the University of Cincinnati. February 15, Cincinnati, Ohio.

Chisholm, S. (1980b). The black woman's response to women's liberation: An interview. Dorothy K. Williamson-Ige, Interviewer. February 16, Columbus, Ohio.

Hancock, B. R. (1972). Affirmation by negation in the women's liberation movement. *The Quarterly Journal of Speech, 58* (October), 269–271.

Haskin, J. (1975). *Fighting Shirley Chisholm.* New York: Dial Press.

Henley, N. M. (1977). *Body politics.* Englewood Cliffs, NJ: Prentice-Hall.

Hicks, N. (1971). *The Honorable Shirley Chisholm.* New York: Lion Books.

Hope, D. S. (1975). Redefinition of self: A comparison of the rhetoric of the women's liberation and black liberation movements. *Today's Speech, 23* (Winter), 19.

Mohrmann, G.P. (1982, May). An essay on fantasy theme criticism. *The Quarterly Journal of Speech, 68* 109–132.

Pinola, M., & Briggs, N.E. (1979). Martha Wright Griffiths: Champion of women's rights legislation. *Central States Speech Journal, 30* (Fall), 228–240.

Solomon, M. (1978). The rhetoric of stop ERA: Fatalistic reaffirmation. *The Southern Speech Communication Journal, 44* (Fall), 42–59.

Stowe, H.E.B. (1969). *Uncle Tom's Cabin.* Columbus, OH: C.E. Merrill. (Reprint of Jewett Publishers, 1852).

Thompson, W. N. (1979a). Barbara Jordan's keynote address: Fulfilling dual and conflicting purposes. *Central States Speech Journal, 30,* (Fall), 272–277.

Thompson, W. N. (1979b). Barbara Jordan's keynote address: The juxtaposition of contradictory values. *The Southern Speech Communication Journal, 44,* (Spring), 223–232.

Whalen, A.C., (1976). The presentation of image in Ella T. Grasso's campaign. *The Central States Speech Journal, 27,* (Fall), 207–211.

Williamson-Ige, D.K. (1984). A critique of two Chisholm speeches on women's rights for black and white females. *Missouri Speech Journal, 15* 50–58.

7

Storytelling Strategies in Mother-Daughter Communication

Deanna L. Hall

University of Maine

Kristin M. Langellier

University of Maine

In everyday life, people tell stories or personal narratives about their own experiences. Researchers on personal narratives (Labov & Waletzky, 1967; van Dijk, 1976; Robinson, 1981) have studied stories predominantly from male subjects and have analyzed stories from a "male-as-norm" perspective. Women's communication experience has not been considered worthy of study by past researchers; or it has been described as deviant or deficient by comparison to male models (Spender, 1980). Such research implies that women cannot tell stories "right" and that what women tell are not "real" stories. Kalčik (1975) states that "some women's stories are not structured in ways that have been commonly studied" (p. 7). There is a limited amount of research on women's stories in general and little if any research on mother-daughter storytelling as an example of women's storytelling.

Baldwin's (1985) folkloristic study of a Pennsylvania family contrasts men's and women's roles in family storytelling. Men's stories are marked, linear narratives with dramatized dialogue and action. They recount a specific, remarkable event "with a point worth tellin.'" To make his point, the male storyteller may alter or omit details of the experience. His purpose is to entertain, to tell a better—funnier or more dramatic—story. In contrast, women tell open-ended stories of descriptive detail from family history. Their stories may frame men's marked narratives or interrupt the story to correct facts, add details, and provide background (geneology, people, places). Women's stories describe a general or usual or typical circumstance rather than a particular event. Their purpose is to present the facts of family history as a context and corrective to the men's entertaining stories. In the family, men and women tell stories simultaneously (team telling) or sequentially. Baldwin argues that together men's and women's distinct storytelling roles strike a narrative balance between dialogued action (the telling) and descriptive detail (the "truth") which results in a complete family story.

Research on women's personal narratives characterizes their storytelling in the following ways. First, women's stories may be structured atemporally rather than in the chronological order of events leading to the most significant point. Kalčik (1975) identifies "kernel stories" that have an emergent event structure dependent upon the conversational context for their development. Second, women's stories may be told for the purpose of self-sharing rather than self-enhancement as storytelling research has assumed. Jenkins (1982) describes a cooperative style of storytelling among women that uses self-denigrating humor and emphasizes similarities between the speaker and listeners. Third, women's stories may have a criteria of tellability different from "remarkableness." Jenkins (1982) states that women's stories focus on commonplace events. Polanyi (1979) presents examples of stories told for their emotional interest rather than their remarkable action. Fourth, women's stories may not display an evaluative function, that is, make a point. Robinson (1981) and Polanyi (1979, 1981) provide examples of women's stories that do not have a point or that develop or negotiate a point in the act of telling. Fifth, women's stories may be gender-specific and context-specific. Yet data has repeatedly been collected on men's storytelling, usually in public places, and generalized to an entire speech community.

From a feminist communication perspective, Langellier and Peterson's (1984) theoretical critique locates two models of women's storytelling implicit in the research—a "traditional" model and a "collaborative" model. The traditional model is characterized by strategies that establish distinctions within a group hierarchy, for example, strategies to get a turn, to hold the floor, and to top the previous speaker's story. The collaborative model, on the other hand, emphasizes differentiation through closeness in a horizontal structuring of group relations. Collaborative strategies such as linking, filling in, supportive responses, and clarifying questions result in the group production of a story and a "shared floor" (Edelsky, 1981). Langellier and Peterson's conceptual analysis of the research suggests the differential use of various storytelling strategies by women in particular speech contexts. Women's strategic communication assumes a rationality of discourse as its explanation (Edelsky, 1981; Kramarae, 1981; McConnell-Ginet, 1980) rather than either sex (biological differences) or gender (social power).

This study provides an empirical investigation of women's storytelling and focuses specifically on storytelling strategies as they are revealed in personal experience narratives of mothers and daughters. Stories were collected from mother-daughter pairs about their experiences with food—preparing food, eating, and dieting.[1] A guided interview technique (Patton, 1980) was used for data collection; however, the traditional interviewer-interviewee dyad was modified to allow for a joint interview with the mother-daughter pairs in order to access their conversational interaction as well as their stories. Oakley (1981) argues that the interview is especially successful in accessing women's experience.

Five mother-daughter pairs of various ages, religious, ethnic, economic, and family backgrounds served as participants. Mothers and daughters were asked to reflect on some of their food-related experiences and to share one of the stories with each other, feeling free to comment on or add to each other's story. From there the conversation spiraled. In effect, the interviewer functioned as an audience to the mother-daughter storytelling, observing what mothers and daughters say to each other and how they say it.

Eighty stories were isolated for analysis of storytelling strategies.[2] The data were analyzed using a phenomenological method.[3] In this article, 10 storytelling strategies are first described and illustrated with an example.[4] Second, the strategies are analyzed for how they construct storytelling roles with unique communicational constraints for mothers and for daughters. Third, we explore how collaborative strategies confirm the mother-daughter relationship.

---

[1] This article is based on Hall's (1985) research, *Mothers' and Daughters' Lived Experiences of Food: An Analysis of Women's Storytelling.* References to the interviewer in the text refer to Hall.

[2] A story is defined as the telling of a lived, memorable event with personal, social, or cultural significance in the narrator's world.

[3] Phenomenological analysis is conducted in a three-step reflective process (Stevick, 1971; Lanigan, 1979): (a) The researcher listens repeatedly to audiotapes of the stories in order to identify and isolate significant interaction units. All significant interaction units are coded on cards; (b) The researcher sorts the cards into clusters of similar statements, carefully checking each strategy against the original story and context and taking care not to impose categories on the data; (c) Each cluster is then described in detail, analyzed for its interaction patterns, and named.

[4] Because this study focuses on storytelling strategies, the stories themselves may be truncated in the transcribed examples. The transcribed data is recorded in the following way. The speech is punctuated and disfluencies removed in order to compose readable statements. Speech errors are retained so as not to alter the participants' language. In the transcribed portion, [. . .] signifies the removal of a pause or disfluency; [. . . .] signifies that a thought has ended and talk not applicable to the telling strategy has been eliminated; [M] signifies the statement is made by the mother and [D] the daughter. [(] indicates an overlap; [/] indicates both the mother and daughter are speaking at the same time.

Storytelling Strategies

Although previous research conceptualizes women's storytelling variously as "team telling," "cooperative," "collaborative," and "shared," few empirical examples are reported. Nor has research analyzed precisely what type of sharing occurs and how it is achieved. The following description of the data reveals that mothers and daughters use a variety of strategies in their storytelling, from individual monologues to collaborative dialogues; and further, that collaboration differs as to degree and type.

Strategy 1: Individual Storytelling

The seven stories in this cluster are told individually by one speaker—the mother in all but one instance. Despite their monologistic quality, most of the stories also include minimal responses from listeners in the form of laughter and phrases such as "yeh" and "uh-huh." For example, one mother reflects on making her husband egg salad sandwiches for three weeks straight, to which both the daughter and interviewer respond with laughter. Told in a humorous way, this story has social interest (Polanyi, 1979) and would probably be funny to most listeners. But in other stories the daughter's laughs of anticipation and recognition represent a more personal recollection of the mother-daughter experience:

M: So Carol [daughter] and Dan would walk down the sidewalk and this was . . . *everyday* ritual. They'd stand in front by the grandparents and I'd watch this from the door . . . . He'd come over and give 'em each some candy and like I used to think,

D: (laughs)

M: If it was me I'd run over behind the grandparents' house and eat it, but, no, they come right back down the street to the house and they'd come in chewing away . . .

In this instance the daughter's laughter anticipates the next image in the mother's narrative and is specifically related to their shared personal experience. The mother "tells on" the daughter, and the daughter contributes laughter during the storytelling.

Strategy 2: Story Requests, Content Correction, and Evaluation

Mothers introduce and conclude more stories than do daughters. For example, one mother asks, "What's a typical meal you ate down there? Tell her about that, I bet she'd [interviewer] like to hear about that [trip to Mexico and the food]." Mothers also correct story content, add information, or provide an evaluation of the story told by a daughter:

D: My grandmother's in the nursing home and sometimes/ was it Thanksgiving? Great grandmother. Yeh.

M: /Great grandmother

M: Yes, Thanksgiving.

D: And something else (too.

M: (They have in the summertime . . . the cookout.

D: Yeh, that's right. They have, well, a Thanksgiving meal there and it's not that day, it's sometime before.

M: The Sunday before Thanksgiving they have (

D: (Yeh, so everyone can come.
[a few minutes later, after the mother and daughter describe the meal and the nursing home, the mother remarks:]

M: That was always nice, a nice time.

Although the daughter tells this story, the mother prompts and guides the telling with her comments. The mother also evaluates the story, signifying its point and importance: "That was always nice, a nice time." There is a degree of collaboration in these stories, but it occurs primarily in introducing and concluding a story between which the storytelling progresses as a monologue.

Strategy 3: Same Event, Different Views

Mothers and daughters recount the same event in these stories, but tell different versions. One story focuses on the importance of food during the potato harvest. The daughter describes breakfast and supper routines and then turns to describe lunch:

D: We did eat a lot then. Of course, people compare what you got in your lunches and everyone would say "what you got, what you got . . ." Everyone was always envious of what we had to eat (laugh). All the other kids would say "I wish my mother would give me that."

M: But after dinner it took quite awhile really to set up the lunch boxes. Washing them all out and drying them well and the thermoses and getting their water containers together. And really you spent x amount of time after dinner was over and dishes were done, then you'd start the lunch bit, you know.

In this example, mother and daughter bring different perspectives to the same event and learn about each other's experience of the potato harvest-time lunches. The mother learns of the specialness associated with the daughter's memory of lunches she packed; the daughter learns of all the work involved in preparing those special harvest-time lunches. Their narrative views are different yet compatible, and both contribute to the meaning of the story.

In another story the mother and daughter's different narrative views lead to incompatible meanings about an experience they share. When the mother begins the story, the daughter challenges its significance by saying, "I was wondering what the hell this has to do with what we're talking about?" Her mother responds in a commanding tone of voice, "Wait, now listen." The mother sounds annoyed at her daughter for interrupting, for using profane language, and for devaluing the story the mother is about to share, especially since the story has special significance for the mother. The daughter responds with some surprise at her mother's annoyance, "All right," and the mother continues:

M: One of the things that we did . . . would be to go to the coast and we would dig clams. And we would have a big fire on the shore and have our steamed clams. . . . That was something that I enjoyed so much that I wanted my kids to have the same opportunity. And I think they've all enjoyed the clams, especially this one [daughter].

D: I remember eating them when I was younger but I got so sick of them. I used to eat so many that now I can't eat them anymore.

M: Really? You mean steamed clams or any kind of clam?

D: Any kind of clams. I just don't care for them at all.

M: Yeh?

D: And it was funny. I never was into digging them because I would see Mom going out with the tide and the tide pulling her back in . . . and cleaning the damn things. And then her [mother] back would hurt her so much for two days, I thought there's no way I'm going to go and do that . . . . I'll watch and sit on my rock. . . .

M: So, that's not one of your loved things, I mean you wouldn't look forward to the coast for clams.

D: Not for clams!

In this storytelling, the mother and daughter discover their different and conflicting views of this family ritual. As in the preceding story on the potato harvest, they emphasize different aspects of their shared experience (the mother, a "loved" family ritual; the daughter, her "hatred" for digging, cleaning, and eating clams). As the daughter participates in the mother's story, she challenges her mother's meaning for the event. By the end of the telling, the story has changed its meaning for the mother.

Strategy 4: Don't Tell

There is only one story using this strategy, but it reveals a significant dimension of mother-daughter storytelling. The daughter has introduced the topic of mealtime for the family and then says:

D: I was telling/ Deanna [interviewer] how it would

M: / What did you have in mind?

D: start off where we'd get to going and you'd end up saying, "I can't sit here and eat" / and you'd go in your bedroom.

M: / Well don't tell this, this didn't happen all the time.

D: And then Tom [brother] would say, "I can't eat, I have a stomach ache now," and he'd go into his room and close the door.

M: This is only a few occasions now, she's telling you the worst times we've had. We really shouldn't be telling this . . . .

D: And I would end up leaving the table because I couldn't eat if you and Tom weren't going to eat. And then my father would sit there and he wasn't going to get up. He can eat through just about anything.

In this story about mealtime tension, the mother says twice that the daughter should not be telling the story. The daughter persists and talks over her mother, successfully finishing the story. Since both mother and daughter in this pair knew the interviewer personally, this may explain why the mother let the daughter finish the story.

The mother and daughter have conflicting meanings for this story. The daughter reflects on the mealtime tension in a humorous way. She laughs during the telling and mimics the voice of her mother and brother. She sees this as a typical, now "silly," family routine. The mother, however, is embarrassed and takes the story more seriously. She tries to argue that it was not a typical mealtime occurrence. As in Strategy 3, mother and daughter present two different views of the same event, but in this strategy there is no indication that they accept each other's view of the experience.

Strategy 5: Repeating Each Other

In these stories the mothers and daughters repeat what each other is saying. In some instances they speak almost simultaneously. In this example the mother begins to describe the dinner she will have for her son Tom and his girlfriend who are visiting:

M: Tonight I've planned as far as that roast with potatoes and carrots (

D: (It's kind of limited because she's Jewish so she/ she can't

M: / All I know is she don't eat pork . . .

D: She can't eat pork and she . . . has allergies, too, so sometimes she doesn't eat because of her allergies/ so the choices are limited.

M: / I know she does eat/

D: / So everytime they come over here . . . nine times out of ten/ we have roast beef.

M: / She won't tell us now what she likes.

D: And when we ask her what she likes/ she says, well,

M: / She likes chicken but [Tom] doesn't.

D: "I don't care, whatever you want to fix. That's all right/ with me."

M: / She says anything that's all right, anything . . . and I tell Tom
      and they eat different things . . . I don't know what . . . I'm going
      to ask this time and put it down, I'll tell you that.

Here, mother and daughter say the same thing almost at the same
time. They compete to tell the cooking story. The mother begins the
story, but the daughter controls its development while the mother
repeatedly attempts to contribute to the telling. The mother speaks
quickly as if to fit her remarks in between her daughter's words. The
daughter continues to tell the story almost as if her mother is not there.
Interestingly, the mother's statements precede the daughter's, although
the daughter's talk is more forceful. Stories using the strategy of repeating each other cannot be categorized as mutually developed, for
although both mother and daughter contribute to the telling, neither
attends to what the other says. Thus the stories in this group are told
more as parallel monologues with similar content than as collaborative
stories.

Strategy 6: Content Agreement

In this group, story content told by one participant is supported by the
other. An equal number of stories are told by mothers as by daughters
in this cluster. In the following example about feeding children nutri-
tional foods rather than candy, the mother shows her agreement with
her daughter:

D: She knew what it was like as a mother having other people
      interfere and try to give your kids little snacks . . . . I never felt
      . . . when they visited her that she pumped them full of grandma's
      wonderful cookies and things, you know, to win their love . . .
      I never had to fight her too much.

M: Yeh . . . when they came to visit I wasn't handing out candy,
      and you know, like basically

D, M: Grandmothers are supposed to do.

M: Oh, you know they don't need it and it just makes it rougher on
      her [daughter].

The mother agrees with the content of her daughter's story and with
her point of view—indeed mother and daughter say the same thing
simultaneously and with the same attitude.

Strategy 7: Similar Experience Support

Similar to Strategy 6, these stories also show support between mother
and daughter. More stories in this group are told by daughters and
supported by mothers. Strategy 7 differs from the preceding strategy
because support is shown not just through agreeing with story content,

but by sharing a similar experience. The story which follows is concerned with dieting:

D: We've tried diets . . . but it's a never-ending theme that we've lived with. . . . Ever since I can remember one of us has been on a diet. You know, it goes in typical stages, doing real well initially and being really hyped up about it and gradually getting lax and before you know it you're back to where you were before/ and you lose your enthusiasm.

M: It's because . . . we say "O. K. we're going to change our lifestyle. We're not going to do this and we're not going to do that as far as food is concerned." And true, you can follow that for a little while and then after awhile you say, "Oh, I'm doing so good I can have this or that," and that's when it all starts in again.

D: And that's what happens too, with me. When Dave and I broke up and I stopped eating and I lost a lot of weight . . . when I started getting my mental capacities back . . . . I realized, "my God, I'm thin!" . . . And it almost gives you this confidence to just really go out and blow it.

This story is introduced by the daughter, supported by the mother, and then the mother's comment further developed by the daughter. The daughter describes her family's trouble with dieting. Her mother provides an explanation for the experience of "getting lax" described by her daughter. The daughter then supports her mother's explanation by providing an example of her own experience. This mother and daughter seem to be engaged in heuristic storytelling as together they articulate and discover one of their problems associated with dieting.

Strategy 8: Recreating a Shared Experience

In this cluster mothers and daughters tell stories together. They ask questions of each other to contribute more information to the overall story. The story which follows is about the parents' twenty-fifth wedding anniversary:

M: I was telling her. . . . I'm sure it will always stay with me because of (

D: It better, it was a lot of work . . . .
(All laugh)

D: What did you tell her?

M: Well, I can't remember . . . what do you remember?

D: Well, I remember everything.

M: You do.

D: Well, of course, I do . . . I was the initiator of this project . . . .
[The daughter continues a few minutes to describe the planning and preparation involved.]

> D: We hired the catering department at the university and they put on
>   a really nice spread of sandwiches. What else did they have, there,
>   Mom?
> M: Oh, fresh vegetable trays and/
> D: Oh, vegetable trays/ fruit trays
> M: / and beautiful fruit trays with lots of strawberries and grapes.
> D: And we went out and got wildflowers and I got two recipes for
>   champagne punch . . . .
> M: Beautiful cake
> D: Yeh, we ordered a cake . . . what else ?
> M: Oh, beautiful music. Anna came and played the piano.

Both the mother and daughter continue to describe the anniversary
party for approximately 10 more minutes. In excited tones of voice, the
mother and daughter together recreate the anniversary party for the
interviewer and for themselves. They laugh together at the events of
the party, ask questions, fill in story information and produce an
elaborately detailed story together. The questions asked and information
added in this story serve a shared goal of recreating the experience
together as exactly and completely as possible. By contrast, questions
in Strategy 2 functioned as requests for the other to tell an entire story.
Story prompting in Strategy 2 functioned more for accuracy than for
elaboration and re-creation of the experience.

Strategy 9: Discovering Relational Conflict

These stories are also told together as in Strategy 8 and they reveal
new information in their telling as in Strategy 3. But rather than bringing
mother and daughter together or to a new understanding, they display
relational conflict. In the following story a mother learns something
about her diabetic daughter's behavior:

> D: I was trying to think, Mom, of the time that I was walking home
>   from junior high and my blood sugar was so low that I just wanted
>   to stop on the side of the road and lay down.
> M: I don't remember that.
> D: And I think I dragged myself home and I had gotten to the point
>   where you needed to help me to get something to eat . . . because
>   of the shakes.
> M: Yeh.
> D: I think you've helped me out on instances before . . .
> M: Yeh. But you're getting better about that, aren't you. I mean you
>   don't (
> D: (I still have them.
> M: But you don't allow yourself to get in that same condition/ do you?
> D: / I have . . . it's happened to me at work.

M: You don't have anything with you all the time, something you can
    just quick take?
D: I just usually have money on me in case I need to get something.
M: You should carry something.
D: Well, you know, you wear a dress, where are you going to put it?
M: In a purse, in a pocket/ you should have something.
D: Let's not start getting on that.
M: O.K. O.K.

Although this story begins as a recollection of a past event that
brought mother and daughter together, its focus shifts dramatically
during the telling. In fact, the past event is left undeveloped as present
circumstances take precedence. Thus their shared telling of a past
experience leads to conflict in their present relationship.

Strategy 10: Mutual Storytelling

These stories show the greatest sharing and combine several of the
preceding collaborative strategies as mother and daughter develop a
story together. This cluster contains more stories than any other group,
suggesting that shared storytelling is characteristic of mother-daughter
storytelling. For example:

M: Like I said when I was pregnant with Laura. I took her [daughter]
    to school in February—what is that, mid-year test? . . . She didn't
    have to be there till 9:30 so I just tossed my coat over my housecoat
    and took her to school. I dropped her off at high school and I said
    to her, "you know, if I keep this up I'll be going to PTA meetings
    when I'm 80."
D: (laugh)
M: Well, all she think of . . . it's a wonder she passed the tests, keep
    think of that, picturing me hauling into PTA.
D: It was the most hilarious thing.
M: Oh God, and the day I had Laura, Carol [daughter] come home from
    school . . . . I told her I hadn't been really feeling up to par that
    day so she told me, "I'll make supper." She made chop suey . . .
D: (laughs)
M: She was puttin' it all together and I was askin' my 16-year-old
    daughter "what . . . do you think I should do?" "Well, I think you
    should call the doctor, Mom. I think you should talk to him."
D: Now this is about five, five-fifteen and my sister was born, what
    six-fifteen/ six-thirty?
M: / Uh huh
D: About an hour or so later.
    (both laugh)

D: Right around supper time, you know, she was thinking of getting through the meal and probably would go to the hospital after supper, you know, and, uh, I said "I don't think you ought to wait," so she called a friend and her friend came down and took her to the hospital.

M: Well, I didn't even feel any labor pains with her, that was the trouble, I had no pain with her. So I said "I don't have to go now. Well, what should I do?" I sort of had a icky feeling, some little feeling there, you know, but here I was asking my 16-year-old daughter what should I do.

D: Well, that morning she had an inclination that that was the day, and said before I went to school that you thought it might be that day. Just some kind of feeling, and I called home about after every class. I'd go to the office and use the phone to check on her to see whether or not she'd gone to the/ hospital.

M: / Well, like I said, about an hour later. So I called the house and told her and, of course, for about 16 years she'd been . . . waiting for a sister and finally she got one.

D: I used to tell people if you wait long enough, don't give up on your dream, it will happen after awhile.

This story is developed by the mother and daughter together. Mother and daughter share the event, the tone of the telling, the perspective on the story, and its point. In a later section, we analyze this story more closely for its collaborative strategies. Like the other stories in this group, the childbirth story is gender-specific and specific to the particular mother-daughter relationship.

Mother and Daughter Storytelling Roles

As mothers and daughters tell stories together, they define distinct storytelling roles as mother and as daughter. In this section, we analyze these storytelling roles.

Mothers function as family historians in mother-daughter storytelling. Like an historian, a mother is concerned with the selection of stories, their accuracy and completeness, and their interpretation and valuation. The mothers' storytelling strategies display their function as family historians: mothers introduce and conclude more stories than do daughters; they request that particular stories be told; they ask questions, add background details, fill in explanations, and correct errors in daughters' stories; and they provide story evaluations.

Mothers monitor the tellability of a family story, using strategies that determine which stories are worthy of telling and allowable to tell. From a mother's perspective, these stories are of interest to the audience, that is, a daughter and the interviewer. For example, one mother asks her daughter, "What's a typical meal you ate down there? . . . Tell her about that, I bet she'd like to hear about that." More often, mothers simply introduce topics and tell more stories than do daughters. Mothers frequently check a story's worth by asking the interviewer, "Is this what you want to know?" Tellable topics include food and its preparation, typical mealtimes and holiday meals, nutrition and health, diet and weight, and cooking for children and men. Conversely, tellability excludes certain topics and particular stories, as suggested by the "Don't Tell" strategy. Notably missing are stories about family or marital disharmony and more political "women's issues."

Mothers also function to keep stories accurate and complete. They collaborate in a daughter's story by filling in facts and details of family history. Strategy 2 exemplifies how a mother patiently prompts and corrects the daughter's story about Thanksgiving dinner for her great grandmother. The story about the potato harvest in Strategy 3 shows a variation on this function. After the daughter tells how the children compared their lunches to see who had the best, the mother details the work involved in food preparation—details unique to a mother's work, omitted by the daughter, and generally invisible in the culture. In Strategy 8, the mother explains why the family "got lax" in dieting.

Analysis of storytelling strategies reveals that in her function as family historian, a mother faces communicative constraints unique to her role as mother. As a family historian, she contributes the details and perspective of the mother to the stories. As a mother she nurtures and supports her daughter's storytelling. But storytelling as a mother also hints at conflict in family relationships—conflict that mothers submerge and deflect. As family historian the mother is constrained to present the family—and her relationship with her daughter—as healthy, happy, and harmonious for the interviewer—or else she risks her identity as a "good mother."

Daughters most often play the complement to their mother's function as family historian. That is, daughters listen to their mothers' stories, additional details, and corrections; they tell stories on request; and they acknowledge the story's meaning and significance within the family. In this complementary position, daughters collaborate with their mothers to present family history. They confirm the mother's function as family historian and themselves as objects of that history. Together mothers and daughters collaborate to define their distinct generational storytelling roles.

But daughters also challenge their mothers as family historians. Daughters challenge the tellability of a story, the accuracy of the mother's perspective, and the story's significance. While mothers are concerned to present a harmonious family, a daughter's story and telling strategies belie conflict. For example, the strategy of repeating each other in the cooking story is played competitively by the daughter as she talks over her mother. We have already mentioned the "Don't Tell" story as an instance where a daughter challenges her mother's rule for tellability. The mother protests, "Well, don't tell this, this didn't happen all the time," and again, "this is only a few occasions now, she's telling you the worst times we've had. We really shouldn't be telling this . . ." These "worst times" refer to tension in the family (perhaps related to the mother) that disrupted mealtimes. When the mother uses "we" in her second protest, she points to the mother-daughter collaboration in presenting family history.

A daughter may challenge the accuracy of her mother's point of view in a story. In the clam story of Strategy 3, the daughter counters her mother's perception that, like her mother, the daughter loves to go the seacoast and dig and eat clams. Even if it is true that she loved to go to the coast, the daughter reveals that she hated digging for clams, and, indeed, now won't eat them. By challenging her mother's storytelling, she contributes a conflicting view of family history from her own perspective and also intimates conflict in the mother-daughter relationship. Conflict is taken more explicitly beyond the level of story content to the level of relationship in the diabetic story of Strategy 9. In this daughter's story, recollection of a past experience changes to a present relational conflict when the daughter reveals that, unknown to her mother, she still has serious episodes of low blood sugar. The mother's discovery turns to concern, which the daughter spurns. The daughter ends the story with "Let's not get start getting on that," suggesting an ongoing issue in their relationship. Consistent with her role as family harmonizer, the mother does not push the issue, at least in the presence of the interviewer.

In her role as a family storyteller, the daughter also faces communicative constraints unique to her role as daughter. As a family storyteller, she participates in the presentation of family history under her mother's guidance. But as a daughter, she challenges that family history precisely by distinguishing her perspective from her mother's. The daughter's challenge to her mother's family history reflects conflict in families or between generations, but it also indicates something more. In failing to corroborate the mother's history, she simultaneously disconfirms the mother's authority, and, by extension, herself as a "good daughter." Faced with these contradictions, the daughters more often chose to confirm their mothers.

It should be emphasized that mother and daughter work together in their different storytelling roles to constitute their experience. Their storytelling does not simply recount past events with sedimented meanings but *makes sense* of their personal history and present relationship. Throughout the description of the strategies, we suggest how mothers and daughters discover new facts, different meanings, and emergent points in their storytelling—what they share and how they differ. As mother and daughter constitute their family history, they simultaneously define their relationship to each other, the subject of the next section.

Mother-Daughter Collaboration

Mothers and daughters collaborate in storytelling to present family stories from their different generational perspectives: mothers function as family historians, daughters as storytellers under their mother's guidance. The generational differences in storytelling roles sometimes reveal conflicting views and meanings for the stories as well as conflict in the mother-daughter relationship. But elucidating storytelling roles does not account for either the variety of strategies mothers and daughters bring into play nor their preference for highly collaborative strategies. Indeed, when perspectives and meanings are disputed, one might expect more monologistic storytelling. Hence, their different storytelling roles must be situated within the mother-daughter relationship itself. As family historian, the mother strives not just to present family history, but also to nurture her relationship with her daughter. As a storyteller, the daughter strives not only to represent herself within the family, but to present herself to her mother. The resulting collaboration is a rich and complex interplay of identification and differentiation between mother and daughter as they define their relationship to each other.

In this section we consider how collaborative strategies function in another way: to confirm the mother-daughter relationship. This collaboration is distinct from the storytelling function in three ways. First, it focuses more on the personal relationship between mothers and daughters rather than their generational roles. Second, it emphasizes the pleasures of storytelling itself for mothers and daughters rather than the concerns of family history. Third, it suggests how mothers and daughters identify as women within the family.

In the anniversary story in Strategy 8, mother and daughter recreate together an event with special meaning for both participants. Mother and daughter produce the story together by asking questions, filling in, and linking statements. They relate symmetrically as equals rather than as complements, even though the story topic depends upon their distinct mother-daughter roles. The story can also be seen to reverse mother-daughter roles as the daughter plans and prepares the party ("I did all the work") which the mother enjoys. The anniversary theme nourishes and confirms their relationship; indeed it dramatizes the success of the mother and the daughter in their family roles. Moreover, the excited and engaged telling itself functions to enact their mutual confirmation of their mother-daughter relationship.

While the anniversary story confirms mother and daughter as successful in performing their family roles, some storytelling strategies cast the participants in mother-mother roles. Strategy 6 presents a story in which both participants share a mother's perspective on an event. The daughter compliments her mother for not giving her grandchildren candy like "grandmothers are supposed to do." Not only does the pair take delight and satisfaction in literally saying this line together, but both speak as mothers: the daughter as mother of her children (not as daughter to her mother) and the mother as a mother (not as grandmother to her daughter's children). This collaborative strategy functions to constitute the pair into a mother-mother relationship.

Being a woman is implicit in the mother-daughter role and relationship. Mothers and daughters also relate as women in a way not directly dependent on their family roles. Although dieting is not a woman-exclusive activity, it has gender-specific meanings in our culture (Spitzack, in this volume). Mother-daughter stories contain themes about eating "good" versus "bad" food, reasons to lose weight, age of weight gain and weight loss, being the "right size," the obsession with food, and difficulties of dieting. In these stories mothers and daughters relate as women who share the pressures to "be thin." The story "we've tried diets" in Strategy 8 shows the empathy and support mothers and daughters communicate to each other. Mother and daughter are involved in heuristic storytelling as they construct and confirm their reality. Although family roles as mother and daughter serve as a background, their bodily identification as women predominates. Collaboration functions here to underline their shared reality as women and the bond that creates women's reality.

Childbirth is an experience unique to women. A closer look at the childbirth story in Strategy 10 shows the highest degree of collaboration and just how complex and creative are the mother-daughter storytelling strategies. One might expect a childbirth story to be narrated from the mother's viewpoint and experience. The mother begins the story, but it is soon clear how central to the narrative is the daughter's perspective, even when the mother collaborates in the telling. For example, on the morning of the birth, the mother jokes to her daughter, "You know, if I keep this up I'll be going to PTA meetings when I'm 80." She continues that "it's a wonder she [daughter] passed the tests [at school], picturing me hauling into PTA." Next the mother tells that her daughter made supper because she [mother] wasn't feeling "up to par." The mothers says and repeats again later, "here I am asking my 16-year-old what should I do." The daughter tells her, "well, I think you should call the doctor, Mom." The daughter also adds clarifying details like "now this is about 5, 5:15" and then collaborates to supply the mother's experience ("she was thinking of getting through the meal and probably would go after supper") and ("she had an inclination that that was the day"). When the mother reports the baby's birth as "well, like I said, about an hour later," she also delivers the point of the story: "of course, for about 16 years she'd been . . . waiting for a sister and finally she got one." The daughter concludes the story with "I used to tell people if you wait long enough, don't give up on your dream, it will happen after awhile." As mother and daughter share this storytelling, they even seem to share the dream. Their collaborative storytelling strategies constitute the childbirth as much a product of the daughter's desire as the mother's action. Notably, no men (husband, father, brother) are mentioned in the story.

This story is clearly a favorite of the mother-daughter pair and they take great delight in its shared telling. There is a sense of their doing a "command performance" of the story for the interviewer. The collaboration is striking in several ways. Mother and daughter tell *each other's* experience of the childbirth. The mother narrates the daughter's experience; the daughter narrates the mothers's experience. In the story content, mother and daughter reverse roles: the mother calls on her daughter for dinner, advice, and decisions. Mother and daughter also reverse roles as storytellers: the daughter adds informative details, supports her mother's storytelling, and provides evaluation of the experience, behavior more characteristic of a mother's storytelling role. The collaboration functions to identify the storytellers simultaneously as mother and daughter and as women in the family.

Conclusion

The mother-daughter storytelling strategies constitute women's communication within the family structure in three ways. First, the stories are gender-specific and present family history from the perspective of women. The stories are not gender-exclusive in topic nor are they especially feminist in their perspective, but they do reflect the particular experience and concerns of women in the family. Second, collaborative strategies are the preferred mode of storytelling for mothers and daughters. And third, their storytelling strategies define the special constraints of mother-daughter communication. While their strategies may constitute storytelling roles and story meanings that are different for daughters than for mothers, their collaboration even more strongly confirms their relationship as women within the family.

Before concluding, it is necessary to interrogate our own position as researchers of mother-daughter storytelling. When mothers and daughters tell stories stategically, they respond not only to their family history and mother-daughter relationship, but to the interview situation as well. We have suggested in the previous discussion, sometimes explicitly and sometimes implicitly, the effect of the interviewer's presence on the discourse. How does the interviewer constrain the mother-daughter discourse? Her position is ambiguous: as a person unrelated to the mother and daughter, the interviewer is an "outsider" to the family; as a woman, the interviewer is an "insider" to their female experience. This double position constrained the storytelling in particular ways, but constraints should not be understood in a negative and simplistic sense as "obstacles, or barriers, or fetters" (Wilden, 1982, p. 186). No communication situation is without constraints. Constraints are an infrastructure that makes possible a particular story organization and communicative relationship. The presence of these constraints provides valuable leads into the complex process in which mothers and daughters construct their reality and express their values through storytelling. Thus the "don't tell" story is, in fact, told. In her double position the interviewer obtained stories that the mothers and daughters might otherwise have considered unworthy or insignificant; and the interviewer did not obtain stories the mothers and daughters considered to be private, family matters. Her double position as outsider-insider helps explain why the mothers and daughters so enthusiastically reflected on the details of family roles, including unpleasant details, but so seldom and so reluctantly criticized those roles, and by extension, their families.

Studying the communication of mothers and daughters suggests a second and more subtle way to interrogate the researcher's position. How did the researchers themselves play a family role in the interview and the analysis? Did we function as a mother or a daughter in relationship to the interviewees? When Chodorow and Contratto (1980) examine recent writing on motherhood, they identify a recurrent theme in which mothers are conceived as totally responsible for the outcome of their mothering, even if their behavior is shaped by patriarchal society. "Belief in the all-powerful mother spawns a recurrent tendency to blame the mother on the one hand, and a fantasy of maternal perfectability on the other" (p. 55). They argue that feminists and nonfeminists alike view the mother-daughter relationship from a daughter's perspective. Daughters participate in "the fantasy of the perfect mother," whether the mother is idealized as perfectly good or blamed as perfectly evil.

We cannot claim to completely avoid "the fantasy of the perfect mother," but we present an analysis of storytelling strategies that reveals the complexity, ambivalence and creativity of mother-daughter communication. By studying how mothers and daughters talk together in a particular situation, we show them responding strategically to the specific constraints of storytelling, to their own relationship, and to the interview setting. This analysis of mother-daughter storytelling strategies in context reveals their capabilities for conflict and conflict avoidance, for control and spontaneity, and especially for collaboration. We suggest that the strategic capabilities of mothers and daughters in storytelling recur in other situations when women communicate.

References

Baldwin, K. (1985). "Woof!" A word on women's roles in family storytelling. In R. A. Jordan & S. J. Kalčik (Eds.), *Women's folklore, women's culture* (pp. 149–162). Philadelphia: University of Pennsylvania.

Chodorow, N. & Contratto, S. (1981). The fantasy of the perfect mother. In B. Thorne & M. Yalom (Eds.), *Rethinking the family: Some feminist questions* (pp. 54–75). New York: Longman.

Edelsky, C. (1981). Who's got the floor? *Language in Society, 10,* 383–421.

Hall, D. (1985). *Mothers' and daughters' lived experiences of food: An analysis of women's storytelling.* Unpublished master's thesis, University of Maine, Orono, Maine.

Jenkins, M. M. (1982). The story is in the telling: A cooperative style of conversation among women. In S. Trömel-Plötz (Ed.), *Gewalt durch sprache: Die vergewaltingung von frauen in gesprächen.* Frankfurt am Main: Fischer Taschenbuch Verlag (ERIC Document Reproduction Service No. ED 238 083).

Kalčik, S. (1975). ". . . like Ann's gynecologist or the time I was almost raped: Personal narratives in women's rap groups." In C. R. Farrer (Ed.), *Women and folklore* (pp. 3–11). Austin: University of Texas.

Kramarae, C. (1981). *Women and men speaking: Frameworks for analysis.* Rowley, MA: Newbury House.

Labov, W., & Waletzky, J. (1967). Narrative analysis: Oral versions of personal experience. In J. Helms (Ed.), *Essays on the verbal and visual arts* (pp. 12–44). Seattle: University of Washington Press.

Langellier, K., & Peterson, E. (1984, November). Spinstorying: A communication analysis of women storytelling. Paper presented at the Speech Communication Association Convention, Chicago, IL.

Lanigan, R. L. (1979). The phenomenology of human communication. *Philosophy Today, 23,* 3–15.

McConnell-Ginet, S. (1980). Linguistics and the feminist challenge. In S. McConnell-Ginet, R. Borker, & N. Furman (Eds.), *Women and language in literature and society* (pp. 3–25). New York: Praeger.

Oakley, A. (1981). Interviewing women: A contradiction in terms. H. Roberts (Ed.), *Doing feminist research* (pp. 30–61). London: Routledge and Kegan Paul.

Patton, M. Q. (1980). *Qualitative evaluation methods.* Beverly Hills: Sage.

Polanyi, L. (1979). So what's the point? *Semiotica, 25,* 207–241.

Polanyi, L. (1981). What stories can tell us about their teller's world. *Poetics Today, 2,* 96–112.

Robinson, J. (1981). Personal narratives reconsidered. *Journal of American Folklore, 94,* 59–85.

Spender, D. (1980). *Man made language.* London: Routledge and Kegan Paul.

Stevick, E. (1971). An empirical investigation of the experience of anger. In A. Giorgi, W. F. Fisher, & R. Von Echartsberg, (Eds.), *Duquesne studies in phenomenological psychology, Vol. 1* (pp. 132–148). Pittsburgh: Duquesne University.

van Dijk, T. A. (1976). Philosophy of action and theory of narrative. *Poetics, 5,* 287–338.

Spitzack, C. (1988). Body talk: The politics of weight loss and female identity. In B. Bate & A. Taylor (Eds.), *Women communicating* (pp. 51–74). Norwood, NJ: Ablex.

Wilden, T. (1982). Postscript to 'Semiotics as praxis: Strategy and tactics.' *Rescherches Semiotiques/Semiotic Inquiry, 2,* 166–170.

8

Coping with Victimization: Portraits of Women in The Drama

Barbara A. Larson

University of Wisconsin-Milwaukee

In *The Philosophy of Literary Form,* Kenneth Burke argues for the development of sociological criticism. Starting with the premise that "social structures give rise to 'type' situations, subtle divisions of relationships" (Burke, 1957, p. 253), Burke maintained that "critical and imaginative works are answers to questions posed by the situation in which they arose. They are not merely answers, they are *strategic* answers, *stylized* answers" (Burke, 1957, p. 3). So he proposed that, ". . . we think of poetry (meaning any work of critical or imaginative cast) as adopting various strategies for encompassing situations . . . insofar as situations overlap from individual to individual, or from one historical period to another, the strategies possess universal relevance" (Burke, 1957, p. 3). Thus, "art forms . . . would be treated as equipments for living that size up situations in various ways, and in keeping with corresponding various attitudes" (Burke, 1957, p. 262). Viewed in this way, critical and imaginative works become "a ritualistic way of arming us to confront perplexities and risks. It would *protect* us" (Burke, 1957, p. 51).

To those who would argue that literature and drama are imaginary and fictive, born of a writer's mind and imagination, Burke answered that "the difference between symbolic drama and the drama of living is a difference between imaginary obstacles and real obstacles. But the imaginary obstacles of symbolic drama must, to have the relevance necessary for producing effects upon audiences, reflect real obstacles of living drama" (Burke, 1957, p. 268).

More succinctly and directly Burke asserted that "human relations should be analyzed with respect to the leads discovered in the drama"

(Burke, 1957, p. 267) and, he added, we should then "apply the results of our analysis to the 'informal art of living' " (Burke, 1957, p. 265).

Burke's concept of sociological criticism carries three important implications for communication studies. First, it recognizes implicitly a heuristic, instrumental function in creative works. Second, it acknowledges a rhetorical dimension involving identification and having a quality of being addressed. And finally, it suggests a socially relevant communicative function in works of art, such as the drama and literature.

The purpose of this paper is to explore Burke's notion of sociological criticism by approaching situations and strategies in the drama as revelatory of real-life human relationships. Specifically, I propose to examine the roles of women portrayed in the drama as they exhibit strategies for coping with situations of victimization.

The term "victimization" comes from Gordon Allport's 1954 study of *The Nature of Prejudice*. In Allport's analysis "victimization" means the suffering inflicted on a person by the arbitrary will of another— suffering inflicted often by the attribution of stereotypic traits and roles on individuals. Victimization may take the form of verbal rejection, discrimination, physical attack, ridicule, denigration. It may be rooted in historical, sociological, cultural, phenomenological, personal, or situational factors. It is directed against anyone who is viewed as "different," "inferior," who is a member of a minority, or an "out" group.

Allport's primary attention centers on prejudice and victimization based on racial and ethnic background. Yet he does, albeit briefly, acknowledge that sex grouping also constitutes an important basis of prejudice. Allport adds that antifeminism reflects two basic ingredients of prejudice—denigration and overgeneralization. For some people, he notes, "Women are viewed as a wholly different species from men, usually an inferior species. Such primary and secondary sex differences as exist are greatly exaggerated and are inflated into imaginary distinctions that justify discrimination" (Allport, 1954, p. 33).

According to Allport, victims of discrimination develop an array of coping behaviors as defense mechanisms, which can be divided into two groups of victimization traits. The first set of traits he labeled *extropunitive*. Victims with these traits exhibit obsessive concern and suspicion, slyness, cunning, strengthening of in-group ties, prejudice against "out" groups, aggression and revolt, stealing, competitiveness, enhanced striving, and blaming causes outside of self for difficulties.

The more introverted, submissive traits he termed *intropunitive*. Victims with these traits exhibit introversion, uncertainty, blaming of self for situation and treatment, passivity, self-hate, neuroticism, sympathy for all victims, symbolic status striving, docility, obedience, desire for approval, and clowning (Allport, 1954, ch. 9).

Often, Allport noted, a single person will display several traits, or blend the two types of coping strategies.

Victimization in the drama, as in real life, evolves from situational factors, group memberships, and role relationships established through communicative interaction. Equally important, communication is a key means of coping with victimization. Thus analysis of dramatic discourse, of women communicating through varied dramatic roles, promises to be productive on two counts: it affords insight into the modes of perception and self-assessment that typify the victimized woman in a given role relationship; and, it provides paradigms for identifying the nature and range of coping strategies.

In the following analysis primary emphasis centers on individual communicative strategies and modes in interpersonal relationships. Several key questions provide guidelines for establishing the background, situational, and relational elements germane to the analysis. These are:

1. What is the situation that sets the scene for victimization?
2. Who are the victimizers?
3. Who are the victims and what is their relationship to the victimizers?
4. What is the nature and mode of victimization?
5. What is the range of responses in coping with victimization?
6. What inferences can be drawn that are relevant to real-life human relationships and experiences?

Analysis from "Leads in the Drama"

The pages of dramatic literature are filled with portraits of women coping with victimization. These range all the way from Antigone and Medea of Greek tragedy to Shakespeare's Ophelia, Desdemona, and Katherine in *The Taming of the Shrew*. They include Ibsen's Nora in *The Doll's House*, Elizabeth Barrett in *The Barretts of Wimpole Street*, *Saint Joan* of Shaw, Mary in Anderson's *Mary of Scotland*, Laura in *The Glass Menagerie*, and Blanche in *Streetcar Named Desire*.

The victimizers include kings, husbands, lovers, fathers, brothers, sisters, sons, priests, princes, and politicians. Their reasons are personal, private, public and political, religious, spiritual, and civic. But in each case three key elements are present. First, the victimizer holds a position of dominance. Second, there is an assumption that the victim is inferior. And third, there is the exercise of power. The strategies for coping range from defiance to deference, rebellion to obedience, submission, and escape.

As it is not possible to examine the entire range of dramatic roles and relationships, I have chosen two modern American plays as representative examples for analysis. These two plays are *The Little Foxes* and *Another Part of the Forest* by Lillian Hellman (1951, 1947). I focus on these for several reasons. First, they were written by a woman playwright and presumably reveal something of a woman's insight into the problems and processes of coping with victimization. Second, the women in the two plays share the same external circumstances of time, place, and people, yet each reveals a different set of coping strategies because for each the intrinsic nature of victimization is different. Thus in this impacted microcosm of relationships we can view a variety of victimization situations met by varied coping strategies.

The dramatic clarity and brilliance with which Hellman's five women illustrate the victimization traits noted by Allport lend special credence to Burke's assertion that human relationships should be studied for "the leads found in the drama" that provide us with "equipments for living."

The action in *Another Part of the Forest* (written and produced in 1946) is set in the reconstructed South of the 1880s. The second play, *The Little Foxes*, thought written and produced first (1939), picks up the threads of life of the same characters in 1900.

The five Southern women portrayed in the plays are entrapped and victimized in two ways—by two kinds of situations which overlap. First, there is the external system of social class, custom, and caste attitudes, of nouveau riche, Southern aristocrat, and servant, that clearly affects their positions and roles. Beyond these nuances of class consciousness and position, there is a second more powerful form of victimization—that perpetrated by other individuals, arbitrarily and knowingly. The women thread their ways through two plots ensnared in a maze of greed, deceit, evil, and ambition. The four white women—Regina, Birdie, Lavinia, and Alexandra—dramatize a range of coping strategies relative to their victimization and the levels of personal evil from which the oppression flows.

A fifth woman, Addie, the black servant woman, portrays victimization by the most obvious, overt kind of oppression, that based on both race and history. Yet it is she who radiates a quiet force, compassion, and understanding. It is she who articulates the theme and thesis of *The Little Foxes*, and indeed the plight of the women in both plays.

Addie's comment comes at the beginning of Act III in *The Little Foxes*, during a singularly quiet moment—Alexandra, her Aunt Birdie, and her father, Horace, are gathered in the parlor on a rainy afternoon. Horace, who has returned home a terribly ill man, is seated in a wheel chair. It is two weeks since his bitter fight with Regina when he refused to give her money for investment in a cotton mill. Addie appears with wine and some special cakes she has baked for them.

These four characters form a small "in-group" as victims of deceit and exploitation, but they share a warm loving relationship with one another. They discuss the effects the new cotton mill will have on the community. Birdie reminisces with Horace about the old times, the music they shared, and recalls when, as a young girl, she was frightened by her Mama's terrible anger at the ways the Hubbards cheated and despoiled people in the community, whites as well as blacks. And Addie comments, "Yeah, they got mighty well off cheating niggers. Well, there are people who eat the earth and eat all the people on it like in the Bible with the locusts. Then there are people who stand around and watch them eat it. Sometimes I think it ain't right to stand and watch them do it" (Hellman, 1951, p. 703). The same thought and theme is reiterated a few moments later by two other characters in different terms. But the significance of Addie's statement resides in the world view it encapsulates. The essence of the human condition involves two kinds of people: the eaters and the eaten, the tyrants and the tyrannized, victimizers and victims—and, more covertly, the doers and the watchers. Implicit in this world view is the assertion that evil and the power to victimize persist only by the subtle assent of those who can or will do nothing to defy them.

Another Part of the Forest is set in the 1880s. The plot centers on the Hubbard family who live in a small Alabama town. The father, Marcus Hubbard, is a well-to-do store merchant. His ill-gotten wealth has been wrung from the hands of his fellow townsmen and the poor blacks whom he charges exhorbitant prices for food and goods.

Hovering in Marcus' past is the shadow of his suspected complicity with Union soldiers leading to the massacre of young Confederate trainees during the war. Marcus and his wife, Lavinia, have two sons, Benjamin and Oscar, and a daughter, Regina. Marcus wields a petty, but powerful, tyranny over the four members of his family. Wife, sons, and daughter are all held in economic bondage as he dominates their lives by keeping tight, penurious control of his wealth.

Regina is the dominant figure in the plots of both plays. In *Another Part of the Forest* she appears as a handsome young woman of 20. In *The Little Foxes,* set in 1900, she appears a woman of 40, still handsome, still iron-willed, still, as her brother Ben characterizes her, "beautiful, warm outside, and smart" (Hellman, 1947, p. 123). Regina's driving concern is to get her own way. As a young woman of 20, she wants two things: John Bagtry for a husband although he doesn't want it, and keeping her father happy so he will continue to supply her with money for clothes and trips. To achieve these two goals she manipulates her doting, domineering father, and scuttles Benjamin's plans to gain Lionnet, the Bagtry plantation. When Ben gains control of the family wealth by blackmailing Marcus, Regina turns from her father, moves to Ben's side, acquiescing to his power over the purse strings and, subsequently, her life. Never one to cling to the losing side or a lost cause, Regina acknowledges Ben's victory over the father and shifts to the winner's side.

When Regina appears 20 years later in *The Little Foxes*, her drive for money and social position has not altered. Now married (at Ben's direction) to Horace Giddens, a banker of good position and family, Regina verbally duels with her brothers over a financial investment to build cotton mills in partnership with a Northern businessman. She sends her daughter, Alexandra, to Baltimore alone to bring home Horace who has been hospitalized for five months. Alexandra is a perfect dupe in the plot to get Horace home, since he dotes on her and will do anything for her. Regina thinks nothing of using her daughter in this deceitful manner to get Horace to a position where he can be driven to put up the money needed for the investment. She even considers sacrificing Alexandra in marriage to Leo, Oscar's weak and dishonest son, as a bargaining lever to gain a larger share of profits. Once Horace arrives home, a terribly ill man, Regina badgers him unmercifully for the money. Horace almost blocks her plot, but has a sudden attack as they are talking. As he chokes and gasps, struggling to reach his needed medicine, Regina stands coldly immobile, unmoved, waiting. Horace's death gives Regina full control of his wealth. With this she blackmails her brothers, wins her price and share of potential profits, and triumphs, rich at last. But the winning is hollow, for there is no one, not even her own daughter, who cares to share the lucrative victory.

So Regina, a woman of the nouveau, prevails. Little in her character elicits sympathy. Her few meditative, reflective moments, suggesting an inner loneliness, fail to alter the overriding image of selfish greed. She stands as kin to Lady Macbeth and Hedda Gabler, with the same iron drive to dominance in a period when women had no avenues through which to channel their ambition and powers. The softening of lines of portraiture, in her last few moments, fails to blur the hard inner core that lies within.

Regina reveals many of the extropunitive traits and coping strategies. There is the slyness and cunning, the suspicion, the aggression against other groups, the competitiveness and rebellion and enhanced striving. Victimized by a social caste system, domineering father, and two Machiavellian brothers, her response is to cope by outmaneuvering the victimizers. Rather than be eaten she has joined the eaters.

These traits are exhibited in her interaction with other characters in the two plays. Her range and style of coping strategies are varied and extensive, though scarcely admirable. Aggression against "out groups" is revealed when she scorns the "high tone" kinfolk of her lover, John Bagtry, yet feels insulted when they take no notice of her. Living in the shadow of her father's treacherous usury, she is defensive about her family and background, flaunts her wealth by boasting that it could buy and sell John's family in a single morning.

In her interaction with the men, Regina's primary communicative strategies center on bargaining and negotiation, in a constant verbal duel of parry, feint, and thrust. With slyness and cunning she manipulates and deceives her doting, domineering father. She flatters him, waits on him, spends Sundays reading to him, and uses his inordinate affection for her as levers to get the money she wants—and the freedom it will buy. The fact that she must resort to these tactics reveals her dependency, her lack of control over her own life, her early victimization. She uses the ploys available—flattery, feigned docility, submission, and affection and deceit.

Just as Regina flattered her father, she charms Mr. Marshall, the wealthy businessman from Chicago, inveigling an invitation from him to visit Chicago where she hopes he will provide her entrée to the socially wealthy and elite.

The charming facade Regina presents to Mr. Marshall contrasts sharply with her treatment of her husband Horace and her two brothers. She harasses Horace, a fatally ill man. At his death she blackmails her two brothers, threatening to put them in jail by revealing their theft of Horace's bonds. The price of her silence is 75 percent of the profits. When Oscar protests that she can't put her own brothers in jail, Regina, now in full control, replies sharply.

> There are people who can't go back, who must finish what they start. I am one of those people, Oscar. Well, they'll convict you. But I won't care much if they don't. Because by that time you'll be ruined . . . Now I don't want to hear any more from any of you. *You'll do no more bargaining in this house.* I'll take my seventy-five percent and we'll forget the story forever. That's one way of doing it, and the way I prefer. You know me well enough to know that I don't mind taking the other way.

To which Ben replies, "None of us has ever known you well enough, Regina" (Hellman, 1951 pp. 716–717).

Regina's interaction with the other women is no less manipulative and deceptive, but it is different. They pose little or no threat and are themselves victimized by her, as pawns exploited to help her fulfill her dreams. Her communicative mode with them, reflecting her dominance and control, is one of command, the use of the imperative voice. As a young woman in *Another Part of the Forest*, she barely tolerates her mother, Lavinia, is embarrassed by Lavinia's eccentricities, treats her much like a wayward child, and tries to force her to go to Chicago—totally ignoring Lavinia's dream of teaching black children in a mission school.

With Birdie Bagtry, who is her own age, Regina is distantly cordial. In *Another Part of the Forest* they meet when Birdie comes to ask the Hubbards for a loan to save her family plantation. But Regina destroys Birdie's efforts to get the loan because it will provide money for John, Regina's lover, to go to South America rather than join her in Chicago.

Twenty years later, in *The Little Foxes*, Regina largely ignores Birdie, who is now her sister-in-law. One singular moment of friendliness occurs in Act I. Regina and Birdie are alone briefly. The deal with Marshall has just been settled. Regina is open, gleeful, expansive. She reveals her plans to go to Chicago, her hopes of joining the wealthy socialites there. She asks Birdie what she wants to do with the profits she and Oscar will get; she then totally ignores Birdie's reply when Ben and Oscar appear. In effect, Regina treats Birdie pretty much as a "nonperson." She does have some awareness of the strong bond between Birdie and Alexandra, however, and at one point chides Alexandra for sounding "just like your Aunt Birdie." Similarly, Regina largely ignores Addie, the black servant woman, or recognizes her presence only to give her orders. That Regina is aware of Addie's closeness and influence with Alexandra is revealed when she refuses to let Addie go with Alexandra to bring Horace home.

With Alexandra, her daughter, Regina's interaction is more complex and dynamic, with their role relationship undergoing a subtle change. Two scenes in particular reveal this alteration. At the end of Act I in *The Little Foxes*, Regina orders Alexandra to go alone to Baltimore to bring Horace home. She tells Alexandra that she is to say that she wants her father home because she needs him. Alexandra refuses. Regina challenges her sharply with, "You couldn't do what I tell you to do, Alexandra?" Again, Alexandra says no. Regina then changes her tactics, using Alexandra's concern for her father as a lever:

> But you are doing this for Papa's own good. (takes her hand) You must let me be the judge of his condition. It's the best possible cure for him to come home and be taken care of here . . . You are doing this entirely for his sake. Tell your papa that I want him to come home, that I miss him very much. (Hellman, 1951 p. 679).

Faced with this incredible lie and the clever manipulation of her affection for her father, Alexandra reluctantly agrees to do what Regina orders.

Although Regina has her way with Alexandra in this scene and is able to use her as a decoy to get Horace home, the lines of doubt and rebellion have been drawn. The interaction marks the beginning of Alexandra's awareness of her mother's duplicity, and of her own defiance of her dominance. That defiance culminates at the end of the play in Alexandra's refusal to go with Regina to Chicago. Regina considers forcing her to go along. Alexandra counters by saying that it wouldn't work, that she will not change her mind about going. With Alexandra adamant, Regina shifts ground, appears to acquiesce, with, "Alexandra, I've come to the end of my rope. Somewhere there has to be what I want. Life goes too fast. Do what you want; think what you want; go where you want. I'd like to keep you with me, but I won't make you stay. Too many people used to make me do too many things. No, I won't make you stay" (Hellman, 1951, p. 719).

In spite of this softened line of appeal, Alexandra is now the one who remains firm, in control, replying, "You couldn't, Mama, because I want to leave here. As I've never wanted anything in my life before."

With grudging respect, tinged with loneliness and, perhaps, a bit of fear, Regina answers, "Well, you have spirit after all. I used to think you were all sugar water. We don't have to be bad friends. I don't want us to be bad friends, Alexandra. Would you like to come and talk with me, Alexandra? Would you—would you like to sleep in my room tonight?" To this Alexandra only asks, "Are you afraid, Mama?" (Hellman, 1951, p. 719). With that final line, Regina moves slowly upstairs and out of sight, as Addie comes to stand with Alexandra.

The communicative pattern in this final dialogue provides revealing insight into the altered mother-daughter relationship. Regina relinquishes the reins of dominance and control and seems to seek to reestablish some sort of maternal bond with Alexandra. Her final question, tentatively offered, contrasts sharply with the bold incisive, calculated speech that characterized Regina previously. Conversely, it is Alexandra's words that come boldly, clearly, intensely in tersely articulated terms of defiance and purpose. The reversal of communicative patterns reflects clearly the reversal of roles and relationships.

Set as foils against the brittle outlines of Regina's character, her dominance, cunning, and patterns of calculated discourse, stand Lavinia, her mother, and Birdie, her sister-in-law. Softened, blurred images, ladies "made ghosts" by the war and its aftermath, these two women represent the aristocratic planter class—which Regina scorned openly yet secretly sought. Lavinia and Birdie show different dimensions of the intropunitive traits of victimization in their communicative inter-actions.

Lavinia, Reginia's mother, appears in *Another Part of the Forest*, a "stooped, thin, delicate-looking woman" of about fifty-eight, with a "nervous, distracted way of speaking." Of gentle folk and gentle ways of another time and place, Lavinia is driven to perpetual nervous despair by her family of vipers with whom she is ill-equipped to cope. She is patronized and ordered about by her children, ignored and derided by her husband, who calls her crazy. Behind Marcus' efforts to have Lavinia declared insane lies his fear that she will reveal his treacherous complicity with Union soldiers.

Only the black servants, Coralee and Jake, care for Lavinia with any warmth and affection. She goes with them to their church, the "colored" church, even though she knows that people don't like her doing it. But, as she says early in Act I to Regina and John Bagtry, "There's got to be one little thing you do that you want to do, all by yourself you want to do it" (Hellman, 1947, p. 9).

Although Regina cuts her off sharply, Lavinia's remark is crucial to understanding her situation and position in the Hubbard household. It discloses both her determination to find a meaningful place for herself and the desperation with which she clings to her religious faith for strength and support. Religion has become the dominant force and center in her life as reflected in her thoughts and speaking. Her comments always circle back to her own plans, her church, the standards of her religious faith. Her husband and children perceive this as a kind of religious "dottiness." But it suggests that her wishes and place as a person have been so long ignored and derided that she has become conditioned to center solely on her own affairs as a means of ego defense and of maintaining some self-identity. So complete is the inward turning that often her comments don't track with the general line of conversation—and she is generally ignored, anyway, or chided for interrupting.

Lavinia, however, is not without concern for others and capable of gentle graciousness, given a chance. Her brief exchange with John Bagtry who responds with equal gentleness and courtesy, and her sympathy for Birdie's plight in pleading for the loan, disclose a capacity for concern for others, a sympathy and empathy.

In addition to concern for other unfortunates, Lavinia's victimization traits include self-imposed blame, guilt, futility, and fear. She is plagued by a sense of shame for sharing Marcus' unsavory past. In an exchange with Marcus, at the end of Act II, Lavinia recognizes that he calls her crazy "just to hurt my feelings" and comments, "I know. We weren't ever meant to be together. You see, being here gives me—well, I won't use bad words, but it's always made me feel like I sinned. And God wants you to make good your sins before you die. That's why I got to go now" (Hellman, 1947, p. 91–92). The reason she has "got to go now" is to try to expiate the sin of Marcus' cruelty to the blacks by teaching in a school for little black children. This she feels is her mission, her appointed way. To this one purpose and goal she clings. It is all she has. And thus her strong religious sense works both as a cross and as a refuge from the monstrous amorality of her husband and children.

Lavinia carries, too, some oblique sense of personal guilt that she has allowed her children to be as they are. She takes their faults upon her soul as her own burden of failure. The sense of failure and futility is expressed in a brief exchange with Ben, her oldest son, who has been ordered out of the house by Marcus. She begs Ben for protection from Marcus and help in getting away to go teach in the school. She pleads, "Take me with you . . . I know you're bad off now . . . *You're my first born, so it must be my fault some way.*" "You've grown away from—I loved you, Benjamin . . . Take me with you. Take me where I can do my little good . . . You know, I should have gone after that night, but *I stayed for you children. I didn't know then that none of you would ever need a Mama.*" (italics added) (Hellman, 1947, p. 94).

And then comes the admission of fear. She speaks of wanting to leave Marcus, but "I've always been afraid of him, because once or twice . . . (to Ben) Oh, I've been afraid of you, too. I spent my life afraid. And you know that's funny, Benjamin, because way down deep I'm a woman wasn't made to be afraid. What are most people afraid of? Well, like your Papa, they're afraid to die. But I'm not afraid to die because my colored friends going to be right there to pray me in . . . And if you're not afraid of dying then you're not afraid of anything" (Hellman, 1947 p. 95–96).

There is self-disclosure and self-cognition in these lines—an awareness that she, a "woman wasn't made to be afraid" has spent her life afraid. Implicit in the cognition is a realization that her identity has somehow changed, that she has become another kind of person from what she was and was meant to be.

Beyond the comfort of her religion, Lavinia's method of coping with the alien world of her family lies in a kind of pretense. When Marcus goes back on his promise to talk with her about plans for her school for black children, she pretends that it didn't really happen. When Laurette, Leo's "worldly" lady friend, calls Marcus a bastard to his face, decries his selling salt at exhorbitant prices during the war, lays open his suspected treachery, and flaunts the fact that he barely escaped death by lynching, Lavinia hides the memory of these facts by assuring herself that "salt" and "death" are "perfectly good words" since they appear in the Bible. In sum, she tries to adjust to a world she does not understand by refusing to face reality, by creating a world of pretend and pretense, by "making herself cheer up."

In her moment of triumph over Marcus, where she reveals the awful truth of his treachery to Ben, Lavinia still remains gullible, wanting to believe the best, almost accepting Marcus' placating lies and promises. When Marcus offers her anything she wants, she asks for a mahogany church pew with her brass name plate on it, and refuses his offer for a gold plate.

She wants money for her school and says her "message" from God suggested a thousand dollars a year "would make my colored children happy." Then, in spite of her religious "dottiness" or perhaps because of it, she is canny enough to suggest that "I think ten thousand a year would make them happier." When Marcus offers more Lavinia remains firm, saying that ten thousand is enough. But then she does extract a promise of two hundred dollars a month for Coralee, who supports a lot of kinfolk. Coralee was also a witness to Marcus' treachery the night of the trainees' massacre.

These are selfless wants. Greed is not in her. Neither is a clear recognition of her situation and her people. Only under Ben's prodding does she recognize Marcus' promises and lies for what they are and have always been—empty ruses to silence her. As Ben blackmails his father into signing over all the family wealth to him, by threatening to reveal Marcus' complicity, Lavinia never really comprehends the gambit that is being played. She holds the key to power—her hand-written eyewitness account of Marcus' complicity on the night of the massacre, with dates, times, names, all spelled out as proof, recorded in her Bible. But she seems not to connect the power of this information with Marcus' sudden eagerness to help her with the school or with Ben's use of the information to strip Marcus of his wealth.

The traits of victimization in Birdie are not readily apparent in her two brief appearances in *Another Part of the Forest*, although her discourse and communicative mode show some early warning signs. When she first appears, she has indeed been victimized, not by prejudice or "arbitrary will of others" but by circumstances beyond her control— the destruction of her family, five brothers and a father lost in the war, and the struggle to survive in a desolated economy. She is, at this point, apologetic and self-effacing, though it is difficult to tell whether her remarks are early indications of victimization or simply ritualistic courtesies typical of Southern custom, or, more importantly, of female discourse.

For example, when Birdie comes to the Hubbards to plead for the loan, she apologizes to Ben for disturbing their Sunday "day of privacy." She speaks of how her "Mama" went all the way to Natchez to try to borrow money for the Lionnet plantation and explains, "She did it to save me, Mr. Benjamin, the trip, I mean. I was such a ninny being born when I did, growing up at the wrong time." Uncertainty and lack of self-confidence are further revealed when Birdie acknowledges to Ben that "it's not good manners to take up all your time saying how sorry I am to take up all your time, now is it?" and then "Oh, and I'm doing it again, too. Mama says I say everything in a question. Oh." (Hellman, 1947, p. 31–32). The blaming of self for circumstances beyond control is a typical intropunitive trait. And, as Lakoff (1975) notes in *Language and Woman's Place*, the tag-question formation is the one syntactic rule that women use more in conversational situations than men. As an intermediate form of discourse it occurs when the speaker is stating a claim, but lacks confidence in the truth of the claim; it suggests a lack of self-confidence, a seeking of confirmation and approval from others (Lakoff, 1975, pp. 15–17). This pattern that typifies Birdie's speech, by her own admission, reveals the "politeness" of speech women are taught as "lady-like" which prevents the expression of strong statements and assertive commitments.

Naive, trusting, and uncertain as Birdie appears, she has some understanding of the basic economic needs her family faces. She asks Ben for a loan of 5,000 dollars, explaining that "It would take that much to pay our people and buy seed and pay debts . . . ." But she is uninformed of the legal aspects involved in who would sign for the loan.

At Ben's suggestion, Birdie and her cousin, John, come to the Hubbards the next evening to speak to Marcus about the loan. When Marcus refuses the loan and suggests that she come to visit some other time when she has no motive, Birdie stiffens. Her firm reply reveals an interesting mix of pride, apology, and desperate determination, not unusual for a sheltered young woman of 20. "Yes, I had a motive. Why shouldn't I have? It was why I was asked here—Oh, I mustn't talk proud. I have no right to. Look, Mr. Hubbard, I'll do anything. I'm sure you like good pictures: we have a Stuart and a West, and a little silver left. Couldn't I give—couldn't I bring them to you . . . (then, softly) I was going to use the first money to buy molasses and sugar. All that land and cotton and we're starving. It sounds crazy to need even molasses . . . ." When Marcus replies that "everybody with cotton is starving" Birdie answers angrily, "That's just a way of using a word. That isn't what I mean. I mean starving." Then her voice changes, she sighs, and apologizes saying, "I should have known I couldn't do anything right. I never have . . . You lose your manners when you're poor" (Hellman, 1947, p. 80–81).

In Birdie's unskilled efforts at negotiating the loan, only Lavinia recognizes the enormous effort, the sacrifice of dignity and pride. She graciously bids Birdie goodnight, urging her to ride over for a visit, or "Come down by the river and we'll read together." Then to Marcus she comments, "Goodness, Marcus. Couldn't you have—it's pig mean, being poor. Takes away your dignity." (Hellman, 1947, p. 81).

Birdie appears in *The Little Foxes*, 20 years later, as Oscar's wife. The 20 years have exacted a costly toll. The nervous, determined, proud young woman who pled for a loan now exhibits the intropunitive traits of victimization. Exploited and despoiled, uncertain, seeking approval, Birdie is ignored and denegrated at every turn. Birdie, as Ben tells Mr. Marshall, the Chicago businessman, is one of the acquisitions bought with Hubbard wealth, along with Lionnet land and cotton. Now Oscar, like his father before him with Lavinia, exercises an abusive tyranny over her, ever chiding, scorning, deprecating. When he overhears Birdie warn Alexandra of the plot to make her marry Birdie's son, Leo, Oscar slaps her viciously for meddling. Indeed, it is apparent that she is the only one he can dominate, as Regina and Ben manipulate his fortunes at will in their game to gain more money.

Birdie, like Lavinia, was raised in another world, a gentle world where people spoke softly and behaved honorably. The Hubbards' world is alien to her, also, and she is not fully able to cope with it or with them. Where Lavinia escaped by means of her religion and her world of pretense, Birdie copes by turning inward, to memories of the past, and of her Mama, and to alcohol. Yet she differs from Lavinia in one important aspect. She recognizes the world of the forest and the foxes for what it is, as it is.

The depth of Birdie's cognition is revealed in the scene at the beginning of Act III as she, Alexandra, Horace, and Addie spend a few pleasant moments together, in an oasis of momentary quiet. The time is two weeks after the bitter quarrel between Regina and Horace, when he adamantly refused to put up a share of money for investment in the mill, leaving Ben and Oscar to find money elsewhere and to close the deal without Regina. As they speak of these matters over elderberry wine, Birdie becomes a little drunk and begins to reminisce. Finally she even admits that she "doesn't like Leo. My very own son and I don't like him." Then Alexandra asks why she married Oscar; Birdie replies,

> I don't know. I thought I liked him. He was kind to me and I thought it was because he liked me too. But that wasn't the reason—Ask why

he married *me*. I can tell you that: he's told it to me often enough . . .
My family was good and the cotton on Lionnet's fields was better. Ben
Hubbard wanted the cotton and Oscar Hubbard married it for him. He
was kind to me then. He used to smile at me. He hasn't smiled at me
since. Everybody knew that's what he married me for. Everybody but
me. Stupid, stupid me (Hellman, 1951, p. 704).

When Addie urges Birdie to rest or she'll get another headache,
Birdie replies sharply, "I've never had a headache in my life. (begins
to cry) You know it as well as I do. I never had a headache, Zan.
That's a lie they tell for me. I drink. All by myself, in my own room,
by myself, I drink. Then, when they want to hide it, they say, 'Birdie's
got a headache again'—Even you won't like me now. You won't like
me anymore." Alexandra protests, "I love you. I'll always love you."
And Birdie furiously warns her,

> Well, don't. Don't love me. Because in twenty years you'll be just like
> me. They'll do all the same things to you. You know what? In twenty-
> two years I haven't had a whole day of happiness. Oh, a little, like today
> with you all. But never a single, whole day . . . And that's the way
> you'll be. And you'll trail after them, just like me, hoping they won't be
> so mean that day or say something to make you feel so bad—only you'll
> be worse off because you haven't got my Mama to remember (Hellman,
> 1951, p. 704–705).

Birdie's comments in this scene are reiterated here in detail because
of their importance in two aspects. First, her discourse reveals her
victimization traits and coping strategies. Second, the comments exhibit
three important dimensions of self-disclosure in interpersonal communication. Nurtured by an atmosphere of love, of trust, and understanding, there is *recognition, self-awareness* that her own early naivete
and trust made her vulnerable to being gulled and deceived. Wanting,
hoping to believe that Oscar liked her, she failed to see in his advances
what everyone else saw. She fell victim, apparently, because there was
no one who warned her of his real intent. There was, then, only those
who "stood around and watched."

From recognition and self-assessment flows the second communicative
dimension, *admission*, disclosure of her efforts to cope, to escape, by
drinking—all alone: a disclosure made in spite of the terrible fear that
now, even those she loves will not care for her anymore. When
Alexandra protests that she will always love her, Birdie responds furiously with the *admonition*, warning Alexandra not to love her, because
in twenty years, as she says, "you'll be just like me . . ."

The strength of her love for Alexandra and the extent of her own despair are reflected in Birdie's syntax and tonality. In turning outward to champion another's cause and need, her speech becomes both direct and directive. The broken unfinished sentences, the tag type questions, and uncertain phrases that change direction are gone. Her sentences are direct, almost clipped, declarative, and, in a unique manner, assertive and strong. Thus, communicatively, in this interchange, involving self-cognition, admission, and admonition, Birdie does for Alexandra what no one did for her twenty years before—she does more than just stand around and watch.

Alexandra, for her part, replies thoughtfully, echoing Addie's words earlier in the scene, in a different way: "I guess we were all trying to make a happy day. You know, we sit around and try to pretend nothing's happened. We try to pretend we are not here. We make believe we are just by ourselves, some place else, and *it doesn't seem to work*. Come now, Aunt Birdie, I'll walk you home. You and me" (italics added) (Hellman, 1951, p. 705).

Birdie does not appear again in the play. But her influence carries to Alexandra, warning her not to marry Leo, not to let "them" make her do it, and leading her to realize that pretense, as though nothing's happened, doesn't work. These realizations are reinforced by Addie's words about the two kinds of people, the eaters and the eaten.

With the words of warning and wisdom from the three people whom she loves and who love her, plus her inheritance from Horace, Alexandra gains the understanding and the independence she needs to get away. This change culminates in the final scene of *The Little Foxes* as Alexandra confronts Regina openly. She refuses to be taken in, ordered, or coerced, and stands firm in her decision not to go to Chicago or anywhere with Regina. Defiantly Alexandra tells Regina:

> You couldn't make me stay, Mama, because I want to leave here. As I've never wanted anything in my life before. Because now I understand what Papa was trying to tell me. All in one day: Addie said there were people who ate the earth and other people who stood around and watched them do it. And just now Uncle Ben said the same thing. . . . Well, tell him for me, Mama, I'm not going to stand around and watch you do it. Tell him, I'll be fighting as hard as he'll be fighting, some place where people don't just stand around and watch (Hellman, 1951, p. 719).

So Alexandra adds another dimension to the qualities of the women portrayed in Hellman's two plays. Although initially ordered about and deceived by Regina, her mother, Alexandra is able to avoid the victimization trap. Warned by Birdie, provided for by her father, and aided by Addie who has promised Horace to look after her, Alexandra is able to escape. She is able to recognize and avoid the futility of pretense of Lavinia, the denegrating victimization of Birdie, and the cold, manipulative dominance by Regina that killed her father.

In a sense, Addie's wisdom is the key that leads to Alexandra's liberation. Addie was the one who commented that there were "eaters and the eaten" and that "it ain't right to just sit around and watch them do it." Almost in direct response, Horace, Birdie, and Addie, each in their own way, *do* do something other than just "sit around and watch them do it." Each does what is possible to defeat the eaters.

Some Conclusions as "Equipment for Living"

In accordance with Burke's notion that imaginative works are "strategic answers, stylized answers to questions posed by situations," the portraits of the five women in Hellman's plays yield useful insights and some "leads" concerning human relationships. All five women are victims to some degree. In dramatically intense situations of victimization, their communicative modes and patterns reveal traits of victimization and examplify coping strategies of response.

Each woman develops a distinctive set of strategies for coping with her situation of victimization. As I have noted, we see in Regina many of the extropunitive traits of victimage noted by Allport. Having been victimized by a domineering father and greedy brothers, she copes by cleverly joining the victimizers, using their tactics to outmaneuver them in their schemes. She herself becomes a victimizer, denigrating her lover and his family, ignoring her sister-in-law, barely tolerating her mother, blackmailing her brothers, and deceiving both her husband and her daughter. Like the other women in the plays, Regina wishes to escape her present victimization. Her goal is to get money and wealth so she can go to Chicago where she believes she will find entrée to a better social position. There is little or no tenderness in Regina, though in the final scene in *The Little Foxes* she does gain a touch of pathos. She recognizes that she cannot force Alexandra to stay with her, expresses grudging admiration for Alexandra's spirit, and reveals that too many people have made her do too many things she did not want to do.

Regina's primary communicative strategy is bargaining and negotiation, typified by slyness, cunning, calculated charm, and deception. In dealing with the other women, whom she orders or ignores, her communicative style is marked by the declarative and imperative mood, assertion, and command.

Lavinia and Birdie exhibit the intropunitive traits described by Allport, as each tries to cope with relationships and situations that are alien. Lavinia, the older, her life and marriage spanning the ante-bellum days and the reconstruction period, hides unpleasantness with pretense, and remains unwilling and unable to recognize the situation as it is. She continues to blame herself for the evil deeds of her husband and children; because of them she carries a sense of guilt and sin, and demonstrates sympathy for other victims. Her strong religious faith, at once a refuge and a torture, becomes her preoccupation. Her sense of guilt for others' sins drives her to escape into another world to try to rectify the wrongs that have been done.

Birdie, on the other hand, was but a child during the war. She lived to see the awfulness of its aftermath and to know the struggle to survive in a changing world. She, too, finds herself caught in a web of malice and meanness with which she cannot effectively cope. But she recognizes the web for what it is and sees the trap that has ensnared her. Docile, submissive, desperately seeking approval, even a singular kindly word, she really has no coping strategy except to drink by herself, as a means of retreating from unpleasantness. Like Lavinia, Birdie, too, wants to go away. But her escape is psychological, perhaps even neurotic. She wants not to go out, but back—back to Lionnet where she believes everyone will be happy and kind again. She seeks escape back into the comfortable cocoon of the past she knew and loved. Her nostalgic dream is all the more pathetic because it can never be fulfilled. It will never happen. She remains totally trapped in her situation, knowing she is caught in a web of evil from which there is no escape.

Alexandra presents a mix of traits. Whereas we see in Birdie a transformation from strength to docility and submissiveness, Alexandra's development moves from docility to strength and defiance. At the beginning of *The Little Foxes*, she is docile, obedient, passive, though reluctant to follow Regina's orders. Then from Birdie, from Addie, and from her Uncle Ben, she comes to see the situation for what it is. She develops assertiveness if not aggression, defiance, and rebelliousness. In the shift from acquiescence to defiance there is both a realism and an idealism. She, too, wants to get away. But the getting away has a purpose: she has the convictions of a reformer; she promises to be a fighter, one who will not just "stand around" and watch others be eaten—foreshadowing perhaps a new breed of woman yet to come.

Addie does not clearly reveal either set of traits in much detail. She, too, is a mix. Though outwardly obedient, docile, passive in her role, there runs underneath a kind of Olympian quality of transcendent understanding and wisdom that lifts her above the external entrapments of victimization. She serves as observer, reporter, commentator, surrogate mother to Alexandra, and a key factor in Alexandra's transformation.

Addie is the realist who sees the foxes in the forest and understands what they are about. Though she herself is powerless to alter the situation, she does offer hope that her wisdom will find its influence in Alexandra.

Thus, each woman copes with her situation. Each seeks a way out, an escape from what is. Each in her own way seeks another ground in which to sow seeds of happiness, suggesting the barrenness of the old plot which gave satisfaction to none and brought to bloom only despair and unrest. The victimizers include a father, son, daughter, brother, husband, mother, wife, and a social system. The victimized are wife, daughter, mother, servant, and husband. The modes of victimization and dominance include denigration, ridicule, deceit, abuse, power, scorn, wealth and social/economic position. The modes of coping encompass deference, defiance, adaptation, submission, striving, and escape, assertiveness, and withdrawal. Money, wealth, dreams, wisdom, defiance are portrayed as providing ways out of victimization.

If Hellman's portraitures of women coping with victimization are to be taken, as Burke suggests, as a "ritualistic way of arming us to confront perplexities and risks", then what inferences are we to draw that may "protect" us?

First, the plays emphasize the presence and potentialities of power. The use and abuse of power is shown to be as much a part of interpersonal, familial relationships as of business, public, professional, or social interactions. Power is shown as establishing dominance: control over one's own life and over the lives of others. In the case of the five women, power flows from two key sources: possession of money and possession of information. Wealth confers control over those who lack it and independence for those who have it. Information confers power because it can be withheld or proclaimed to manipulate the trust, fears, or ignorance of others.

Second, Hellman's women reveal an important element of power. Power depends on cognition, on a clear perception and understanding of realities—concerning self, situations, and others. Those who acquire and exercise power effectively see things as they are, not as they wish or hope them to be. Those with the least power tend to fantasize or withdraw.

Integral to the exercise of power and cognition is a third key factor: communication. The communicative patterns of the five women reflect a range of possible responses in coping with victimization, some of which are self-defeating. These responses include: acquiescence, defiance, transcendence, suppression and pretense, and/or enlistment. *Acquiescence* is reflected in submissive, docile, approval-seeking talk. *Defiance* is expressed through rebelliousness, risk-taking, and insistence on self-determination. *Transcendence* is revealed in discourse that expresses a move of the spirit to some higher order of concerns and some supra-situational sense of self-worth. *Suppression* entails communicative pretense and deliberate refusal to acknowledge realities. Such responses may be born of hope, naivete, or both. *Enlistment,* joining the victimizers, is portrayed as entering a maze of bargaining and negotiation with the will to acquire power and the desire to use it to control self and others. Most importantly, Hellman's portrayal of women acting and communicating shows that *the choice of responses to victimization lies with the individual*—although the situations may vary greatly in degrees of subtlety and circumstance.

The centrality of individual choice in role-power-response relationships raises some larger questions. Are there only eaters and eaten? Must one join the victimizers to avoid being victimized? Beyond acquiescence and enlistment are there alternatives for freedom from victimization? Is there some middle ground or some other ground and stance that one can take to secure control over one's self and life and future without denigrating and deceiving and dominating others? The full playing out of such alternative responses is not developed in Hellman's two plays. But in Alexandra and in Addie there is a suggestion that alternatives to submission or dominance *do* exist. Insofar as the women in Hellman's two plays have illuminated some strategies for coping with the foxes in the forest, they offer us some "leads" for real-life human relationships and provide, in Burke's terms, some "equipments for living."

References

Allport, G.W. (1954). *The nature of prejudice.* Cambridge, MA: Addison-Wesley.

Burke, K. (1957). *The philosophy of literary form.* (Revised edition). New York: Vintage Books.

Hellman, L. (1947). *Another part of the forest.* New York: Viking Press.

Hellman, L. (1951). The little foxes. In M. Bloomfield and R. Elliott. (Eds.), *Ten Plays: An introduction to drama.* New York: Rinehart & Company, Inc.

Lakoff, R. (1975). *Language and woman's place.* New York: Harper & Row.

9

Shared Leadership in the Weavers Guild

Nancy Wyatt

The Pennsylvania State University

Shared Leadership in the Weavers Guild

This essay reports the results of a research study of leadership that I conducted in a women's group as a participant-observer. The group was the Weaver's Guild, a group of approximately 40 women who belonged to the group because of a common interest in handspinning and handweaving. The Weavers Guild was composed mostly of quite traditional and conservative women, who are for the most part middle-class and married. The main goal of the group was to meet the individual goals of the members; the Guild had no serious aspirations to bring culture to the community or to educate the public on the virtues of their craft. In this way the group resembles many other women's social groups throughout the United States.

I joined the Weavers Guild shortly after I arrived in the community because the members shared a common interest in my own avocation—spinnning and weaving. My initial impression of the Guild was a very pleasant one, because the Guild seemed both friendly and active. There were spinners and weavers at all levels of expertise, and the interests of the individual members were very diverse. Moreover, the atmosphere of the group seemed to me one of sharing and learning. The attitude was that you brought what knowledge and experience you had to the group, and everyone learned from each other. Failure was as instructive as success, and there was a notable absence of overt competition among members. I was a member of the Guild for five years until I left the community.

My formal study of the Weavers Guild as a social unit grew out of the confluence of my interest in the group itself and my vocational interest in studying group behavior. As a weaver I enjoyed the participation in the group; as a student of group behavior I was interested in discovering and describing how the group was run. I had noticed that the Guild operated very differently from other groups of which I had been a member. For example, the military wives' groups to which I had belonged had been very status conscious. Each military wife took on the status of her husband. When groups met, you would find the colonels' wives talking to other colonels' wives and the lieutenants' wives talking to other lieutenants' wives. When the wives took part in charity work, the field grade officers' wives supervised, while the company grade officers' wives did the work.

Furthermore, I couldn't identify any cliques in the Weavers Guild like those I had found in graduate school. Among the graduate students I had noticed divisions into different "camps" divided by emphasis: rhetoric, social science, and mass communications were the main divisions. But students also became identified with the professors with whom they worked; students were often referred to as "a Schwarz man" or "a Whiffle student."

Everything went very smoothly on the surface in the Weavers Guild. For example, I had noticed that there was little or no discussion of issues during the formal monthly meetings of the Guild. Proposals were made and approved and slates of officers were elected with a minimum of discussion. Clearly decisions were being made by someone, but I couldn't immediately discover who was making them. I wanted to find out what processes were going on behind the scenes to produce the illusion (or reality) of cooperating, sharing, and friendliness I perceived in Guild activities.

The clues to power and influence that I had learned from my formal studies of communication—formal position in the group, status in the community, control of resources—weren't particularly useful in identifying who was influencing the decisions that were being made in the Weavers Guild. Individual members of the group were willing to work on committees, but they carefully avoided even the appearance of taking charge. No one member held office more than one year. I wanted to find out how this group operated so well without anyone claiming leadership.

The notion that the Weavers Guild was exclusively a women's group and therefore might differ from the men's groups or groups of mixed gender described in the communication literature only dawned on me slowly. After all, the Weavers Guild wasn't consciously constituted as a "woman's group" because male weavers were certainly welcome. There just weren't any. And none of the women in the Guild were vociferously feminist. On the contrary, they were mostly married and quite traditional in their views on family and community. A year after my study of the Weavers Guild was completed, Carol Gilligan's *In a Different Voice* (1982) was published, and it provided an admirable description of the values and behavior I had already described for the Weavers Guild. This essay is an account of my research and of my search for explication of what I found, mostly in light of what I have learned since I completed the study.

I am still not ready to state unequivocally that the Weavers Guild operates the way it does because it is composed entirely of women. I hold open the possibility that men could conduct themselves in the same fashion, if they found it to their benefit. Hunter (1953) presents some evidence that men do share leadership in communities. I know also that women are capable of behaving in the "masculine" model when the opportunity and training encourages that model. I resist the easy definition of people into gender categories, agreeing with the wag who observed, "There are just two kinds of people in the world: people who divide the world into two kinds of people and the rest of us." In this essay I will describe the study of leadership I conducted in the Weavers Guild and discuss possible explanations for my findings.

The Weavers Guild

The Weavers Guild is a group of approximately 40 women who are in some way interested in or involved in the crafts often referred to as "fiber arts." Most of the members are handweavers, although some are spinners or do basketry or lacemaking. Most of the members pursue weaving as a hobby. The ages of the members range from early twenties to seventies. Most of the members could be described as middle class; few are employed full time outside the home. Weaving is a comparatively expensive hobby, because the tools and materials are expensive. Hand-weaving is also relatively labor–intensive as a hobby. Although many of the Guild members sell their weaving, few could claim to make a profit.

The Weavers Guild was organized in 1973 and has remained relatively stable in size and function since that time. Officers are elected in the spring, and the Guild meets monthly from September to May. There are five elective positions in the Weavers Guild: chair, secretary/publicity, treasurer, program chair, and newsletter editor. These officers constitute an Executive Board that meets as necessary to plan the activities of the Guild; they usually meet monthly. Other members volunteer to provide services as the Guild needs them—keeping the coffee pot or the Guild equipment, for example.

Guild meetings, held in the homes of members, consist of a business meeting followed by a program. After the meeting coffee and tea are available and there is an opportunity for informal conversation. There are several smaller informal groups within the Weavers Guild. The largest of these groups is the spinners, who meet monthly to spin and visit. The Guild also sponsors annual study groups that consist of three to six members who are interested in a particular weaving technique. These smaller groups organize themselves and meet at each other's homes. At the last meeting of the year in the spring, each study group reports to the whole Guild and brings samples to show what they have learned. Committees are formed on an ad hoc basis as they are needed to organize sales or demonstrations or to consider matters of policy. Committee members volunteer their services.

The Guild collects dues for operating expenses. The money is used to cover the costs of monthly newsletter and materials for demonstrations. Speakers for the meetings receive a small honorarium. Costs for workshops are paid by the workshop participants, and publicity costs for the sales are paid from the proceeds of the sales. The Guild sponsors various activities as the members evince interest in them: programs, study groups, workshops, sales, exhibits, demonstrations for the public, and so on.

The Study

Any study of decision making in groups must define the nature of the processes under consideration. Traditionally, studies of leadership have focused on the system of rewards available for leaders: status, power, economic gain. Most studies of leadership seemed to make the assumption that leadership was a good thing; everyone would want to be a leader if they could.

The group that I was studying was entirely voluntary and membership or leadership conferred neither status nor power in the larger community. Members of the Guild were pursuing individual goals; there were no important economic or political rewards available for members. In fact, members seemed to try to avoid taking leadership roles. Thinking of leadership in the Guild in terms of rewards had led me to conclude that the only real reward for participation and responsibility was the continued existence of the group itself. The goal of the group members was to maintain the individual relationships within the group that constituted the Guild. I needed a different conceptualization of leadership. I wanted to see if I could find a basis for leadership by looking at the relationships among the members of the group.

For this study, I used a theoretical conception of power in groups drawn from the work of Homans (1974). Homans postulated power in groups as a private system of relationships among group members. Homans asserted that such a system of relationships could be described by the members of the group. This conceptualization of power emphasized the situational nature of leadership and allowed the definition of power and leadership to emerge from the group itself. This theory took account of the relationships among individuals in a group; it allowed for persuasion as an important aspect of decision making. In order for individuals to be identified as leaders, they would have to persuade the other members that they were qualified and capable of leadership. Additionally, Homans' assertion that the members of the group could articulate the system of agreements that constituted power or leadership made it particularly appropriate to a communication-based study.

Homans defined group status as public acknowledgement of a private system of power relationships among group members. Some members, he asserted, are able to provide rare or highly valued goods or services to other members. The action of providing such highly valued goods or services elicits approval and/or compliance from other members, and this exchange is defined in terms of power. The person who provides the highly valued goods or services has power to influence others, and consequently has status in the group. But control of resources is not in itself sufficient for the exercise of power in a group. The person must be willing to provide or use resources for the group; the willingness to enter into an exchange is requisite for the exercise of power.

Homans said that the differential status of members (which represents the public acknowledgment of their relative power in the group) is revealed by language. The members of a group can report the relative status of other members to be "higher" or "lower" or "better" or "worse" in relation to each other. This talk can be either natural talk like that in conversations and meetings, or it can be responses to questionnaires or interviews. In either case, group members are able to describe a status hierarchy for their group. Talk is also the way differential status is ratified in the group. Labeling a certain person as having higher or lower status, Homans explained, is an action like any other action, subject to reinforcement or extinction, depending on the reactions of other group members. Talk reveals and ratifies differential status in groups.

Not only can individual members of a group describe a status structure for members of their group, but there is usually a consensual agreement on the basis for status ranking of group members. This consensus can be articulated by group members. Group members will be able to tell why some persons have higher status than other persons. Reports of this kind can be used as a research tool to study relative status in groups. Homans' theory of power in groups seemed particularly appropriate for a communication-based study of leadership.

I had three sources of data for this study: (a) a formal interview study of 10 weavers mutually identified as the leadership of the group; (b) my own observations of the group as a participant in the group; and (c) the documentary history of the group in the form of meeting minutes, newspaper articles, and other written or published information about the Guild collected by the Guild's unofficial historian since its beginning in 1973.

For my first interview, I chose a member who was well known in the community for her weaving. She was also one of the founders of the Guild and had been an active member since the Guild's inception. I asked this woman to identify women who functioned as leaders in the Guild. Beginning with her list of such members, I interviewed women identified as leaders in the Guild until I had interviewed all of the people who had been named at least three times by different members. In all, I conducted 10 interviews. Only one person was too busy to be interviewed.

I used an interview schedule of 25 questions that began with demographic questions about the weaver herself, progressed to general questions about the Guild, and ended with a request for the respondent to rank the top members of the guild according to their status in the Guild. The interview schedule appears in Appendix I.

During the interviews, I used the formal questions to focus attention on specific issues, but if the interviewee raised other issues, I pursued those issues. Often I asked the women to explain or give specific examples of their statements. Because the specific words were not important to this study, I did not use a tape recorder. I felt that such machinery would lend too formal a note to the occasion. I tried to set the atmosphere of friendly conversation for the interviews, which were held in the interviewees' homes at their convenience.

In interpreting my interview data, I called on my own experience and observation of the Guild activities, and I searched the records of the Guild's operations since it had been formed. Using these three techniques to gather information about the Guild, I could check my observations and inferences for accuracy.

Since this study of leadership is also a study of the personal relationships among the members who provided leadership in the Guild, I will provide a description of the cast of characters you will meet in the following discussion of the data analysis for this study. The names used in this account are, of course, pseudonyms.

Sonya is a young weaver, new to the group. She had a bachelor's degree in textiles and had been a professional weaver before coming to this community, but she had taken a job here and had very little time for weaving. She was very quiet, pleasant, and unassuming at the meetings.

Rachel is one of the founders of the group, and one of the oldest and most highly respected members of the group. Whenever the topic of weaving came up in the community, her name was always mentioned. She has a reputation for knowledge of traditional weaving, and a loyal following who purchase her weavings at the sales. She is quite pleasant and friendly and willing to share her knowledge to weavers who asked.

Janet is another young professional weaver, who was at the time of this interview working as a weaver. She works hard in the Guild to organize workshops and shows, and is always thinking of ways to increase public awareness and understanding of the craft. She also organizes well and understands group process.

Winnie has been a member of the Guild for many years. Every year she seems to take up another kind of weaving. She looks on the Guild primarily as a social group, although her products always are purchased at the sales. She is also the unofficial historian of the group; she has records of all the meetings and publicity for the Guild since it was founded.

Frances is best known for her rugs. She is a meticulous craftsperson, who has extensive experience working with other crafts groups. She is quite knowledgeable in committee work and often volunteers her home for meetings.

Paula is the only weaver to call herself an expert. Self taught, she has an extensive knowledge of technique. She also is familiar with committee work.

Susan doesn't really do much weaving, but is active as an organizer and works on committees. Her vocation is in another craft. I am not sure why she is interested in the Weavers Guild, but she is a loyal member.

Analysis of Data

My analysis of the data I gathered—responses to questions in the interview—took two forms. First, I analyzed the responses to my requests to identify and describe leadership in the Guild, and then I analyzed the interview transcripts to discover how leadership was conceptualized by the members of the Guild themselves. The traditional metaphors for the exercise of leadership used by researchers in communication have been borrowed from sociology or psychology and are based on conceptualizations of power or influence as either force or commodity. These metaphors seemed inappropriate to the discussion of leadership I discovered in my interviews, so I was compelled to redefine the shared leadership I had described by another metaphor of connections or systems of agreements.

In order to describe how leadership functions in the Guild, I tried to find several different ways of configuring the interview responses to find patterns or consistencies in the data. In the end I used several different methods for analyzing the data gathered from the interviews and observations. I graphed the responses of interviewees who ranked the members of the Guild by status (Figure 1) and counted the number of times each person was named as holding status in the Guild (Figure 2). I made sociograms of the members who named each other as holding status and of the members who said they knew each other best (Figures 3 and 4). I counted the times each person was named as a good committee member or as a good officer (Figures 5 and 6). I listed the qualities members identified for good leaders and good committee members (Figures 7 and 8).

As might be expected, my findings were not entirely consistent. One interview question asked Guild members to rank the leaders by status in the Guild. By this ranking Janet came out clearly ahead; she ranked first five times, while Susan was named twice, and Rachel once. But when I counted the total number of times a member's name was mentioned in the interviews, Rachel received seven mentions, Janet and Frances six each, while Susan was mentioned five times.

Janet was named more often than anyone else as a good officer and committee member, but Esther, Sonya, Paula, Bonnie, and Lynette were all identified as good committee members. Janet was also named most often as a person knowledgeable about technical matters of weaving

Figure 1. Ranking of Members in Ordinal Positions*

	First	Second	Third	Fourth	Fifth
Janet	5			1	
Rachel	1	2	2	2	
Susan	2	1		1	
Frances			2	2	2
Paula		1	1	1	2

* Members named at least three times by other members as having status

Figure 2. Ranking of Members by Number of Mentions

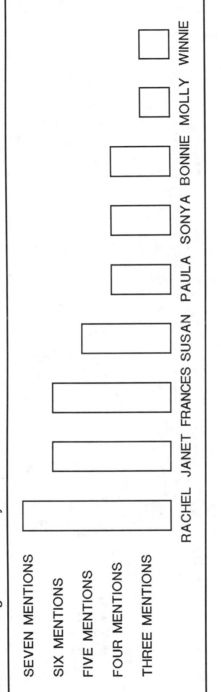

155

Figure 3. Members Identifying Each Other as Holding Status

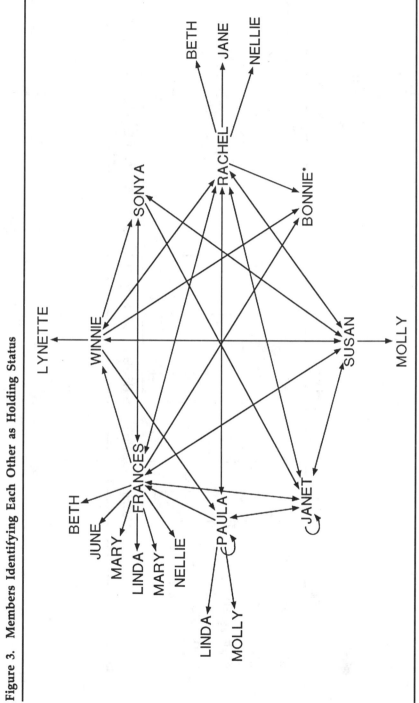

* Bonnie did not participate in the interviews.

Figure 4. Members Who Know Each Other Best

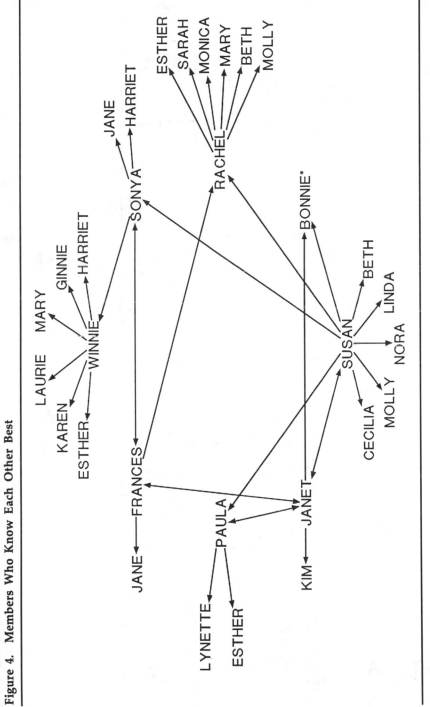

* Bonnie did not participate in the interviews.

Figure 5. Members Identified as Good Committee Members

Figure 6. Members Identified as Good Officers

FOUR MENTIONS

THREE MENTIONS

TWO MENTIONS

JANET SUSAN CECILIA PAULA RACHEL LINDA JANE BONNIE SONYA

Figure 7. Qualities of a Good Leader

Enthusiastic	Organized
Technical competence in weaving	Dynamic/energetic
Follows through	On top of everything
Inspiring	Inspires confidence
Capable	Knowledgeable
Hard-working	Sincere
Does the job	Gets everybody to work together
Says what she thinks	Assertive
Participates	Dependable
Flexible	Thorough
Interested in the group	Not wishy/washy

Figure 8. Qualities of a Good Committee Member

Good organizer	Capable
Experienced in weaving	Cooperative
Gets things done	Enthusiastic
Dependable	Easy to get along with
Has good ideas	Follows through
Competent	Good worker
Has a relaxed attitude	Willing
Works hard	Dedicated to the group
Experienced in education and	Has contacts with other groups
shows	Thorough

and organization, but Paula, Frances, Sonya, Susan, Rachel, and Esther formed a subgroup who were nearly equal in second place.

When I looked at who knew each other best in the Guild, Rachel knew more members than did Janet, who named only a few other women in the leadership group. That wasn't entirely surprising since Rachel had been a member from the beginning, and this was only Janet's second year with the Guild. When I looked at members who were named specifically as good weavers, Janet and Rachel were at the top, and Rachel was identified by the group as providing the most services to the group.

In the end I was able to identify a group of eight women who shared leadership in the Guild. These eight women made decisions for the Guild and persuaded other Guild members to accept and act on those decisions. Most of these women were or had been officers or committee chairs, and they attended executive board meetings or participated in business discussions in the meetings.

Clearly, two forms of leadership existed in the group, distinguished partly by function. Janet and Rachel served as opinion leaders, members who identified and articulated a vision of what the group should be or could become. The other six members organized and carried out the activities of the group. Janet also worked in this second group, but Rachel did not serve as an officer and seldom served on committees. An analysis of the group records revealed that a similar organizational pattern had existed throughout the group's history.

Rachel had been one of the original organizers of the group. She was one of the oldest members of the group, and she articulated the opinions of many of the older members who thought the Guild should be primarily a social group for women who pursued weaving as a hobby. She represented a conservative point of view, supporting the activities that had become traditional for the group. These activities included an annual Christmas sale and various demonstrations. Janet was a young professional weaver, one of a series of younger weavers who had served as leaders of the group over its history. These younger women tended to move in and out of the Guild as their husbands' careers brought them into the community and took them out of it. These women served as energizers for the Guild. They made plans for shows, workshops, classes, and demonstrations in an effort to promote an increased knowledge and expertise of weaving among the members and an increased awareness of the craft in the community. Over the years the Guild had reflected these two visions in a dynamic balance that favored first one side and then the other.

To illustrate this balance of power in operation, I will use the issue of the weaving done for demonstrations. During the first year I was a member of the Guild, we had a very positive, dedicated, and professionally-oriented weaver as chair. Harriet had come from a very active Guild in another city, and her impatience with the relaxed pace in this Guild was apparent. One of the interviewees commented that Harriet kept the meetings real short. She just made up her mind on an issue and presented it to the group.

One of the first things she wanted to change was the type of weaving done on the demonstration loom. In previous years, this loom had been threaded in a traditional pattern, and weavers brought their own thread to the demonstrations and wove what they pleased. When the warp was used up, the weaving was discarded and the loom was threaded with another pattern, usually the favorite pattern of whoever volunteered to warp the loom again. Harriet felt that this practice was wasteful; she introduced the notion of weaving rag placemats that could be sold to help finance the costs of the demonstration. Although Rachel spoke against the change, the Guild went along with Harriet during the time she was a member of the Guild. When Harriet left the Guild, demonstrations reverted to the previous practice of weaving for fun, not for profit.

My interviews revealed that both of the women who served as opinion leaders in the Guild were committed to the Guild as an organization. My observation of the Guild leads me to believe that there exists an unstated understanding among the members of the Guild that both points of view are valuable to the group, and that neither should be allowed to dominate the group. Both opinion leaders told me in interviews that they were very careful not to take a strong public role in the Guild's operation. The conservative leader told me, "I never offer my opinion unless someone asks." Nevertheless, everyone seemed to know she was the person whose opinion mattered. The innovative leader explained that she was careful not to appear to take control of the Guild, because she wanted to share power with the other members. She told me that she had been a strong leader in a guild before, and when she left that guild it could not continue to run without her leadership. She said it "just fell apart." She didn't want that to happen to this Guild. She named another member whom she was training to act as a leader for the group.

My most important observation of this group was that both opinion leaders carefully monitored their behavior to maintain a balance within the Guild. Neither publicly opposed the other, and neither tried to take control of the group. Since the Guild existed to meet the needs of the members, this balance allowed different members to work toward their different goals without overt conflict. The members who were most interested in social interaction could find community in the Guild, and the members who were interested in pursuing weaving professionally could also find activities that supported their goals.

In my interview with Janet this topic came up in association with a question about leadership. Janet observed that the current chair was "too nice" to be chair. "The meetings are too long," she observed. She named another member who would take charge more forcefully, but noted that this member would offend people. She commented that the Guild used to be "just friends who didn't do anything." In changing that attitude she feared some members had been offended, and she wondered whether allowing everyone to speak in an informal atmosphere helped the members to feel better about the Guild. She was, however, committed to getting the Guild members more active in weaving and more visible in the community.

The other opinion leader, Rachel, didn't speculate about leadership or group process. Instead she described the usefulness of individual members to the group. Janet, she observed, was knowledgeable and experienced in education and shows. She characterized Paula, another

of the innovative members, as maybe a little too thorough, but enthusiastic. Her highest terms of praise were *pleasant, nice, enthusiastic,
willing to work.* She was adamant that members should not hold office
more than once: "The position should be passed around in the group,
because that would give the group a lot of variety of talent and interest."
What she did not say, though she may have known it, was that passing
the leadership around would help prevent any one member from gaining
power in the group.

The other six members of the leadership group who managed the
practical business of the Guild also orchestrated their behavior carefully
so that no one exercised more influence or took more credit than any
other member. Chairship and membership of the committees rotated
yearly. Last year, for example, one of my friends who had explained
to me in the original interviews that she didn't want to spend the time
and energy necessary to be an officer of the Guild was serving as the
chair. When I asked her why she had changed her mind, she replied
that it was "her turn." The women described good officers and committee members as being "cooperative," "enthusiastic," "easy to get
along with," and "dependable." The maintenance of good relationships
within the Guild was an important goal of all 10 women in the leadership
group.

My discussion with Frances on the topic of leadership was very
instructive; I think it summed up the consensus of the members on
this topic. Frances stated that she was uncomfortable with the word
"power" applied to the operation of the Guild. While she understood
that someone had to get things done or there wouldn't be a group,
she suggested "responsibility" was a better word than "power" to
describe how the Weavers Guild was run.

I have chosen two issues as exemplifying the operation of the Guild.
Each of these issues arose and was resolved during the time I was a
member of the Guild, so I had personal knowledge of the deliberations
and decisions of the Guild in each case. In each case the resolution of
the issues illustrates the attitudes of responsibility and caring as the
basis for leadership that were illustrated in the interviews.

One of the most important issues to the Guild was the operation of
the annual Christmas sale. The sale was important to some weavers,
because it provided them the opportunity to make enough money to
buy more thread for weaving during the next year. A few members
depended on the sale to bring in extra pocket money; several of these
weavers were retired on fixed incomes. Many members, however, never
wove for sale. The first issue, then, was one of equity: who should
bear the cost of publicity for the sale? When I first joined the group,
the costs of the publicity for the sale came from the general funds of

the Guild. The next year, this policy was changed, and weavers who sold were charged a ten percent fee on all sales to cover the cost of the sales. During the last year I was a member, the fees gathered from the sale exceeded the publicity costs, and the extra money went back into the general funds of the Guild. I could foresee that an adjustment might be made again in the future, if the weavers who sold began to feel they were carrying more than their own weight in financing Guild activities.

Another issue associated with sales was that of the quality of the weaving. Some members of the Guild felt that it was necessary for the Guild to monitor the quality of what was sold, so that the Guild's image in the community would not be impaired and sales could continue to be high. Perhaps not coincidental is that this concern surfaced the year a new member made a great deal of money (more than anyone else) with a new product called "Wheat Weaving." This "Wheat Weaving" was in actuality not weaving at all, but consisted of small ornaments braided of wheat stalks and decorated with ribbons and lace. Before the next sale, rules were formulated about what was acceptable and what was not acceptable for sale; the "Wheat Weaving" was not acceptable.

I watched the rules for what was acceptable for sale renegotiated every year. In the last year I was a member, the rules were carefully renegotiated to allow one of the Guild members to sell some small articles that really did not meet the specifications for the sale. This person had never been active in the leadership, but was a loyal member and one of the friendliest and most pleasant women in the Guild. She also lived on a fixed retirement income. I believe these personal considerations influenced the Guild members to grant special allowances to this member for the sale. In this way, the Guild negotiated rules, but tailored the application of the rules to individual cases.

Through a combination of research techniques—interviews, participant-observation, study of documents—I was able to identify and describe a process of shared leadership in the Weavers Guild. Two types of leaders emerged in the study: opinion leaders and organizers. I could find no differentiation in status between these two types of leadership. The individual members who made up the leadership in the Weavers Guild carefully orchestrated their behavior to maintain a balance of influence and responsibility for the group that would enable all of the members to meet their individual goals in the Guild. Discussions of leadership were inevitably discussions of individual contributions and relationships within the group.

Discussion

Since I completed this study in 1982, I have been pondering the significance of what I found. My original study simply compared what I found in the Weavers Guild to what Hunter (1953, 1980) had found in the community he studied. Since that time, I have been looking at my study through lenses provided to me by studies of women's values (Gilligan, 1982) and studies of powerful and powerless groups (Kanter, 1977). Each of these three explanations takes a different theoretical perspective on human behavior, and each rests in a different context. Hunter's concerns were primarily political; he was looking for informal power behind the public power structure in a community. Gilligan explored differing value systems for men and women, so an explanation from Gilligan's viewpoint emphasizes women's values of responsibility, connection, and caring in the Weavers Guild. Kanter studied human behavior in large organizations; an explanation from her viewpoint emphasizes the organizational aspects of the Weavers Guild.

When Carol Gilligan's book first appeared, I recognized the Weavers Guild in her description of women's values and behavior. Gilligan (1982) described women's values as emphasizing connection and caring. The women she studied emphasized responsibilities over rights when they talked about the decisions they made in their lives and work.

The talk in the Weavers Guild was consistent with Gilligan's observations. The weavers were uncomfortable talking about power or status. The women I interviewed refused to claim or wield power, and they resisted placing themselves and others in any kind of hierarchy. In all their descriptions of the members who provided leadership to the group, they emphasized the individual qualities of each member that made her particularly valuable to the group. Esther was mentioned as a good worker who could get along without conflicting. Frances was described as a good worker, competent, cooperative, easy to get along with. Janet had technical competence in weaving. Although she was not an active weaver, Sonya had experience with running other groups. The talk also emphasized caring for the particular needs of the members. One interviewee mentioned that it was necessary to be careful not to hurt Winnie's feelings. "She gets on her hobby horse and goes off on a tangent," one interviewee observed. But she had been with the group for a long time and so deserved our loyalty.

In response to my direct question about status, respondents politely provided information, but a ranking based on responses to that particular question was not confirmed by the other analyses of the data. While members told me that Janet had highest status in the Guild, they mentioned Rachel most often as an influential member. My own observations and examination of the Guild records revealed that other members had been more active in the Guild than either of these two women.

I was unable to describe a hierarchy of leadership in the Guild. Instead I was able to describe two different forms of leadership: Rachel and Janet served as opinion leaders, who voiced differing visions of what the group should be, while other members carried out the practical work that kept the Guild in business. But the responses in the interviews and my own observations led me to the conclusion that neither of these forms of leadership was valued more highly than the other by Guild members themselves. Instead, the women located themselves in a net or web of relationships, and they shared both the responsibility and the credit for making the group successful. They explained who did the work that was necessary for the Guild to continue to function as a group, but there was no consensus that any individual among the leadership group I identified was more important than any other. My analysis of the two types of leadership—opinion leaders and organizers—does not necessarily imply a difference in status or power in the minds of the women in the group.

The women I interviewed in the Weavers Guild seemed both comfortable and very skillful at balancing the demands of differing values, goals, and relationships to make the group a place where all members could get at least part of what they wanted from the group. The examples of how the Guild members dealt with the issues of sales and demonstrations illustrate this point.

But I am also forced to observe that the type of group that I observed, a support-social-informational group, is one where the skills of caring and maintaining connections are invaluable to the continued maintenance of the group. Pursuit of personal political or economic goals are inappropriate in this kind of group. Overt conflict would destroy the group. My observation that women are skillful at maintaining such a group does not preclude the possibility that men so placed couldn't be equally as skillful at balancing relationships. I would need to find studies of men similarly placed and motivated, perhaps in hobby clubs like model airplane clubs, stamp collecting clubs, or singing groups, in order to make any estimation of the relationship between gender and behavior in groups. I am not aware of any studies that have been conducted on such men's groups.

When I reported my study and its possible implications for women's communication at a meeting of the National Women's Studies Association, I was challenged by a member of the audience who remarked that my findings were almost equally well described by Kanter (1977) in terms of power and powerlessness, where gender was not a salient factor. Kanter described powerless groups of coworkers within the organization she studied as focusing on peer relationships and developing a supportive group culture of their own. Women in clerical and secretarial jobs typically qualified as powerless in the organization, but so did older men in positions outside of the main career advancement ladders. The peer networks developed by powerless employees of the organization provided rewards and recognition within the group to people denied rewards and recognition in the larger organization. Kanter's descriptions of behavior in the powerless groups in organizations were also consistent in many ways with what I observed in the Weavers Guild.

The comparison of the Weavers Guild and a powerless work group might seem tenuous, but an understanding of the community in which the Weavers Guild is located will make it more compelling. State College is a small urban area where many highly competent married women find themselves without opportunities to pursue their own careers. They are like the older men or secretaries in an organization who can't advance in the system, so they find other ways to satisfy their own needs for recognition. Statements made by members and my own observations confirm that several members of the Guild left the Guild when they found full-time employment. One friend in the Guild discussed this problem, explaining her frustration at not being able to pursue the career for which she had trained. Instead she turned to weaving as a substitute pursuit, and worked for the Weavers Guild because she needed an organization to support her in her work. Women who found full-time employment didn't necessarily quit weaving, they just quit coming to meetings. Whether they quit because they didn't have time or because they no longer needed the support is a question that at this time I have no data to answer.

More support for Kanter's explanation as a possible interpretation of my findings came quite unexpectedly when I met one of the most active members of the Weavers Guild in a locker room. She told me that her youngest child had entered high school, and she had suddenly realized that she was 40 years old and was not qualified to hold a job. She said she was thinking about going back to school because "the Weavers Guild isn't going to do it for me anymore." I interpreted her account as evidence that she had looked to the Weavers Guild as an outlet for her energies and a source of recognition for her abilities. In the larger context of the whole community, the Weavers Guild seemed to function as a peer support group for a powerless group of women. The Guild also provided a basis for personal identity for women whose life choices had tied their own identities to their families and denied them opportunities for personal recognition and advancement.

During the interviews one weaver remarked to me that one of the Guild members who had worked as a professional weaver seemed less inclined to share information about her craft. This professional weaver, the member reported, seemed to consider her knowledge as private. When I thought about this comment, I found it a logical extension of the necessity to conform to a different situation and set of rules. To sell successfully as a weaver, one has to establish a persona—a particular style and quality of weaving—and build a clientele interested in that particular group of products. If other weavers produce the same products in the same style and quality, it's impossible to maintain the kind of reputation that will support a professional career in weaving. This issue surfaces regularly in the weaving magazines, where readers are encouraged to experiment and adapt the designs that appear in the magazine. The editors of the magazine remind readers that they should not copy a design from the magazine for reproduction and sale.

The question of data interpretation becomes a question of whether the women in the Weavers Guild choose to emphasize caring, responsibility, and sharing because they prefer that style or because they must. It is not a simple question. Kanter's question in the organization she studied was whether women are unsuccessful in competition because they are inexperienced at the game or because women are different.

The interpretations of Gilligan and Kanter are not mutually exclusive, because historically women have been a powerless group in society. Descriptions of the political and social bondage of women have been eloquently detailed by writers for centuries (Spender, 1982; Janeway, 1971, 1980; Kramarae, 1981). Women may be more comfortable in supportive relationships than men, or more likely to form associations based on mutual support. But the goals of the group, whether chosen voluntarily or forced by institutional forces, seem to me more relevant to interpretations of behavior in groups than either gender or power alone. It makes more sense to me to argue that the women in the Weavers Guild behave as they do, valuing responsibility and connection, because it serves their interests best to do so in the situations in which they find themselves. The issue of why and how these women find themselves in such situations seems to me another question altogether.

There is, however, still another point of view to consider. Hunter's (1953) description of men's behavior in the community he described closely paralleled in some ways the behavior of the women in the Weavers Guild. Hunter identified three levels of power in the community that he studied: (a) a small group of influential men he designated as opinion leaders who set the goals of the community; (b) a larger group of men who were publicly active in carrying out the decisions of the leaders; and (c) a much larger group of members who worked for the community but had no influence to shape policies in the community. On a much smaller scale, I found a similar situation in the Weavers Guild; there were two types of leadership, opinion leaders and organizers, while the rest of the members worked for the Guild occasionally.

There are some important differences between Hunter's findings and my own. The opinion leaders Hunter identified worked informally to shape the values and goals of the community, but they were the most wealthy and most politically powerful members of the community. Their contributions were more highly valued by the community than were the contributions of the men who carried out the activities in the community. There was clearly a hierarchical structure even in the informal relationships of the community (1953, p. 102), but women in the Weavers Guild did not value the contributions of the opinion leaders over those of the people who organized the activities, and opinion leaders were not socially or economically different from the other members.

But comparing communities and clubs is comparing apples and pears. What I found most interesting in Hunter's account was that he could not describe a hierarchy of power among the second level of leadership, the people who implemented the decisions in the community he studied. Instead, he found a fluid grouping of people who voluntarily worked for and with one another according to whatever projects were being undertaken at the time (p. 66). The reciprocal relationships described by Hunter closely paralleled the reciprocal relationships I found in the Weavers Guild. When the goals of the people in groups are to preserve the community from which they draw their identities and support, both women and men seem capable of cooperative behavior.

It is not possible to determine from Hunter's account whether the men in the second level of the community he described managed their behaviors with the concern for connection and caring that characterized the women's behavior in the Weavers Guild. His concern was mainly political, so his descriptions did not address individual relationships within the groups. Possibly the interaction among the men in this group more closely resembled the teamwork commonly found in sports. The point that men are capable of organizing themselves in nonhierarchical arrangements when they find such behavior appropriate seemed to me important enough to comment on.

In all three instances—the community, the work group, and the Weavers Guild—people with differing goals and values have to coexist in harmony; members do this by careful attention to maintenance of good personal relationships and by compromise and cooperation. In any of these situations, if any one person or subgroup decided to run things their way, the group itself would disintegrate into splinters. What all of these groups have in common is that the group itself is necessary for the individuals to meet their own goals.

Conclusions

This study has been an account of my attempts to make sense of observations I have made of the behavior of one particular group of women. My search for explanation has used interpretations of human behavior in terms of differences between women and men (Gilligan, 1982), in terms of power or powerlessness (Kanter, 1977), and in terms of political goals (Hunter 1953, 1980). Each of these interpretations has shed some light on my observations, but none has proved compelling. More useful, I believe, is a perspective that takes situational constraints into account.

The situations in which both women and men find themselves and the goals they set for themselves in those situations have a major influence on their behavior in any group. Humans are social creatures, and they adapt their behavior situationally. Consequently, any explanation of human behavior that focuses exclusively on any one factor, like gender or power, will not suffice to explain human behavior in groups. Women in the Weavers Guild did exhibit the concerns for relationships and caring that were described by Gilligan, but I have no compelling evidence that their behaviors did not change when they entered the workplace and found themselves with an increased responsibility or opportunity to shape their own lives. Careful reading of Kanter leads me to believe that the powerless groups in the organization she studied did not intentionally choose those powerless positions; instead, they found their behavior constrained by powerlessness in situations beyond their control.

The possibility that a powerless group like the Weavers Guild might change its goals to become a force in the community is an interesting problem in speculation. What if, for instance, the Guild decided to change from being inwardly focused on fulfilling the needs and interests of the members to being outwardly focused on creating a market for the members' weaving? Would there be a corresponding change in the patterns of leadership in the group? What if the group decided to become an artistic force in the community and initiated activities to bring about an increased awareness of weaving as an art form? Would the members still value equally the contributions of the opinion leaders and the organizers? Or would other patterns of behavior emerge and be differentially valued? Answers for such questions can come from study of other groups focused mainly on sales or focused mainly on bringing an increased awareness of their art to the community. Such organizations already exist: the Pennsylvania Guild of Craftsmen, the Potters Guild, and the Art Alliance are all such groups, and studies of these groups might provide more data for a discussion of these questions.

Humans are both social and purposive beings. The study of beings that are both socially responsive and purposefully oriented must be a complex undertaking. The way that we go about such study will to a large extent determine what kinds of conclusions we draw. Studying humans by comparing their behaviors on one dimension—gender or power—can distract us from other aspects of their being and behavior that have powerful influences on their thought and behavior. Such studies can shed light on *some* human behaviors *some* of the time, but they can't account for more than that. Such studies are useful, but we cannot stop there.

Study of humans that focuses on single motivations or single attributes can lead to a proliferation of "factors" like gender and power, until we find ourselves confronted by a veritable jungle of factors. The research we have already done can be valuable, and the research we will continue to do will be even more valuable if we remember that the "factors" being studied are ideas, not categories in external reality. Like "intelligence" and "group," these factors exist only as ideas that are useful to explain some human behavior some of the time. Instead of hypostatizing "gender" or "power" and studying these ideas as though they existed—we even try to measure them!—we should use those ideas as heuristics to discover meaningful patterns in human behavior.

If I take my own advice and apply the concepts of gender and power as heuristics to the study of decision making in the Weavers Guild, I find that the construct "gender" proved valuable in explaining what I found. The concept "power," on the other hand, was not valuable in my analysis of that group. Examination of "group goals" led me to some helpful comparisons of behavior in the Weavers Guild with behavior described by Hunter in a larger community. The women in the Weavers Guild were evidently influenced by the situation in which they found themselves—compelled to create a group in which they could find community of interests, an arena for achievement, a social identity of their own. The organization that the weavers created was a nonhierarchical association based on careful attention to relationships and support for individual members to maintain the group.

Power is best conceptualized as one aspect of interpersonal relationships among the members of the group. Unless someone acts in a group, nothing will be done and the group will cease to exist. The Weavers Guild found itself constrained to have officers and committees that exerted power to get work done.

But I couldn't describe a hierarchy in the Weavers Guild. Instead I found a web of interconnecting relationships that constituted an agreement among the members about how work should get done. The "powerful" members of the Guild did not issue orders or directives. They didn't trade services or goods for status. They talked about the welfare of the group and of the members of the group, about group goals, and about the identity of the group and of its members. They were respected in the group because they held strong opinions and could articulate those opinions, but also because they didn't try to influence others to share those opinions.

People emerged as powerful through negotiation about how things are and how they should be; power is more conferred than exercised. The leaders were people who had a clear vision of what the Guild should be like and what the members could do to achieve their goals. Those people who could articulate what the members wanted were the people accorded respect and influence by other members in the group. But one of the most important attributes of a leader in the Weavers Guild was that she should respect different goals and values. Had any of the leaders tried to exert her conferred power to take control of the group, I believe her power would have disappeared.

Women often shun power in groups because of its attendant costs. Power has traditionally been a male concept, associated with control over other people. Power, therefore, is almost always destructive of those relationships that hold people together in social groupings. Power was a dirty word in the Weavers Guild.

Even if we reconceptualize power as leadership, being a leader takes a lot of time and energy, and leaders expect to be repaid for their work by rewards of some kind. Leadership is often repaid with status. Differentiation by status can also be destructive of relationships in a social grouping. The commanding officer always has to leave the party before the troops can begin to have a good time. The members of the Weavers Guild worked out ways of sharing leadership, so that everyone could claim to contribute and everyone could claim to benefit. The structure of the Weavers Guild as I have described it was horizontal, not vertical. Leadership was conferred on members who were able and willing to provide the services necessary to keep the group going. But the leaders shared responsibility and power and were careful to maintain a balance between differing interests and goals that might have come into conflict. The leaders were careful to exercise their authority on behalf of the group, not in their own interest or in the interest only of a part of the group.

From the knowledge gained in the study of this group, I may now go on to the study of other groups in which power is not a particularly relevant construct, to see whether there are meaningful similarities between those groups and the Weavers Guild. The logical next step would be a study of a social-informational-avocational group that includes men and women as members (maybe my own computer users' group?). I would also like to examine a women's group that is actively pursuing goals of influencing the larger community politically or socially.

The issue of interpretation of research findings is an important one, because the metaphors we choose to define and explicate our experience also shape and guide our plans for the future. The arguments over abortion and nuclear disarmament are essentially arguments over metaphors for human experience. It is important to be aware as researchers that we have choices to make in how we conceptualize, carry out, and interpret our research. The topics of gender and power seem particularly difficult to analyze and interpret, and asking the question "Is it gender or is it power?" may be inappropriate. This research finding of shared leadership in a women's group has led me to conclude we should be asking questions about situation and context instead of gender and power. Instead of asking "What kinds of people are there?" we should ask "What kinds of situations do people find themselves in?" It's an interesting idea.

References

Gilligan, C. (1982). *In a different voice.* Cambridge, MA: Harvard University Press.

Homans, G. C. (1974). *Social behavior: Its elementary forms.* New York: Harcourt, Brace, Janovich.

Hunter, F. (1953). *Community power structure.* Chapel Hill, NC: The University of North Carolina Press.

Hunter, F. (1980). *Community power succession.* Chapel Hill, NC: The University of North Carolina Press.

Janeway, E. (1971). *Man's world, woman's place.* New York: William Morrow.

Janeway, E. (1980). *Powers of the weak.* New York: Knopf.

Kanter, R. M. (1977). *Men and women of the corporation.* New York: Basic Books.

Kramarae, C. (1981). *Women and men speaking.* Rowley, MA: Newbury House.

Spender, D. (1982). *Women of ideas and what men have done to them.* London: Routledge & Kegan Paul.

Appendix 1

Interview Protocol

When I interviewed members of the Weavers Guild, I followed this procedure:

(1) I described the results of my research on the group goals of the Guild and how that research led to this study.
(2) I asked for the interviewee's cooperation in this research.
(3) I said that, although I would use real names in the collection of data, only pseudonyms would appear in any research reports.
(4) I said that I would be happy to share the findings of this research with interviewees and with the Guild at large.
(5) I asked the interviewees the following questions:

1. Name
2. Age
3. Address
4. Occupation
5. Husband's occupation
6. Formal education
7. Length of residence in this area
8. How long have you been a weaver?
9. How would you rate your expertise as a weaver?
10. Do you sell your weaving? Can you estimate how much money you make annually from your weaving?
11. How long have you been a member of the Guild?
12. What official positions have you held in the Guild?
13. In what other capacities have you served the Guild?
14. What other groups do you belong to?
15. In what official capacities do you serve in those groups?
16. What other interests do you have besides weaving?
17. Which members of the Guild have you called for advice about weaving?
18. Which members of the Guild have called you for advice about weaving?
19. Which members of the Guild would you get to work on a project or committee for the Guild? Why them?
20. Which members of the Guild do you think would make good officers? Why them?
21. Which members of the Guild do you see socially outside the Guild?

22. Do you have any social contact with members of the other organizations you belong to?
23. Which members of the Guild do you know best?
24. Rank the members of the Guild by status. Why did you make those choices?
25. Do these people work in public or behind the scenes?

10

Jock Talk: Cooperation and Competition within a University Women's Basketball Team*

Melanie Booth-Butterfield

West Virginia University

Steve Booth-Butterfield

West Virginia University

American girls grow up in a culture where their success is often measured more by their ability to get along with others and be well-liked than by individual ability or achievement. When these well-socialized girls reach adulthood, they may find that although their relationship (especially their cooperative) skills are appropriate for family life, these skills are not well-rewarded by the larger society (Weitzman, 1979). The most successful career people are often highly competitive and ambitious rather than cooperative and "nice." Therefore the expectations which were ingrained during childhood in preparation for womanhood may conflict with skills needed as a functioning adult in the professional world.

Some writers describe this phenomenon as "role strain" (Garnets & Pleck, 1979; Stockard & Johnson, 1980; Weitzman, 1979). Women may feel pressured when traditional expectations for their communication contradict what is demanded of a competent, career-oriented adult. Indeed women may even be punished when they communicate in ways which are inconsistent with traditional expectations (Anashensel & Rosen, 1978; Wiley & Eskilson, 1982). Adult women do not outgrow and forget the cooperative, emotional communication skills thoroughly learned as children. Instead the traditionally socialized roles present an alternative set of communication expectations—coexisting and conflicting with demands for assertion, self-reliance, and decisiveness.

* The authors would particularly like to thank Rosie Jones, Jackie Harris, and Coach Jorja Hoehn for their support in this project.

177

Wood and Conrad (1983) label the role strain "paradoxes." Paradoxical messages are inconsistent and conflicting communication injunctions, of which one is typically communicated indirectly. The recipients of such messages cannot comply with both injunctions simultaneously and consequently find themselves pulled in opposing directions (Wilmot, 1980: Wood & Conrad, 1983). For example, a husband may tell his wife, "I am in command here, do as I say," while at the same time he acts in a submissive fashion. In addition, a third injunction completes the paradoxical situation in that message recipients are prevented from removing themselves from the situation entirely.

To illustrate, Wood and Conrad apply the model of paradoxical communication to professional women who face contradictory expectations to act as a "woman" and to act as a "professional." Since their employment occupies a necessary and major portion of the women's lives, removing themselves from the situation is not a viable alternative. Neither do they want to sacrifice their self-image as women in order to achieve in the professional world. Thus, a paradox involves contradictory "rules" or norms within an ongoing communication environment.

Such conflicting messages may cause distress for communicators caught in the middle. However, as Smythe (in press) notes, the messages in real life may not be as conflicting as researchers have concluded. It is therefore important to examine (a) whether women do identify inconsistent expectations as stressful, and (b) how they adapt to contradictory communication injunctions surrounding them.

Competitive women athletes exemplify a group of women facing paradoxical messages. Just as the term "professional women" exemplifies contradictory societal expectations, so too does the term "women athletes." (See Gerber, Felshin, Berlin, & Wyrick, 1974). Society's injunctions for women include being cooperative, supportive, nurturing, and not physically dominant. But the expectations for athletes are typically at odds with expectations for women. Successful athletes are required to be competitive, aggressive, ambitious, and physically dominant—characteristics traditionally deemed inappropriate for women.

Similarly, within the athletic context itself, participants are confronted with contradictory messages. Individual prowess, ambition, and dominance are rewarded in competition, but the interconnected "team" aspect of many sports demands cooperation, coordinated effort, and group support. The dilemma here is whether any competitive athlete can subordinate individual performance goals sufficiently to participate in a cooperative team effort.

These competing messages make women's athletic teams conceptually interesting from a communication perspective. How do women team members respond and adapt to these expectations and how does their communication reflect such adaptation?

Many aspects of team communication were examined during the course of this research, but two major questions guided the analysis of cooperation and competition: (a) *How does a women's basketball team deal with competitive and cooperative aspects of team play in a university environment?* (b) *How does team members' communication reflect competitive and/or cooperative tendencies?*

Smythe (in press) discusses problems associated with generalizing from the typically-studied white, middle-class, mixed sex interactions. Such investigations may not be exploring a salient and extensive range of communicative behavior. Since successful university-level women's basketball teams are unique subjects for communication studies, it was appropriate to broaden the range of communication under study, attending to potentially important but unanticipated responses. Thus, a third research question was posed.

(c) *What communication themes or stylistic characteristics are identifiable in the team's interaction?*

Competition was defined for this study as a zero-sum orientation wherein one party's success or gain means that another party loses. In addition competition implies an external "opponent" rather than simply internally-based drive toward achieving a goal. Cooperation was defined as working together toward a common goal so that all parties benefit, even if one person may not accrue as many rewards as she might if she acted directly for her own success.

In order to examine these constructs it was important to study both women's answers to direct questions about competition and cooperation, as well as the way the structure of their communication reflected competitive and/or cooperative styles. Since on-court communication is highly directed by coaches, we judged the locker room following practice sessions as the best and most natural location in which to communicate with all players simultaneously. We later conducted additional individual interviews.

To answer the specific questions we (a) analyzed the content of players' answers to specific questions asked, (b) examined the characteristics of their language during the discussions, and (c) studied the patterns of talk when the players interacted with each other and the interviewers. In the last step we focused on patterns of turn-taking, interruptions, and nonverbal indicators of interest and attentiveness in discerning a pattern of communication among these women athletes. Additionally, since the association of a basketball "team" involves both a major task to be achieved and the maintenance of satisfying social relations, we noted features of the women's communication which offered insight into the human relations and cohesion of the group.

Methodology

Participants

Not all women's basketball teams would constitute examples of successfully competitive female athletes. At many schools women's teams are minimally supported and result in weak, almost intramural-level play. However, the Jennies of Central Missouri State University had exhibited high levels of success for the four years prior to the study, each year winning both conference and regional championships. For the last three years they had competed in the NCAA Division 2 nationals and in 1984 won the NCAA Division 2 national championship. This clearly demonstrates a pattern of successful competition.

The men's basketball team and the women's volleyball team at Central Missouri State have also experienced success at the national level. Thus, the Jennies were not an isolated "success group" on the campus. At the time of primary data collection the Jennies were in the middle of a successful season and ranked first in national polls.

Measures and Data Collection

Filstead (1979) emphasizes the importance of employing multiple methods of data collection in research to best understand the context and meaning of the communication. Thus both qualitative and quantitative measurement was employed: (a) a focused group interview with observer-count of initiated statements; (b) individual written responses to Likert-type questions; and (c) follow-up individual interviews.

The group interview allowed respondents to interact spontaneously among themselves and provided the interviewers an opportunity to observe ongoing interaction. However, we recognized that this technique might inhibit some players' input due to anxiety, channel overload, or self-monitoring resulting in high levels of agreement. Thus the scaled, individual responses were employed as a measure which allowed the women to anonymously disagree with previous oral responses if they wished. Face-to-face individual interviews, the third measure, have the advantage of eliciting relatively spontaneous and unrehearsed answers to questions, as well as communicating the individual's perspective without other teammates present. The mailed questionnaires provide other advantages still in their total anonymity and time allowed to think through responses. The use of multiple measurement should balance out potential drawbacks of any single technique and result in a realistic, authentic picture of the Jennies' communication.

The interviews consisted of all-female interactions in order to minimize cross-sex self-presentational effects. These interactions took place in naturalistic settings. The group interview was held in the team's locker room following practice during the regular season, a setting in which the team spent a great deal of time communicating and in which they felt at home. All 13 team members participated in the group interview. The individual follow-up interviews took place in various settings, both on campus and in the team members' homes. Face-to-face interviews were conducted with all who could be reached on campus during the summer sessions and interview questions were mailed to those off campus. All but three of the Jennies were reached for these follow-up individual interviews. The focused group interview and the follow-up interviews employed a few central questions, but encouraged free-flow of interaction in order to avoid limiting participants' responses to those the researchers anticipated (Patton, 1980). The probes were designed to encourage the players to talk with each other about their team play and their communication and to minimize obtrusiveness in the interview setting.

The questions were constructed following discussion with the head coach about the competitive and cooperative aspects of team play, examination of sports psychology writing, and integration of women's communication literature. The interviews were transcribed from audiotape into written form to enhance accuracy and detail of analysis.

Following the group interview each team member also responded to 20 scaled questions employing a 9-point Likert-type format assessing cooperation, competition, and aggression. The purpose of this questionnaire was: (a) to assess correspondence between the public statements generated during the group interview and the private feelings and opinions of each team member, and (b) to assess aspects of team play and/or communication which may not be amenable to group interviewing, for example how the women feel about themselves in relation to their teammates or potentially sensitive areas regarding intra-team conflict. The means and standard deviations for each item were then analyzed for intensity and homogeneity of agreement or disagreement. (See Table 1 for these results.)

Results

Overview

We analyzed the content of the interviews looking for indicants of the two major categories: competition and cooperation. In addition three

Table 1. Jennies Questionnaire

1 = strongly agree 9 = strongly disagree			
	Mean	S.D.	S.E.
1. The school supports this team.	3.75	1.356	.376
2. Physical skills are the most important for a winning team.	5.83	1.898	.525
3. I pass off to my teammates more than they pass to me.	4.33	2.309	.64
4. I could take anyone on this team in a one-on-one game.	2.67	2.229	.62
5. I get enough chances to shoot the ball.	4.08	2.644	.73
6. The more physical the game gets, the better I like it.	2.75	1.865	.517
7. I dislike it when the coach takes me out of the game.	2.83	1.851	.513
8. Starting is very important to me.	2.75	1.712	.474
9. I like basketball because it is a finesse game, skill counts more than toughness.	4.16	3.186	.883
10. This team respects me as a person.	1.83	1.114	.308
11. This team works together even when it means someone has to make a sacrifice.	1.167	.577	.16
12. I'd rather shoot the ball than make a good assist.	6.25	1.138	.315
13. I am a cooperative player.	2.58	.668	.185
14. This team respects me as a player.	2.00	1.595	.442
15. Even if I don't start the game, just getting some playing time is okay with me.	6.167	2.725	.755
16. I like a referee who lets the game get a little rough.	3.92	2.644	.733
17. Even when we're getting beat, I give 110%.	2.00	1.758	.487
18. Some people on this team have more skill or talent than I, but I help the team play well.	1.50	1.167	.323
19. It bothers me if the fans don't know me as well as some of the other players.	6.75	2.302	.638
20. A winning team cooperates more than a losing team.	1.83	.389	.107

themes emerged which ran through the cooperation and competition categories: (a) the coach; (b) the players' awareness of public perceptions of the team, and (c) emotional responses to team play and membership. These three themes will be briefly discussed at the outset because they enhance the reader's understanding of the team's communication perspective. In addition players' direct quotes will be included throughout to illustrate themes and provide insight into the communication of the "Jennies."

The team members discussed their coach in two ways. First, the women disclosed their expectations of the coach, rules about what she should and should not do in response to the team members. They also described a need for the coach to break out of the professional role from time to time and become a friend and advisor. But the coach appeared to play a more subtle role in the team's communication as well.

The Jennies frequently expressed their beliefs concerning proper team play and execution. In the interviews each player took responsibility for the belief, but later her statements or statements by other players indicated that the coach exerted a strong influence on team-stated attitudes. "Self discipline," "team concept," and "self motivation" were strongly endorsed by the players, but the origin of those themes appeared to be communication messages from the head coach to the players.

> . . . I think from this interview it's obvious that we listen to her a lot.
> . . . what she says is right, and we've learned it.

> Like when she first says stuff we might think, "oh no, she's wrong," but then when you sit down and start thinking about it—things start coming together and making a lot of sense.

The second major theme concerned the team's awareness of observers' perceptions of the team—to a great extent also filtered through the perceptions of the head coach. The players spoke of a need to maintain a "class act" when in public. This meant a clear dress and behavior code with the head coach providing a role model for these codes. She set high standards of conduct and achievement for the team, but she presented a consistent communication image by stringently following these standards herself. Nowhere was this more apparent than in her public speeches and interviews where she regularly thanked God for her achievements. This orientation is reflected throughout the Jennies' discussions.

Further evidence of the team's awareness of public perceptions is seen in their discussion of grades and coursework. The players spoke with pride of their team's grade point average, a statistic that clearly has little to do with winning basketball games. They also compared their style of play with the men's game, speaking of the men's "glory game" with "slamming" and "dunking," as opposed to their own focus on defense and selfless team play. The women are cognizant that others are watching them and they are concerned about how the team is perceived.

Finally, the teammates discussed emotional aspects. They talked about playing with anger and aggression, about "psyching up" before a game, and about dealing with the pressure of a long winning streak or a close game. Affect is also an important element of the social interaction off the court. The Jennies like each other. They spend a great deal of free time together, as roommates, going to movies or playing cards, so prospective recruits are judged both on their athletic ability and their relationship ability.

What emerges from these general themes appears to be a group of rather traditionally oriented females in a very untraditional setting. Their coach and their awareness of others' perceptions strongly influences the team and its members' communication. The women orient strongly around their emotions, again as a team and as individuals. When their discourse is analyzed more closely focusing on cooperation and competition, the same traditional themes appear.

Cooperation

The women place a very strong value on cooperation. This theme was evidenced in several ways as they discussed both the sport and their individual lives. The strategy of this team is to work as many players into the game as possible, rather than relying on one or two main players. There was strong consensus that the Jennies are not a "selfish team." This is not just because they are cooperative people, but for the pragmatic reason that opponents "can shut down" an individual's scoring, so cooperation is essential.

> Well, like another team can't just focus on one of our players that have to play all the time. Like say, you're depending on one person doing all the scoring and they're not hot that night—their shot is off, then that's gonna throw the whole team off if you're always relying on them to do all the scoring.

To further illustrate this group concern the team members explained that "ego trips," fighting, or "not passing off the ball" to teammates would cause them to go on a losing streak. The questionnaire revealed that most team members would rather make a good "assist" in a play than shoot the ball. They believe it is absolutely necessary to remain a cohesive unit in order to continue winning.

The group also compared themselves to other basketball teams on which they had played, noting the lack of close communication and positive regard on those other teams. They linked the team's success to communicating, cooperating, and respecting each other. Scale items, "This team respects me as a player" and "This team respects me as a person" received strong endorsement with very little deviation (See Table 1). Thus, even in nonpublic statements the team members report strong and uniform feelings of being respected and valued by their teammates. In addition, both public and nonpublic responses indicated that the Jennies realize that some people on the team may have more skill or talent, but that all players help the team to succeed.

> We're one. We're many bodies but act as *one*. We all have our strong points and our weaknesses, but we accept those and work together toward our one goal—to be national champions.

> We're 13 young ladies with different personalities, but with one goal. I'm sure everyone has different goals as far as life, but the same goals as far as the *team*.

> The players are ladies who can be open-minded because the team's success usually counts on that. We all realize we need to give in a little and try to understand one another's needs, most of all *talk it out*.

The team also seemed to value communication as a tool for team success. They reported that when they talked more among themselves, about the game, problems, relationships, and so on, they won more. In the individual follow-up interviews the women noted a wide range of topics discussed among teammates, everything from sex, to religion, to racial issues, to family members, to homosexuality. However, these discussions did not always involve the entire group but perhaps three or four people at a time. Topics were avoided or the subject was changed if they perceived that a member was hurt or embarrassed by the discussion. In other words topics were not usually deemed inappropriate in themselves, but only eliminated from discussion if they seemed inappropriate in the current situation. Further, it appeared that players "knew" when something was inappropriate by reading the nonverbal cues of the involved participants.

> Like, you just *know* when someone's upset. You can tell by their face— or they just get quiet.

Cooperation was also a major theme in discussions of "team goals." As a unit the team set goals for effective competition. At a minimum they planned to win the conference championship, but long-range goals included the national title. The importance of setting high team and individual goals was also emphasized in the follow-up interviews. They reported that the coach pushed them to set high goals for themselves and then to *work* to achieve.

> Well maybe other coaches don't push their teams so hard, set such high goals for them.

All players clearly believed they had to convince themselves to win and then they would be able to accomplish it.

> Everything is mental.
>
> You do what you want to do as long as you think you can.
> Yeah, yesterday she (the head coach) said it was 75% mental and 25% physical.
>
> Cause you have to have self-discipline to get into the team concept.
>
> She plays mind games with us.
>
> Yeah, she tell [sic] you you don't have heart, you don't have intensity and (you think) What do you mean I don't have heart!

A cohesive group philosophy is also apparent as they develop their team through recruitment. Being a good basketball player is not enough. Players who would not fit in off the court are not signed onto the team. Recruiting involves team communication. When a prospective player comes to campus, she is informally interviewed by the team. A strong predictor of whether the new member will actually join the team is an assessment of how well she will fit in with the group's selfless team play and principles of the team which include not drinking and partying during the season, a Christian attitude, and being willing to work extremely hard.

> (What do you look for?)
> Just to be able to get along. I mean you can tell right away whether they're going to fit in or not. If the first thing they ask is where they can party—
>
> Well, they (coaches) ask us how they fit in and stuff and if we like them or whatever.
>
> Yeah, cause we have to play with them. You know, they could be the greatest basketball player in the world, but if they can't communicate or get along with their teammates, then how are we going to play with them?
>
> Yeah, if they can't get along with everyone else then they're no use."

> I feel the key [to our success] would revolve around recruiting athletes, maybe not the most talented, but athletes who are dedicated and willing to work hard. Basketball is one of our top priorities, along with education. I feel that our faith in God is also important and has kept us closer together.

Religious themes running through the Jennies' team experience are apparent. The belief in and adherence to a Christian lifestyle appears to be a unifying element on the team. While the university itself is not a church-related school and the players are from various denominations, group Bible study in the home of one of the assistant coaches was not uncommon. Further, the Christian ethic served as a standard for behavior and attitudes. The Jennies explained.

> We're supposed to be a class act.
> Yeah, like on the court and off the court.
> 'Cause we're all Christians and we're supposed to reflect that Christian attitude. It hasn't hurt us.
> No, never hurt anyone.

Leadership was cooperatively defined on this team and group leadership included several dimensions. Leaders were seen as, ". . . someone aggressive. To be a leader you can't be quiet."

> Some people are just natural—by how they act, you can just follow that.

To a great extent, leadership functions appeared to shift around the team members with members perceived as group leaders if they accomplished what was necessary at a given time. Providing humor was one such necessary leadership function.

> Like if we're in a pretty tight situation and we need some humor, whoever is good at jokes will be focused upon.

> Everyone has something to offer to the group.

Although several people mentioned in both interviews and writing that leaders were not necessarily the "stars," one clear leader was a senior who was named the NCAA Division 2 Player of the Year at the end of the season. This person was a model because of her athletic ability, her work on self-improvement, and her spirituality. She was also regarded as a spokesperson if players wanted to bring up an issue with the coaching staff. She, in turn, recognized this as one of her group roles and made personal, gatekeeping decisions as to whether the issue was valid.

> If it was important enough to take it to them (the coaches) and talk about it, I would. If it's something, I don't—well, if it's something *stupid* like, "Hey Rosie, why don't you go in and see if Coach will let us out of practice early today," now naturally I'm not gonna go in there.
> [It had to be] important not only to me, but important to us as a team. Like say there was a time schedule conflict where the whole group had

something else planned, like a concert they were going to, and the coach wanted us to go to a dinner or something."

Like Steak Night. They're having Steak Night in the dorms and that's a big deal. I want to go eat steak! And no one's saying anything, and so I say, Hey Coach . . . and she let us out early or moved practice up.

Finally, the Jennies exhibited cooperative tendencies when contrasting themselves with the men's basketball team. They viewed the men as "harsh" with each other, berating teammates and calling them names. The Jennies, on the other hand, encouraged each other in a positive, supportive style. At the same time the women again recognized the influence of the coach in this style of team communication.

I think that's the way they really reinforce one another. Really scream at each other. You know, like "get your act together." They really get motivated that way.

Isn't that like expected of men though. That's how society says you're supposed to encourage one another.

Yeah, like they'll call themselves a bunch of pansies or something.

But then you have to look at their coach. It's like with their coach you have to do it right.

What the coach lets you do, you're gonna do. If their coach lets you get away with something then why not.

Their coach will call them a pansy while our coach will say you don't have heart or desire.

Cooperativeness is a dominant pattern among the team members' communication. They appear to strongly endorse supportive, cooperative strategies in encouraging each other, developing team play, forming team goals, interacting off the court, and incorporating new players. This focus is exemplified by uniform and strong agreement with the questionnaire statement, "I am a cooperative player."

Competition

While the Jennies clearly value cooperation, this conviction must be qualified. The primary task of this group is to win. They have established themselves as winners, a fact that cannot be overlooked in interpreting their communication. The powerful record of success this team and coach has enjoyed during the past four years is a strong indicator of the competitive strength of the squad. In this sense task attainment and evaluation are very direct and clear: they are successful as a team if they have a winning record; they are accomplishing their group goals if they triumph over other teams. Thus, it seems reasonable that the team exhibits a pattern of cooperative communication as a means to the end of winning basketball games.

Competitiveness was evidenced in the recurring theme of setting high goals, both as a team and as individuals.

> When I was recruited, coach asked me, was it my goal to start a game? And I knew I wasn't going to start and I didn't know what to say and she said that if one of my goals wasn't to start, then she really didn't want me there.

> Yeah, we talk as a team. We make a goal and our next goal is to make (achieve) another goal.

> Everyone agrees to this, and it's in their hearts, and you have the potential,—then it's, 'let's do it!'

> Step by step, you work to achieve that goal.

In addition, any "pressure" from being on a winning streak was reported as positive and exciting, adding an edge to the game. These women appeared to enjoy the "spotlight" afforded by the team's success and were willing to work hard and sacrifice in order to maintain their high standards. It should be noted that this mutual determination can also be viewed as team cooperation.

Aggressive play was a positive and enjoyable aspect of competition. However, distinctions were drawn between "necessary" and "unnecessary" aggression. Necessary aggression helped the team to win. Aggression was viewed as negative if it got the player in foul trouble or caused her to play poorly.

> When you foul you make aggressive mistakes on defense and then there are fouls you make when you're just stupid.
>
> Yeah, like a situation in a game towards the end and if it's close and you stop the clock then you get a foul and then that's a smart foul.

> You got to think about it too, cause it could be a strategy. Like if you're in foul trouble and somebody is in your face or pushing you or something, then you're gonna want to push them back and then there goes another foul. And you get fouled out or get four fouls and get taken out, so you just try hard, you know.

Tolerance for and even enjoyment of aggressive play was also evidenced on the individual questionaires. As Table 1 indicates, most players agreed with the statements, "The more physical the game gets the better I like it," and "I like a referee who lets the game get a little rough." Physical contact and the sometimes "rough" nature of the sport were considered fun among the Jennies.

The issue of "playing time" probably generated the most intra-team competition. This issue clearly highlights the zero-sum nature of competition (Hocker & Wilmot, 1985) in that (a) there are only a limited number of minutes in a game, and (b) if some players are on the floor most of that time it cuts down on the playing time of others. The members voiced strong agreement that length of playing time was very important, yet it was not a topic of open discussion among team members.

Frost and Wilmot (1978) suggest that women are taught to avoid open conflict. Indeed, several players noted privately that conflicts sometimes arose when someone felt she wasn't getting to play enough. Communication about this issue appeared to be an exception to the general pattern of openness on the team. While team members tossed most other topics around freely, they did not broach the subject of players vying for the same position.

> No one really openly discusses that they would like to beat out their teammate at a certain position. Maybe we discuss that we would like to improve certain skills to get more playing time, but we never say I would like to beat her out because I'm better or I work harder. That is something that is more or less a silent competition between teammates that share the same position.

One questionnaire item further illustrated this "silent competition." Team members strongly disagreed with the statement, "Even if I don't start, just getting some playing time is OK with me." Just getting to play wasn't really enough, a starting position is what everyone strives for. Thus, while everyone agreed they wanted to be in the starting line-up, their competition for those positions was not openly discussed. This may be an accommodation strategy, common among women, which occurs when "the individual puts aside his or her own concerns in order to satisfy the concerns of the other person" (Hocker & Wilmot, 1985, p. 43). The Jennies all understand that each player can't be a "starter," so in order to maintain team cohesion they minimize communication about competition for positions.

The coaches played a strong role in minimizing the competitive nature of the team's communication when it was focused on areas judged to be dysfunctional: teammates, the men's basketball team, or team/school rivalries. The head coach also exerted control of communication channels by telling the players not to read about games in newspapers. The explanation for this was that quotes may be inaccurate.

But we surmise that such instructions also served a protective function and prevented intra-team conflict if certain players were singled out for attention.

> . . . at the end of the year we were asked not to discuss what the men's team have or get compared to us.

> Shoot, the coaches don't let us find out stuff they don't want us to. Heck, they keep things from us so well.
> Don't even read the paper.
> Yeah, don't read the paper cause they may misquote. Just let it go in one ear and out the other and don't let it bother you.

The team's high goals and standards of play, the excitement generated by a winning record and aggressive play as a means of winning all illustrate the Jennies' competitiveness. However, such competitive inclinations were viewed as dysfunctional when they turned inward and became rivalries over playing time, especially exacerbated by media attention. Therefore these latter aspects were suppressed by team and coach norms.

Structural Aspects of the Interviews

The nonverbal and paralinguistic behavior of this unique group were also of interest because of reported differences in men's and women's communication (Eakins & Eakins, 1978; Hall, 1984; Pearson, 1985; Scott, 1980). Generally, the Jennies displayed those physical and paralinguistic behaviors expected of the "women's role" in society: attentiveness (Rosenthal & DePaulo, 1979; Hall, 1984), politeness (Jay, 1980), and general conversational rule-following (Zimmerman & West, 1975; West & Zimmerman, 1983).

The team members exhibited very attentive, polite, and open postures in all interviews. They were attentive not only to interviewers but to each other as well, maintaining eye contact most of the time. They appeared very relaxed: sprawling, slumping, legs stretched out in front of them, leaning forward with elbows on knees, lying on their sides. Such postures are suggestive of the "masculine" and physical nature of their sport but their attention remained focused on the interaction.

During our interaction with the players their turn-taking behavior was polite as well. There were many talk-overs, but this appeared due to their eagerness to contribute and their comfort with each other rather than to competitiveness with the team. Interruptions tend to be a masculine and dominant aspect of communication (Zimmerman & West, 1975) but the Jennies also encouraged each other to participate, at times directing questions to one another. According to the count of initiated interactions, every member participated with seven or eight team members' statements central to most of the interaction. To illustrate, at one point in the group interview one member "shushed" everyone, admonishing them not to all talk at once so everyone could hear what was going on.

Team members also demonstrated cooperative and feminine behavior in their high level of agreement (Aries, 1982). Many statements were prefaced with "yeah" and contained paraphrases, extensions, or additional examples of the first reply. (The quotations included thus far give ample evidence of this agreeing pattern). The few times dissent emerged, it tended to be voiced as humor/joking or an agreeing response followed by differentiation.

> We thought we'd be sick of each other by now, since we spend so much time together, but we get along great.
> Yeah, great.
> That's not what I heard. (laughter)

> (interviewer) What's the coach like outside of her "coaching role"?
> You know, kind of like a friend.
> Someone to talk to.
> Yeah, a friend, but you can't get too buddy-buddy with her because then I think fairness suffers.

The women also employed effective communication skills in the form of perception-checking each other and the interviewer, as well as the use of clarification strategies. All communication evidenced was polite and nonconfrontive.

This nonconfrontive communication was reinforced in individual interviews. The team handled conflict in a roundabout manner. The team members consistently emphasized that they did not "ignore" conflict, but time was allowed to "cool off" and only when the issue remained salient, affecting team play, did the team deal with it. The coach was not brought into conflict unless the issue was with her— typically conflict with the coach centered around "playing time."

> If the persons involved are unable to talk it out truthfully and openly, team leaders may help. But the parties involved usually try to come to an agreement. It is usually never ignored. Something that I believe helps is that other members of the team may step in and help you to understand the other person's point of view.

> Usually the coaches stay out of it. I would say that we try to keep most of the conflicts just between the team. We were fortunate not to

have conflicts, because in my past experiences nothing can tear a team apart more than interpersonal conflicts. When they occur, it's difficult to have everyone end up happy.

A final point concerning the structure of the team's communication is in order. Smythe (in press) suggests there has been a homogenization of profanity norms for males' and females' communication. However, profanity was totally absent in all interactions here. In fact, a player in one interview corrected herself for starting to label mediocre play "half-assed." While this may, to some extent, be a result of the "interview" setting and presence of a tape recorder, minimal use of profanity also has been reported in other studies (Selnow, 1985) and appeared to be the status quo here. In other areas of talk the women did not seem to be guarding their responses and the group interaction particularly was characterized by spontaneity and laughter. This absence of profanity may be due to the strong Christian orientation and self-image as "feminine" and a "class act" which the Jennies maintain. The players repeatedly referred to themselves as "ladies" who are "feminine" as well as athletic. Thus it seems probable that these women use coarse language very infrequently, if at all, in their daily interactions.

Summary

Here again the emerging pattern of interaction structure is predominantly cooperative and "feminine." With the exception of their casual, "masculine" postures, the polite language, attentiveness, and turn-taking were clearly consistent with the image they endorse as "ladies who are also athletes."

Conclusions and Implications

Several communication patterns are consistent among the Jennies. First, the Jennies appear to communicate according to traditionally female expectations. As a team and as individuals, communication patterns all strongly emphasize cooperation, working and getting along together. Competition, by contrast, appears to be directed at opponents in a formal context of the "game." When intra-team competition occurs, it tends to be deflected or suppressed.

Second, although cooperation is the higher value, competition does play a powerful role. These women enjoy, expect, and look forward to aggression and competitive pressure. This presents an interesting bind for the researchers. On one hand, the players seem to ascribe to traditional feminine values. Yet, these women eagerly anticipate a form of behavior that is the antithesis of "feminine" behavior: physical aggression. Furthermore, there seems to be no role strain in this apparently "paradoxical" situation. The players exhibit no discomfort, frustration, or confusion regarding societal expectations. This outcome is consistent with recent survey results concluding that role-strain was not evidenced in a high school women's basketball context (Hoferek & Hanick, 1985). Simply put, societal expectations may not be as stereotypic and limiting as some of the traditional literature assumes.

Therefore, in answering our research questions we need to examine why these college women do not perceive societal norms regarding competition and cooperation as contradictory for them. Possible explanations include (a) methodological limitations of this study; (b) societal change; (c) situational adaptation; and (d) the efficacy of a "team culture."

First, methodological limitations of the case study approach must be acknowledged. These individuals were not randomly selected for participation and variables surrounding the communication situation were not controlled. We intended to study naturally-occurring communication interaction in an intact ongoing group. In such cases self-selection stands as a potential explanation for the team's ease of communication (Campbell & Stanley, 1963). Specifically, women who are members of successful athletic teams may arrive there because they are the type of people who are able to engage in both cooperation and competition without feeling role strain.

It may be that any successful women's team would demonstrate similar patterns. Further it should be noted that college women may be at the least "restrained" time of their lives and that noncollege women may be more susceptible to role strain. It would be informative to conduct similar studies with other successful, as well as unsuccessful teams, and women's groups who are not "teams" or are not in college to determine whether the same patterns emerge.

Societal change is a second possible explanation for the Jennies' communication. It may be that our culture as a whole has altered traditional expectations for women and athletes and that the findings of Hoferek and Hanick (1985) and the incorporation of both competitive and cooperative communication styles by the Jennies reflect this wider definition of women's communication. Wood and Conrad explain, "It may be argued that the traditional woman is but a particular manifestation of womanhood which is a far broader, richer concept than can be captured in any singular embodiment" (1983, p. 317). Within this framework, the cooperative "feminine" aspects of the team members' communication are not at odds with the competitive aspects; they are situational adaptations.

The athletes' responses to questions about perceived inconsistencies between the expectations of an athlete vs. expectations of a woman support this interpretation.

> No, I don't think most people see us as "weird" or anything. Maybe 10 years ago or so. But now it's really accepted to be an athlete, people look up to you.

> Now, unlike 5 to 10 years ago, people don't view us as "jocks." All of our team members keep themselves looking feminine while still being an athlete.

While this explanation sounds ideal, it is not entirely satisfying. Recent trends indicate that societal norms for women have not altered as much as we might have hoped. Certainly the upswing of political conservatism does not reflect broadening traditional expectations for women. A 1980 survey of college students indicated a trend toward more conservative attitudes toward women in general. Further, a recent study (Philips & Gilroy, 1985) found sex-biased expectations for mental health more than a decade after the initial Broverman, Broverman, Clarkson, Rosenkrantz, & Vogel study (1970). The authors of this replication concluded that the previous results may have been due to statistical artifact and that changes in expectations had occurred. However, a closer look at their analysis indicates very similar expectations from 1970 to 1980 and not the liberalization Philips and Gilroy suggest.

Therefore, if we assume that some societal pressures remain for women to conform to traditionally feminine roles, a third explanation of the Jennies' cooperation and competition is that they adapt their self-presentation to fit various situational expectations. The team members emphasize that they are more than just "players" and that they enact many other roles in their lives.

> I don't like people to respond to me only in the role of a player. I mean, I have many more aspects than that. There's Jackie the athlete, but there's also Jackie the student, Jackie the employee, etc. When I'm in those roles the athletic part doesn't affect me that much.

> There's the constant question, "aren't you a Jennie?" and sometimes you want to let them know you are much more of a person than just a basketball player.

> There's one thing I can say about our team, we know that after basketball there is another life out there.

> There are the men and they have a Pro (league) to go to and there

isn't anything for us right now. But each one of us know that and we want to get our education.

It may be tempting to interpret this perspective as a type of communication which perpetuates a double bind. The players appear to be "adhering to alternative injunctions in different situations" (Wood & Conrad, 1983, p. 312), a problematic form of adjustment due to the requisite vigilance and constant "switching." If caught in the "wrong" communication style for a situation the actor appears incompetent and role strain heightens. However, there is no indication that the Jennies significantly change their overall self-presentation by situation. In other words, they do not seem to communicate exclusively as athletes or as females in any situation. Instead they acknowledge both cooperative and competitive tendencies, accept them, and direct those communication strategies into appropriate areas.

The most encompassing explanation of the Jennies' pattern of communication appears to be the creation of a "subculture." The Jennies do not need to alter their communication patterns to fit societal expectations because the team provides sufficient interpersonal validation and reinforcement. In this subculture the group redefines the appropriateness of cooperation and competition for the members and minimizes the impact of wider societal injunctions.

It is clear that the primary reference group for the women is the "team" itself. Team members act as closest friends and roommates, and this reference group, headed by the coach, decides what communication norms are necessary for success. The women reported an awareness that their athletic endeavor was a barrier to sharing relationships with many other women. The Jennies reported often feeling stereotyped as "jocks" by other women. Furthermore, they believed that these stereotypes interfered with relationship development and served to isolate the team members from other women. (Interestingly, the team members did not believe that men engaged in similar stereotyping.) Thus, in the subculture of this women's basketball team cooperation and competition are not gender-linked communication, but appropriate or inappropriate as defined by the team. The Jennies appear to cooperate on an intragroup level and focus competition on opposing teams. Competition and aggression within the group are clearly discouraged and at least currently, effectively dispersed so the team can act as "one."

To illustrate, the contradictory demands of team/individual play, previously noted as one of the paradoxes, remain in existance. However, the dilemma appears to be resolved by (a) accentuating cooperative norms leading to "team unity"; (b) avoiding or suppressing competition where it might be disfunctional, for example, among team members;

and (c) redirecting competition toward opposing teams. Communication injunctions are separated and redirected so they are consistent with the needs of the team.

Thus, the case of the Jennies illustrates that a cohesive group may form a subculture in which communication injunctions from an external society have little influence. The "team" acts as the society to which members look for salient messages. As long as members remain within the team culture the team will define appropriate and inappropriate communication. Players can communicate in a highly cooperative manner without threat to the competitive or aggressive elements demanded of successful athletes. Conversely the Jennies' highly competitive communication does not undermine their status as women in the group. Thus, the cohesive team supports and defines competent communication patterns, and minimizes potential role strain.

References

Aries, E. (1982). Verbal and nonverbal behavior in single sex and mixed sex groups. *Psychological Reports.* *51*, 127–134.

Anashensel, D., & Rosen, B. (1978). Sex differences in the educational-occupational expectation process. *Journal of Social Forces, 57*, 164–186.

Broverman, I., Broverman, D., Clarkson, F., Rosenkrantz, P., & Vogel, S. (1970). Sex-role stereotypes and clinical judgments of mental health. *Journal of Consulting and Clinical Psychology, 34*, 250–256.

Campbell, D., & Stanley, J. (1963). *Experimental and quasi-experimental designs for research.* Chicago: Rand McNally.

Eakins, B., & Eakins, R. (1978). *Sex differences in human communication.* Chicago: Houghton Mifflin.

Filstead, W. (1979). Qualitative methods: A needed perspective in evaluation research. In Thomas Cook and Charles Reichardt (Eds.), *Qualitative and quantitative methods in evaluation research.* (pp. 33–48). Beverly Hills: Sage Publications, Inc.

Frost, J., & Wilmot, W. (1978). *Interpersonal conflict,* (1st Ed.) Dubuque, IA: William C. Brown Publishers.

Garnets, L., & Pleck, J. (1979). Sex role identity, androgyny, and sex role strain analysis. *Psychology of Women Quarterly, 3*, 270–282.

Gerber, E., Felshin, J., Berlin, P., & Wyrick, W. (1974). *The American woman in sport.* Reading, MA: Addison-Wesley.

Hall, J. (1984). *Nonverbal sex differences: Communication accuracy and expressive style.* Baltimore: Johns Hopkins University Press.

Hocker, J., & Wilmot, W. (1985). *Interpersonal conflict.* (2nd Ed.) Dubuque, IA: Wm. C. Brown Publishers.

Hoterek, M., & Hanick, P. (1985). Woman and athlete: Toward role consistency. *Sex Roles, 12*, 687–696.

Jay, T. (1980). Sex roles and dirty word usage: A review of the literature and a reply to Haas. *Psychological Bulletin, 88,* 614–621.

Patton, M. (1980). *Qualitative evaluation methods.* Beverly Hills: Sage Publications.

Pearson, J. (1985). *Gender and communication.* Dubuque, IA: Wm. C. Brown Publishers.

Philips, R., & Gilroy, F. (1985). Sex-role stereotypes and clinical judgements of mental health: The Brovermans' findings reexamined. *Sex Roles, 12,* 179–193.

Rosenthal, R., & DePaulo, B. (1979). Sex differences in accommodation in nonverbal communication. In R. Rosenthal (Ed.), *Skill in nonverbal communication: Individual differences.* Cambridge, MA: Oelgeschlager, Gunn & Hain.

Scott, K. (1980). Perceptions of communication competence: What's good for the goose is not good for the gander. In C. Kramerae (Ed.), *The voices and words of women and men.* New York: Pergamon Press.

Selnow, G. (1985). Sex differences in uses and perceptions of profanity. *Sex Roles, 12,* 303–312.

Smythe, M. J. (in press). Analyzing sex differences in communication behavior. In B. Dervin (Ed.), *Progress in communication sciences.* Norwood, NJ: Ablex.

Stockard, J., & Johnson, M. (1980). *Sex roles.* Englewood Cliffs, NJ: Prentice-Hall.

Weitzman, L. (1979). *Sex role socialization.* Palo Alto, CA: Mayfield Publishing Company.

West, C., & Zimmerman, D. (1983). Small insults: A study of interruptions in cross sex conversations between unaquainted persons. In B. Thorne, C. Kramarae, & N. Henley (Eds.), *Language, gender and society,* Rowley, MA: Newbury House.

Wiley, M., & Eskilson, A. (1982). Coping in the corporation: Sex role constraints. *Journal of Applied Social Psychology, 12,* 1–11.

Wilmot, W. (1980). *Dyadic communication.* Reading, MA: Addison-Wesley.

Wood, J., & Conrad, C. (1983). Paradox in the experiences of professional women. *Western Journal of Speech Communication, 47,* 305–322.

Zimmerman, D., & West, C. (1975). Sex roles, interruptions and silences in conversation. In B. Thorne and N. Henley (Eds.), *Language and sex: Difference and dominance.* Rowley, MA: Newbury House.

11

Women's Ways: Interactive Patterns in Predominantly Female Research Teams

Marie Wilson Nelson

George Mason University

In recent years activities in which most women participate have expanded. In *The Second Stage* Betty Friedan (1981) cites women's progress toward fuller "participation, power, and voice in the mainstream, inside the party, the political process, the professions, the business world." But participation is merely the first stage of change, Friedan claims; for to realize both "the limits and the true potential of women's power" requires more of women than merely learning to act like men. Equal participation in society requires women to learn new ways of interacting; it also requires a reciprocal commitment from men. True equality requires no less, according to Friedan, than literally "changing the terms" by which society operates, a goal she believes will improve institutions for women and men.

In this study I describe interactions typical of five successive teacher-research teams who took part, between 1981 and 1985, in the qualitative program evaluation of a university writing center. The study was conducted in the Composition Tutorial Center (CTC) at George Mason University, a state school of 17,000 in the Virginia suburbs of Washington, DC. Selections from transcripts of Team I's final session illustrate interactive patterns familiar to females on all teams but unfamiliar to the males who occasionally joined these teams. Follow-up interviews with members of Teams IV and V confirmed Team I's conclusion that their team functioned differently from most academic and professional groups. They also confirm similarities between Team I and later teams.

This study found several groups of women changing the terms by which academic groups have often operated. It also shows the men who joined them adapting to the unfamiliar women's ways and finding personal, professional, and academic advantages in doing so. Its goal was not to compare male and female interactions definitively, however, but to describe interactive patterns recurring on these largely female teams, to show how those patterns differ from those of traditionally male-led groups, and to document those patterns' importance for the men and women who experienced them.

The Context in Which Teams Operated

The Composition Tutorial Center, housed in the English Department, was established in 1981 to offer small-group tutorial instruction to undergraduates having problems with university writing. There graduate teaching assistants (TAs) led mixed groups of four or five native and second-language (ESL) speakers in writing workshops meeting twice a week for a semester. My job as center director was to design and administer the program, train the TAs to teach writing, and supervise their work. The teaching assistants were selected on the basis of experience as writers, experience in teaching or applied linguistics, and non-elitist attitudes. Most knew little about the center approach when the training began, for it was based on recent discoveries about how language abilities develop and was grounded in writers' testimony about how they learn to write. As a result, the program contrasted with the writing instruction most TAs had experienced themselves.

Tutor training, therefore, had several components. For two weeks in August new TAs attended a daily seminar to prepare them to start teaching the small tutorial groups. Training continued weekly throughout fall semester in a three credit-hour graduate course, and the teams met spring semester in regularly scheduled staff meetings and in occasional in-service or research sessions. To help TAs learn to help their students grow confident and independent, the training included several strands: reading and discussing recent writing research and theory, writing extensively and examining their own writing processes, and conducting qualitative teacher-research to learn how their students actually wrote. The personal experience on which teams drew in analyzing writing processes and in brainstorming methods of teaching from which they themselves would have benefitted as writers contributed to the trust and cohesion that developed on these teams. So did the one rule I make clear in all my writing classes—that because writing often dries up in the face of harsh evaluation, responses to each others' work should be honest but supportively phrased to avoid making light of any writer or her work.

To encourage classroom interactions from which TAs could learn about learning, I modeled from the first day of class the kinds of interactive processes that would help them experience first-hand the rewards of collaborative work. I knew that if they had experienced the motivation collaboration brings (Kohn, 1986), they would be more likely to use it in their own teaching. I therefore modeled the kinds of oral and written responses to writing that research has shown encourage developing writers at all levels. I shared personally motivated as well as professional writing of my own to demonstrate that they could do many kinds of writing in my class. To illustrate the critical stance I hoped they would assume toward their teaching, I revealed problems I experienced and asked for their suggestions. Modeling the kinds of risk-taking from which teaching and writing improve, I examined inconsistencies between how I write and how I teach, told them when I tried new approaches, and asked for help with writing I was doing that term.

I also praised or otherwise focused classroom attention on the kinds of behaviors I expected of students. I praised well-thought-out experiments, even when they failed, reinforcing students for taking risks and illustrating that classroom failures help people learn from mistakes. I focused team attention on strengths in what students were doing by pointing out thoughtful responses they gave to each other, saving time for talk about "breakthroughs" that followed risks taken with writing or teaching, noting developing commitment and motivation in their "learning logs," asking for (and dealing with) constructive criticism. I also modeled the process of dealing with negative feelings that emerged to reveal how doing so could help students work through common resistances to studying writing. And lest TAs misunderstand why I taught the course this way, I explained that trust and closeness functioned *not* as teaching goals but as serendipitous by-products of successful collaboration and as powerful rewards that motivate students to work hard (Kohn, 1986).

Team Participants

Team membership varied yearly but typically included six to 10 first-year tutors (ranging from 22 to 50 years of age) and (in all but the first year) one or two interns or doctoral students who joined the team because they were interested in the research. The first team, for example, included five female TAs, a female professor (myself), and a 23-year old male who adopted (and commented on) the women's interactive style. In only one case were there two males on a team, and in five years the total number of males was five.

The roles the male tutor and professor played deserve special mention as they were somewhat different from those of others on the teams. As a negative (non-female) case, the male TA Arthur[1] said this group was different from others he had been in:

> I just love being in here with all you women. You make it such a nice place to work. You're so warm and supportive that I never feel stupid when I make a mistake. It's different in here from how I've seen people do things before. Most graduate students are so competitive.

Arthur's comment echoes the view of female teammates that this group was different from academic groups they'd been in before. As one woman said: "It's so nice and relaxing to work with *women* for a change!"

This comment was part of a lunchtime chat about the team's approach in which the women of Team I described

1. their collegiality ("how much we learned from each other");
2. the noncompetitive atmosphere ("it motivates me more");
3. support they gave each other ("emphasizing strengths as well as weaknesses");
4. their relatively co-equal status with the professor ("you include us in decisions"); and
5. benefits of emotional openness on the team ("It was talking about the anxieties we all felt that made me realize I wasn't alone in having failures and doubts").

All of these traits have been found to be common in women's inter-actions by other recent research on gender-related behavior (Gilligan, 1982; Miller, 1976; Pearson, 1985).

My position of authority in the university hierarchy—that is, my dual teacher/supervisor role—gave me disproportionate power on these teams though I tried to minimize authoritarian behavior. In general, therefore, talk and decisions were collaborative and collegial. To provide some background on my perceptions as participant-observer, let me also say it was my intent to treat teammates as colleagues and my hope that they would respond in kind. I'd chosen this approach in part because former students and friends had noted that they felt happier and more productive working in supportive, collaborative women's

---

[1] All names except mine have been changed.

groups. Another motivation, however, was that such a group was professionally important to me. It was my first year at GMU, and my office was distant from those of others in my department. With the team of graduate students whom I would see daily, however, I hoped to create a supportive environment for myself and them by treating them as a group with whom to discuss professional issues, a group who might come to take an interest in my work, a group who might offer the support I needed to be most productive, a group from whose varied experience I might also learn.

Among traits sometimes disparaged as "soft" or "weak" or "feminine" were two I had found helpful in growth- and learning-oriented groups and which writing research and theory indicate facilitate writing development. One was maintaining a nonthreatening atmosphere to make possible the frankness and risk-taking characteristic of successful learners. The other was dealing with whatever feelings arose in response to interpersonal interactions or to the group task itself. I therefore wove these into the fabric of the teacher-research teams. Only vaguely aware of specific studies (Miller, 1976; Pearson, 1985) showing that my preferences were typical of women (though experience told me this was probably so), I was trying to create the environment in which my students and I could best learn. My success at achieving this goal outstripped my expectations, expanded my awareness of the rewards of collaborative work, and convinced me of a point I hope to make in this essay—that the interactive patterns into which I as a woman had been socialized offer substantial benefits to academic and professional teams.

On the assumption, then, that conditions that helped me learn might also help others, I tried to create for the TAs and to model for them as tutors the kind of supportive, collaborative groups in which I am most comfortable and productive. I knew from other women that the kinds of interactions I sought were widely perceived as more typical of female than of mixed groups. The sewing circle, for example, and the quilting bee, were often mentioned as examples of traditional women's groups having collaborative production and mutual support as their primary goals and a lateral rather than hierarchical pattern of organization. Even the name "sewing circle," like the name of my mother's church group, reflects a nonhierarchic, context-dependent, shifting, lateral structure in which skillful group members (with neither position nor rank assigned) help less proficient groupmates develop skills as the need arises.

Such behavior is not regularly associated with male-originated groups. In Masonic orders, for example, or on many athletic teams, the division of labor and responsibility is determined by rank in a hierarchy or by direct competition for defined positions or roles. In football, coaches plot strategy; quarterbacks direct the team; and experienced first-string players, who need game practice the least, play more often than others because competition produces the need to win. In baseball, weaker players may be cut from the roster and sent to practice in the "minors" rather than getting a chance to work with more skillful members of the team. But even for the survivors, who make the final cut, it is coaches (near the top of the hierarchy) rather than proficient teammates who are designated responsible for improving player skills.

Aware of these different tendencies of female- and male-led groups, I chose the interactive style with which I was most at home to create a supportive learning/working atmosphere for the center staff and to improve my own chances of success.

Team Goals

Together—in the graduate course, in staff meetings, and in special research sessions—five successive teacher-research teams tested and refined a program to help basic and ESL writers master academic writing. Though these three types of meetings went by different names, interactions in all were similar; for pedagogical, administrative, and research issues were (as one tutor put it) "not distinct." Three goals for the program shaped interactions on all five teams:

1. To help beginning TAs improve their teaching by studying it for patterns of greater or lesser success.
2. To conduct a program evaluation through which the tutorial program could be progressively adapted to meet the needs of basic writers.
3. To examine similarities and differences in ESL and native writers so an approach based on native-language writing research and theory could be adapted as needed for non-native students (40%) who enrolled in the CTC.

The Data

Patterns of team discussion, analysis, and decision making grew evident when I examined several types of data: research reports and other writing done for the tutor-training courses; audio-tapes of classes, staff meetings, and research sessions; and interviews with male and female members of several teams.

The Findings

During fall semesters, Teams I through V exhibited similar patterns of interaction:

1. All groups demonstrated a problem-solving orientation, the goal of which was helping students learn.
2. Decision making tended to be collaborative and field-dependent, with administrative, instructional, and research-related decisions influencing each other and rooted in concensus rather than authority.
3. Despite constraints (like evaluation) imposed by the university hierarchy, teams tended to function collegially, as laterally organized groups, with information being generated by and flowing to and from all members.
4. Analyses were as much emergent as preplanned, were more collaborative than individual, and involved intuitive and holistic as well as linear patterns of reasoning.
5. Teammates tended to offer each other emotional support and constructive criticism, interact good-naturedly, deal openly with negative feelings, and avoid competitive behaviors that threatened what they called the "sanctuary" atmosphere.
6. Positive and negative evaluation were balanced and sequential, tactfully phrased (to protect self-esteem and prevent defensive reactions) and designed to nurture growth more than to eliminate the weak.

In the remainder of this essay excerpts from Team I's final session illustrate the six patterns which characterized team interactions. The excerpts are followed by confirmatory interviews with members of Teams IV and V to show the extent to which these findings are supported by contrasting participant views.

Team I: Excerpts from a Typical Teacher-Research Session

The following excerpts illustrate the six patterns that typified interactions on research teams I through V. For example, the following segment shows the extent to which decision making was holistic and nonlinear, how research, administration, and instructional issues were (as Francie notes) "non-distinct," and how group problem solving focused on helping others. Here Lynn's concern about a common method (instruction) grows out of her close observation of student writing behavior (research), elicits advice for making the method work better (instruction), gets collaboratively refined to accommodate conflicting evidence (research), and eventually leads to a new center policy arrived at by concensus (administration).

What seems most striking in this sequence, however, is that the collaboration involved and was largely led by Lynn and Francie, the two strongest personalities on the team, who from the first day of school had experienced strongly competitive feelings. Strong feelings were common on the teacher-research teams as they were in the TA's tutorial groups, and channelling them constructively was one of my teaching goals. In most cases, teammates rose above negative feelings and prevented personal conflicts and loyalties from affecting their group's success. In this case, for example, aware that their feelings threatened the group's safe atmosphere, Lynn and Francie monitored their interactions, came independently to me for advice, and spent a morning near midterm in conflict resolution. During that time they openly expressed and confronted their troublesome feelings, explored why they made each other uncomfortable, and collaborated to keep their conflict from threatening the work of their team.

From that morning on I no longer detected tension in Team I, though both Lynn and Francie struggled to remain mutually supportive all year. Five years later in a chance meeting, Lynn, now teaching high school, confirmed that both had worked hard to maintain what Francie herself first labeled the "sanctuary" atmosphere. I told Lynn I was writing this essay and said I'd like to include their experience to show how, in a supportive environment, women often work to keep personal feelings from affecting the work of a team.

"Well, it's true, we really did," Lynn proudly replied. "We both had negative feelings, but we didn't let them interfere at all!"

The following excerpt shows Lynn and Francie at the end of the year collaborating successfully despite their history of competition. When Lynn suggests a controversial change in teaching methods, Francie supports her against the objections of Caroline, Francie's closest friend. Even while contributing conflicting evidence, the group helped Lynn qualify and refine her ideas by specifying conditions under which they did and did not hold true. And though she openly revealed what others may have seen as failures, at no point did Francie or other teammates show anything but respect for Lynn's careful work. In short, evaluation emphasized potential rather than weakness and constructively helped each tutor improve her success at helping students learn.

Lynn: I'm concerned about something. I don't think we should keep working on assigned papers with students. I started out doing it last fall, but I've changed my thinking.

Kate: But what if they come into the center only for that?

Francie:	These issues are not distinct. One thing hinges on another. I listed a suggestion under "administration" that relates to this. If we could only get students [enrolled] in here before they get assignment pressure, we could avoid this conflict.
Caroline:	Just for the record, I've had *great* luck working with papers for classes.
Lynn:	I've had very poor luck.
Marie:	What makes the difference?
Caroline:	I've been able to show the writing process through assigned papers. I find the grade motivates them to go through the entire process of drafting, revising, editing . . .
Lynn:	I have students who aren't interested in learning. They just want their papers corrected.
Marie:	What if you told them we don't do that in this program?
Fran:	Yeah. Once they try freewriting, they see that it works.
Lynn:	Most of mine have not had that insight.
Caroline:	I would hate to lay down an edict that we *can't* work on [teacher-assigned] papers, because it has really, really worked for me. Maybe we just have to emphasize process when we let them do it.
Marie:	Yeah. Or you could say that "Working on assignments isn't helping your writing at this point. You need to back up and practice writing about things you *know* about first."
Caroline:	That's what I did with one student, and it worked, too.
Lynn:	I worked on [assigned] papers all year, but after watching them I think they need to learn the process separate from assignments, on writing *they* control. Then with luck they can transfer what they've learned to their coursework.
Caroline:	For someone who wants to be writer, what you say makes sense. But what about students who're just trying to get through freshman comp?

While clarifying what their varying observations meant, Team I identified a problem—the way students' negative attitudes interfered with teaching success—and collaborated to develop an administrative solution. As did other teams, they pursued the goal of helping students learn until they reached consensus about how it might be achieved rather than letting one solution win out over others. The way conflicting opinions were openly discussed shows teammates searching for fuller understanding through collaborative problem-solving rather than focusing on who was right or wrong, an evaluative stance more typical of more competitive groups. This pattern of conflict resolution was similar to that Lynn and Francie used when working through their personal conflicts outside the group setting. In the sequence that follows, the pattern of logic is associative and unfocused, inching toward consensus in a holistic, intuitive, nonlinear way:

Lynn:	Maybe we need a statement of what the CTC does because some composition teachers call and say their students need help with assignments "because of grammar problems."
Fran:	Yeah. Students get mixed expectations because the composition teachers don't always understand what we're trying to do.
Marie:	Maybe we need to clarify our approach to part-time faculty and TAs who teach our students in Freshman English.
Caroline:	When students have been told by teachers to get help on papers, and we don't address those papers, there's a lot of emotion, a panic. You can see it in their faces.
Marie:	Maybe a memo to writing teachers. . . .
Lynn:	People may be offended if they teach differently from us.
Francie:	They may get angry, so you need to lay out developmentally just what it is we are trying to do and why!
Marie:	I want us all to agree if we're making a policy statement? Tell me what to say.
Francie:	Sure! We're a place that focuses on the process of writing. We believe writing is developmental, that many factors affect writing, not the least of which are affective. We find that attitudes are very important, and that building motivation takes time. Also, about multiple revisions . . . . Say that writing isn't perfect the first time.
Lynn:	To some literature specialists who don't know new ways of teaching writing, you will have to explain—maybe in a footnote.
Marie:	"Note: see me for meaning of this memo" [much laughter].
Lynn:	How about, "I think that writing is developmental and that one draft does not a paper make."
Francie:	"And twenty lashes with a wet noodle if you tell students we correct papers."
Marie:	Perhaps I should reassure them that we do, in fact, work on grammar and mechanics—but through the writing itself.
Caroline:	And say that we do that toward the *end* of the process.
Marie:	What about "We work on grammar whenever the papers have been revised to the point that they are ready to be edited"?
Francie:	Oh, beautiful!
Marie:	Alright. Thanks. That's what I needed to know.

The excerpt above shows how Team I dealt good-naturedly with feelings, how collaborative analysis and decision making gradually led to concensus, and how teaching methods, administrative policies, and empirical observation all interacted in complex ways.

The following critique my teammates gave of the training program shows the supportive but constructive stance we teammates took toward each other. How the program benefitted from our frankness can also be seen in our discovery of a valuable research tool—"the records" or "the casework"—which later teacher-research teams came to call "log-keeping." We discovered its value when Lynn revealed that she had stopped doing assignments for my course in order to pursue her study of students because she learned more from them. As the observational logs she kept increased her teaching success and added to the whole team's knowledge of how natives and non-natives write, I decided to assign observation logs to members of subsequent teams and those they produced (on some 90 tutorial groups) became the project's most valuable data source. Without the openness and freedom encouraged by the lack of competition and evaluation anxiety, however, we might never have discovered the full potential of teacher-research.

Despite my mantle of "authority" and the risks it implied for students, we teammates, Lynn and Francie included, worked together toward a common goal—building the best program we could to help basic writers develop. Notice in the sequence below how secure the TAs seem to feel: Even when Francie asks *in my presence* whether Lynn has done all the readings, Lynn assumes (correctly) that the question is not a trap and exposes her lack of compliance with assignments for the course. The risk Lynn takes is warranted only because she is right in assuming that both Francie's and my behavior are less evaluation- than learning-oriented. Though Francie is her competitor and I determine her grade, Lynn apparently trusts we are not trying to judge her negatively but are looking for new methods of helping students learn.

Marie: I'd like advice on improving tutor training for next year.

Lynn: The most helpful thing I did in your course was writing everyday about the students in my notebook—aside from what I wrote in their folders. I wrote pages and pages and pages: "Today Timothy came in, and he did this and he did that. *And this is what I think it means.*"

It was *great!* I learned so much. It helped me learn how to teach. A wonderful help! [Voice subsiding again] It's a lot of work, however.

Marie: Maybe I should try to give tutors some scheduled time to do that kind of writing. Maybe we could shift to four groups of five students instead of five groups of four.

Lynn: [excited] If they wrote about students all semester long, they could do case studies as part of the course. Oh, I think it's a *wonderful* idea!

Francie: I do too, but you're going to have to let something else go because it would be more work than anyone could do. [To Lynn] Were you able to do all the readings?

Lynn: No! I didn't do all the reading because I was very involved in keeping all these records for the case studies. I thought they were more important.

Francie: I'm not putting you on the spot, Marie, but something would have to give.

Lynn was not the only TA using writing to teach herself to teach.

Through these discussions the functions writing served in tutor learning became clear, with exploratory and observational writing assuming important roles and influencing the assignments I would give the following year:

Arthur [who had come in late]: One thing that would help is separating the reading [response] journal from the writing in which we study students. Some of it needs to be kept as records of the teaching, but the rest is to figure out what we think about what we read.

Fran: Thinkwriting!

Marie: Discovery writing.

Arthur: I read a lot in people's journals that was not good for records and stuff in the records that should have been in the private journals.

Lynn: I didn't put any personal reactions to students in the records because students have access to them.

Marie: Maybe it would be better not to keep the records in students' writing folders from now on.

Such feedback, conflict resolution, and negotiated planning led to other changes in the research process and in the structure and emphasis of the following year's course:

Kate: I think it would take some pressure off by not talking about writing [the research] up. Instead just say, "This is to help you keep track of students' progress." That's what it really was for.

Caroline: I disagree. I don't think Marie should wait until the course is over to encourage TAs to publish. In my [other graduate] classes, I never felt like I knew quite what was going on in the field, but this class made me feel like I was contributing something new. Not talking about publication at first is great, but later saying, "Hey, you could publish this if you work on it a little"—that's a really important motivator. It was really important to me.

Francie: Yeah. Toward the end of the semester you can point out ideas that just jump out at you because they're so good, and then encourage the tutors to publish.

Caroline: It might be quite a surprise to find that you could write it up for something. That makes sense to me—not trying to get things to happen too fast.

Marie: I guess I did talk a lot about publishing, but you had such incredible evidence. I mean, I was learning more from reading your notes than from reading published research.

My early acceptance of these master's level students as colleagues in research (and their ability to fulfill that role for me) apparently produced anxiety for some, for none had any experience with educational research. Soon, however, they began to see themselves as I saw them—as professionals basing decisions on carefully collected and considered evidence:

Lynn: I didn't know why you thought our findings were so remarkable until Fran and I presented our stuff at the developmental writing conference, and I'm telling you [voice rising], we were the only people talking about anything like this! That's what finally convinced me it's publishable stuff.

Marie: Several of you got published, and [nodding] you two got reprinted!

Francie: If [next year's tutors] keep their casework up, they shouldn't have any trouble writing up their results.

Informed by this discussion, the team helped me revise the research report assignments for the following year. The goal was to improve my training of tutors, thereby improving instruction basic writers would receive:

Marie: If four groups of five were scheduled instead of five groups of four . . . they'd have more time for the casework. You keep saying slightly larger groups work better anyway . . .

Tutors: Yeah!
That'd be good.

Marie: Maybe I should have several short researchy papers due every once in a while—so they'd could pull findings together a little at a time.

Tutors: Sure.
Yeah. That's a good idea.

Marie: What's reasonable to assign? If we made schedule changes, they'd have two [working] hours out of ten for the records, so the analysis and writing would be all they had to do for the course . . .

Tutors: Yeah.
Fine.

Marie: Do you think I should ask them for three shorter papers? One at midterm, one a few weeks later, and one at final time? Then they could build on each other.

Tutors: Sure.
That sounds fine.

Fran: I think you should split it in thirds. Then they can use the first two as drafts for the final one.

Arthur: Yeah, they might get something out of that.

Marie: Okay, good idea! And on the drafts I could give suggestions on how to tighten and confirm the analysis.

These excerpts illustrate the six patterns that characterized research-team interactions. They also support other research which suggests that women's interactions tend to be rooted in emotional openness and reciprocity (Ferguson, 1984; Miller, 1976; Pearson, 1985), that women are more cooperative than competitive (Ferguson, 1984; Gilligan, 1982; Lever, 1976; Miller, 1976; Pearson, 1985; Sassen, 1980), that women generally prefer helping others to self-enhancement at others' expense (Ferguson, 1984; Miller, 1976; Sassen, 1980), that women are more reluctant than men to be judgmental (Gilligan, 1982), and that women engage productively in honest but respectful conflict (Ferguson, 1984; Miller, 1976; Pearson, 1985).

These transcripts show what Miller (1976) calls "productive conflict"—conflict which benefits all participants rather than producing a single winner. Team success is enhanced by the women's "affiliative" habits (Gilligan, 1982; Miller, 1976) which lead to honest but supportive criticism (Miller, 1976; Pearson, 1985) and help teammates deal with negative feelings in supportive but direct ways (Miller, 1976; Pearson, 1985). A carefully honored commitment to protecting each other's self-esteem creates an environment in which these teammates feel safe exposing weaknesses, ask unselfconsciously for help in order to improve their work, and give each other generous support, all traits Miller (1976) found typical of women involved with learning. Cooperation subordinates self-advancement to the good of the group (Ferguson, 1984; Gilligan, 1982; Kohn, 1986; Miller, 1976; Sassen, 1980). It also improves the help TAs give learners in their care (Miller, 1976).

Observations and tapes of the five teams also lend support to Gilligan's (1982) and Ferguson's (1984) findings that women tend toward inclusive, lateral networks of relationship rather than toward more typically male hierarchies of power. They show women sustaining these networks by nonaggressive verbal conflict-resolution (Ferguson, 1984; see also Amidjaja & Vinacke, 1965; Vinacke, 1959) rather than by adopting a competitive (and exclusive) win-lose principle (see also Uesugi & Vinacke, 1963). Gilligan concludes that women's interactions are motivated by a morality of responsibility rather than by a more typically male ethic of individual rights and that women value relationship and connectedness over individual achievement. The interactions of these five largely female teams lend support to her conclusion.

I am not alone in my view of how the five teams operated. Many other teammates came to similar conclusions. Most women openly welcomed what one called the "sanctuary" atmosphere, stating that it was rare in academia: One wrote SANCTUARY in bold letters on a sign and hung it on the center door, and several wrote letters and/or poems expressing gratitude for the supportive learning atmosphere of the class. Apparently only the women had experienced such interactions before, however, for several men expressed surprise at my "unfamiliar" approach. The next two sections of this essay present one male and one female perspective showing that similar interactions characterized later teams: In both cases these students, Carey and Benyam, confirm and elaborate the findings I've offered here.

Team IV—From a Male Perspective

Arthur was but one of several males who participated on the teams; exactly three years later Benyam, a poet, joined Team IV. A bilingual Ethiopian of thirty, Benyam had lived in the United States or Europe since the age of six and had received an entirely English-language education. After settling in the United States during his early teens, Benyam completed high school and college before taking an M.A. in poetry writing from Brown University. He became interested in the CTC program and applied to tutor in it while working on a second master's in applied linguistics.

As one of five male team members during the five-year project, Benyam's multicultural/multilingual background and reflective bent brought many valuable insights to his team's analysis. Also, as a male who was unaware of my study of gender and communication, he offered an ideal perspective against which to check my preliminary analysis. When he wandered between semesters into the office where I was drafting this essay, I at once inquired about his perceptions of Team IV. I refrained for some time, however, from bringing up the gender issue. I didn't want to influence the comments Benyam made.

To my surprise, Benyam had thought deeply about the issues I'd been studying. Like Arthur, he saw his team as different from groups he'd known before—in "openness," "equality," the way "everybody was a leader," and "evaluation approach":

Benyam: [The team] was different in that everything was out in the open and everybody was a leader. The participation was very equal because there was no fear of evaluation attached to responses we gave each other, including those we gave you. In fact, the equality started with your coming to our level.

Benyam said his teammates gradually grew confident, cooperative, and willing to take risks to achieve a common goal. And because such participation was voluntary, the team differed from another group in which an employer had tried unsuccessfully to mandate "equality" from above:

So we became equal, and sources for each other, and the goal was to produce something of value based on everybody's input. Each had to be open to everybody else as well as contributing all we could individually.

That's the cooperative environment we sought, which made us different from other groups. Once another employer insisted a group I was in participate as equals, but it didn't happen in practice.

Competition was missing, said Benyam, but the team "challenged" each other to be open and trusting, take risks and give support, and "help" each other feel "secure" enough to learn:

> I'm not talking about *competition* but about *challenges* to resistances we felt against being judged. In most groups fear of evaluation inhibits learning by making us hide our ignorance, and at first that happened in this group too. So the challenge was not competition but to learn to help someone feel comfortable revealing themselves so they could learn from experience—because that kind of activity entails admitting your ignorance.

Benyam saw his team as "emotional," "open," "emergent," and "anticipatory," a view consistent with my observations of teams:

> It was intense, happy, energetic, emotional at times. And there was openness of interactions. It was anticipatory too. We were always waiting for the meeting to happen, and we tried to be as open as possible, to set aside the preparation we had done, so that spontaneously produced things—like the products of interactions, inspirations, problems—could be recognized and built upon. These became challenges and opportunities for learning.

In short, he said, course structure was different from that of other courses. Instead of being determined by a preset structure imposed by the content, much learning emerged from teammates' interaction with new material and from its connections with their past experience. Benyam also said he felt rewarded by Team IV's willingness to deal openly with feelings:

> Another difference is that in this approach transfer of content relied on individual reactions to the content as well as on its objective presentation. And since it involved us emotionally, the content became more involving. This made it much more meaningful and easier to learn.

Benyam saw other benefits in the openness: It led to learning that was lateral, holistic, and participatory:

> The group was a haven for expressiveness, but the purpose of expressing feelings was not only communication. Its other goal was presentation, or *modeling*, of how we learned. Our task was to observe what went on in others so we could learn how people think, feel, and especially learn. In

that environment, people could expose their feelings, so others could observe and respond honestly without feeling they were attacking or being attacked by anyone. We felt secure. If someone expressed a feeling against us, we didn't take it personally but saw it as something to observe and learn from.

Because instruction was organized in nonhierarchical ways, students became teachers of each other, independently providing experiences they—and I—could learn from:

> The openness set up a metacommunication for us to learn from in place of the typical "Let me tell you what I know" you usually get from teachers. For example, I felt threatened by experienced tutors from previous years, but I was able to express my fears about teaching—not for the purpose of *communicating* them but so afterwards I could see them as others did, could *get distance* on my anxiety, and *learn* from it. I knew that afterwards I would feel like the rest of the group had felt when they looked at the feelings I'd exposed.

Benyam saw benefits in the more lateral, interactive organization that let students share control of learning, and he confirmed what I had noticed—that such sharing led to emergent learnings unlikely to occur through top-down teaching alone.

> Exposing myself this way felt safe, and there were long-term rewards that made me do it more. I learned things that worked for me beyond that particular group. I learned that I could learn *by myself*, for example. So it's different from an authoritarian environment where somebody else decides what I have to learn. In this group I learned that I can motivate myself. In other groups you're usually led, in very concrete ways, and revealing incidents that emerge, when welcome, are secondary to planned instruction. This group balanced planned content with incidental learning.

Benyam was describing the kind of atmosphere I had tried to create, and his words confirmed my analysis of how the teacher-research teams functioned. After seeing that his perceptions were close to mine, I asked if he thought differences between this group and others might be gender-related. Benyam said he'd suspected a connection from the start when he was first exposed to the unfamiliar interactive patterns:

> Considering differences I've observed in how men and women behave, our group had a strongly "feminine"[2] way of interacting. And this is not

---

[2] In editing transcripts, I have preserved speakers' diction wherever possible, even when there is a chance their intentions will be obscured by connotations of which they are apparently unaware.

the first time I've brushed up against this masculine/feminine question in my thinking about that group. It's something I thought about from the beginning when asking myself, "What is going on?" and "How is this group different from groups I've been in before?"

Benyam saw his team as "feminine" in content as well as in process:

> So far I've talked only about our interactions, but the group was also "feminine" in the content we built—both from our experience and by studying our students. And the methods that uncovered this material were different from what I'd been used to. By that I mean the course content was produced *together*, from shared research or experience.

The "feminine" aspect also showed up in the supportive atmosphere.

> Here's where the feminine shows up again: In our emphasis on an unthreatening environment, we focus on a feminine principle—a safe and supportive setting where risk-taking leads to learning. (Many people have drawn analogies between the feminine principle and a vessel or container, and our work fits that metaphor in its emphasis on the *environments* in which learning take place.) But its feminine nature also shows up in the *content* of that learning because in part it's the drives and motivations of the people in the environment. By dealing with their feelings and personal motivations, we help each other find an internal driving force to learn.

Benyam's experience in a women's supportive, open-ended learning environment is consistent with Miller's (1976) contention that women may know how to nurture learning in ways that men do not because "change and growth are intimately part of women's lives in a way in which they are not for men" (p. 56). It is consistent with Nancy Chodorow's (1978) conclusion that many typically female traits develop from the traditional women's work raising children. And it supports Gilligan's (1982) assertion that women's reluctance to judge others harshly is rooted in their commitment to inclusive networks of relationship rather than in a more typically male drive for individual achievement, particularly if achievement must be gained at others' expense. Benyam echoes female perspectives documented by Ferguson (1984), Miller (1976), Friedan (1981), and Pearson (1985), all of whom suggest that men can learn much from women's ways of interacting; for though he found them initially unfamiliar, Benyam saw "feminine" interactive strategies as valuable alternatives for men:

> As the only male, I learned that it's not important whether you're a man or woman because the "feminine"/"masculine" aspects of learning are available to anyone. What's "feminine" or "masculine" is the way

of interacting and the method of generating and transferring content and information.

Benyam's words support my analysis of how teams worked co-equally, for through his team experience and his research on the twenty-odd tutorial groups he had taught, he had became convinced that

1. students in a "feminine environment" take more responsibility for learning and
2. they therefore begin to feel "equal" to their teachers.

That my own data confirm this view can be seen in the case of Lynn, the TA who openly ignored assignments to do unassigned writing of her own because she saw learning (rather than pleasing a teacher for a grade) as the goal of the course. Benyam explained how nonhierarchic interactions fostered growing independence in learners:

> The sense of equality comes from letting me be responsible for my learning, for in doing so I become equal with the teacher. The teacher remains the teacher, so it's not quite true equality, but once I go inward and get in touch with my own motivation instead of looking to an authority to tell me what I should learn, equality and hierarchy *as issues* disappear. Then whether I'm technically *equal* or not becomes irrelevant, for equality is not an issue when I control my learning.
>
> So you see, there's also *unlearning* that must take place: Inequality is perceived to the extent that we bring a hierarchical perspective to relationships, but when that perspective changes, the equality/inequality issue vanishes.

In the nonhierarchical "security" of his "strongly feminine" group, Benyam "unlearned" past perceptions of inequality and freed himself to adopt emotionally risky "feminine" ways of interacting:

> An example of not feeling equal was the baggage I brought to our group as a male. Being foreign was also part of the baggage. Those were two of my insecurities. Being black was the third. But I overcame them in that safe atmosphere.
>
> For example, I responded emotionally to something a woman wrote about a piece I'd written. Part of it showed admiration for my writing, but she also took liberties, making false assumptions about my African background. That was the first time I ever gave someone freedom to be expressive even though she was wrong. It was the first time I was able to take a negative expression as it was *intended* instead of taking it personally.

In a protected environment Benyam grew aware of interactive alternatives he had never chosen before, and because he was feeling less unequal than he had in the past, he was able to take the kind of risk that leads to learning:

> What saved me from responding irrationally was that the supportive environment helped me get *above* my feelings and see that they were natural. I asked, "What can I do with this comment?" and realized I had a choice: I could judge her and say "No! You're wrong!" or respond supportively. So I decided to respond to her enthusiasm for my writing rather than to her erroneous projections about my past.

By deciding to comment first on strengths in his teammate's response to his writing instead of attacking her ignorance or insensitivity, Benyam shifted from negative to more balanced evaluation approaches which were more protective of his teammate's self-esteem. By taking a risk (exposing himself further, despite her insensitivity), he turned a potentially hostile exchange into a learning experience for himself, the woman concerned, and others in the group. What he learned was to shift the focus and sequence of his evaluative response to protect the supportive atmosphere necessary for her to continue the risk-taking and collaborate in extending the learning opportunity he'd begun.

Marie: Are you saying this new kind of interacting became possible for you *because* of the supportive environment?

Benyam: Yeah. In that nonjudgmental atmosphere I was able to separate my preoccupation with her errors from that which was genuine and positive in her self-expression. Actually, what I learned was to address these issues *in a different sequence*. First I looked for the overall positive intention of her response and *accepted* it. Then I responded to the negative. To address her errors, I had to expose myself again, but *because I did*, her error resulted in a double learning situation which applied to us both and effectively caused her error to vanish: It no longer existed except in memory and in my understanding of what happened in our exchange.

Taking risks in a protected environment, Benyam experienced the kinds of rewards many women say they regularly get from women's groups. These motivated him to continue learning unfamiliar patterns of interaction that he referred to nonjudgmentally as "feminine":

> This is the kind of learning that the feminine environment made possible, that the feminine way of interacting allowed us to learn. And this was one of the first steps I took in changing my way of interacting.

Benyam's words supported my own analysis of gender-related differences. So did an interview with Carey, a female member of Team V. Though this essay is too short to present interactions from all five teams, Cary's testimony is revealing; for as my research assistant she had transcribed tapes from earlier teams and was therefore familiar with part of the data on which my analysis is based.

Team V: The Problems of Maintaining "Women's Ways" in the Face of a Hierarchy

Though Carey's experience on the fifth teacher-research team was similar to Benyam's on Team IV, she had a less positive experience than his when adapting to a cross-gender interactive milieu which did not encourage teamwork. Her experience illustrates vividly how, as Alfie Kohn (1986) notes, structural competition "cannibalizes cooperation" (p. 30). Not long after Team IV dispersed at the end of school, Carey took a job teaching English as a second language to non-native speakers employed by a fast-growing Washington Beltway corporation. Working in one branch of a larger training department, she and two other ESL teachers taught classes for entry-level employees and worked individually with non-native members of management. This interview documents Carey's struggle, and that of her female colleagues, to maintain collaborative interactions within a corporate hierarchy. These women struggled against great odds because, at least in Carey's view, the rewards of collaborative "women's ways"[3] outweighed the drawbacks of competition, not only for the women themselves but for the company as well. Interestingly, however, they apparently took the struggle for granted, for according to Carey they never talked about it. Despite their silence, Carey had thought a lot about her teams' interactions and without prompting was able to speak analytically of them.

Carey's case contrasts with Benyam's in another way. When interviewed, Benyam knew nothing of my study of gender-related behavior. As my research assistant, however, Carey transcribed audiotapes of several team sessions and critiqued early drafts of this essay (with Benyam's perspective omitted).

After transcribing the Team I session excerpted here as well as several tapes from other teams, Carey offered further impressions of team interactions. Later, after reading a draft of my analysis, she again

---

[3] Like many women Carey (consciously or unconsciously) avoided referring to women's communicative patterns as "feminine," a term which has often been used in uncomplimentary ways. Instead she consistently used the terms "women's styles" and "women's ways" to refer to collaborative, supportive, nonhierarchical patterns of interaction. It is therefore Carey's language, not my own, that the title of this essay reflects.

confirmed my conclusion that the teams had adopted an open, supportive, collaborative, emergent, and non-hierarchical style. Some time later, I showed her Benyam's response and found that he'd said nothing that conflicted with her view.

After reading an early draft of the first part of this essay, Carey first volunteered her perspective on my analysis:

> Carey: I agree with what you have written because of my experiences in the corporation, in your class, and also transcribing all those tapes. The transcripts showed me so clearly how the class I took came to be, how you learned what you taught us from your students, and why you had us write logs. They also showed how the teaching process we used with our students had gradually evolved.
>
> All resulted from the collaborative findings of many people, and a good example is how you learned to assign logs. I hadn't realized it before, but there it was on the tapes! The TAs taught themselves and then taught you and you taught me!

The corporation was different from the female working groups Carey had known. Like Benyam she found negative evaluation and individual competition distinctive to the hierarchy and found that, by contrast, collaboration and balanced, sequenced evaluation were strategies women tend to rely on when helping students learn. Carey and her colleagues had tried to maintain women's values and interactive patterns within the hierarchy.

> I see examples of what you're writing about where I'm employed. Three professional women, in a corporation, are forced to integrate women's styles with very different corporate rules. This corporation emphasizes only negative aspects of performance, but we female teachers have been used to stressing the positive first. Our emphasis has always been on what students do right—to help students build on what they do well instead of discouraging them. In addition, we've all been used to using collaborative methods: As long as it's successful, who cares whose idea it is! The point is not who owns an idea, but working together to help students.

Like Benyam, Carey said balanced, sequenced evaluation had characterized the women's groups she'd known; and as on the teacher-research teams, a common goal of helping everyone succeed replaced win/lose competition in female working groups. In the company at large, by contrast, negative evaluation and pressure for individual achievement inhibited workers' ability to reach company goals, a finding supported by numerous studies comparing competition with cooperation (see Kohn, 1986, for a synthesis of related research):

My job is to teach employees, and if I do well, they will be better employees and the company will benefit. When I share with experienced colleagues, my ability is increased, but when rewards come only for individual achievement, workers stop emphasizing the goal and focus on themselves. Unfortunately, emphasizing negatives and pushing individual achievement also threatens to eliminate our ability to collaborate. It hasn't destroyed mine yet, but I've seen others lose sight of the goal that the company do well.

Carey's response to her company's highly competitive style contrasted with male teammates' feelings about the female-led teams: While the men welcomed benefits from the collaborative interactions they were learning, Carey experienced a loss of contentment and productivity. Her words contrast with Benyam's earlier assertion that learning to rely on peers led to greater confidence in himself. Carey's experience in the company was the opposite, she said. Instead of feeling individually empowered by collaboration, Carey found her success limited by the pressure to work alone:

The effect on the individual—on me—is to realize that all I have left is me and my own resources. I lose access to the experience of all the other women in my department.

Reading my analysis helped Carey explain bad feelings resulting from the company's emphasis on negative evaluation.

Lately I've wondered why I strongly dislike so much about my job when I *love* teaching and *know* I'm good at it! But reading this made it clear: It's the *policies* I hate—like being evaluated only on individual achievement and emphasizing the negative.

I was surprised when in a training seminar it was stated that evaluations are "always unpleasant"! In six years of teaching I'd never found giving or getting them distasteful. Then two weeks ago I got my first corporate evaluation, and it was indeed an unpleasant experience. They were told to include as many negative comments as positive, and no new employees—like me—were to be rated "outstanding."

Regardless how good or bad we were, we all got the same score— the lowest we could get and still qualify for a raise. So even while they were begging me to go full time, I got what I consider a bad evaluation. This is very different from my experiences with women.

Despite company pressures limiting their success, Carey's colleagues struggled to maintain a collaborative approach:

Time is a problem, but though we've never talked about it, we work hard to ignore the pressures for individual achievement. For example, we were ordered to give specific sections of a seminar and told our evaluations would reflect our individual success. Now, what we've done in cases like this is collaborate as much as we can, fully realizing we'll get no credit for helping each other do well.

One thing that strikes me about Carey's experience is that though she and her colleagues collaborated to maintain their interactive work, they never explicitly talked about doing it. When the issue arose in my paper, however, Carey lamented losing support for the work she did, said she felt stress from the competitive policies, and observed that women friends in the corporation also suffered from pressures to abandon "women's ways."

> When women enter corporate environments after working mostly with women, we have to adjust to high stress on individual performance. It's not easy, and this may explain why so many successful women have had so much trouble helping other women—they felt forced to reject women's ways in order to succeed.

Like Benyam, Carey saw less competition and more learning-oriented risk-taking on female than on male-led teams:

> So what you say in this essay, Marie, is that women *are* team players, and my experience confirms the collaboration you write about. Successful women teachers share their methods a lot, depending on each other to solve classroom problems. But in my corporation there is very little sharing. I sometimes hear of successes, but *nobody* talks about *failures*. It would make them too vulnerable on performance evaluations.

Carey saw verbal commitments to teamwork imposed from above, but like Benyam said that in practice, workers did not take them seriously:

> The company emphasizes verbally that you're supposed to be team playing, but because of the evaluations, everything you do is for yourself— it's just that you do it under the *guise* of team playing.

Apparently the corporate competition Carey observed was fueled by a hierarchically conditioned principle of *exclusion* which made employees see themselves in vulnerable win/lose situations. By contrast, an *inclusive* assumption of universal potential convinces many women like Carey to help everyone succeed.

> This is different from my experience of how women work together because in our minds, at least, we aren't so self-serving. On the [teacher-

research] team, we emphasized helping students write better, but an indirect result was making me a better teacher. Students benefitted, but the school and I did too.

Competition, Carey concluded, was a primary difference between corporate and women's teams. Rejecting a common deficiency theory which attributes inadequacy to corporate women who choose not to compete, Carey defended such behavior as a strength from which companies could benefit. Her experience confirms views of many feminists who have studied women in corporations (for review of this literature as it relates to this issue, see Ferguson, 1984):

> I was impressed, in transcribing your research tapes, at how well women on those teams functioned as team players, at how they worked without the competition that permeates my corporation. They were in direct contrast to a book called *Games Mother Never Taught Us* which says that women are not taught to be team players and that's why they have problems in corporate settings. What I'm saying is that women *are* team players who *can* work together, and your transcripts of these teams give evidence for that.

Later, after reading a transcript of Benyam's comments, Carey "agreed strongly" with his conclusions, particularly those related to competition, vulnerability, the role of the affective environment, the importance of *helping all succeed* as a goal, and the counterproductive effects of harsh evaluation. In response, she elaborated her view of the role of negative evaluation in learning and in reducing her colleagues' ability to achieve the company's goals, thus supporting Kohn's (1986) conclusions about the drawbacks of competition:

> What Benyam says confirms what I am also saying—that women's ways reduce anxiety about evaluation and make people more secure learning. As a woman I experienced these differences from the other side and saw that, at least in my corporation, the emphasis on negative evaluation and individual achievement threatened women's ability to collaborate for *the company's good*.

The women's groups Carey had experienced and the transcripts she had studied revealed a learning-oriented goal, a typically female approach to learning that the men in her company did not know, but which men on the research teams came to value after experiencing their rewards firsthand:

> So, when I read your draft, Marie, this was my response: You're talking

about team playing. That's what this chapter is about. These women, and an occasional man, are truly collaborating, but without the *competition* I see in the corporation. And the interesting thing to me is that the women know how to do it, while both of the men you quote say they've never done this before. Even so, both men are willing to learn the women's ways because they find they benefit personally and professionally.

Carey's conclusions were broader than mine, for I lacked her corporate perspective, but her descriptions were consistent with some of my observations in academia. (For example, a former female professor of mine, on being granted tenure, wrote to apologize for maintaining a distant professional role for several years and to offer the support and friendship she had wanted to offer all along. Having watched numbers of talented female colleagues fail to earn tenure, she said, she felt obliged to postpone offering friendship and support to students she cared about until after she herself had passed the tenure hurdle.) Carey stressed the very traits of hierarchies that had made me set up, in two universities, supportive learning/working groups that function in "women's ways." Her words support the conclusions of a number of theorists (Ferguson, 1984; Gilligan, 1982; Kanter, 1975; Miller, 1976; and Sassen, 1980) who note how women's approaches to learning and their definitions of success are shaped by the value they place on networks of relationship. Drawing on Gilligan, Kathy Ferguson (1984) summarizes this polarity between the values she and Gilligan find to be typical of most women and men:

> The differences between the two worlds can be summarized . . . in terms of an identity of connection and an ethic of responsibility versus an identity of separation and an ethic of rights. (p. 159)

Pressures Placed on Women's Ways by a Hierarchy

Carey found that women's ways were hard to maintain in a hierarchy because evaluation rewarded only individual achievement. But hierarchical pressures against women's ways come not only from above. In a hierarchy they can also intrude from below. Moreover, women don't always follow their own interactive paradigm. My students didn't follow women's ways perfectly; nor, I admit, did I. If Carey found collaborating difficult because of corporate competition, the TAs and I faced similar challenges in academia. Not only was evaluation pressure on students strong at evaluation time (just as one might predict from Carey's and

Benyam's analyses), on several occasions students susceptible to those pressures also tried to put pressure on me.

To reduce the pressure my students felt I followed a practice common in writing classes—giving one grade at the end of the term and relying on formative evaluation to guide students during the term. Once each semester, however, my position required that I shift from formative to summative evaluation, from helping students develop potential to judging how well they had done so. Though the grades and recommendations I wrote were based on the formative critiques I'd given, two TAs seemed taken aback at this shift in focus and angrily withdrew support from me and from their teams. After this happened, I also felt pressure at having my nonhierarchical work evaluated by a hierarchy unattended to women's ways.

For example, when a woman got a lower grade than she expected, she stopped contributing at staff meetings, which continued throughout the year, making our second semester's work less pleasant and less productive. The same TA later tried (but failed) to challenge her grade, though she used the opportunity to attack my competence. In another case a diffident young man who had failed to receive an assistantship took the training course and an internship to gain teaching experience and confidence. When a faculty team of which I was a member agreed for the second year not to hire this person to teach in our freshman program, his teammates came to warn me of vindictive rumors he had spread.

Apparently these students failed to realize my support of their learning had been rooted not in personal loyalty but in a sense of responsibility for *all* the learners in my care, responsibility that commited me to hiring the best teachers available and to rewarding only outstanding progress with outstanding grades. In retrospect, I now can see that these not-very-confident teachers, who'd improved considerably in the absence of harsh negative criticism, might have felt betrayed by receiving less than outstanding grades. I can also see how this false expectation, naive from my perspective, could have led to later hostility. The hostility they felt seems to indicate a "convert effect" whereby people assume with intensity new feelings or beliefs the opposite of those they have previously held. The intensity of these students' reaction to evaluation also seems to be related inversely to their developing sense of potential, a common result of the kind of learning supported by women's ways. Whatever the causes, however, these hostile incidents taught me to devote more attention, in the tutor-training course, to clarifying for future students the roles of formative and summative evaluation. I did so in part to make clearer my expectations of TAs, in part to help them avoid similar misunderstandings with their own students.

In short, my ability to create a sanctuary where women's ways could prosper was weakened by behavior mandated by my assigned position in the hierarchy and by my failure to anticipate the effects it would have on students. Though in subsequent semesters I successfully prepared TAs for the shift to grades, these events showed me some of the problems of hierarchies as learning contexts, for it is not only at grading time that evaluation intrudes.

In addition to disrupting collaboration after the end of first semester, evaluation anxiety caused noticeable end-of-term regression in two otherwise productive teams. The pattern by which teams typically developed is significant here. Early each semester I worked to establish a protective atmosphere in which the risk-taking that leads to learning could take place. As each term progressed and trust levels grew, teammates gradually set aside what Benyam called their "perceptions of inequality" to interact more as equals and to grow more independent of me. Twice at the end of the term, however, slight regressions occurred when one or two less confident TAs began competing with others, making team collaboration somewhat superficial and tense.

The dilemma of grades was one I had struggled with for years after feeling their negative as well as positive effects. I had felt ambivalence as a student and a teacher when I realized they brought negative as well as positive results, but I'd never thought to question the necessity of their role until experiences like these helped me recognize the relationship between control and ownership of learning in hierarchies.

Before incorporating women's ways deliberately into my teaching, I had invested less energy in formative evaluation and in implementing the assumption that everyone can grow and learn. In those days I taught more as my own teachers had, uncritically accepting traditional assumptions about learning and judging product quality without balancing that concern with attention to production processes. Students rarely misunderstood my familiar, traditional grading. Nor did any grow hostile when they failed to do well. It was almost as if weaker students *expected* to get bad grades. Certainly for many years I expected them to.

More recently, however, weak students in my classes regularly show dramatic growth, and the expectations I now communicate reflect this change or the two weak tutors who became hostile would not have felt betrayed. But even dramatic progress and the motivation it produces do not automatically deserve strong recommendations or grades. Freshman writers, for example, no matter how they improve, deserve continued help in learning to write until they are able to succeed on their own with university assignments. At the graduate level even stricter standards are appropriate, for only very capable teachers should be tapped to teach the writing courses most freshman need. To help my graduate students gain critical distance on their teaching so they will not feel betrayed by well-deserved but mediocre grades, I have therefore begun, several times a semester, to have them draft thorough summative critiques of their teaching and learning to date. These self-evaluations allow them to set their own goals for improvement and help them develop realistic expectations for the grades they eventually receive. Placing responsibility on students in this way is one strategy I've developed through trial and error for protecting women's ways of supportive evaluation within hierarchical bounds.

It happens occasionally that some women and men, who say they might otherwise prefer using women's ways, express the conviction that in a dog-eat-dog world, women's ways are unrealistic because they leave those who don't compete vulnerable in the face of hierarchy. Of course, one might reasonably argue, competition leaves folks vulnerable too (and widespread anxiety about nuclear war would seem to support this view). I don't discount the validity of the objection, for it takes only one dissenter to threaten the sanctuary atmosphere on which noncompetitive teamwork depends. In fact, I have experienced my share of evaluation anxiety because of my efforts to offer learners the benefits of women's ways. To make matters more difficult, the women I've studied (including Carey and myself) have lacked reliable strategies for protecting women's ways from competition. Let me give two examples from my experience.

I learned a lesson from incidents occurring on two teams and from noting how my responses affected them differently. In each case, a woman, who collaborated well into spring semester, abandoned the team's ground rules by which she had operated up to that point. The first, a beginning poet, whose considerable talent I had encouraged, grew hostile when I backed away from a friendship she began to flaunt, an action that threatened the trust and equality her team had pains-takingly built. Whereas all fall this woman rejoiced in the team approach, writing poems to celebrate an awakening she experienced in my class, in April staff meetings she sat rigid, stonewalling all discussion, making group interactions uncomfortably strained.

The sanctuary quickly vanished as we teammates errected barriers, reducing trust and risk-taking in that hostile atmosphere. By the end of spring semester teammates were interacting just enough to complete the work for which each felt accountable. This team's reduced effec-tiveness was surely caused in part by my unprepared response to the poet's hostility, for when our easy and trusting interactions suddenly broke down, I retreated to a more familiar (i.e., authoritarian) administrative stance by calling fewer staff meetings and seeking less input from the group.

The experience, though unfortunate, was instructive. It forced me to develop strategies to protect teamwork in the event competition again threatened the sanctuary on which women's ways depend. When another TA defected from Team IV (once again in the spring), what I'd learned from my work with the poet led to positive results. This time instead of retreating from a student-led power struggle, I worked harder to buttress collaboration by reinforcing the positive habits of the team and by demonstrating my own willingness to continue taking risks. This time, apparently taking their cue for how to respond from me, Team IV closed ranks to compensate for the threat to their success. In fact, this group went on to complete a second course together, a course in which we continued our collaborative research.

In both cases teams felt vulnerable when teammates seeking control tried to change team ground rules single-handedly. I lost the competition with the poet by participating in it. In the latter case, however, I acted on my preference for women's ways by shoring up the "sanctuary" and continuing to take risks. I thus gave Team IV an option the poet's team had not had. They could retreat to self-protective strategies common in hierarchies or maintain nondefensive teamwork despite a member's competitiveness. Team IV, as Benyam's interview suggests, maintained women's ways.

"Women's Ways"—Are They Only *Women's* Ways?

I make no claim that only women interact in "women's ways," that those who do so do so consistently, or that men rarely do so at all. In my data, however, women's ways are distributed unevenly across genders, with women being more likely to know and use them than are men though several men in the sample picked them up easily.

To perpetuate themselves hierarchies must exclude the weak. Women's ways, by contrast, enhance an opposite result, for they create environments in which all can succeed. In universities like mine, therefore (and in corporations like Carey's), incompatible interactive paradigms co-exist. One is highly aggressive, rewarding only winners, even when winning means someone else has to lose. The other paradigm de-emphasizes success at others' expense in favor of cooperating to enhance progress for all by rewarding collaboration and mutual support. As others have noted, competitive approaches threaten such cooperation and are not only less efficient, they tend to subvert the goals for which they are pursued (Kohn, 1986). In light of these findings, universities (and other institutions as well) might increase their effectiveness by studying women's ways.

Many critics find the current dominant interactive paradigm inadequate, and this study supports their calls for change by showing how hierarchies are limited and limiting vis a vis women's ways. Friedan (1981), for one, calls for change in "the old, unequal, polarized male and female sex roles." "What's needed now, she asserts is to "transcend" those terms, to "transform the structure" of the institution itself (p. 40).

Friedan is not alone in maintaining that abandoning gender-typical interactions will improve society. Reviewing research on gender and language, Pearson (1985) concludes that communication will improve when women and men achieve interactive flexibility by developing less stereotyped repertoires of communicative skills. Miller (1976) goes further to assert that by treating women's concerns as trivial, "male-led society" may have placed itself in jeopardy, unwittingly delegating to those it keeps powerless "not humanity's 'lowest needs' but its 'highest necessities.' " As a result, says Miller, women offer society hope in the form of "emotionally connected cooperation and creativity," traits she believes "necessary for human life and growth" (pp. 25–26). Like Friedan and Pearson, Miller believes women's ways will improve institutions by providing a "new framework" that is "inevitably different" from male-led hierarchies (p. 27).

Others also see women playing active roles in change. Affirming the need for institutional restructuring and asserting that survival for all people depends on this, Georgia Sassen (1980) proposes a "new agenda" for women in organizations: "Affirming the structures and values they bring to the question of competition versus relationships and . . . reconstructing institutions according to what women know" (p. 22). Her perspective is echoed by Kathy Ferguson (1984) who calls for recognition and use of women's "subjugated knowledges" (p. 156). Rejecting the false separation between public and private life, for example, Ferguson details the contributions of emotion to rational thought. This study confirms that her assertions have important implications for learning communities.

Consistent with theorists' calls for change are assessments of popular values which signal growing readiness for change in society at large. Friedan (1981) found support for change among men as well as women, and research confirms the existence of a "significant subculture" which holds alternative values "generally accepted as positive" and consistent with a "female language style" (Pearson, 1985, p. 203). Kramer (1978) found communicative traits associated with women perceived by women and men alike as close to ideal speech. Apparently there is readiness among the public at large for securing the rewards of women's ways for all.

Kohn's (1986) book *No Contest: The Case Against Competition*, describes scholarly echoes of that readiness. Synthesizing findings from studies in fields as diverse as linguistics, psychoanalysis, cultural anthropology, business, and biology, Kohn concludes that by contrast with competition, cooperation leads to greater learning, athletic achievement, productivity, enjoyment, efficiency, and psychological health. Even in nature, the concept of survival of the fittest—often offered by advocates as evidence that competition is inevitable—occurs at the group, not the individual level, Kohn states. Like Miller, Kohn concludes from his study that the safety of society stands in jeopardy unless it abandons its competitive ways.

Though research refutes the myth that competition is rooted in human nature rather than in learned behavior, Kohn explains, hierarchies create economies of artificial scarcity that inevitably lead to structural (i.e., hierarchically-induced) competition. Eliminating competition is therefore necessary, he believes, to create an environment in which healthy, safe, and productive interactions can survive. In so saying Kohn echoes female theorists' calls for sweeping change in the terms by which institutions operate.

Addressing the practical issue of how such change might take place, Friedan (1981), Gilligan (1982), Miller (1976), Pearson (1985), Sassen (1980) and Ferguson (1984) make similar suggestions. In Ferguson's words, instead of accepting current "dominance/subordinance relations" in which "constellations of instrumental and expressive traits [are] allocated . . . by gender," we must view such traits "as complementary dimensions of all individuals, male and female." In other words, she continues, in a changed society, the "tensions between [instrumental and expressive traits] would be more effectively expressed as tensions within individuals rather than tensions between groups."

Against this backdrop of suggestions that we change institutional terms by offering men and women more flexible "repertoires of communicative skills," this study shows that such changes have begun to appear and that, in learning contexts, women's interactive approaches are both possible and worthwhile. By showing women and men adopting new interactive strategies, it records solutions emerging from conscious efforts at change. Carey shows female teachers using women's ways to achieve a corporate goal, and Benyam explains how teachers and students can, by working together, alter "dominance/subordinance relations." To support his conclusion that "perceptions of inequality" and the defensive responses they provoke are rooted in acceptance of the "hierarchical perspective," Benyam cites evidence that in a protected environment, people adopt new and emotionally risky interactive approaches by choice. As men in this study were willing and able to adopt the constellation of behaviors and attitudes Carey called "women's ways," it becomes inappropriate to see such interactions only as *women's* ways. For as Benyam concluded, people of both genders can choose how they interact once they become aware of the options available:

> I learned that it's not important whether you're a man or woman because the "feminine"/"masculine" aspects of learning are available to anyone.

Again, I make no claim that all women interact in "women's ways," that those who do so consistently, or that men rarely do so at all. Though women's ways are apparently distributed unevenly across genders, with women being more likely to know and use them than are men, interactions documented on these largely female teams show men also being empowered by the "sanctuary atmosphere" which replaced the competition with which the men said they were more familiar.

Apparently enough dissonance exists between competition and women's ways that the latter have difficulty surviving within hierarchies unless those in power sponsor them. To complicate matters, lack of experience has left women few strategies for protecting women's ways. This can be explained historically, for women have traditionally worked around the fringes of the hierarchy or (in this case) within one or two levels (Ferguson, 1984). Chances to use women's ways across levels have therefore been rare, and women are just beginning to share strategies they have developed for protecting noncompetitive ways in the face of aggressive ones. Containing competition without reverting to authoritarian approaches, for example, was absolutely critical to my work with the teacher-research teams, but my knowledge of how to do so grew slowly, and largely by trial and error, for I had no known role models for what I was trying to do.

Though I speak of sharing strategies for protecting women's ways from their more aggressive counterparts, I don't mean to suggest that women's ways should be integrated into hierarchies, for they are in direct conflict with several assumptions on which hierarchies are based. Some aspects of the dominant paradigm may not be inconsistent, however, and blending the strengths of each paradigm might lead to a useful synthesis. Successful extended interactions require attention to both task and group maintenance functions—to producing quality results and to maintenance, climate, and interpersonal skills. These have been the respective emphases of hierarchy and women's ways, and both are required for the conduct of humane and efficient activity. Fortunately, blending positive aspects of these paradigms may not be as large a task as it might at first appear, for though studies like this one dramatize problems caused by the paradigm clash, they also confirm the potential of collaborative problem-solving. In doing so they eliminate the need to rely on competitive strategies when negotiating the terms by which restructured institutions will operate, for ground rules exist for productive conflict in which no one group dominates at another's expense.

References

Amidjaja, I. M., & Vinacke, W. E. (1965). Achievement, nurturance, and competition in male and female triads. *Journal of Personality and Social Psychology, 2,* 447–451.

Chodorow, N. (1978). *The reproduction of mothering.* Berkeley: University of California Press.

Ferguson, K. (1984). *The feminist case against bureaucracy.* Philadelphia: Temple University Press.

Friedan, B. (1981). *The second stage.* New York: Summit Books.

Gilligan, C. (1982). *In a different voice: Psychological theory and women's development.* Cambridge: Harvard University Press.

Kanter, R. (1975). Women and the structure of organizations. In M. Millman (Ed.), *Another voice.* New York: Doubleday/Anchor, pp. 34–74.

Kohn, A. (1986). *No contest: The case against competition.* Boston: Houghton Mifflin.

Kramer, C. R. (1978). Men's and women's ratings of their own ideal speech. *Communication Quarterly, 26,* 2–11.

Lever, J. (1976). Sex differences in the games children play. *Social Problems, 23,* 478–487.

Miller, J. B. (1976). *Toward a new psychology of women.* Boston: Beacon Press.

Pearson, J. C. (1985). *Gender and communication.* Dubuque, IA: William C. Brown Publishers.

Sassen, G. (1980). Success anxiety in women: A constructivist interpretation of its sources and its significance. *Harvard Educational Review, 50,* 13–24.

Uesugi, T. K., & Vinacke, W. E. (1963). Strategy in a feminine game. *Sociometry, 26,* 75–88.

Vinacke, W. E. (1959). Sex roles in a three-person game. *Sociometry, 22,* 343–360.

12

Redwood Records: Principles and Profit in Women's Music

Cynthia M. Lont

George Mason University

In the last 20 years we have seen a proliferation of alternative institutions, developing out of the antiwar, antiestablishment movement of the mid-1960s. They were constructed among a system of established organizations and continued to burgeon at an enormous rate, resolved to exist without the bureaucratic authority and profit motive found in standard organizations. Formed in direct opposition to traditional profit-making business, these "worker-managed, worker-controlled, anti-profit organizations" attempted to function nonhierarchically and maintain their political and social change goals (Vocation for Social Change, 1976). Yet, in order to survive, many alternative institutions have had to modify their original goals, become more profit-oriented, or cease to exist. Often, alternative institutions faced with this problem are women-owned, women-controlled organizations. This chapter is an analysis of one such alternative institution, Redwood Records.

Redwood Records is viewed through three frames of analysis. First, Redwood Records is an example of an alternative institution. Yet unlike other alternative institutions which have stagnated or gone out of business, Records has evolved and grown. Second, due to the direction of the founder of Redwood Records, Holly Near, the creation of coalitions among various political and social change movements is highly valued within the organization. Third, the alternative institution structure of Redwood Records and its commitment to coalition building among various groups insures a tension between political/social change goals of Redwood Records and the need for profit in order to exist. What this tension insures is a dissatisfaction with Redwood Records' policies and decisions by various political and/or social groups. How Redwood has dealt with these issues and groups while continuing as an alternative institution which builds political coalitions is detailed throughout this chapter. A final analysis is presented based on descriptive data collected during a qualitative study of Redwood Records in 1984.

Method

The most effective and efficient way in which to obtain the type of necessary data for an analysis of Redwood Records was through naturalistic inquiry. Taking this approach, the researcher looks for "theoretical constructs through the systematic study of everyday life in everyday settings" (Anderson, 1981, p. 2). One looks at how tasks are accomplished, what rules govern behavior, what patterns are seen, and so forth.

Primary data were obtained through interviews with the staff of Redwood Records and interviews with participants in the women's music industry. In February 1984, I spent a week at Redwood Records to observe and inquire about the organization's day-to-day operations as well as its past experiences. With few exceptions, the staff was extremely receptive to my presence, as indicated by unexpected opportunities to observe meetings and the unveiling of a new album cover. Although busy, all members of Redwood made time to talk about their work and motivations. Since my 1984 visit, I have maintained ongoing contact with the staff. Each piece I have written concerning Redwood has been previewed by the entire staff. I have carefully considered all their written and oral comments.

Secondary data provide the foundation for the history of Redwood Records and Holly Near. This data includes press releases, newspaper and magazine articles, album covers, inserts, recordings, and state and federal documents.

Redwood Records 1973–1984

To discuss the history of Redwood Records requires an understanding of its founder, Holly Near—her music and goals. Near expresses her goals in her first album, *Hang In There* (1973), through to her most recent release, *HARP* (1985). The albums, listed in Appendix I, demonstrate the diversity of Near's political and social change goals.

Redwood Records was founded in 1973 as a support system for Holly Near and her music. Near had sought a contract with a major label and although she had found interest in her substantial following, most major recording companies were too uncomfortable with her politically motivated lyrics, especially her controversial anti-Vietnam War songs. Although Near had the popular folk madonna style of the day (long flowing hair, blue jeans, and soprano voice), she refused to give up artistic freedom and control over her work for mainstream acceptance. At one point, an executive from a major label told Near it was doubtful she could be a hit female singer because she didn't have any element of submission in her voice. With the majors uninterested and the demand for her music unfulfilled, Near and Jeff Langley, piano accompanist, co-composer, and friend, recorded *Hang In There*, the first production of Redwood Records.

While Near and Langley toured, Ann and Russell Near (Holly's parents) handled all the business operations of Redwood Records from their home in Ukiah, California. Redwood, at that point, was a part-time, family-run business with no defined organizational structure—literally, a "mom and pop" business. Profit was of little importance; rather, Near's aim was to get her political words to others. By 1974, though still meeting with major labels, Near and Langley grew impatient and recorded a second album, *Holly Near: A Live Album*. Although this album still focused on the antiwar movement, Near was becoming increasingly interested in feminism. *You Can Know All I Am*, her next album, reflected her new consciousness.

Near's message differed from other female political singers of the 1970s such as Joan Baez or Joni Mitchell. These women sang songs lamenting women's oppression; Near sang about an end to that oppression. Two examples of this difference are reflected in the following lyrics.

> I'd tell you to go find yourself another woman
> But I'd hate to pass you on.
> That'd be like passing on to a sister
> A pretty packaged bomb.
> ("Get Off Me Baby." *Holly Near: A Live Album*, 1975)

> Honey, you been lagging behind.
> The time has come for me to either call or fold.
> ("Winner Takes All." *You Can Know All I Am*, 1976)

This new musical message caught the attention of "women's music" artists and fans, the majority of whom were lesbians. These women listened and accepted this "straight" woman's songs.

Women's music is usually defined as music "for, by and about women" as well as economically controlled by women. In the United States, women's music developed as a separate industry which included its own recording labels (Olivia Records, for example), its own nation-wide distribution system (WILD—Women's Independent Labels Distributors), local concert producers, and local retail outlets (usually feminist bookstores). In fact, for many years, the women's music industry was a self-contained unit, dealing only with women's music artists who recorded on women's music record labels, which were distributed by WILD to feminist bookstores and bought, primarily, by women. Music festivals in Michigan, Illinois, and California supported new women's music talent and brought together thousands of women every year to see what one performer called "the big cheeseburgers"—Margie Adam, Meg Christian, Cris Williamson, and Holly Near (Gaynes, 1983). Although not started as a women's music recording label, Redwood Records and Holly Near soon became an important part of the women's music industry.

In 1975, Near for the first time performed with women's music artists, Cris Williamson, Lily Tomlin, and the Alice Stone Ladies Society Orchestra, in a benefit concert to save the Los Angeles Women's Building. In a tour that followed, Women on Wheels, Near worked closely with women's music artists. The tour was a political statement concerning feminism and lesbian-feminism, one of the first tours of its kind. But Near learned that this music frightened many people, especially some of her antiwar fans:

> . . . As the music moved out into the world I was surprised by the controversy that erupted as a result of this culture. The songs were often too radical for the radicals, not because they were anti-male, but simply because they weren't about men (Near, 1983).

Near found herself between two political movements, a place in which she learned to be comfortable. During the same time, she decided to change the structure of Redwood.

Evolving as an Alternative Institution

From 1976 to 1978, significant changes occurred in Redwood Records. As Redwood grew, Ann and Russell Near decided they would prefer to act in more supportive roles rather than as the main representatives of the business. Redwood needed a new organizational structure. Near, her parents, and Jeff Langley discussed various alternatives: a family business, a collective, a cooperative, or a partnership? Yet, as Near explained:

> All the while these business decisions were being made, political/historical

events were taking place of which I was a part and these events affected every decision I made (Near, 1986).

Therefore, in the spirit of feminism, Near restructured Redwood Records into an alternative institution: an all-woman, worker-run, nonhierarchical organization dedicated to social and political change. Each woman shared the stamp licking as well as the decision making. Characteristic of the alternative institutions of the 1970s was commitment to a nonhierarchical structure, an antiprofit ideology, and dedication to social or political change (Lont, 1983).

The nonhierarchical structure usually meant a lack of structure in direct opposition to traditional businesses. Unlike these businesses, alternative institutions used consensus decision making and were worker-controlled and worker-managed. Again, in opposition to traditional businesses, alternative institutions' main concern was their political and social change goals. Profit was unimportant and in fact, their antiprofit ideology assumed that all workers had the right to a decent wage for their work but whatever was left over after operational expenses should be returned to the community in the form of lower prices or as a contribution to another organization within the movement.

During Redwood's structural change to an alternative institution, Near fell in love with a woman, and her first album released under the new alternative institution structure, *Imagine My Surprise*, reflected this new emotional and political connection to the lesbian-feminist community. Dedicated to the women's community, this album was seen as Near's first "women-identified album." The lesbian politics of the album were obvious in its lyrics, its cover, and Near's discussion of her own lesbianism:

> One surprise was discovering that, for many women, lesbianism is more than "sexual preference" as it is often so narrowly defined. For me, it opened many doors . . . emotional, spiritual, cultural, and political. These new songs came through these doors (Near, 1978).

Women produced, recorded, engineered, and distributed the album, and sold it to women. Jeff Langley and Holly Near amicably ended their eleven-year partnership prior to this album. Near began to work solely with women musicians.

The change to an alternative institution brought with it many difficulties—inconsistent service, high member burnout, and slow decision making. This resulted in a debt of $75,000 by Redwood as well as internal conflict. Near, tired of working in the business aspect of Redwood, felt it drained too much energy from her music and political work. During this time, Near toured nationwide with the help of two women's music producers/distributors, Joanie Shoemaker and Jo-Lynne Worley. By January 1980, Worley and Shoemaker had convinced Near to give Redwood Records one more try but with a new structure. The three partners made most of the decisions and kept the all-woman staff but started to view Redwood as a business as well as a political/social change mechanism. This partnership resulted in a total change in organizational structure, a more commercial image for Near, and a more commercial sounding album, *Fire In The Rain*, yet a political message was woven throughout. By 1982, Redwood Records had recovered from its $75,000 debt and showed a profit. The quality of the music mix and record vinyl improved without significant increases in prices. Redwood Records was heralded as one of the few companies to survive the slump in the recording industry, "with an ease unknown to most independents in that field" (Johnson, 1983). The new partnership and structure seemed to produce good politics and a profit.

Although Redwood became more structured, other characteristics, positive and negative, of the alternative institution remained. The women who comprised the growing staff of Redwood intentionally created a work atmosphere of informality and support for one another. Near stated:

> We want work to be a positive experience. We spend a huge percentage of our lives doing it. So we (Redwood Records) try to have a concern for safety, good lighting, music in the air and celebration of birthdays (Near, 1986).

Although informal and homey, the climate of Redwood was also somewhat chaotic. All staff members were busy with business tasks. Space was cramped and upon entrance to Redwood, one was met by the ringing of phones and the movement and talk of members. As these negative aspects continued, Redwood evolved, mixing business and social change goals until it arrived to its present state. One major change included Redwood's responsibility for Holly Near. For the first 11 years, Redwood was the production-management service for Holly Near and as one of three partners, Near made decisions in all areas of Redwood. Now Redwood has become a distribution/promotions company for many other artists and is no longer the booking agent for Holly Near. In addition, Near no longer participates in the business aspect of Redwood.

> Until last year (1985), I [Near] still had a major influence over decisions—especially artistic and philosophical questions. Now I'm not even involved

in that. This feels wonderful to me. I trust and care about Redwood staff. That doesn't mean they always decide to do it like I would do it. It means they do it the way they feel is best for Redwood. That's very healthy (Near, 1986).

Near receives her percentage of the profits of Redwood as one of the three owners, plus a touring income. In the past, any money Near received from tours went back into Redwood Records. Now Redwood, like any other record company, must exist on the profits from the sales of albums.

Another change in Redwood has been its communication system. Members of Redwood found themselves under a lot of pressure due to the many albums they released. To keep up with the demands they made on themselves, they needed to modify the organizational structure. They changed some of the informal systems in order to become more focused and more efficient. Shoemaker explained:

I think in the past a lot of what we had done was processing and discussing what the problem was. Now we are into fixing it rather than talking about it (1986).

Ultimately, the staff created a management team.

The new, more efficient organizational structure of Redwood resulted in a more formal means of day-to-day communication. Members' days are structured with meeting times set days in advance and requiring as few people as necessary. Agenda items for all staff meetings are collected in advance and fall into three categories: announcements, reports, and discussion. Routing forms, memo sheets, requests for action or information are found in each staff member's mail box. A form must be filled out when shipping materials (to whom, from whom, charged to which department). A blackboard once used for the collection of meeting agenda items is now a message board—who is out and where.

These practices are normally found in traditional businesses. When asked if she felt Redwood was becoming more like a major record company, Joanie Shoemaker replied:

Yes, and that's ok. In order to do what it is we wanted to do, we had to do it more efficiently. I think women are, by their nature or by training, more efficient than men in many ways. I think it bothered us when we were not being efficient and organized (1986).

Yet decision making remains consensual, which is much different from major record companies. If consensus cannot be achieved, the staff at Redwood talks it out. Disagreement is not seen as destructive. The staff tries to talk out differences and change people's minds, but if they can't, the staff lives with the final decision. At times, a decision has to be made quickly and the partners make those decisions, then explain why staff input was not ascertained. This is done rarely because, as Shoemaker explained:

> We don't railroad a project through because the emotional energy that everyone comes to work with needs to get channeled into a positive way in order for it to come out the best it can (1986).

Making decisions without staff input in not considered positive for staff members and, therefore, not positive for Redwood.

In 1984, the majority of the seven full-time members and three partners were lesbian, white, Anglo-Saxon women, from middle-class backgrounds and ranging in age from 20–35. Four of these seven members have moved on but of the nine members of Redwood in 1986, these general demographics still hold true. Although one would assume that similar demographics would insure more cohesion within the staff, this has not held true. Near explained that early in Redwood history, the staff "was trying to run a business, define and develop a political perspective and struggle with oppression—external and internal—with varying degrees of experience. That didn't simplify things—it complicated it" (Near, 1986).

Coalition Building

In 1975, when Near worked with women's music performers, she discovered that her antiwar followers were threatened by her connection with another political group. This continued when she began working with antinuclear coalitions. Her previous audience felt they would lose her to another political group. Near felt she was connecting these groups and not "leaving" any of them. She showed them that each group had similar problems and could be of help to each other. Since this first connection between antiwar advocates and lesbian-feminists, many coalitions have been formed through the records Redwood produces and distributes. For example, Near's first two albums were aimed toward antiwar advocates. *You Can Know All I Am,* her third album connected these antiwar advocates with feminists. Her fourth album, *Imagine My Surprise,* was produced for the lesbian-feminist community but included much for the straight feminist as well. The next two albums more clearly demonstrated Redwood's desire to bring together various political and social change groups. In particular, *Speed of Light,* produced in

1982, exemplified this position, as the lyrics to a song entitled "Unity" indicates:

> One man fights the KKK
> But he hates the queers
> One woman fights for ecology
> It's equal rights she fears
> Some folks know that war is hell
> But then they put down the blind
> I think there must be a common ground
> But it's mighty hard to find
> Hang on, don't give up the ship
> Hang on, don't let the anchor slip
> We are all sailors and we're in mutiny
> The safety of this journey depends on
> Unity

Speed of Light clearly connected political movements and brought together diverse audiences. The album was followed by an antinuclear tour, BE DISARMING. Old fans (antiwar activists and lesbian-feminists) rubbed shoulders with new fans (environmentalists and anti-nuke activists) to listen to Holly Near.

This emphasis on connecting groups continued with Near's next album, *Lifeline*, in collaboration with Ronnie Gilbert. Jeff Langley joined Near and Gilbert on this album and the subsequent tour. Old Left and Weavers fans came to see Ronnie Gilbert and Near's other fans joined them.

In 1984, Near sought an international message through an album entitled *Watch Out!* Recorded with traditional folk musicians, John McCutcheon and Trapezoid, this album had clear political intent:

> When we were writing this song Ronald Reagan was sending troops and "advisors" all over the world—especially to Lebanon, Grenada, El Salvador, Nicaragua. For as long as we support systems of government that think they must control the world there will always be a "man like that" (Near, 1984).

The last album of that year, *Sing To Me A Dream*, was a cooperative effort between Inti-Illimani, a Chilean all-male ensemble, and Holly Near. On the album insert, the Redwood staff explained:

> It is not by chance that a North American is making music with a Chilean ensemble. Nor is it by accident that these seven men are performing with this one woman. It's not merely coincidence that a feminist/progressive record company in the U.S.A. is working with a Chilean cultural organi-

zation in Europe. And it was completely intentional that the fifteen-city U.S. tour by Holly Near and Inti-Illimani brought together strikingly diverse communities to share an evening dedicated to peace in the Americas (Near & Inti-Illimani, 1984).

This collaboration was a defiant political statement. It actively contradicted the assumption that people must live apart and at war when conflicts with the United States and South American countries were at their peak.

Holly Near's latest album is *HARP*, named for the first initial of each of the artists who recorded it: Holly Near, Arlo Guthrie, Ronnie Gilbert, and Pete Seeger. This live album resulted from a sold-out tour and included political and nonpolitical songs from many eras. Pete Seeger, a builder of bridges himself, stated:

> There are a lot of good people, but we have allowed ourselves to be separated from each other a little more than is necessary. And so here we are, trying to draw together an audience of these different kinds of people and see if we can't find some common ground (Near, Guthrie, Gilbert, & Seeger, 1985).

By 1985, Redwood Records no longer produced music exclusively for women. Redwood's products included albums by many performers beside Holly Near. Although owned and staffed completely by women, Redwood no longer sees itself as a purely women's music recording label. Joanie Shoemaker defines Redwood more accurately as:

> . . . a socialist, feminist, anti-imperialist company and wants its work to totally be within that context . . . and it comes from the heart and that's basically because of our structure . . . that Holly, Jo-Lynne and I make these decisions based on the world situation and economically what we can afford (Shoemaker & Worley, 1984).

New albums that elaborate the world situation include two albums by a Nicaraguan artist produced by Jackson Browne, a new album by Inti-Illimani, and two albums by Australian Judy Small. Redwood, however, has not excluded women's music. Popular and established women's music artists Linda Tillery, Mary Watkins, and Ferron continue to have their music distributed and promoted through Redwood. Ronnie Gilbert released a new album through Redwood and a new artist, Hunter Davis, will release an album in 1986 with Near, Ferron, Linda Tillery, and Teresa Trull as vocalists.

As is obvious from these various albums and tours, Redwood Records works innovatively to build political coalitions. Yet coalition building, itself, can be seen as either profit or politically motivated. From a political perspective, coalition formation builds a broader political base from which to make social change. Redwood tries through Near's music and political work to make various groups see their common problems. At the same time, with coalition work, Redwood reaches out to new audiences and creates new markets in which to sell records.

The Tension Between Profit and Politics

The tension between profit and politics is imbedded within the structure of the alternative institution. One characteristic of an alternative institution is an anti-profit attitude. This usually leads to a lack of material reserve, low wages and low job security for the employees, and dependence on the political community for its continued existence (Lont, 1983). Thousands of alternative institutions fell to these problems, many closing their doors, others returning to the hierarchical structure in order to survive. Redwood Records was among those in financial decline in the mid-1970s. Many alternative institutions, like Redwood Records, tried to find the middle ground where they could accomplish their political work and still survive as a business.

Although not completely antiprofit, the need for profit at Redwood Records does not seem to affect the political and social goals set by the Redwood staff. This doesn't mean that profit is not important to the staff of Redwood Records. The majority have worked in women's music as producers, distributors, and artist's managers for very little or no money. They came to Redwood Records with the desire to integrate their politics with their work, but for many economic stability has assumed greater importance. The newer members have very strong political ideals, yet they too understand the necessity of an economically viable organization. Suzanne Harkless, who had been at Redwood for two years, described her past experience and her reaction to the balance between politics and profit when she worked with a women's music production group which consistently lost money. When she left that organization, she sought a politically motivated women's organization not haunted by financial problems. She endorsed Redwood's willingness to lose money on an event "if it's a trade-off . . . if a production is worth doing and part of our [Redwood's] goals." She suggests that some events are "considered successful because they bring somebody new to the area and because the audience loved it and the artist loved it." She went on to note, however, that these events "have to be covered by more saleable events that do make money" (Harkless, 1984). Many women in Redwood had experience with mismanaged women's music organizations and realized the devastating and crippling effects.

Many members seek security, not huge salaries but the promise that the employing organization will continue to exist for a few years.

The desire for political purity versus the desire for profit may be perceived by some as an either/or proposition. Redwood Records seeks to find a middle ground by becoming economically solvent without losing the political value of its message. Interestingly, the individuals of the Redwood staff personally embody the dichotomy between profit and politics. Some members lean more toward profit and others lean more toward politics, most stay closer to the center. Betsy York, a former WILD distributor and National Distributor for Redwood, exemplifies one primarily interested in profit for the organization. York deals primarily with many business components of the industry and sees the political goals in Redwood Records. While many distributors talk in terms of the audience or "participants," York spoke in traditional terms of the "market," the development of the market, and increased sales. Yet York's interest in Redwood is not purely business oriented:

> I don't want to grow up and be a record distributor. I have no interest. If I wanted a career, I'd be something else. I'm in this from the women's movement. Now my business is at a point where I can use it as a tool that I've always wanted. Which is to promote the product anywhere I can because there's still a message to it as far as I'm concerned (1983).

And although the Redwood message is somewhat less explicit than in the past, to York it is enough.

On the other extreme is Amy Bank, firmly committed to Redwood Records' political goals. She came to Redwood, first and foremost, to work her politics, yet Bank could also combine the politics and profit needs. As she stated, the two components are tied. For example, a success indicator for Redwood Records, she explained, "has to do with money because money means support and then we can do some of the projects we want to do." Bank explained there were many projects that Redwood wanted to initiate but what "distinguishes between possible and not possible is usually time and money" (1984). York and Bank represent the extremes in Redwood, but most members fall somewhere in the center.

A nonprofit organization of Redwood created in 1983 reflects Redwood's direction toward the middle ground between profit and politics. Originally known as CWI (Cultural Work, Inc.), CEF (Cultural and Educational Fund) provided an organizing tool for Near's political work, giving her the opportunity to expand her political, educational, and cultural work. Two factors motivated the formation of CEF. First, Near wanted to do political work that was not always profitable. CEF can sponsor these tours and activities and do its own fund raising. Previously, Redwood sponsored these events and either absorbed the loss or spent time fund raising. Second, CEF benefited those who wanted to particularly contribute to Near's activities. This political organization gave supporters the opportunity to make tax-free contributions.

CEF does two very important things. It gives Near and Redwood the freedom to work on activities that may not be income-producing but that are political/educational work. Redwood no longer has to fear for its survival every time a politically important event needs to be funded. Second, CEF has brought together various people who all support some part of Near's political work. A listing of supporters demonstrates the coalition building that Near has accomplished over the past twelve years. Among the well known names are Ed Asner, Dennis Banks, Del Martin, Bonnie Raitt, and Alice Walker.

Discussion

Redwood Records has been viewed through three frames: as an evolving alternative institution, as a coalition builder, and finally, as an organization caught between the need for profit and the goals of political and social change. Yet Redwood Records is not an unusual case. In the late 1970s, thousands of alternative institutions became victim to their own lack of structure. Jo Freeman stated, " 'structurelessness' caused other organizational crisis" (1976), particularly in the feminist movement from which many alternative institutions had sprung. The unstructured nature of the organization and the antiprofit ideology had negative effects: inconsistent service to the community, a high turnover rate among staff members, and financial problems. Yet structurelessness brought with it many positive aspects. Because everyone made decisions together and information was imperative to decision making, communication among members was high. Since information is power, each member of the organization shared equal power.

Alternative institutions which have continued into the 1980s have retained much of their basic philosophy but have modified many practices in order to exist. Redwood is one example of an alternative institution which continued to exist by finding a middle ground between a lack of total structure and the hierarchical structure of traditional businesses.

Organizational communication researchers have noted that the quality of work life and the consideration of human consequences of organizational arrangements are as important to a system and its effectiveness as economic indicators. High absenteeism, alienation from the job, and hostility towards leaders are but a few symptoms of the dissatisfaction workers have with traditional structures. Some experts have stated that these symptoms are caused by low opportunity, low mobility, powerlessness, and tokenism, among other factors. Some companies have incorporated various programs at homes and at work to try to help the employee feel more a part of the system. Alternative institutions had taken care of many of the above problems that traditional businesses are now just dealing with through equal power among members, a leaderless structure, and personal attention to each staff member. Many traditional organizations have looked to alternative institutions for direction. At the same time, alternative institutions have looked toward traditional businesses for help with efficiency and speed of production. Yet to continue as an alternative institution, profit must be secondary to political goals.

The importance of the political and social change goals to the alternative institutions, though less radical, continues to be of prime importance to the staff members and their supporters. Food co-operatives are still dedicated to providing healthy, non-chemical, natural food for their consumers. Women's health clinics are dedicated to providing non-sexist, self-help, comfortable, holistic health care for women. Redwood is no different. The staff members still feel their goal is to provide music which will help change the political and social system. The one difference in Redwood is the inclusion of various political movements. Instead of narrowing in on one group (antiwar, feminists, lesbians, antinuclear), Redwood and Holly Near seek more universal goals which includes all these factions. In the same way that the New Right has brought together its forces to gain their demands, so too does Near try to bring together these various groups on the Left to have more impact. Coalition building, traditionally a women's task, may be imperative for the Left to gain strides, politically, culturally, and economically. One may see Near at a pro-choice rally in Washington, an environmentalist concert in Des Moines, or a Hispanic celebration in Los Angeles, yet her music and message are the same.

As stated earlier, in order to reach various factions, Redwood has watered down and widened its political message. Its less direct message may make it appeal to many groups and thus increase sales and profits for Redwood. Depending on one's perspective, this compromise of Redwood's message and political structure may be positive or negative. Lesbian separatists who were devoted to Near's *Imagine My Surprise* album felt Redwood "sold out" when it became a partnership, watered down its lesbian message, and started to work with male institutions. In order to build coalitions and expand its audience, Redwood worked with male musicians, producers, distributors, and retailers. They eliminated women-only concerts and expended energy and profit on male groups and mainstream audiences. Various articles criticized tactics which sought mainstream listenership (Kort, 1983).

Another faction that would consider Redwood's structure and music negative would be mainstream record companies. A few would like to produce, promote, and profit from Holly Near's music but would need to have her water down her music even more. Near refuses and continues to record with Redwood solely.

Somewhere between these two factions rests Redwood, one of the few alternative institutions which continues to survive and grow without completely eliminating its political/social goals. This is not to ignore the desire of Redwood to make a profit, though the profit usually ends up in another Redwood production or project. But it is this author's perspective, a hopeful one perhaps, that Redwood has chosen a positive path—one which few alternative institutions involved in political or social change goals have uncovered. Instead of dealing with the profit issue, many alternative institutions closed their doors. Others dealt with profit versus politics by taking on a traditional business structure. Redwood has found something in between. Some would say that Redwood Records has failed in its goals (Kort, 1983) but if the proof is in the end result, than Redwood Record has shown that, although not easy, the tension between politics and profit can be dealt with and juggled successfully. There are very few alternative institutions which have the staying power of Redwood Records. Fewer yet have continued with their original political goals and continued to grow. For that reason alone, the study of Redwood Records is imperative—to search out the way in which at least one organization not only makes money but is of social and political worth to the world.

References

Anderson, J. A. (1981, May). *Evaluative principles for naturalistic inquiry or: How do I know that you know what you're talking about?* Paper presented at International Communication Association Convention, Minneapolis.

Bank, A. (1984, February 10). Interview. Redwood Records, Oakland, CA.

Freeman, J. (1976, July). The tyranny of structurelessness. *MS.*, p. 76.

Gaynes, S. (1983, June 3). Interview. Ninth Annual National Women's Music Festival: Bloomington, IN.

Harkless, S. (1984, February). Interview. Redwood Records, Oakland, CA.

Johnson, H. C. (1983, September). Datelines: California Redwood Records rock rolls along. *USA Today.* p. 15.

Kort, M. (1983, July). Sisterhood is profitable: Some sing the songs and some balance the books. *Mother Jones*, pp. 39–44.

Lont, C. M. (1983, March). Alternative institutions: Model for social change. Paper presented at the Fifth International Communication and Culture Conference, Philadelphia, PA.

Near, H. (1973). *Hang in there.* Oakland, CA: Redwood Records.

Near, H. (1974). *A live album.* Oakland, CA: Redwood Records.

Near, H. (1976). *You can know all I am.* Oakland, CA: Redwood Records.

Near, H. (1978). *Imagine my surprise.* Oakland, CA: Redwood Records.

Near, H. (1982). *Speed of light.* Oakland, CA: Redwood Records.

Near, H. (1983). *Journeys.* Oakland, CA: Redwood Records.

Near, H. (1984). *Watch out!* Oakland, CA: Redwood Records.

Near, H. (1986, September). Solicited documents.

Near, H., Guthrie, A., Gilbert, R., & Seeger, P. (1985). *HARP.* Oakland, CA: Redwood Records.

Near, H., & Inti-Illimani. (1984). *Sing to me a dream.* Oakland, CA: Redwood Records.

Shoemaker, J. & Worley, J. (1984, February). Interview. Oakland, CA: Redwood Records.

Shoemaker, J. (1986, January). Oakland, CA: Redwood Records.

Vocation for Social Change. (1976). *No bosses here.* Boston, MA: Vocation for Social Change.

York, B. (1983, June 4). Interview. Ninth Annual National Women's Music Festival: Bloomington, IN.

Appendix I

Hang in There

Holly Near (1973)

Hang In There was Redwood Records, and Holly Near's first album. Produced with Jeff Langley and friends, Near's album demonstrated the historic spirit of the antiwar movement. While Near and Langley toured, the business end of Redwood Records was run by Ann and Russell Near (Holly's parents).

Holly Near: A Live Album

Holly Near (1974)

While awaiting a major label recording contract, Near, Langley, and friends recorded this album which included songs of Near's childhood as well as songs about people's changing lives. This antiwar album contains one of Near's best-known songs, "It Could Have Been Me," a tribute to international struggles for freedom.

You Can Know All I Am

Holly Near with Jeff Langley (1976)

This album clearly demonstrates a more feminist perspective on the part of Holly Near and Jeff Langley. Songs revolve around the rights of women and look at relationships between women and men.

Imagine My Surprise

Holly Near (1978)

This was the first Redwood Records album produced and recorded by women only. Meg Christian (a women's music performer) was the album's music arranger. Considered Near's first "woman-identified" album, this multiple award-winning LP presented a tribute to the power of lesbian-feminism. *Imagine My Surprise* was the first album produced under an alternative institution structure.

Fire in the Rain

Holly Near (1981)

A more mainstream album in both content and cover, this album demonstrated Near's many singing talents and styles. Although the album was still produced and recorded by women only, the organizational structure had changed.

Speed of Light

Holly Near (1982)

This LP was musically Near's most adventurous. The first album since *You Can Know All I Am* that included male musicians, this album was acceptable to various audiences.

Lifeline

Holly Near and Ronnie Gilbert (1983)

This live recording captures the personal warmth, artistic power, and electric excitement of the historic collaboration of Holly Near and Ronnie Gilbert (of the Weavers), which was prompted by the overwhelming response to their scene together in the Weavers reunion movie, "Wasn't That A Time!" These two major figures of their respective generations sing songs by Holly and by some of the finest songwriters of past and present. They are accompanied by Jeff Langley on piano and Carrie Barton on bass.

Journeys

Holly Near (1983)

This retrospective album includes 12 songs from Holly Near's first six LPs. It offers the variety of musical styles and lyrical content that is Near's trademark, and features the work of over 60 musicians. The four-color insert includes stories and photos. A few songs were rerecorded for better sound quality or updated lyrics.

Watch Out!

Holly Near (1984)

Blending complementary talents, Trapezoid and John McCutcheon join Near to produce a new, acoustic sound. Includes political and nonpolitical songs.

Sing to Me a Dream

Holly Near and Inti-Illimani (1984)

For both English and Spanish speaking listeners, this album brought together Holly Near's vocals with Inti-Illimani's instrumentation. Songs feature solos and exciting vocal combinations, backed by the unique wind and string instruments of the Chilean ensemble. This album clearly demonstrates the coalition building direction of Redwood Records and Holly Near.

HARP

Holly Near, Arlo Guthrie, Ronnie Gilbert, Pete Seeger (1985)

Live concert album from their sold-out tour. HARP blends these voices in magnificent harmony on old favorites and introduces five new songs as well. The album is a connection between old Left, new Left, antinuclear, environmentalists, feminists, and lesbian-feminists.

13

Ideology, Contradiction and Change in a Feminist Bookstore

Lynette Seccombe-Eastland

University of Delaware

With the resurgence of the women's movement in the early 1970s, women's businesses began to emerge both as an alternative work environment for women and as a means of gaining economic independence. Record companies, publishing firms, bookstores, and coffeehouses were established with the ultimate aim of providing a network through which women could market their talents and products, opportunities which women felt they had been denied through traditional patriarchal organizations.

Because feminist businesses can be regarded as the product of a specific ideology, they provide a unique opportunity to examine how feminism is enacted in an organizational setting. It is in practice, as evidenced in day-to-day life, that theory is accomplished. "Without feminist organizations, feminism is limited to an abstract concept. At our workplaces it becomes a living reality" (Freeman & Macmillan, 1980, p. 263).

A study of the *processes* whereby feminist theory is enacted in the communication of organizational members can serve three purposes. First, it can make a contribution to organizational theory in that it provides a means to examine the distinction between organizational ideology (theory) and organizational action (practice) or between what organizational members *say* and what they *do*, and the relationship between this dichotomy and the process of organizational change. Second, because the theory-practice contradictions in the enactment of separatism within this organization reflect the same contradictions discussed in the writings of radical feminists, this study may also act as a real-life illustration of how this contradiction works, the means whereby it is managed, and the impact it can have on collective feminist effort. Third, focusing this study on an all-woman feminist business enables us to see how feminism is communicatively enacted in the day-to-day life of a group of women attempting to serve the ideological needs of a community and at the same time stay in business. Such an examination may also provide us with some understanding of the possibilities of feminism as an ideology operating within a capitalist framework. I hope to provide some insight into the claim of some feminists that feminism and capitalism are antithetical[1], by examining the interplay between ideology and action in a specific feminist business.

Theoretical Considerations

Process and Contradiction

Traditional organizational studies have focused on concrete organizational entities that can be measured and assessed in terms of organizational outcome or productivity rather than on the processes through which organizational structures are created, sustained, and modified. J. Kenneth Benson (1977) maintains that "established perspectives fail to deal with organizational arrangements or to analyze the entanglement of theory in those arrangements" (p. 1).

Benson proposes an approach that focuses on those processes by which organizational arrangements are produced and maintained. The organization is conceptualized as a multileveled phenomenon laced with contradictions that undermine the existing features. The direction of change depends "upon the interests and ideas of people and their power to produce and maintain a social formation" (p. 1).

Linda Putnam (1986) argues, in a similar vein, that contradiction is a viable means for understanding subtle as well as dramatic organizational change. Contradiction, she says, is a natural outgrowth of change. It "evolves from the circumstances we encounter, i.e., from attempts to cope and adapt to a continuously changing environment" (p. 151).

An approach that focuses on communication processes provides an opportunity to study how, in the natural process of change, contradictions emerge in the interaction; how organizational members respond

---

[1] Many feminist theorists regard the concept of feminist business as problematic. Some contend that feminist business is contradictory. Feminism and capitalism, they argue, are antithetical because capitalism is a patriarchal framework. It is even regarded by some as an advanced stage of patriarchy. Feminist business will not work without compromising the ideology. See Al-Hibri (1981).

to or manage those contradictions; and how the nature of those responses in particular organizational settings determines the nature and direction of change.

Process and Ideology

Most organizational examinations of ideology[2] regard it as a variable that has an impact on the organization.[3] Some studies have focused primarily on the constraining features of ideologies (Dunbar, 1982; Brunsson, 1982) while others have addressed the functions that ideology serves in organizational settings (Starbuck, 1982; Meyer, 1982).

None of these studies, however, have dealt with the processes by which ideology is created and sustained. "The social world," Benson says, "is in a continuous state of becoming—social arrangments which seemed fixed and permanent are temporary arbitrary patterns and any observed social patterns are regarded as one among many possibilities" (p. 4). The approach adopted here proceeds from the assumption that reality is socially constructed through words, symbols, and behavior (Berger & Luckman, 1966). It is within the patterns that emerge that contradictions arise, render the current sense-making inconsistent, and are managed or fail to be managed by organizational members.

The Organizational Focus

Description

Of the women's businesses that have emerged during the last 15 years, women's bookstores have provided the greatest number of opportunities

---

[2] I am using Clifford Geertz's conception of ideology here because it is not value-laden and focuses on the constraining and enabling features of ideological systems. Geertz regards ideology as a cultural model. It functions as a template or blueprint for the "organization of social and psychological processes, much as genetic systems provide such a template for the organization of organic processes." Ideologies, Geertz says, attempt to render "otherwise incomprehensible social situations meaningful, to so construe them as to make it possible to act purposefully within them." See Geertz (1964).

[3] Roger Dunbar (1982) sees ideologies as instruments of stagnation, Nils Brunnson (1982) describes them as retrospective justifications for irrational decision making. William Starbuck (1982) regards them as concepts invented to meet crisis situations. An alternative definition is provided by Alan Meyer (1982) who contends that organizational ideologies "legitimate certain actions, render other actions heretical, evoke historical reinterpretations and create meanings for events that have yet to occur."

for individual women to become involved in a feminist experiment.[4] It is a women's bookstore and coffeehouse in Salt Lake City, Utah that is the focus of this study.

Twenty Rue Jacob served as a primary gathering place or community center for feminists, particularly lesbian feminists in Northern Utah, during the years of its existence. Founded in February of 1980 as a three-member partnership, the combination bookstore and coffeehouse changed to a collective system in 1982 and then returned to a three-member partnership shortly before it closed in April of 1984. Like so many other women's bookstores, the Rue, as it was called by its owners and patrons, was primarily a political rather than a financial venture.[5]

The Rue was located about four or five blocks from the downtown area of Salt Lake City. The coffeehouse/bookstore was housed in a small leased building that occupied a corner lot with parking for a few cars in back. The front door opened into the bookstore. The kitchen, dining area, and a small office were located in the back. Two small front windows housed book or pottery displays that were changed periodically. A string of bells attached to the front door announced the arrival of customers.

Directly across the room from the door was a large bulletin board that served as a communication center. It was filled with the business cards of women therapists, chiropractors, lawyers, printers, and artists as well as handwritten signs offering French and music lessons and trade skills such as carpentry, plumbing, and so on. Often there were announcements of special events, petitions or lists for special orders; advertisements for roommates, or personal notes for individual women.

The bookstore was housed in this front room. Unfinished wooden bookshelves took up much of the space and displayed an assortment of popular lesbian literature, woman and child-oriented health care texts, feminist political texts, and books of poetry. One bookshelf was used to display an assortment of t-shirts, some bearing the logo of the establishment. On a rack to the right just inside the front door was a selection of feminist and lesbian records featuring artists such as Meg Christian and Holly Near.

---

[4] Women's Bookstores began to appear with the establishment of feminist presses and the growing interest in women's subjects. Early business efforts ranged from volunteer-staffed one-room stores to tables set up at conferences, in women's buildings, and on university campuses. In 1983, there were approximately 80 to 110 such stores in the United States.

[5] In a 1983 article on women's bookstores in *Ms.* magazine, Jeanne O'Connor claims that "almost every women's bookseller will say that her motivation for starting the store was political, rather than financial. Abby Maestas, co-owner and founder of Twenty Rue Jacob often jokes with customers, "What! Do you think I am in this to make money?" The reality of it is, she says, that "you don't do this to get rich, but it would be nice."

Both in the bookstore and the coffeehouse, the works of women artists were displayed on the shelves and walls. Included were pottery, jewelry, weavings, paintings, woodworking, greeting cards, and tie-dyed shirts. A framed poster of interwoven threads bearing the words "sister threads—20 Rue Jacob" hung on the wall in the coffeehouse. A limited edition silkscreen done by a bookstore patron and donated to the Rue, this poster sold out all of the sixteen copies at $10 apiece.

A doorway to the right at the rear of the store led to the coffeehouse, and an open area in the wall allowed whoever was minding the kitchen to keep an eye on the bookstore as well. Two booths, two tables, and a counter with six stools provided seating. A doorway behind the counter led to the kitchen which was equipped with a refrigerator, a microwave, and two long preparation tables. Another doorway at the far end of the coffeehouse led to a short hallway where two bathrooms were located.

In the dining area, bright tablecloths and vases of silk and sometimes real flowers decorated the tables. Women's artwork hung on the walls around the room. Over the counter was a stained glass piece with the bookstore's logo etched in the glass. A blackboard menu hung at one end of the counter advertising such items as turkey, ham, veggie, and roast beef sandwiches, bagels, a soup of the day, nachos, and veggie tostados. An assortment of herbal teas, soda pop, and a variety of juices were stocked on a shelf behind the counter.

Twenty Rue Jacob was open Tuesday through Saturday from 11 a.m. to 6 p.m. During the first year it was often open evenings. Most of the owners held employment elsewhere during their period of involvement, although at times one owner would be working full-time in the store. Most of the time this was Alex, the founder and primary owner during most of the Rue's existence.

Every Friday evening during the academic year, the Rue was open on a "women only" basis for special activities. These included poetry readings, musical performances, political meetings, discussion groups, art show openings, or parties. Classes in such diverse subjects as assertiveness training, poetry writing, and stained glass art were sometimes held in the evenings after the business closed.

Clientele

Most of the regular clientele were lesbians. They ranged in age from 17-year-old high school students to a 63-year-old school teacher who had just retired. The largest number of women were in their twenties and thirties, some were college students, others were blue-collar workers; there was also a large number of professional women and graduate students. Many stopped in over the lunch hour for a bowl of soup or chili or a sandwich and to visit with friends. Others came in to study or relax and had only a drink and an occassional snack. During the summer it was not uncommon to have visitors from as far away as New York or California. Most of these women had heard of the business from friends, had read about the place in *Ms.*, or had gotten the name and address from a gay guide.

The establishment served a need in the community for those women who were too young to get into the bars, for those women who were just "coming out" and were hesitant or troubled, and for many professional women who preferred not to patronize the bars. It also served as a connecting point for women with children who felt a need to do much of their socializing during the day.

There was a strong emphasis on the notion of community, and collective members worked hard to provide a safe haven for those who needed one. This notion of community was unique because of the complex social environment in which the business operated. Salt Lake City provides a predominantly conservative political and social environment because of the influence of the Mormon church. Ironically, because of this strong conservative element, alternative communities in Salt Lake City have become more active and cohesive than would be usual in a more moderate community. These rather visible communities have gathered strength in the past decade of enormous growth in the Salt Lake area. One reason for this is the influx of people and businesses from Southern California. Another is the animosity between the members of the Mormon Church and non-Mormon residents of the area. There is an atmosphere of quiet toleration, but there is enough tension to stimulate a visible cohesive community among non-Mormons or ex-Mormons. Unfortunately, lesbians within the Mormon Church and many from Mormon backgrounds find visibility difficult or impossible.

This complex, larger environment affected the business at Twenty Rue Jacob in three ways. First, it definitely made it difficult for some women to utilize the bookstore for fear someone they knew would see them going in or coming out. They perceived their family and job situations as unable to tolerate disclosure. Second, for many feminist women, patronizing the business served as a political statement in what was perceived as a larger hostile, environment. If a woman perceived her position as "safe" either because she felt the chances of discovery were slim, or because disclosure really didn't matter to her, then her involvement in the Rue was a point of pride. Third, for a large number of women, the Rue served as a connecting point between a repressed past and a hopeful future. It was not unusual for rather nervous mature women to come in looking for someone to talk to. Many were referred to the organization by therapists or trusted friends—for example, the retired elementary school teacher who drove around the block several times before she finally came in. It was this function of the organization that made it an invaluable community resource.

Methodology

Given the emphasis in this study on the naturally-occurring communicative behavior of organizational members, and the assumption that reality is socially created, sustained and modified in interaction, the most appropriate methodology was participant-observation. This method enables the researcher to adopt a member's viewpoint and thereby gain an understanding of the collectivity's shared knowledge of what is going on. The method calls for the researcher to participate in the interaction of the group under study on an ongoing basis and have some "nominal status for them as someone who is part of their daily lives" (Zinn, 1979, p. 111). In engaging in participant-observation, the researcher immerses herself in the data to learn the actor's definition of the situation by thinking and acting as the actor does, seeing things as she sees them and then distancing herself from the data, transcending the experience, permitting her to see what the actor doesn't and to analyze it for patterns, process, and common denominators.

As a participant-observor, I attended business meetings and social organizational functions and was considered an "honorary," nonvoting member of the collective. Occasionally, I assisted in maintaining the kitchen, making sandwiches, and waiting on customers. Often I helped customers in the bookstore or answered the phone. I achieved membership status and in effect, became an insider[6] in the organization. I often took field notes while in the business; sometimes I reconstructed events soon after they had concluded, and occasionally I conducted unstructured interviews. Often, I taped and then, later, transcribed meetings or interviews.

---

[6] Whether research can be more fruitfully conducted by an outside or an insider is a major methodological issue in discussions of participant-observation. The argument basically involves the contention that the insider's proximity to the data precludes her ability to be objective. On the other hand, those who advocate an insider stance maintain that the insider is "endowed with special insight into matters necessarily obscure to others, thus possessed of a penetrating discernment." (Schwartz & Jacobs, 1979, p. 46) The insider stance was essential in this study since an outsider would have been regarded with suspicion and never permitted the access to information and interaction that I, as a community member and honorary collective member, was afforded. It was also essential because much of the decision making and discussion that goes on occurs in social rather than business settings.

My data for this study, however, encompass more than these observations. In constructing my analysis, I also utilized feminist literature
with which organizational members were familiar, inasmuch as that
literature provided an intellectual and social context for the naturally
occurring interaction. I also used as data my own personal experiences
and responses to the observations I made. In a sense, over two-and-
a-half years spent in the business, I became one of my own key
informants. My data were broader than the recorded observations of
talk and social action. The physical space of the business, the texts of
the organization (signs, newsletters, etc.), my personal experiences and
responses, and feminist literature on ideology and organization also
served as data. My analytical task was to integrate the varied texts to
provide an understanding or interpretation of the way in which feminist
ideology and organizational action played themselves out in this particular organizational setting. The text functions as the empirical data
and the study is a critical analysis of that text.

Analysis

This analysis will focus on one major contradiction which emerged
between theory (ideology) and action (practice) in the interaction of
organizational members, discuss the nature of that contradiction, and
examine the responses of organizational members and the ways in
which those responses determined the direction and nature of organizational change.

This major contradiction existed between the notion of separatism,
which was a fundamental component of the organization's ideology,
and the notion of business[7], which defined day-to-day organizational
life. Organizational members were tied into enacting, what for them,
were mutually exclusive alternatives. The contradiction between separatism, which is essentially exclusive, and business, which is essentially
nonexclusive, was evident not only in the theory-action dichotomy, but
pervaded the organization and emerged clearly in several levels of
organizational understanding.

An examination of the contradictory understandings of the concept
of separatism within feminist writings is essential to an understanding
of the contradictory nature inherent in its enactment in this organization.
Marilyn Frye (1983) characterizes feminism as kaleidoscopic—"some-

---

[7] Organizational members constantly referred to the Rue as their "business," and
whenever they discussed anything to do with the marketing or financial aspects of the
organization, they always used the term "business." I have used it throughout to reflect
their perspective.

thing whose shapes, structures and patterns alter with every turn of feminist creativity." The one element she sees as present in every change is separatism, and it assumes "different roles and relations in every turn of the glass . . . depending on how the pieces fall and who is the beholder" (p. 95).

Adrianne Rich (1981), in her assessment of separatist ideas in *Sinister Wisdom*, addresses the relationship:

> In trying to come to some clearer view of what separatism means, I have realized that for me, at least, theory and practice are constantly tugging at each other, often entangled with each other, but they are by no means the same. I find myself wondering if perhaps the real question is with what kind of conscious identity it is practiced (p. 85).

Twenty Rue Jacob served as what Sasha Gregory Lewis (1979) refers to as a "workshop of separatism" (p. 96). It provided a rich opportunity to examine separatism as it is enacted and to understand the relationship between theory and practice and the nature of the conscious identity with which it is practiced.

Many radical feminists consider the issue of separatism to be dead. Lucia Valeska (1981) notes, "From the West Coast a friend writes that the very word elicits deadpan hostility or an active curse. Yet, she adds, 'while so many are outwardly against separatism, they continue to live it' " (p. 95).

This contradiction between theory and practice renders separatism one of the most problematic aspects of feminist theory. What makes this examination of the separatist contradiction valuable is that it so beautifully reflects the theory/practice contradictions that exist in theoretical discussions of separatism, and provides a means to examine how that contradiction is managed or fails to be managed in the day-to-day lives of individual feminists.

The women of Twenty Rue Jacob were well acquainted with the issues involved in discussions of separatism. The bookstore setting contributed to their theoretical understanding. When there was talk, it focused on new books or arguments found in older literature, but the diversity of opinions reflected the diversity in the literature. Some members would consider themselves separatists, while others would not consider themselves separatist at all. Despite the broad understanding of the issues there was never any discussion that explicitly tied that theory to organizational life.

Thus, among radical feminists in general, and among those in the organization, there was not simply a question as to *how* separatism should be enacted, but a question as to whether it should be enacted at all. This same confusion was evident in the enactment of separatism in Twenty Rue Jacob, and can be organized around two major claims about that enactment. The first claim is that the organization's goal was inconsistent with the chosen means of reaching that goal. It was not possible for them to be a business and be separatist at the same time. The second claim is that the explicit recognition of this contradiction would have necessitated a radical change in the organization. To remain a viable business entity, it would have been essential for organizational members to renegotiate their separatist purpose. To renegotiate their "business" definition of the organization would have meant a major restructuring and would have made it necessary to seek other avenues for financing that were perceived as unavailable. It became essential, therefore, to address the problem only indirectly. To explicitly recognize the contradiction would have meant to have to deal with radical change. What results is a separatist/capitalist dilemma which is only partially evident in the talk, but never explicitly addressed.

There was a consensual understanding of what "being a business" meant. Although there were differences in attitude when it came to business procedures, it was generally agreed that the Rue was there to exchange merchandise or service for money as a means of economic survival. No one debated the necessity of keeping records or doing inventory, of issuing receipts or making deposits, of stocking up on kitchen supplies or of taking turns working.

There was, however, no consensual meaning when it came to how to meet the goal of "providing a separate place for women." In fact, since the meanings for separatism were never explicitly addressed, they emerged instead in talk of who the clientele should be, or who should attend the Friday night activities or whether or not the "Others" sign on the second bathroom should be replaced with a "Men's Room" sign. Consensual meanings of separatism were indirectly negotiated in these interactions. The focus was on how some *aspect* of separatism should be enacted in the organization, how it should figure in decisions.

The contradiction between being a business and being separatist emerged most clearly in the process of defining the organization's clientele. It often took the form of a problem to be solved, and organizational members developed communicative strategies for managing the contradiction. Among those discussed here are (a) strategies for explaining fluctuations in business, (b) strategies for redefining the potential clientele, (c) strategies that made potential changes appear consistent with the separatist goal, and (d) strategies which allowed organizational members to recognize one level of the contradiction, while ignoring the other.

Explaining Fluctuations

For the business to survive it needed the support of a community. The women's community did not provide enough support to sustain the business. Only a small minority of women patronized the Rue with any regularity. To make it even more difficult, women usually have less money than men. Therefore, to survive, either more women in the community needed to begin using the business or the definition of who constituted the potential clientele needed to be reworked. Attempts to increase patronage all met with minimal success. Those efforts included book sales, specials, advertising, and coupons for free food with a book purchase.

There were specific times when business was characterized as particularly "good" or particularly "bad." As is the case with business in general, Christmas was a "good" time. Extra merchandise was ordered in anticipation and if additional merchandise was going to be added, it was done then. Summer business was characterized as "bad" and explanations are similar to explanations one might typically expect from other businesses: people want to spend time outside, they are on vacation, and so on. Friday evening activities were suspended and little if any new merchandise was ordered.

Organizational members, when asked, usually defined their clientele as the Salt Lake women's community. However, when business problems were being confronted or lack of support was explicit in the interaction, strategies were developed for explaining things.

Alex used one such strategy by explaining fluctuations in business in terms of uncontrollable community-related phenomena. "People aren't coming in because they think we are too political," or "Everyone's down on Carol (the owner of a local women's bar) so they're coming in here now," or "Business has been good this month because everyone is going through annual bar burn-out," or "Because several of the collective members have a lot of education, they think we're elitist," were typical explanations. Explanations, which functioned to reduce the uncertainty and lack of stability, were usually accompanied by a story which supported or verified the contention. At the same time, these explanations of phases allowed for the uncertainty that existed because they usually addressed the temporary nature of the situation and could not be proven inaccurate, which would have called for new explanations later when good business turned bad or bad business improved.

Explanations of day-to-day business fluctuations were not as carefully constructed, perhaps because day-to-day unreliability was not as threatening as trends which were noted month to month. Regardless of who made the comment, "I wonder what kind of day it will be?" the answer was always, "Who knows," often accompanied by a shrug of the shoulders. For awhile, Thursdays were exceptionally busy, but even that could not be counted on.

> I guess yesterday was a departure from the last few Thursdays—only $9 business. It never fails, whenever Melanie is here, it gets real busy. I guess she has been super busy the last few Thursdays.

One volunteer had the perception that every second Friday when people got paid was very busy, but I never was able to see that. Receipts and the number of people that came in seemed as unreliable to me as those on any other day.

There was little relationship between the number of women who came in and the cash receipts. Thirty women might come in and out during the day and order only coffee or five could come in for lunch and buy a book or a record and bring in the same amount of money. More than once I heard a comment similar to this one: "If every woman in the community (meaning the Salt Lake women's community) would come in here and have lunch or buy a book even once a month— we'd be doing great."

There was no way to obtain accurate statistics on the number of lesbian feminists in Salt Lake City who made up the potential clientele of the bookstore, but there was the perception among organizational members that the number of women who came in regularly were only a very small percentage of the community. Comments that indicated amazement were common:

> Scarcely a day goes by that some dyke I never saw before comes in here. Do *you* know those women in the bookstore?

> Everytime I go to the bar, I don't know 90% of the women in there. Never saw them before in my life. I don't know where they come from.

Regardless of where they came from, there was some surety of where they didn't go, at least on any regular basis, and that was Twenty Rue Jacob, and that was a source of considerable pain and frustration for organizational members. A general feeling of "where are they?" (the customers) prevaded many business days. The community was described as "fickle" or "politically unaware" and there was often a bitter note in efforts to organize activities.

> It bugs me a lot; people expect this place to cater to their needs. I get the impression that they feel they can come in here and be relaxed and uh, interact with one another on a freer level—and yet they don't expect

to want to pay anything for that, like they don't even wanta pay commitment to coming in here a lot.

Redefining the Clientele

Between attempts to bring in more lesbians, there were attempts at redefinitions of *who* constituted the potential clientele, which was variously described as lesbians only, feminist women, gay males and lesbians, and anybody who happened to come in.

Occasionally, particularly around the time of involvement in a women's conference at the university or at the time of the publication of an article on feminist bookstores in *Ms.*, which mentioned the bookstore, there was increased interest in pulling in more feminist women. Ads were placed in feminist-oriented publications with both lesbian and heterosexual feminist readers, and a booth at women's conferences stressed the feminist nature of the business. When non-lesbian feminists did come in, their presence was greeted with enthusiasm and hope.

> Five women came in today. I saw them coming and thought, 'Oh no, relief society women. [Relief Society is the women's missionary society of the Mormon Church.] They don't know where they are.' They looked like they'd just come from a meeting, but they came in and had lunch and bought a bunch of books—feminist, not lesbian. They seemed real comfortable. I made them extra special sandwiches, extra chips, the works. It was great.

Carol: That was *another* woman who read about us in *Ms!*
Jill: Great!

A more practical solution to the money problem emerged in the effort to attract more gay males. This solution, however, presented a problem in terms of separatism. The possibility of catering to the gay male population emerged as problematic because it clearly violated the separatist goal, yet organizational members often talked about attracting gay male patrons as if no problem existed. "We need to get those men in here spending money." On the other hand, the positive, beneficial aspects of the Rue were conceptualized in women-to-women terms. "The Rue is a space for women." "There isn't any other place here where women can just be with other women."

At one point when money was very low and taxes were due, a proposal was presented at a collective meeting by a woman who later became an owner, to open the business as an after-bar breakfast place on weekends. The extra money it would bring in outweighed the ideological considerations, for the collective owners.

Jane: My only concern was, when she said it first, was 'Oh great, we're tryin' to clean up our act to have a more, uh, nicer image and we're gonna do this thing! But then I thought about it and well, it's a completely different time of day, the people aren't gonna interface with our other customers, our book buying customers and, uh, ya know, so I was able to deal with it.

Ann: It sounds like maybe we should beef up our gay men's selection.

Lynn: Then maybe they'll come back in during the week to buy books!

Jane: That's what we're thinking, that's what we're talking about, that's what we're hoping and that's why, if we can make it look nice they'll wanna come back.

Meg: Yeah, we need to open ourselves to gay men.

Ann: Two came in yesterday and said, 'Oh, you have our favorite table,' like they come in here all the time. I was sitting by the window.

Mary: Well, you missed the guy that came in with chains all over his body who wanted to know if Jane knew any women who were really into reading the Bible. (laughter)

Jane: You wanna hear the worst part? I go 'No, I don't know any women who are really inta that . . . and the women who come in here wouldn't be interested.' Then, I had my back to him, I was at the cash register and he moved and I swear I jumped a mile. I just finally said, 'Hey, I really don't like your energy.'

Ann: You said that?

Jane: Yeah, and ya know what he said—"I'm not surprised, you shouldn't.'

In this example, the dilemma created by the breakfast suggestion was made explicit. Even though the after-bar crowd, which was likely to be heavily male, wouldn't interfere with the daily customers, there was nonetheless enthusiasm about them returning during the day to have lunch or buy books. The concern was more with the rowdiness of an after-bar crowd than with the gender of the people coming through the door, until Mary brought up the incident the day before. What the story served to accomplish was concern with the uncertainty that accompanied the changes. Even with the recognition of the need to cater to gay males, there was still a lack of understanding as to what it would mean if men began coming in regularly.

The concern was not so much with the after-hours proposal, but with the possibility that such a move would mean a loss of control over who came in and out and with what groups of individuals might come to feel comfortable in the Rue. While not explicitly mentioned, it was understood that during the day the clientele could be regulated by the presence of and reception given by the women in the business. At night, the staff would be a mixed group with very different ideas as to what purpose the business was there to serve. The response to the proposal was a rather grudging willingness to agree, "with conditions." The women were willing to approve the proposal, but the enthusiasm of the group was low. The woman who presented the proposal soon lost interest and let it drop.

Consistency Strategies

In day-to-day organizational life, theory and practice were not consistent. Organizational members might say "I'm not a separatist anymore," or "We can't afford to be separatist," but when men came in, particularly men who were not perceived as gay, conversation usually ceased and the atmosphere was tense until they left. Sometimes the uncomfortable quiet would be broken with a comment after they were gone, such as "and don't come back." This was not always the case and depended on several factors, such as the nature of the conversation that was interrupted and who happened to be there when they arrived. In general, though, male presence was usually regarded as intrusive, and there was enough inconsistency to make it next to impossible to decide who should be there and who should not.

Inconsistency was evident in this conversation that occurred among three women who were involved in redecorating the coffeehouse during the summer of 1983. The three were painting and discussing plans for the changing image of the business:

Alice: Where's the vacuum and I'll clean up this stuff?

Susan: It's in the "other."

Alice: If we're goin' ta try to attract some of the men we're going to have to change that—ya know? If I was a woman and went into a male bar—and the sign on the women's room said 'other,' I'd be offended.

Susan: Ann has made some jewelry for men—and we're gonna get some books for men.

Janet: (surprised) So, are we gonna try to *attract* the men? (everyone laughs) I mean, I think . . . .

Susan: Phoenix [a local transition center for women] has one bathroom and a women/men sign—you can just flip it over.

Alice: When those friends of Alex's came in they wanted jewelry made, a lambda, I think—then a woman came in later and asked to have some made for male friends.

Susan: Well, they're over 50% of the population and have well over 50% of the money. . . .

Alice: So business-wise . . . .

Susan: Yeah, we're cutting our own throats.

Alice: As long as we keep Friday nights "women only" and I think the men will understand that. . . . It's a tradition—they're into tradition—they have a few of their own.

Susan: Some of them are really nice—like that retired English professor—
he came in here with his lover.

Several things are going on in this interaction that made the im-
pending changes (the practice) appear consistent with the ideals (the
theory) of organizational members. This was done in terms of explanations and justifications and by redefining separatism. There was an
effort here to reconceptualize separatism, or the manifestation of separatism in the Friday night ritual as tradition. This reconceptualization,
talking about separatist activities as ritual or at least the suggestion that
it might be *explained* that way to the men, allows one to transcend the
separatist/capitalist dilemma.

This example suggests that redefinition was working at two levels.
The changes occurring at the event level were explicit. The sign on the
bathroom door, "others," had to be changed and new books and jewelry
had been ordered. The changes at the individual level were harder in
coming and still needed justification and qualification.

"They're over 50% of the population and have well over 50% of
the money" addressed the capitalist in the speakers, the implication
being that the Rue was a business and it was there to make money.
Hanging on to a strict separatist definition proved to be at odds with
a "business" definition of the Rue. So they redefined the Rue, too. The
Rue in this piece of interaction was not an enactment of feminism, it
was a business, and so in redefining just what separatist meant, what
the women were doing was approaching it from a "business" standpoint
to make it okay, and reconceptualizing the ritual from a male definition.
Explaining the Friday evening events as "traditional cultural rituals" to
gay male patrons made the separatist evenings appear acceptable since
the men had "traditions" too. This could be done on a business level,
but not an ideological level. Organizational members reconceptualized
the ideology, at least appeared to reconceptualize it, to survive.

When Susan brought up the bathroom sign at Phoenix she was not
suggesting an alternative solution for the Rue, because this solution
didn't meet the criteria for the problem. The Rue had two bathrooms,
not the one bathroom problem that the sign was a solution to. What
was being accomplished in the talk was an understanding that *not*
being strictly separatist was okay. Phoenix is feminist and it's not
separatist so maybe it's okay.

The attempts at making things appear consistent allowed organizational members to make some changes as long as they could be
explained, but they made any widespread campaign impossible, because
not all aspects of the possible changes could be made to appear
consistent. Some of the changes, the painting for example, were completed. Others, such as the orders for new books and records, were

instituted half-heartedly. The sign on the bathroom door never was changed.

Ignoring Contradictions

Contradiction was evident not only in interaction among the owners, but in conversations with customers. This next interaction occurred on a day that I was volunteering. Cindy and I were behind the counter. Tom, the only regular male, was sitting in a booth and having a cup of coffee while he read his paper. A couple of women were sitting around the room. A woman walked in, ordered coffee, and sat quietly at the counter. Tom paid for his coffee and left.

Customer: What was he doing in here?
Cindy: Having a cup of coffee and reading his paper. (pause) He comes in here a lot.
Customer: Oh, I thought this was a woman's place.
Cindy: It is.
Customer: Oh, I thought maybe things had changed. (shrugs shoulders)

This customer explicitly addressed the dilemma. If this was a woman's space, then why was a man in here? It became obvious to her that there was some knowledge she didn't share. Apparently, this separatism thing was more complex than she thought. She was working from the assumption that separatism had a radical separatist definition in this business, that men were not allowed or at least not welcome. The fact that Tom was there at all confused her, but the fact that Cindy seemed calm about that fact confused her even more. Presence she could explain: he might have stumbled in and Cindy not asserted herself to let him know the rules, or he might be gay and waiting for a friend, but acceptance she could not understand. She anticipated a different response from Cindy than she got—at the very least a negative one. "I don't know, the jerk was probably checkin' us all out," would have encompassed her understanding of the separatist aspects of the business, but a straightforward description of his activities did not. It became obvious that she was dealing with knowledge she didn't possess so, rather than pursue it, she backed off.

On some levels, organizational members were aware of the contradiction. On others, they appeared to be oblivious to it. Gay males often found it difficult to decide if this was a place they should patronize. The following conversation occurred about lunch time after one collective member had just answered the phone.

Lynn: You'll *never* believe this! You'll never believe. (Lynn staggers through the door laughing hysterically, and falls into a chair.)
Cindy: What? What?

Lynn: That was *Allen* on the phone!
Cindy: Yeah?
Lynn: He called to ask *permission* to come down for lunch.
Cindy: What?
Lynn: (still laughing) He said, "I was wondering, ah, is it all right if I come down for lunch today?"
        (There is a stunned silence.)
Cindy: (with a serious expression) So, what did you tell him? (everyone in the room breaks into laughter.)

We evaluate human behavior in terms of consistency and predictability. Organizations that send contradictory messages or appear inconsistent are regarded as unreliable or directionless despite the fact that contradiction is part of the natural process of change. It is this ambiguity that people respond to, that makes it impossible for either message to be successful. From this perspective, Allen, calling to see if he could come in for lunch, was perfectly understandable. It seemed preposterous to organizational members because the ambiguity was often not clear to them, but the aspects of the message that qualified the situation, that made it perfectly okay for Allen to come in for lunch, could hardly be evident to Allen in light of the ambiguity. Organizational goals were both separatist and nonseparatist, and this emerged in decision-making interactions with patrons and in most aspects of organizational enactment.

While certainly seldom this explicit, the contradiction was obvious because the reputation of the bookstore was decidedly separatist—it was referred to by gay males as a "lesbian place." One gay male said to me, "Isn't that the lesbian place?" Another came in one day and jokingly said, "Excuse me, is this the Lebanese bookstore?"

The contradiction then, between separatism and capitalism, prevented the organization from establishing a clear direction, because at the same time it was trying to satisfy the goal of providing a separate place for women, it was trying to become a successful business entity. The organization was locked into pursuing what were for them cross-purposes. To survive as a business, it was necessary to sacrifice or at least reconceptualize the ideology; while to serve the purposes of the ideology, it was necessary to somehow limit the clientele. Neither course of action seemed viable, or at least viable enough for organizational members to commit themselves to one course of action to the exclusion of the other. Rather than directly confronting the contradiction, organizational members developed strategies involving avoidance or compensation which either explicitly ignored aspects of the contradiction or at least made practices appear consistent. These management strategies worked in handling the contradictions in day-to-day interaction, but didn't provide enough change in any clear direction to allow the business to survive. Organizational members made the decision to close Twenty Rue Jacob four years and two months after it had opened.

Theoretical Implications

Organizational responses to contradiction are not predetermined. Organizational members can respond in any number of ways when confronted with inconsistency. The most useful way to talk about responses in this organization is to talk about them in terms of accomplishment. What did the strategies formulated to manage the contradiction do for organizational members and how did they do it? Two major responses to contradiction were evident in this business: suppression and dispersion.

Suppression refers to the degree to which organizational members failed to explicitly recognize contradiction in the organization's enactment. What suppression accomplished for organizational members was that it allowed them to ignore the problems inherent in the contradiction, while it also limited their ability to deal with contradiction or manage its effects, because they were constantly striving to understand what was going on.

The second major response to contradiction was dispersion. Contradiction that is not explicitly recognized cannot be successfully managed and tends to be dispersed throughout the system, resulting in the "existence of multiple inconsistencies across organizational events, levels and boundaries"[8] (Putnam, 1986, p. 164).

The suppression and dispersion of organizational contradictions have important implications for the nature and direction of the process of organizational change. Both Putnam and Benson locate organizational change in the processes of social construction and regard contradiction as the moving factor which regulates the production and maintenance of social formations. It functions as a catalyst for change. For Benson (1977), the organization is characterized by "ruptures, breaks, and

---

[8] While I am primarily addressing contradictions between theory and practice, Putnam contends that contradictions within organizations may emerge from any number of relationships. For example, she maintains that the verbal-nonverbal, literal-metaphorical, abstract concrete, and content-relationship dichotomies also provide fertile grounds for incompatibility in organizations. It is true, however, that theory-practice contradictions may also lead to contradictions *within* theory and practice, so that often there are contradictions between what organizational members say they believe at one time and what they say they believe at another, as well as the ways in which they enact those beliefs at different times. This dispersion of contradictions is discussed in the analysis.

inconsistencies in the social fabric" (p. 2), to which he applies the general term contradiction while acknowledging that such rifts may be of different types. Putnam, however, delineates several categories or types of rifts. She centers her discussion on the concept of paradox. The term comes from the Greek word para + dokein which means "to think twice; to reconcile two apparently conflicting views" (p. 19).

Putnam discusses contradiction in terms of specific types of paradoxes. The type of paradox that has the most relevance in this study of Twenty Rue Jacob is the pragmatic paradox. In this paradox, contradictions are mutually exclusive alternatives that evolve over time. As an example of this, Putnam points to orphanages and welfare systems. These agencies exist to place homeless children in healthy home environments, but they often develop rules and regulations which preclude them from placing children in many excellent home environments. In the process of accomplishing their goals, "they create standard operating procedures that defy their very aims for existence" (p. 153). Contradictions such as these are created communicatively by organizational members as they go about attempting to accomplish their goals. They evolve over time through interaction.

One specific kind of pragmatic paradox is of particular use here—the systems contradiction. A systems contradiction emerges when an "organization's practices (ways of getting things done) become incongruent with an organization's structures (rules, procedures, goals, and policies for operating)" (p. 154). This construction can be applied to the dialectical relationship between theory (ideology) and practice (enactment) in this organization. At Twenty Rue Jacob the organization's business structure was incongruent with the separatist practices which emerged as a result of the organization's ideology. The women of the Rue were "being a business" so that they could meet the goal of providing a place for women, but these two actions could not be accomplished together.

The major location of systems contradiction is in the "clash between prevailing objectives, goals, or structures and the constraining effects of these creations," which define the limits of change within a particular period or within a given system. "When created social arrangements become dysfunctional, they are transformed, only to find that the cure for the ill becomes the ill" (p. 162).

One example of the constraints imposed by the existing system is in the change generated by efforts to enact successful business by attracting a new and different group of clientele. The organization's morphology is the officially enforced and conventionally accepted view of the organization as embodied in the prevailing objective and goals. Within the ongoing process of social construction, alternatives to this morphology are constantly generated. According to Putnam, the nature of these alternatives or innovations is seated in the process of organizing:

> Organizational members create their procedures and policies; these enactments operate for a period of time until they become dysfunctional. Some members then, begin to organize differently—to create new procedures and structures that run counter to the prevailing ones, so that innovations, whether officially sanctioned or not, frequently oppose the prevailing way of "doing things around here" (p. 161).

Contradiction, then, may lead to organizational crisis, which makes the search for alternative organizational arrangements imperative. When these alternative structures collide with the established morphology, the structures in place work to constrain changes in the organization.

Such was the case with Twenty Rue Jacob. As it became apparent to organizational members that the "women's community" was not supporting the business, that the current way of doing things was dysfunctional, some members began to talk in terms of innovations. Some of these innovations, efforts to attract more women through advertising, coupons, new activities, and so on were consistent with the organization's morphology, but could not operate to increase business because they were aimed at clientele that could not or would not respond. Others, such as attracting gay male customers, were in opposition to the prevailing way of doing things, which was constituted in the organizational goal of providing a "place for women." This aspect of the morphology was resistent to change. It allowed for the entertainment of creative alternative because of the contradictions. Thus, organizational members could paint and redecorate the interior, order new merchandise, and talk about redesigning the logo, but even these innovations were often limited by the established morphology and therefore could not function as catalysts for change. For example, the redecorating included the framing of signed women's music posters and the talk of the new logo included women-oriented flower images despite the fact that organizational members talked most often about attracting gay male customers. Contradiction in Twenty Rue Jacob, then, emerged in the relationship between the established organizational morphology, practices that ran counter to it, and the constraints it imposed on the system.

Dispersion was also manifested in communication levels. Putnam contends that the verbal-nonverbal, literal-mataphorical, abstract-concrete, and content-relationship dichotomies provide fertile ground for incompatibility in organizations inasmuch as meaning is derived from an aggregate of different levels of interaction. In fact, systems contradictions frequently emerge in the organizational enactment of these different levels. One location of this, related to the theory-practice dichotomy, is in the message-action relationship. This is descriptive of some of what was going on in Twenty Rue Jacob and provides a possible explanation for the failure of the innovations.

When organizational members became quiet or exchanged glances as men came into the business, when they posted signs for "womyn only" activities or maintained that the Rue was a space for "womyn" and then placed orders for male-oriented books and jewelry, message-action contradictions emerged. So that, while organizational members were making some changes to attract gay male patrons and make the Rue a "space for everyone," they were also retaining organizational practices and delivering organizational messages which clearly said, "this is a space for women only."

We enact organizations and our enactments, in turn, impose on us and limit our behaviors. In Twenty Rue Jacob, the enactment of the organization's ideology imposed limits on the behavior of organizational participants within the context of the business, constraining the nature of change. Communicative responses to contradiction can generate an awareness of the limitations imposed. By entertaining alternatives and reframing events, organizational members *can* reconstruct the prevailing system in such a way as to overcome limitations. Contradictions then can function as opportunities for change, but in Twenty Rue Jacob, because they were often suppressed, they dispersed throughout the system and functioned as problems to be explained and then resolved, strategized, and gotten around. They could not fully function as opportunities when they were not explicitly recognized as contradictions.

William Starbuck (1982) contends that organizations that cannot entertain competing ideologies are unable to adapt to their environment and wither and die. This provides a possible explanation for the death of the business. The social arrangements which arose from their enactment of separatism constrained the business and limited transformation enough that radical change was not possible, contradictions were system-destructive and the business eventually had to close.

Linda Putnam (1986) says that through the study of contradictions, perhaps we can "discover how organizations pull themselves out of self-made quagmires by their own bootstraps" (p. 166). A study of Twenty Rue Jacob shows how some organizations *cannot*, not because of the rational actions they do or do not adopt, but because the contradictory elements were antithetical.

In this organization, contradictions which could not be managed successfully were system-destructive and caused the closing of the business, rather than emerging as system-integrative which would have enabled the organization to continue in new and radically different ways.

Both Benson and Putnam, while they are aiming at different ends in their treatment of contradiction, link organizational success with the continuance of the organization. Both aim at discovering how organizations can *overcome* contradictions. Their perspectives, as well as traditional approaches to organizations, proceed from the assumption that the resultant structure is the central feature of an organizing process.

To simply say that the contradictions were system-destructive and the business failed is not particularly useful here, because it ignores the troublesome logical problem presented by the concept of organizational death. It assumes that if organizational members had been successful in managing contradiction and the ideology had been less constraining, continuous construction would have possible and the organization would have been successful at least in remaining a viable business entity. As it was, because the organization died, it failed. I see this assumption as problematic. First of all, it does not take into account that the enactment of feminism was a primary reason for the founding of the business in the first place. As is the case in many feminist businesses, becoming a part of an alternative structure was the reason for the involvement of many organizational members. Alex, the founder and only original owner left at the end, said the hope was to "stay one step ahead of the wolves."

Second, assuming that the closure of the business meant failure does not address the issue of organizational integrity. At what point in undergoing change does the organization cease to exist? Herbert Kaufman (1976), in his work on organizational change asks, "How many changes can an organization make before it is regarded as a totally new organization?" (p. 23). Had organizational members defined and redefined the ideology to accommodate the contradictions, at what point would the Rue have ceased to exist?

On April 23, 1984, Twenty Rue Jacob conducted a moving sale and the business closed down by 4:00 that afternoon. On one wall inside the coffeehouse Alex hung a large sign on which was the following message: "Women of the Salt Lake Community—We won!" Organizational members speculated on the possible meaning. One organizational member said to me "It's a contradiction. It sounds like the kind of thing you say before you give in to ultimate change." This explanation was based on the assumption of success as continuance.

There is, however, an alternative explanation, based on the assumption that success can have different meanings for organizational members than continuance, and that is that organizations can still meet their goals but ultimately fail in the traditional sense. This was definitely the case at Twenty Rue Jacob. Organizational members went along successfully accomplishing their goal to "provide a place for women" for several years. Unfortunately, that goal was inconsistent with business success for this organization. They *won* because they accomplished the original purpose of the organization. Some members may have regarded the effort as a failure, but Alex preferred a different explanation. From her perspective, while the need was there, the Rue would somehow continue. She reconciled the contradictory elements by not seeing the two organizational goals as working against each other. If the need was really there, the support would be there: if it was not, then that meant to her that its time was over, its organizational task accomplished. On the ideological level, she saw the business not as a failure, but as a completed task. It succeeded on one level, even if it failed on the other.

In her closing letter, published in a local newsletter for women, Alex said:

> If there were a need for the Rue, someone from the community would have come forth to continue. Inasmuch as no one has at this time, it seems clear that Twenty Rue Jacob is no longer meeting the needs of this community. Perhaps something like the Rue will exist in the future when the time is right.

> We need to give ourselves positive strokes for the three years we had with the Rue. We did what we knew how, the best we knew how. As Debbie Lempke writes in her song "Nicole" (Berkeley Women's Music Collective)
> "but I know now, what I didn't know then
> That you do know how, but you gotta know when."

References

Al-Hibri, A. (1981). Capitalism is an advanced stage of patriarchy: But Marxism is not feminism. In Lydia Sargent (Ed.), *Women and revolution* (pp. 165–193). Boston: South End Press.

Benson, J. (1977). Organizations: A dialectical view. *Administrative Science Quarterly*, 22, March 1.

Berger, P., & Luckman, T. (1966). *The social construction of reality.* Garden City, NJ: Doubleday.

Brunsson, N. (1982). The irrationality of action and action rationality: Decisions, ideologies and organizational actions. *Journal of Management Studies*, 19(1), 29–44.

Dunbar, R., Dutton, J., & Torbert, W. (1982). Crossing mother: Ideological constraints on organizational improvements. *Journal of Management Studies*, 19(1), 91–108.

Freeman, J., & McMillan, C. (1980). Building feminist organizations. In *Building feminist theory: Essays from Quest.* (p. 263). New York: McMillan.

Frye, M. (1983). *The politics of reality: Essays in feminist theory.* New York: The Crossing Press.

Geertz, C. (1980, Spring). Blurred genres: The refiguration of social thought. *American Scholar, 49,* 165–179.

Geertz, C. (1964). Ideology as a cultural system. In David Apter [Ed.], *Ideology and discontent* pp. 47–76. London: Collier McMillan. Ltd.

Kaufman, H. (1976). *Change in organizations.* New York: Harper and Row.

Lewis, S. (1979). *Sunday's women: A report on lesbian life today.* Boston: Beacon Press.

Meyer, A. (1982) How ideologies supplant formal structures and shape responses to environments. *Journal of Management Studies,* (1983). 19, 45–61.

O'Connor, J. (1983). What makes a feminist bookstore special? *Ms., 12,* 79–82.

Putnam, L. L. (1986). Contradictions and paradoxes in organizations. In L. Thayer, [Ed.], *Organization-Communication: Emerging Perspectives.* (pp. 151–167). New York: Ablex.

Rich, A. (1981). Notes for a magazine: What does separatism mean? *Sinister Wisdom, 18,* 83–91.

Schwartz, H. & Jacobs, J. (1979). *Qualitative sociology: A method to the madness.* New York: Macmillan.

Starbuck, W. (1982). Congealing oil: Inventing ideologies to justify acting ideologies out. *Journal of Management Studies, 19,* 3–27.

Valeska, L. (1981). The future of female separatism. In *Building feminist theory: Essays from Quest* (p. 95). New York: Longman.

Zinn, M. B. (1979). Field research in minority communities: Ethical, methodological and political observations by an insider. *Social Problems, 27-2,* (December) 211.

14

Implementing Feminist Principles in a Bureaucracy: Studio D The National Film Board of Canada*

Anita Taylor

George Mason University

Introduction

This chapter introduces Studio D of the National Film Board (NFB) of Canada, a women's filmmaking unit, and presents a description of members' communication related to decision making, leadership strategies, and methods of dealing with conflict as they existed in early

---

* The introduction to a news release prepared by Studio D as part of a "celebration" of beginning the eleventh year in existence, contains the following words:

"We profoundly believe in the films we make. The objectivity we practice is that of not letting one's own set of vested interests interfere with another person's telling of her own truth. But we do not believe there is value, at this time, in the kind of 'objectivity' that pretends detachment when dealing with matters of life and death, of justice, truth and human well-being.

When John Grierson founded the National Film Board in 1939, there was a war being fought, and films were made with the passion and commitment appropriate to a war effort. We make our films with the passion and commitment appropriate to fighting the war against sexism, racism, and the other political and economic tyrannies which impact on all ordinary people and on our collective future as a Human race."

After my introduction to Studio D and most of its members, I bring a similar inability to be "objective" about the group and its work. To pretend otherwise would be a fraud, though it would be possible to write "objective" prose about the Studio that would support the pretense. Such a style, however, not only would be dishonest, it is unnecessary. The insights in this report are those of a stranger who was welcomed into the group and to whom doors were opened without defenses solely because she was a feminist researcher. They are, I believe, accurate, having been largely confirmed by those who

1986. As any group is, of course, constantly in process, no conclusion about its rules, roles, and patterns is accurate for all time. This is particularly true of Studio D. It is a young group in many ways; it is a group in which membership varies so that it differs as its members differ. It is a group currently under both external and internal pressures that threaten its survival. Any description, therefore, is grounded in a specific time, and the exact conditions of 1986 may not have existed 12 months earlier nor will they be present 12 months hence. In spite of the transient nature of the conditions, however, a portrait of Studio D at one moment in time can contribute to understanding how women communicate. Studio D, a predominantly female group, established in 1974 to make films by, for, and about women, by 1986 had existed 12 years. It provides, therefore, a unique opportunity to observe the interactions of women with each other in an ongoing, successful enterprise.

This study describes how members of the group interact under the specific circumstances of late 1985 and early 1986. Though one's knowledge of a group, especially one undergoing significant changes, can never be perfect, the methods used permit accurate reporting. I reviewed many written materials about the NFB, Studio D, and the films. I viewed most of the recent films made by the Studio. I spent several days with Studio D members, at work and informally, on two different occasions in January and in June 1986. I was included in Studio meetings; I recorded and have transcribed structured interviews with the executive producer and with many others—directors, producers, editors, and writers. I conducted the first set of interviews, all in January 1986, in private using an audio recorder unless the person requested that it not be turned on. During these conversations, which lasted from 30 minutes to two hours, each person responded to the same basic questions. I asked them to describe how decisions are made within the Studio, to describe the leadership within the group, and to discuss how conflicts are dealt with. The comments of each led to somewhat different follow-up questions, but I talked with each interviewee until she, and I, believed those three areas had been thoroughly covered. Citations from my transcripts of these interviews occur throughout the study, without identification and citation of source, because respondents were promised anonymity. The second set of interviews was "public," in the sense that they were recorded by a television camera with the expectation that a tape would be created for classroom and other uses. Citations

daily experience the reality of the Studio, but they are also conclusions of a writer who shares members' vision. It is possible, I believe, to present information and insights through art that may eventually result in changes in the status of women in a world currently generally inhospitable to the idea of equality between men and women.

from these interviews are referenced. These latter conversations did not focus on internal workings of the Studio, though subjects often voluntarily commented on such matters. In the video-recorded interviews I asked respondents to describe their background in filmmaking, to discuss their work at Studio D and the Film Board, and to "answer any question I should have asked about the Studio but did not." Appendix A includes a list of all films reviewed and interviews conducted.

In preparing this account, I utilized a method adapted from the process of filmmaking used by Studio D. Each of several drafts of the paper has been circulated for reactions by members of the Studio; their corrections and insights have been incorporated where appropriate. In so doing, I have increased the accuracy of description and been assisted in seeing the Studio operations through the eyes of those who work within it. My technique was to observe, ask questions, learn all I could about how members saw themselves, their studio and their work, and then seek reactions to my perceptions from those persons. I report here my learnings about three specific aspects of group members' interactions. No a priori framework was used to locate the members' interactions within any particular theoretical structure. Rather, I framed open-ended questions and drew my conclusions based on the group members' own ways of framing their experiences. Thus, what is presented here is a largely descriptive presentation of women in natural settings, dealing with daily problems, communicating with one another.

Studio D

History and Environment

The National Film Board of Canada, established in 1939 to record the diversity of Canadian culture and "to interpret Canada to Canadians," has become one of the world's premier public filmmaking organizations. Among its solo accomplishments is the 1974 creation of Studio D, the only government-supported women's filmmaking group in the world. This study focuses on the development and current structure of this unique group of women. I pay special attention to how its members deal with each other and with the dilemma of being a feminist group within a larger bureaucracy that is largely uncommitted to serving women as a distinct audience and much of which is at least covertly hostile to Studio D's feminist goals.

In 1938, reacting to seeing primarily U.S.-made films with U.S. content in Canadian theatres, the Parliament commissioned a study to "survey and make specific recommendations for the development of Canadian government film production." There followed the National Film Act of May 2, 1939 creating a National Film Board (hereafter, NFB) and the appointment of John Grierson as its first commissioner. Grierson, already internationally respected as a film critic and historian and one of the world's first producers of documentary films in England, was described as a dynamic and forceful man. Today he would be described as a charismatic leader. His development of what has now become a national institution began with one assistant, two secretaries, and a supervisor of production. By 1945 when he left the Board, it had a staff of 787 in 12 production units that had created 500 films being shown throughout Canada and in the United States as well (Evans, 1977).

While the NFB had not been created because of the war consuming Europe at the time and rapidly moving to do the same to North America, that war permeated the intellectual and social environment, thus inevitably influencing how the new institution would develop. Grierson enunciated two goals for the Board: to make films to cover the historical aspects of the war and to "secure the future" by making films about the "everyday things of life, the values, the ideals which make life worth living." Grierson wanted NFB films to show Canadians (and others) that there was "something worth fighting for, worth going back to" (Nash, 1982).

In spite of a strong identification with the war effort and the necessity for government "sanction" of NFB films, Grierson saw clearly that the filmmakers must remain free from government restraints. He was certain that creativity could be easily eliminated by government regulations. Moreover, he was anxious that the NFB perform a dual role. Not only was it a means for the government to maintain morale in a nation at war, but he wanted it to be a mode of information flow in the opposite direction as well. He hoped to be able to "translate the needs of the Canadian public into Government policy."

At the close of the war there was considerable sentiment to disband the NFB, but that never occurred. The National Film Board of Canada still operates under a legal mandate to "produce and distribute, and to promote the production and distribution of films in the public interest. Specifically, it must "interpret Canada to Canadians" and to other nations, represent and advise the government in matters pertaining to film, conduct film research and disseminate its findings" (McKay, 1964). NFB films are made available to Canadians through libraries, or through the distribution division of the Board itself. In its early years, Board distributors took the films to local churches, schools, and libraries, maintaining a direct link with Canadian audiences. Later, during the Board "Challenge for Change" film project, filmmakers and audience interacted directly, developing a strong synergy between NFB filmmakers and those who "consumed" the work, perhaps a more direct interaction between artist and audience than exists anywhere else. While this practice has largely disappeared in most NFB studios, a similar kind of direct interaction between filmmakers and women audiences has been maintained at Studio D.

Kathleen Shannon entered this special environment in 1956, joining the Board as a sound editor. She demonstrated the talent for filmmaking that later would permeate the works of Studio D as she did both picture and sound editing for more than 200 films before she was permitted to work as a director/producer. In the early 1970s she began creating "Working Mothers," a series of films focusing on women whose lives involved the difficult juxtaposition of paid work outside the home and motherhood. The women of Canada responded with unprecedented enthusiasm to this series which remains popular with NFB film users in 1986. The series has, comments Shannon, "remained unfortunately current" (1986). Due in part to this strong audience reaction to "Working Mothers," in part to the personal influence of Kathleen Shannon, and in part to the excitement of women everywhere about International Women's Year, the NFB in 1974 created a new studio, Studio D, and gave it the mandate to meet the "particular needs of women filmmakers and audiences." The creation and charge of Studio D acknowledged both a need to improve the status of women within the Board (a strong need, as the Board's own Equal Opportunity Report reported a few years later) and the absence of films among the NFB catalog that suitably addressed the women's audience (Brassard, Nash, St. Arnaud, & Tremblay, 1978; Denisko, 1975).

Studio D has since evolved beyond its early mission of making films by, for, and about women, though it still does that. It is now a largely female filmmaking group implementing a feminist philosophy that has, with technical and other support from the rest of the NFB, created many award-winning films, two of them winners of Oscars from the U.S. Academy of Motion Pictures. The best known Studio D film, at least in the U.S., is probably "If You Love This Planet," the film that received wide U.S. publicity when our Department of State initially labeled it as propaganda and attempted to prohibit U.S. distribution of the film. Also a well known Studio D film is the widely circulated and controversial, "Not a Love Story," a searching examination of the pornography business.

Now more than 10 years old, Studio D is still at work creating important educational and artistic films. In 1985, the NFB released two other Studio D films destined for controversy—"Speaking Our Peace," an introduction to Canadian women involved in the international antinuclear movement, and "Behind the Veil" a searing exposition of sexism in the church—and Studio D members were at work on films about women's spirituality, incest, and survivors of the Holocaust.

Studio D now overtly identifies its feminist goals. In an April 1985 news release intended to celebrate the "Second Decade," Studio D restates its original multi-part mandate of: providing "training for women with emphasis on the film crafts from which women have been traditionally excluded"; increasing the employment of professional women filmmakers; addressing the "specific information needs of women audiences"; bringing "women's perspectives to all social issues through the medium of film"; and maintaining "an environment where women can explore a female esthetic" (National Film Board of Canada, 1985). A slick, tri-color publicity brochure prepared about the same time makes the feminist philosophy more explicit: "We acknowledge feminism as an important political force which needs continued support and exposure," and the Studio pledges to contribute a feminist viewpoint, whether its films are made by men or by women. The brochure continues, "We are determined to continue making films and engage in other activities directly connected to the feminist movement . . . we believe that nothing less than full equality between men and women can liberate humanity as a whole," and asserts the essential role of film as a part of "that long process of changing attitudes" (National Film Board of Canada, n.d.). Studio members believe that "films and other art by women helps us learn to trust our own seeing, and we need to support, encourage and respect that in each other" (Shannon, n.d.).

In 1986, with a conservative government in Ottawa, a growing national debate about "privatizing filmmaking" (Richmond, 1985), and perhaps as well a backlash against the feminist Studio D films, the entire concept of government-supported filmmaking is under attack. Though Studio D films clearly meet the early goals enunciated by Grierson (making films about the "everyday things of life, the values, the ideals which make life worth living"), a desire to cut government funding overall makes support for filmmaking an easy target. Especially easy to charge with being inappropriate for government funding are feminist films that challenge established ideologies. In 1986, many Canadians fear that survival of the National Film Board and all its units is in question.

Though an overt move to eliminate the NFB would be politically unpopular, changes in budget and bureaucratic processes have affected morale and staffing throughout the Board, including the membership of Studio D. Members now live with the dissonance of receiving warmth and strong popular support from women across the continent who respond positively to Studio D films, of having achieved broad critical acclaim, and (in contrast) perceiving absence of support from government and within the NFB itself.

In many public statements, Studio D has reiterated its intention to create a supportive working environment for women (Women's Programme National Film Board, 1981), its goal of providing "an environment where women can work together in a collective atmosphere of mutual support" (NFB, n.d.). Studio members work hard to implement that philosophy but in recent months have found themselves increasingly under attack. They have begun to fear for their survival as a separate unit within the Board. These stresses affect their internal processes, causing some to question whether the basic philosophy of the feminist group is possible or even appropriate. Comments one member in words echoed by many others, "When people were not all working, they were feeling insecure, and they began to become quite paranoid about it."

Structure

To examine the structure of a group, it is useful to see that group within the system of which it is a part. Table A presents the formal organizational chart of the NFB, and as previously noted, Studio D is one of six currently organized within the Montreal headquarters of the English Production branch. (There are also four regional offices or studios within English Production that are located throughout Canada.) As with any bureaucracy (a term used descriptively, not pejoratively, in this essay), the units are strongly interdependent. All production units work with personnel in Technical and Production Services and rely on that divison for making their films. Moreover, many of Studio D films are made in French and French-language versions of many others are made, so constant interaction with personnel in the French Production branch occurs as well. The chart aptly places Distribution at the center, for all production units rely upon the services of the Distribution branch. Studio D may rely more heavily upon Distribution than most studios since the interaction between filmmaker and audience is especially important to the women of Studio D (Brassard, et. al., 1978).

Associated with Studio D, and considered a part of its "membership," though not part of the formal structure (at least not part of the budgetary structure), is the Federal Women's Film Programme. This program uses many Studio D personnel and shares its physical space. Studio D provided the leadership and personnel in developing the Federal Women's Film Program, a program in which the NFB matches funds provided by other federal departments to produce needed films related to women's

Table One. National Film Board of Canada

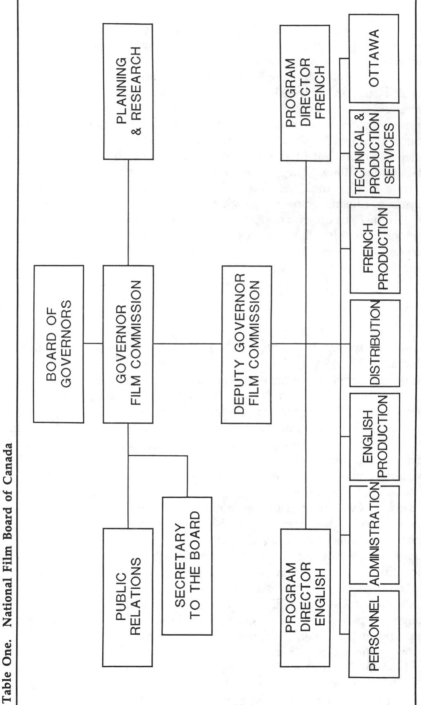

* Brassard, C., Nash, M. T., St-Arnaud, M., & Tremblay, M. (1978). Women at the National Film Board: An equal opportunity study. Montreal: National Film Board of Canada.

issues. These might be internal training films, but generally have been films that departments use for educating important parts of their own constuencies, such as a current series on spouse abuse. Other FWFP films have dealt with nontraditional employment for women, employment for native women or for physically disabled women, women and microtechnology. During the 1985–86 fiscal year, a Studio D training project was initiated through the Federal Women's Film Programme and partly funded by one government agency. To mark International Youth Year, 25 young Canadian women were selected to participate in the project that provides instruction in filmmaking by Studio D staff, using NFB space and technical support and staff. While this on-site training exercise is a new venture for Studio D, it is seen as an extension of the mandate to provide training for women filmmakers and is a source of real pride and some solace for Studio D members buffeted by budget cutbacks and tensions within the bureacracy.

Each NFB studio is headed by an executive producer, the position Kathleen Shannon holds within Studio D. Within the civil service (as well as within a film crew comprised of contract staff) positions within the studios range from producer, through director, editor, writer, and a variety of technicians and assistants. In describing the membership of Studio D, Shannon and most others take pains to stress that membership in this studio extends beyond the civil service employees. Many "free-lance" or "contract" filmmakers, some of whom work on premises at the NFB and some working outside in their own studios or in other locations, are considered members of Studio D. One such free-lancer comments, "People always think I belong to the Film Board. They never kind of say 'oh, you are a free lancer!'"

Studio D members, though committed to being a collaborative group and anxious for even free-lance filmmakers to feel part of that group, understand that the Studio is not a collective in which all parts are theoretically equal. Several members referred to studio discussions that had occurred specifically on that point. Though few echoed the words of one who said, "To say it's not a hierarchy is ridiculous," all agreed that Studio D has a clear formal structure of authority and a nearly as obvious status structure that is not completely due to its location within a larger bureaucracy. Members recognize the structure and are generally comfortable with it. Most are aware that the formal organizational structure endows specific positions with more responsibility and, as a result, more authority and impact on decisions. Others agreed with one who said that there are "real attempts made in the studio to try an do away with that [the hierarchical pattern] as much as possible. Sometimes we are more successful than other times." Some sense of dissonance between the reality and the feminist theory exists: "As women, I feel we are dedicated to the idea of a nonhierarchical pattern" is a typical comment. And the difference between what one person describes as "the rhetoric and the reality," bothers some members more than others. Though most members support the idea of a nonhierarchical system, most recognize that it does not exist in Studio D and agree that it could not exist in a single unit within a larger, quite hierarchical organization. Moreover, some at least, are not sure that such processes would ever be totally compatible with filmmaking.

Due to the NFB structure, the executive producer is the responsible authority of the Studio. She has the highest rank, and all members agree that she is not merely first among equals. The current executive producer founded the studio, has been its philosophical, psychological, and artistic leader. This rank and status is not questioned by any member of the group to whom I spoke, and all believe it is not questioned by any member of the Studio. This rank and status are not due solely to structure within the bureaucracy, however. It reflects a combination of legitimate, referent, and expert power as described by French and Raven (1979), being an authority earned by talent, success, experience, and personality. One long-time studio member described this characteristically: "Historically . . . she did an incredibly good job." With Kathleen Shannon, the current executive producer, considering retirement in 1986, studio members are having, for the first time, to consider alternatives in the position of executive producer. That this possible transition is coming at a time of external stresses on the NFB and Studio D makes these troubling times for members. This transition issue arose often when I raised questions about decision making and conflict resolution processes within the Studio.

After the top positions, producers have the highest staff rank within the NFB, but their position within the larger hierarchy does not grant them highest status with Studio D. Members respect some producers as they would normally someone at the highest rank in the group or as they would respect the position of producer in "outside" filmmaking, but when they do, it is, as several pointed out, because of the individual involved, her personality and talent.

Generally, within Studio D at least—and Studio D members believe this true to a large extent throughout the NFB—films are associated with a director. One result of that is that, after the executive producer, directors have the highest status within the group. Within this NFB bureaucracy, the role of producer is somewhat different from that in private filmmaking. Here, a producer usually does not conceive the film "idea" and does not need to engage in fund-raising. Rather, a producer's role is to see that the necessary details in bringing a film from conception to finished product are attended to and, in Studio D, is often described as a "housekeeper." An interesting incident illustrating both the structural relationships among roles and how conflict issues are dealt with occurred in accepting the Academy Award for "If You Love This Planet." Terri Nash, the director, by all accounts within the Studio, deserved the award. She had conceived the film; worked with the executive producer to arrange for its support by Studio D and for clearance to distribute it through the NFB; had supervised the shooting, editing, and in-house production. The award, however, in keeping with the Academy policies, was made to the producer of the film. After considerable correspondence with the Academy officials and discussion within the Studio and the NFB, Nash was designated co-producer of the film and jointly received the award. For her to do so, however, required that the man originally designated as producer write a letter refusing to accept the award, since his name was listed in the film credits as producer of the film when it was submitted to the competition.

Nash, interestingly, is one of the "free-lance" filmmakers at Studio D. She has been associated with the NFB and Studio D in a variety of roles and in an off and on time-frame almost from the beginning of the Studio. Throughout, the Film Board relies heavily on these contract or "free-lance" filmmakers. In 1978, 25 percent of the total NFB workforce were contract staff (Brassard, et. al., 1978). That meant some 240 free-lancers and temporary employees worked along side 950 permanent (civil service) employees. Some of the contract personnel are casual employees, hired only on a temporary basis for a specific job and not around long enough to become an integral part of the Board. Others, however, have long-term relationships with the NFB, separated by their contractual status from the "regular" staff. These contract personnel have no job security and no benefits such as paid holidays, sick leave, and medical insurance. The Board was, throughout, so rife with this perceived abuse of the contract status that it was taken to court in 1975 by the staff union, with the result than many "free-lancers" were required to be added to the civil service employment status. Three "regulars" joined Studio D as permanent employees as a result of that suit.

Within Studio D, the commitment to using women throughout the filmmaking process results in having a proportion of free-lancers somewhat higher than the rest of the NFB, and while such distinctions among filmmakers are problematical in all NFB studios, they cause additional difficulties within the feminist studio that attempts to involve all its members in collaborative decision making. Two typical comments, one by a staff member, another by a free-lancer, illustrate. Replying to a question whether the distinctions cause conflict, the staff member responded, "Not interpersonally. I've never encountered that. I would say that the people on staff feel badly. You know, it's a position of privilege. . . . The most awkward situation is that (such as) you were in the room yesterday: some people are on staff and are secure, and some people aren't and they work side by side. It is just awful. And there is no solution." The free-lancer's comments basically agreed: "It's funny, you know, but I'd say that if there was ever a cause for real conflict and bad feelings, it is just a fantastic cause, but it very rarely comes up. We all know that a lot of people on staff are aware of our position and feel badly. . . . It is not a major issue." Yet it is clear that the differences do create simmering resentments. Free-lancers pointedly noted their lack of security and benefits; staff members that it is often galling to see free-lancers' contracts consuming limited studio money when money is insufficient to support projects the staffers would like to be doing. One member noted with some irritation that free-lancers' contracts result in higher hourly rates than staffers receive and Shannon observed that often neither staffers nor free-lancers remember that she intends for higher rates paid to free-lancers to compensate for their absence of benefits.

Members' Interactions

That Studio D was created and has survived for more than a decade is itself a remarkable story. I was specifically interested, however, in how this unique group of women interact with one another. How, I asked members of the group, does it operate? How do decisions get made? What processes of leadership and followership exist? How are conflicts dealt with? The questions are interrelated, but the answers reveal much about the problems of women, not just as filmmakers, but in dealing with an internal and external environment filled with contradictions.

Hierarchy and decision making. As noted above, a clear hierarchy exists within Studio D. It exists and owes its existence to much the same sources as hierarchy within any organization or group: rules of the larger system, individual members' talents and inclinations. Even its feminist vision of collaborative processes has not freed Studio D from the bureaucracy, with much of its hierarchy and decision structure ruled by that bureaucracy. That an executive producer is appointed by the authority of the Film Board itself and that she, not other members of the Studio, is held accountable for Studio D money and products leads inevitably to some hierarchy within the Studio. That almost all Studio members are women generally committed to collaborative processes rather than hierarchical authority structures has not (cannot, I would argue) freed it from the organization's structures. As numerous management and organizational studies have demonstrated, climate and methods throughout an institution depend heavily upon the vision and practice of top management (Barnard, 1968; Bennis & Nanus, 1985; Likert, 1967; Peters & Waterman, 1982). Climate and role performances within any unit of an organization need not coincide totally with other units or the "rules" laid down by top management, but the degree of divergence possible or permitted is limited. Therefore, even though committed to implementing feminist interactive processes, Studio D members have been unable to fully accomplish the goal.

Though an executive producer is ultimately responsible for decisions made by a studio, everyone I talked with agreed that on most issues Shannon tries to involve members of Studio D in decision making. One result is that resolving some issues takes longer than some members believe is necessary. A telling incident occurred near the end of a Studio meeting in January 1986. A staff member from another division of the Film Board interrupted briefly (invited to do so as the group was waiting for a guest to appear) and asked which Studio member would be its representative in a word processing seminar being made available to NFB employees. Shannon's response: "Oh, Michael, we usually take at least 30 minutes to decide something like that." Ultimately, unless only one member of the Studio wishes to attend, Shannon will choose the representative. She will talk with several people and a number of people will devote considerable time before the issue is resolved. The ambiguity of this process, coupled with the inevitable delays caused by such efforts at reaching consensus, tests Studio members. On larger questions, the time required will be greater and the emotional investment higher, with the resulting test of commitment to collaborative processes more severe.

The bureaucracy alone, however, does not totally account for the hierarchy within Studio D. The process of filmmaking itself is historically, if not inherently, hierarchical. Most of the decisions made within Studio D are involved in the process of filmmaking: What films will be made? What will their budgets be? What personnel will be involved? What will be the content of the film? What film will be used, what discarded? What will be the script, the sound, and so on? Within Studio D, these decisions involve collaboration on various levels, but when the collaboration does not easily evolve into consensus (and it often does not), ultimately the person "in charge" at the appropriate point in the hierarchy makes the decision. For some members of the Studio, this "fact" of the filmmaking process does not cause distress. For others, it highlights the dissonance between the reality of Studio D and the feminist vision and is, therefore, a source of distress. In yet other cases, the processes work as members would desire. Comments one director,

"I'm really conscious of what it feels like to be at the bottom of that ladder of hierarchy . . . so we have tried really hard on this production to make it a circle. I see my role as the director as maybe one that has to take the responsibility for a great number of decisions about the film. However, I really do that in conjunction with everyone else. Everybody who has worked on this production has been invited into the ideas and the decisions. . . . In that way, inasmuch as I can control things, you know, I'm trying to do in my little way what I can in terms of working in film a little differently."

She continues by pointing out that although some directors believe they should be more hierarchical than others, she believes "that every other director will probably say the same thing, I mean that in their way, as they can figure things out, [they] have also tried."

Similar dichotomies between the desire to work collectively and the necessity to succeed at their tasks of filmmaking appear in other major issues upon which decisions are required. Perhaps the most important decisions ever made in the group are the choices about what films are produced, since budget almost always places a funnel between ideas for films and support for their creation. Film ideas come from a variety of sources, of course: directors inside and outside of the studio, audience suggestions, and in the early years from Shannon herself. For many years, the NFB process involved a Board Programming Committee whose members signed off on all proposals for filmmaking from all studios. In recent years, film decisions have been decentralized to each studio with the executive producer in each responsible for determining how her/his budget is distributed among various films to be produced. Thus, Shannon is responsible to the bureaucracy for making appropriate responses to film proposals. Beyond that structural requirement, however, is the consensus within the group that Shannon's film judgment is excellent. Thus, while most film ideas originate with others, many suggestions for refinement of the ideas are Shannon's, and though the studio often discusses as a group the films to which its resources will be devoted, all respect her judgment regarding what will "fly" with both the audiences and the bureaucracy. Noted a long-time studio member, Shannon has "a very good intuitive feel about audiences." This person believes that is because Shannon has "always been so clear on where her commitment is . . . [It is] not to us as filmmakers, which frustrates some, and it's not to say she's not committed to us, I mean a big part of the studio has been to train women in film. But her primary commitment is to women as audiences. And that really has, I think, given her a kind of guiding sense of what films, you know when a proposal comes in, of what films really need making." In short, ideas are aired and collaboration occurs, but ultimately, the executive producer decides what films will be made.

Once the studio has decided to move forward with making a film, personnel must be assigned to the effort. These decisions usually result from collaboration among the executive producer and the director involved; rarely will the entire studio be involved in this kind of choice. It is these personnel decisions that may most dramatically reflect the implementation of Studio D's feminist philosophy. Several instances exist of allowing inexperienced directors to direct important projects, as do instances of selecting staff from "lower status" roles for important production roles.

The Studio exemplifies its feminist philosophy in such staff choices. This most striking implementation of the Studio's vision is a stringent test of commitment to that vision, because when inexperienced filmmakers have important responsibilities, the problems that result in the filmmaking process can be significant. For many creative artists, a degree of insecurity inheres in the process. One's creativity, and hence self-identification, is tested each time one's work is "put on the line" for inspection and approval of others. This vulnerability only increases when people with relatively little experience have important responsibilities. It is not uncommon for such situations to result in one member of the Studio extending help to others, as would be expected in any similar situation. Dissonance results, however, from the inconsistency members see (often within themselves) between the nurturant vision and the resulting very real (and understandable) desires for "credits" for the help extended. As one director explained, "You have to be very gifted as an editor to say, 'you know, I think that I'm making a major contribution here.' I don't think any director in Studio D would say, 'No, you're not.' They would acknowledge you are, and I really appreciate it, thank you." But, she continued instantly, the film is credited "in the world" to the director, and concluded, "I mean, I'm happy I'm a director and not an editor." Coping with such issues is one of the major sources of conflict in the Studio as well as being a situation that brings members face to face with the difference between the vision and the reality.

Many other important decisions occur during the process of creating films. In many respects, these decisions reflect the model described above, that of consultation among those involved with the "authority" in the situation holding final decision power. Thus, as films are made, the collaboration to which the studio is philosophically committed occurs, but in large part the hierarchical nature of filmmaking remains the *modus operandi*. As noted in the discussion above, films are largely identified with a director, and when differences of opinion cannot be resolved by consensus among those involved, directors decide. Indeed, in many aspects of filmmaking, no consensus is sought. The director decides and production staff do not question that decision authority.

Some crucial points in the filmmaking process spotlight the collaborative/authoritative dichotomy: in the cutting and editing stages and when film rough-cut is screened. When a film has reached this latter stage in production, available members of the studio gather for review of the materials or viewing the screenings. Suggestions come from all and studio members speak favorably of the creative power that results from this collaborative process, described by a director as "one of the key processes in the studio. . . . It's a great moment, or potentially a great moment. . . . Showing a film to other respected colleagues is an incredible experience, because what happens is that when you are editing a film you are very close to it and you're still working with what you hope it's doing and what you're trying to do. And then suddenly, other eyes come in and see things that you've never seen. Respond to things differently, have feelings you didn't imagine they'd have. And when they come, you accept that input, obviously according to your feelings about that person's judgment."

As this member's comments suggest, the hierarchical nature of filmmaking and the studio itself is never far from the surface. Even though members attempt to adhere to the desired collaborative processes, ultimately the hierarchy persists. Many suggestions are made to the director who may or may not agree with them and implement them. How she responds to suggestions is partly a function of her own judgment regarding the idea and her respect for the person making the suggestion.

Shannon as executive producer is often involved in these screenings; her suggestions carry the weight of her office as well as the strength of her demonstrated skill in filmmaking. She is sensitive to the influence she has with studio members and is not seen as heavy-handed in suggestions she makes. But, ultimately, when she expresses an opinion that is strong and differs from that of another member of the studio, only very secure and convinced directors or editors will persist with a film decision that differs from that of the executive producer.

Other aspects of life within Studio D highlight this dissonance between philosophy and reality. For example, the staff distinctions discussed earlier lead to problems with which the Studio must deal. Members see commitment to the feminist philosophy of the Studio as variable, and even some of the permanent staff describe the commitment as higher among free-lancers than among permanent employees. Yet sometimes contract staff are unable or unwilling to attend Studio meetings and are thus less informed about policies and plans. The difficulty if not impossibility of wielding a completely cohesive studio membership under those conditions reduces the effectiveness of the efforts at collaborative decision making. Almost inevitably in a group where such distinctions exist, resentments between the different categories of staff will exist. In a group that wants to see itself as a sisterhood, not only as committed to improving conditions for women within the film industry but as doing something about it, such distinctions present difficulties.

Dealing with conflict. Perhaps the most striking fact about the permanent employee/contract staff distinction is how studio members deal with these differences. It is virtually a model for other cases in which conflict-producing issues are handled. Without exception, the people to whom I talked were troubled about the two categories of staff and about the resentments and conflicts generated. An undercurrent of guilt pervaded much of the talk by members who were permanent staff. One overtly described the guilt she felt when working side by side with contract staff; another somewhat defensively referred to the higher pay rate contract employees could negotiate to compensate them for absence of benefits. Yet, when I asked if these problems were openly discussed, most commented in terms similar to the director who replied, "Well, let's see. What can I say more to a person? And I don't bring it up. I mean, how do I deal with it? . . . I know all the staff would feel very, very awkward, and, guilt's not the right word, but to be living in an unequal situation is terrible. So, what is there to be discussed?"

Throughout our discussions, Studio D members made clear that they recognized that many conflicts existed among them and, almost without exception, overtly or otherwise communicated some sense of guilt because the conflicts seemed to challenge the basic feminist philosophy of the group. One member used almost exactly those words in commenting that one expects such conflicts in a patriarchical system and therefore is less bothered by it. That they have been unable to eliminate conflict within Studio D is a source of considerable tension for members. The situation creates considerable dissonance as members recognize the inconsistency between their aspirations as a feminist group and the actuality of their situation.

In the spirit of their feminist philosophy, members discuss, in small groups or sometimes in Studio meetings, whatever issue may be causing the problem, but most believe the discussions are not totally honest. Such openness is believed especially difficult for free-lance filmmakers who may fear that their speaking out will jeopardize their next assignment. But almost all recognized that it was common not to openly air disagreements of virtually every kind.

Many cited this tendency to avoid uncomfortable discussions when I asked how group members deal with conflict. They largely agreed that members of the group attempt to avoid discussing unpleasant issues or matters in which conflict inheres, even though such disagreements eventually emerge, often in heated arguments or emotional confrontations. One member recalled an effort once made to cope with these problems. She described a studio meeting during which Shannon had "tried her best to get out all the dirty laundry." Shannon had asked that members with a gripe, any gripe, write it on a piece of paper without identification. The papers were all put into an envelope, and taken out one at a time. Then each member in the meeting was to say, "Does this apply to me or not?" The particular incident was described in relating how studio members talk about a director's "ownership" of a film. As she noted, in many films it is really the editor who "makes" the film, but that it still is the director's film. She said, "I wouldn't like that if I was an editor," but admitted to talking that way even though sensitive to the issue.

Many studio members admit that they personally tend to avoid discussing issues of disagreement, and say that other members of the studio behave similarly. Commonly they explained the tendency to avoid confronting conflict situations by saying they don't like to hurt the people involved. Most attributed this sensitivity to the fact of their female membership. Interestingly, however, members did not distinguish clearly what particular sensitivity they were describing. Was it that of the person who avoids bringing up an issue of conflict because she perceives that the other person will "be hurt by the statement?" Or the sensitivity that causes people to feel hurt when it is pointed out to them that someone else disagrees with them or when someone criticizes their work? The members' terms for describing the hurt feelings seem to encompass both aspects of the matter, as illustrated by this typical statement. "I think we've produced more films with less conflict, probably than most filmmakers. I mean, there are horrendous stories in the film industry . . . it is inherent . . . [filmmaking] almost nourishes and fosters prima donna behavior. . . . Just putting it in perspective, I think we've done a remarkable job." She noted that much conflict in the studio stems from "the incredible gap between what we need to do, what the public perceives that we are able to do and what, in fact, we are able to do and how our institution [the NFB and Studio D] exists. And, she concluded, "we are terrible" at confronting conflictual situations before they "become terribly painful." In short, she said, "there's a lot of nurturing that goes on in terms of how we handle conflict." This person reflects a typical sense of dissonance, however, as illustrated by her further comments. She stated that she feared that, in thus attempting to create a supportive working atmosphere, they had somehow shortchanged themselves. Had they limited their own development of interpersonal skills and ability to "negotiate with men?" she wondered.

Many members attributed their conflicts to the "emotionality" of women, and for those with comparable experiences in other kinds of groups, it was common to compare the emotionalism with which conflict situations are dealt in Studio D to what they remember as the more dispassionate discussions of difference they had experienced in other situations. Some members attributed the emotionality to lack of experience, indicating that insecurity often creates excessive strains in the interpersonal relationships accompanying a creative process that ultimately measures the individual by the quality of the product. Others, usually those with experience in other work situations, related the issue of inexperience to lack of experience in using power. These two explanations are of course related.

Most members also noted that the conflicts are usually discussed, even if not among those parties who may be at odds. Several used the same term to describe the resulting communication pattern as gathering in "affinity groups." While most recognize that such groupings are not unusual in organizations, almost all communicated a sense of guilt about the existence of such subgroups within the Studio, primarily because the origin of the subgroups is attributed to avoidance of conflict, not just normal interpersonal interest sharing. Members also saw the relationship between such subgroups and conflict, and believed them contradictory to the Studio feminist philosophy. Individuals are uncomfortable with the existence of conflict because they perceive it as an indication of their fallibility in achieving Studio goals of a warm, supportive, caring atmosphere in which women may learn and practice filmmaking.

Conclusion

Most striking about Studio D is its survival for 12 years as a predominantly female, feminist filmmaking group operating within a large and patriarchial governmental bureaucracy. Even though members have found themselves unable to change the larger bureaucracy or even to escape its pervasive influence, they have struggled to implement their mission of making films that, in the words of a Studio producer, "change the status of women" (Janes, 1986). They not only have survived, but have produced award-winning films and films that rank among the most popular ever created at the NFB. A recent survey of circulation of NFB films reported that, even when excluding "Not a Love Story" and "If You Love This Planet," the NFB received more requests for Studio D films than for those produced by any other NFB studio (Shannon, 1986).

For those interested in women as communicators, Studio D provides a remarkable case study. It shows that, even in a situation where women are vulnerable to forces of a superordinate structure that is at best indifferent and at worst hostile, feminist visions and processes can survive. The processes will be modified, the reality will not perfectly reflect the vision, and individual members will experience often severe dissonance; but feminist goals and outcomes can be achieved. Similarly, Studio D reflects much that the literature about women and about communication would lead us to expect, especially in a self-consciously feminist group.

While I have avoided framing the description of Studio D with any specific theoretical perspective, the work of important theorists provides explanations for the phenomena of Studio D. For example, I have noted that members believe that commitment to an idea must be carefully balanced with the effect of one's behavior on others. The constant references by Studio D members to their concern for the effect of their work on each other, and to their concern for how the films impacted the lives of those filmed as well as those to whom the film will be shown, reflect women's morality described by Carol Gilligan (1982). As filmmakers, members of Studio D set out in 1974 to celebrate and solidify their connections to other women. They describe their work as an effort to "present issues in their interconnectedness" (Shannon, 1985). They consciously seek to create a work atmosphere of caring and concern for each other. Maintaining good relationships among those making films has always been important to these women. The desire to maintain such relationships and to emphasize the connectedness of women everywhere can also explain the reluctance of Studio members to confront conflicts among themselves. While no Studio member spoke openly about fearing to "break up" the group by such a confrontation, concern for others' feelings was often mentioned and they talked a great deal about not wanting to hurt someone. Thus, members demonstrate the mature morality described by Gilligan; they determine and evaluate their behavior based upon the effect of the actions on other people, not according to abstract rules and principles.

I have also noted that members prefer cooperative behavior as a mode of interaction, but do not invariably behave cooperatively. The intense unease of Studio D members when they have recognized the sometimes broad gaps between the actualizing of their feminist philosophy and the reality of their working world illustrate more than the argument of Gilligan. Doubtless their unease stems in part from a recognized violation of their own morality, but this discomfort in the face of dissonance and the resulting behaviors to restore imbalance also can be explained as examples of Festinger's (1957) cognitive dissonance theory and Heider's (1958) balance theory at work. When the inconsistencies between belief and behavior are recognized, and they usually are, the discomfort of members is explained by the existence of dissonance, which members seek to reduce in a variety of ways, not all of them positive.

Conflict among members exists, but they avoid confronting it when possible, generally personalizing the sources of the conflict, even in cases when the factors generating the problems are neither internal nor personal. Differences are perceived more often as differences among personalities than as arguments about abstractions or differences of belief. Differences that may inhere in different beliefs (e.g., definitions of the studio's feminist goals or level of commitment to those goals) get described most often as differences of personality.

Studio D also illustrates a typical response to paradox (Watzlawick, 1977) as well as what Kanter (1977) has suggested is a reaction to powerlessness. While Studio D members strongly resist blaming themselves or each other for the problems they identify, strong forces pressure them to do so. Even though most members attempt to locate the sources of their difficulties within the patriarchy of the Board or of the larger society, many members (if not all at least some times) question whether their own weaknesses, as women, have created the problems. In that most Studio D members are conscious feminists and many are well read, they are (perhaps) excessively sensitive to blaming a victim for her own difficulties. Thus, they wrestle with the paradox of the existence of inevitable human shortcomings that impact upon their work, but which cannot be openly identified or discussed outside (and often inside) the group.

Kanter, again, (1980) provides an explanation for their resistance to openly identify and discuss problems of the Studio. Studio D is a "first," and studio members are quite conscious of their uniqueness. Not only are women filmmakers a minority at the NFB, and not only is the Studio only one of six production units within the English Division in Montreal, but it is probably the only government-supported women's filmmaking unit in the world. For these feminist filmmakers to be less than perfect (as a group of women, not as filmmakers) can be magnified into failure by perceived enemies—those in the patriarchy who hope the Studio will demonstrate the negative stereotypes about women. Any human failing can be translated into a failure for all women.

The attempt at keeping private their own failures to perfectly exemplify their feminist philosophy, however, itself presents a paradox for Studio members. Thus, when a weakness or problem is identified that cannot be attributed to the patriarchy, it may be inevitable that it is personalized. Failures are explained in inherently paradoxical ways. Problems that may be caused in large part by external forces are attributed to personal weaknesses; or conversely, problems that stem from personal behaviors are attributed to forces beyond one's control— for example, the bureaucracy.

Whether or not there is a full second decade for Studio D, and regardless of what form it takes in response to a different environment in the nation and in the NFB, it has created a remarkable legacy. It has created 70 films—many of them popular, uncompromising feminist films that remain largely timeless. It has offered to dozens of women the opportunity to learn and mature in the arts and craft of filmmaking, an opportunity that would not have been available to many of those women had Studio D not existed. And finally, it has presented an opportunity for a case study of women communicating that I have only begun to tap.

References

Barnard, C. (1968). *The functions of the executive.* Cambridge, MA: Harvard University Press.

Bennis, W., & Nanus, B. (1985). *Leaders: The strategies for taking charge.* New York: Harper & Row.

Brassard, C., Nash, M. T., St-Arnaud, M., & Tremblay, M. (1978). *Women at the National Film Board: An equal opportunity study.* Montreal: National Film Board of Canada.

Denisko, O. (Ed.). (ca. 1975). *4 days in May (6 to 9) a report.* Montreal: National Film Board.

Evans, G. (1977). *The war for men's minds: Government film propaganda in Britain and Canada, 1914–1945.* Unpublished doctoral dissertation, McGill University, Montreal.

Festinger, L. (1957). *A theory of cognitive dissonance.* Stanford, CA: Stanford University Press.

French, J. & Raven, B. (1979). The bases of social power. In D. Carwright (Ed.), *Studies in social power* (pp. 150–167). Ann Arbor, MI: Institute of Social Research.

Gilligan, Carol. (1982). *In a different voice.* Cambridge, MA: Harvard University Press.

Heider, F. (1958). *The psychology of interpersonal relations.* New York: John Wiley & Sons, Inc.

Janes, B. (1986, June). (Video Cassette). Interview.

Kanter, R. M. (1977). *Men and women of the corporation.* New York: Basic Books.

Kanter, R. M. with Stein, B. A. (1980). *The tale of "O": On being different in an organization.* New York: Harper and Row.

Likert, Rensis. (1967). *The human organization: Its management and value.* New York: McGraw-Hill.

McKay, M. T. (1964). *History of the National Film Board of Canada.* Unpublished manuscript, National Film Board of Canada, Montreal, Quebec.

Nash, M. T. (1982). *Images of women in National Film Board of Canada films during World War II and the post war years (1939–1949).* Unpublished doctoral dissertation, McGill University, Montreal, Quebec.

National Film Board of Canada. (1985, April). *Studio D of the National Film Board of Canada: Starting the second decade.* Unpublished news release, Montreal, Quebec.

National Film Board of Canada. (n.d.) *Studio D.* Descriptive brochure available from National Film Board of Canada, Montreal, Quebec.

Peters, T. J., & Waterman, R. H., Jr. (1982). *In search of excellence: Lessons from America's best-run companies.* New York: Harper & Row.

Richmond, T. (1985, December). *A proposal to form a women's market development group at the National Film Board of Canada.* Unpublished draft, National Film Board of Canada, Montreal, Que.

Shannon, K. (1986, June). (Video Cassette). Interview.

Shannon, K. (1985, March). *This is about objectivity, objections and some objectives.* Address to conference of the Centre for Investigative Journalism, Toronto, Ontario.

Shannon, K. (n.d.) *As we see our selves.* Unpublished manuscript, National Film Board of Canada, Montreal, Quebec.

The Women's Programme National Film Board. (1981, March). *Speaking of women's culture.* Unpublished manuscript, National Film Board of Canada, Montreal, Quebec.

Watzlawick, P. (1977). *How real is real?* New York: Random House.

Appendix A

Interviews

Gloria DeMers, January 10, 1986

Dorothy Todd Henaut, June 7, 1986 (video recording)

Barbara Janes, January 13, 1986 (audio recording); June 6, 1986 (video recording)

Bonnie Sherr Klein, January 13, 1986 (audio recording); June 9, 1986 (video recording)

Terri Nash, January 11, 1986 (audio recording); June 6, 1986 (video recording)

Margaret Pettigrew, January 10, 1986

Donna Read, January 20, 1986 (audio recording)

Gerry Rogers, January 10, 1986; June 7, 1986 (video recording)
Beverly Shaffer, January 11, 1986 (audio recording)
Kathleen Shannon, January 10, 1986; January 13, 1986 (audio recording);
    June 6, 1986 (video recording)
Ginny Stikeman, February 12, 1986
Margaret Wescott, June 6, 1986 (video recording)

Films

Chatwin, L. (Producer), & Shannon, K. (Director). (1974). Luckily I need
    little sleep. Montreal, Quebec: National Film Board of Canada.
Chatwin, L. (Producer), & Shannon, K. (Director). (1974). Mothers are
    people. Montreal, Quebec: National Film Board of Canada.
Shannon, K. & Chatwin, L (Producers), & Shannon, K., Angelico, I.,
    & Henderson A. (Directors). (1975). ". . . And they lived happily
    ever after." Montreal, Quebec: National Film Board of Canada.
Shannon, K. (Producer), & Beaudry-Cowling, D. (Director). (1976). Maud
    Lewis: a world without shadows. Montreal, Quebec: National Film
    Board of Canada.
Shannon, K. (Producer), & Guilbeault, L., Brossard, N., & Wescott, M.
    (Directors). (1977). Some American feminists. Montreal, Quebec:
    National Film Board of Canada.
Yoshida, Y. (Producer), & Shaffer, B. (Director). (1977). I'll find a way.
    Montreal, Quebec: National Film Board of Canada.
Pettigrew, P., & Pearson, A. (Producers), & Klein, B. S. (Director).
    (1978). Patricia's moving picture. Montreal, Quebec: National Film
    Board of Canada.
Henaut, D. T. (Producer), & Klein, B. S. (1981). Not a love story: A
    film about pornography. Montreal, Quebec: National Film Board
    of Canada.
Le Lorrain, E. & Nash, T. (Producers), & Nash, T. (Director). (1982).
    If you love this planet. Montreal, Quebec: National Film Board of
    Canada.
Singer, G (Producer & Director). (1982). Portrait of the artist as an old
    lady. Montreal, Quebec: National Film Board of Canada.
Johansson, S. & Singer, G. (Producers), & Singer, G. (Director). (1984).
    Abortion stories from the north and south. Montreal, Quebec:
    National Film Board of Canada.
Johansson, S. (Producer), & Wescott, M. (Director). (1985). Behind the
    veil nuns. Montreal, Quebec: National Film Board of Canada.
Le Lorrain, E. & Shannon, K. (Producers), & Shannon, K. & Stikeman,
    G. (Directors). (1984). Dream of a free country: A message from

Nicaraguan women. Montreal, Quebec: National Film Board of Canada.

Klein, B. S., & Pettigrew, M. (Producers), & Klein, B. S., & Nash, T. (Directors). (1985). Speaking our peace. Montreal, Quebec: National Film Board of Canada.

Johansson, S. & Janes, B. (Producers), & Horne, T. (Director). (1986). Speaking of Nairobi. Montreal, Quebec: National Film Board of Canada.

15

Themes and Perspectives in Women's Talk

Barbara Bate

Drew University

The women described in this book are a diverse lot. Within that diversity, however, their communication reveals four elements that both confirm and redefine past generalizations about women's talk. The four unifying elements that emerge from these studies are: (a) an honoring of the communication process itself; (b) an awareness of multiple perspectives; (c) a search for identification with others; and (d) a delight in creativity. Selected examples will show how each of these themes emerges in various communication situations.

Honoring the communication process

In every study of women organizing to complete a task, the women themselves express an awareness that the way they interact with each other is as important as their end result. Redwood Records, Studio D, the teacher-researchers, and the bookstore collective all make substantial (some may claim excessive) time commitments in order to work out their plans, procedures, and responses to changing events. The foundation of most of the conversations examined in this book is respect for the communication process and a willingness to invest personal time in that process. Speakers from each group cited above treat ongoing consultation and problem solving with each other as the only way to establish and maintain cooperative relationships. A climate of fear or judgment would deprive all the members of reality checks on their own perceptions and would hinder creative women in particular from taking the risk of self-expression. Never in these varied studies do we encounter people who have given up on interacting. Repeatedly we meet women who believe they can work on life issues better in the company of sisters and colleagues.

Awareness of multiple perspectives

To be aware of multiple points of view about a situation or relationship can be both an advantage and a disadvantage for a communicator. The evidence from these studies suggests that women choose to take into account opinions other than their own, with all the demands on the conscious mind that such inclusion entails. The process begins with careful listening to others; it usually entails affirming others' rights to differ with the self; and it can lead to immobilization when choosing between alternative opinions or actions. Workers at the Emma Goldman Clinic for Women can convince their clients to think differently about medical personnel precisely because they recognize the patriarchal approach to doctor-patient relationships and can counter it with constructive new symbols. The feminist humorists, the mother-daughter pairs telling stories, the Redwood record producers, and the weavers all show evidence of taking other views into account as a means to further their joint endeavors. On the other hand, the negative impact of multiple perspectives becomes clear when the women in "Body Talk" discuss their shameful bodies. While they can articulate the voices of unidentified Others who call them overweight, unkempt, or unattractive, they must struggle to retain a self-affirming view of their situations.

A search for identification with others

Identification between individuals or groups can involve intentional efforts to join one's interests with others, or it can occur through unplanned or even unconscious feelings of oneness with another (Burke, 1950). Shirley Chisholm's speeches to black and white women's audiences reveal a speaker who is intentionally seeking identification through her use of evidence that will reach both her black and white female audiences. She takes account of the fact that some issues of social custom bother white women—the use of Mrs. vs. Ms., for example—but do not matter as much to black women. Chisholm centers her talks on demonstrating to both audiences that sexism makes all women victims. Having showed she is aware of multiple perspectives, she can foster an identification among all women which can transcend racial boundaries.

Ways of collaborating on tasks show how people identify with each other. When mothers and daughters tell stories together to an interviewer, each is an individual adult, a family member, and an informal historian at the same time. As Hall and Langellier demonstrate, both members show their connection to each other in the small details of collaborative storytelling. Even where there is conflict about what to include in the story, the partners' efforts to "get it right together" indicate a valuing of their shared interpersonal constructions of family events. In a more public setting, the Jennies team members show a surprising approach to being basketball stars, for they neither seek nor reinforce individual self-aggrandizement on or off the court. The researchers imply that some within-the-self conflict may arise in the players who get less playing time than they would like, but these players express frustration only rarely, in a written questionnaire for the researchers, never in discussion in front of their peers. Identifying with the team as a unit and with the coach as a moral as well as athletic leader, the Jennies moderate the expected desire for personal glory by defining the team, not the individual player, as the focal symbol in their current lives.

Humans often use identification with others to moderate the impact of inequalities and to transcend conflicts. In the Weavers Guild, Studio D, Redwood Records, and the teacher-research team, leaders act in ways that submerge their dominance and place more responsibility on others in the group. It is as if they recognize the problem of dominance and choose a process that will moderate its effects.

Delight in creativity

Women's communication reveals a spirit of delight in creativity in both obvious and subtle ways. Creative freedom and flair are obvious in the needlework and porcelain plates of "The Dinner Party," and the ingenuity evidenced in unearthing and highlighting heroic women through the ages is awe-inspiring in itself. Creative activities are the foundation for the Weavers Guild, Redwood Records, and Studio D. Other women delight in feminist puns like "pap smear envy" and in remembered stories that reveal character in a light or loving moment. Emerging from many of these accounts is an image of personal creativity as an option at any moment. Some of these people genuinely experience their communication together as an open process, one which can produce renewed or radically altered realities among the participants. Pervasive in these studies is the suggestion that verbal and visual creativity is a major emblem for the communicative competence women can enjoy and respect, even in settings where women cannot control the structure or outcomes of their effort.

From a different methodological framework, the research review of Mary Jeannette Smythe (in press) sheds an interesting and largely supportive light on the studies in this book. Examining the results of the few quantitative studies of female dyads, Smythe found evidence (a) that in conversations with one another women exhibit lower levels of dominance, dealing with each other in a more cooperative or synergistic manner than they do with men; (b) that during initial interactions with each other, women are less guarded and more relaxed than are men with men; (c) that women together discuss more personal matters, focusing on family, relationship problems, and (hence) men; and (d) that women talking with women exhibit a high rate of verbal back-channel cues, behaviors demonstrating active attentiveness and perhaps supportiveness. With different wording, these results suggest a similar flavor of pleasure, trust, and support between women, as suggested above, concerning both identification and creativity.

Four Perspectives on Studies of Women's Talk

The research studies in this volume can also be seen from a more general and philosophical vantage point. Four different perspectives have been the recognized or unrecognized bases for defining, describing, and evaluating the communication of women (Bate, 1988). The four perspectives are the biological, the cultural, the power-based, and the rhetorical or strategic. Each of the four directs attention toward a different emphasis as one examines how women communicate with each other. By revealing the varying filters on our perceptions of women's (and men's) talk, each perspective opens the way to greater understanding of both the constraints and the possibilities facing women communicating. Each exists in both a patriarchal form, assuming male dominance as social foundation, and a feminist or alternative form, assuming that women's outlook on experience is essential and constructive. Brief descriptions of each and its relevance to this volume show how themes and issues are interwoven across the various studies.

The biological perspective assumes that differences in biological makeup—particularly reproductive capacity in women, muscular strength in men—produce significant differences in communication behavior. A traditional version of the biological viewpoint asserts that size differences between men and women not only do but ought to affect their behavior, making the man act either more protective or more aggressive, and making the woman more quiet and passive since she is expected to be unable to defend herself against attack and vulnerable as a potential carrier of (his) children.

A feminist alternative within the biological perspective on communication claims that women's bodies (a) are not weak or shameful, (b) are in fact stronger than men's in longevity and disease resistance, and (c) are appropriate for women ourselves, not men, to define and evaluate. Biological difference between the sexes remains important in this viewpoint, though with strikingly different conclusions. The musculature and hormones of men are seen from a feminist perspective as problematic, for many more men than women commit violent crimes and suffer injuries from attempts to demonstrate their physical superiority. In contrast, the reproductive capacity of women provides a basis for woman-to-woman intimacy and support, and it makes possible an act of creation that is unparalleled in human experience.

The cultural perspective emphasizes the different assumptions, languages, nonverbal codes, and spheres of interest that are believed to characterize the distinctive development patterns of females and males. In its traditional or patriarchal form, the cultural viewpoint suggests that men "belong" in the world of paid employment and public leadership, while women "belong" at home with children and private interests. Underlying this traditional system of beliefs is the idea that people communicate best when they are functioning in their "natural" place or situation. "Natural" as a term unites cultural directions with biological differences, implying that those who can create children can only interact appropriately within the family.

From a feminist standpoint, cultural awareness is important because boys and girls have in most cases been taught to think of themselves in two distinct communication cultures: he is to look as large as possible, swear to show his bravery, and never cry; she is to look as petite as possible, avoid profanity to retain her status as a "lady," and cry when angry, frustrated, or fearful. The feminist view of these phenomena is that they place severe constraints on both sexes in attempting to become competent adult communicators. Women have fewer chances to organize, carry out plans with others, and manage conflict effectively, while men have fewer chances to work as equals, care for children, and admit vulnerability to another adult. But the situation of difference has positive potential as well: among feminist artists, creating new symbolic forms offers a way to reach other women and thus develop a new, more affirmative female culture through poetry, music, film, painting, and other media. (See also Johnson, 1986).

Viewpoints based on power show dramatic differences between the patriarchal and the feminist views. Power-based approaches to communication deal generally with one's control or one's efficacy in communication situations. The patriarchal perspective on power is that it is a resource for controlling the behavior of others. Two people cannot have equal power, for one will be dominant or be attempting to gain superiority over the other. In this older view, hierarchy is natural and everyone is expected to want to have more power than some others around them.

The feminist concept of empowerment denotes the sharing and distributing of power, and power itself is seen as the ability to attain goals regardless of whether one has higher or lower status than another. Power is a finite commodity in the patriarchal view, but potentially limitless in the feminist view; thus to feminists egalitarian communicative relationships are not only possible but sought after. Though many men and some women are skeptical that this second form of power is feasible, many women describe their communicative relationships with other women as highly pleasurable and self-affirming because the issue of dominance has been absent.

The rhetorical or strategic perspective is the fourth approach to women's communication. It starts from the premise that any person makes strategic decisions about how and when to communicate in particular circumstances. Using basic concepts from rhetorical theory and criticism, this approach assumes that communication is situational; speakers make choices of what to say in a situation according to what they believe will accomplish their goals in that particular situation. Where situations are perceived by both sexes similarly, women and men may respond to them in similar ways; but because the constraints of history, attitude, and personal experience often differ widely between the sexes, men and women often make extremely different choices about what to say, to whom, or whether to speak at all (Kramarae, 1981).

Traditional studies of rhetoric focused on the communication of men because women were either not seen, not welcomed, or not listened to as public speakers. Only recently have rhetorical studies of inter-personal communication applied rhetorical concepts to the private communication settings where women have been expected to appear. One contribution of the research in this book is to illuminate many of the complex circumstances in which actual women make choices about their talk. Feminists often face not only the immediate demands of accomplishing a task but also the unstated urgency of representing "Women in General" with sufficient dexterity to avoid being stereotyped as either too strong or too weak a communicator. To recognize complications and paradoxes in women's rhetorical situations is to move toward an appreciation of the rhetorical skills women must exhibit simply to survive.

Describing the research studies in this volume in relation to the four viewpoints is done to illustrate how new knowledge can be composed not only of individual bits of information, but also of new angles of vision, new points of view, new paradigms. Many of these studies are illuminated by more than one of the four perspectives. The present choices of emphasis are made to show major ideas and connection points across individual essays.

Spitzack's essay on body talk is founded on the traditional version of the biological perspective: young women see their bodies as battle-grounds between the ease and comfort of eating and the mortification of starving oneself to reach a slender cultural ideal. Contemporary news reports reveal the extreme results of desiring a perfect body: thousands of fitness centers and health spas on the one hand, and a major increase in disorders such as anorexia nervosa and bulimia, both centering on the individual's terror of being overweight. For the women Spitzack interviewed, the physical body itself takes on characteristics of both an object to be subdued and another person with a will of its own.

Owen's study of the Emma Goldman Clinic reveals both patriarchal and feminist viewpoints about the body. The patriarchal view has kept women confused and powerless in dealing with their own reproductive systems; the feminist view gives them matter-of-fact knowledge of the body and personal support for controlling their own physical being.

Foss's study of "The Dinner Party" combines a feminist approach to female biology with elements of the cultural, power, and rhetorical viewpoints as well. Central to the artistry and the controversy of "The Dinner Party" are the decorated porcelain plates, the centers of which resemble female labia. The sexual component of women's identity is presented in a way that violates the usual split between sexuality as private and social communication as public. Dinner parties are tradi-tionally a social activity involving women; but if one admits the bodily images in most of the dinner plates one must acknowledge women's sexuality—both as sexual partner and as birth-giver—as a reality to be celebrated rather than hidden. From a power viewpoint, Judy Chicago and her co-artists have asserted their right to create images of historic women that can be interpreted either as sociable or as obscene, de-pending on the expectations or stereotypes of viewers about what is "beautiful." Woman in this case is both the artist's object and the Artist herself, empowered to speak visually about her own biological reality.

Several of the essays in this volume examine cultural perspectives in women's communication. Among them, Secombe Eastland's study of the feminist bookstore-coffeehouse makes vivid the contrast between the goal of having a separatist meeting place and the constraint of having to open their doors to gay men and nonfeminist women in order to have sufficient income. For the women in Eastland's study, a feminist culture seems possible only if the members all share lesbian-feminist values and symbols (e.g. "womyn only"). In contrast, the women in Redwood Records adapt their communication patterns in significant ways to win and maintain outside support for their feminist projects. As Lont reports, the task of being a cross-cultural organization with feminist values places heavy demands on a communication process. Participants must reach across the feminist/nonfeminist culture boundary and try at the same time to maintain trust established within their feminist community.

Taylor and Nelson both portray ongoing groups of women who nourish a "feminist culture" of communication within larger institutions that do not model or promote those ways of interacting. In Studio D, the filmmakers attempt to support each other's creative visions while operating within the limits of a civil service organization. In the writing lab research teams, the leader tries to model collegial, informal transactions that avoid negative judgments about individuals and promote a maximum of innovation and trust. Both groups attempt to embody a feminist communication culture within a nonfeminist institution, presenting participants with the tensions of living amid two value systems at once.

Issues related to power, hierarchy, or competition emerge in all of the studies reported in this volume. The primacy of these issues may derive from the fact that patriarchy historically restricts women's knowledge and exercise of power. Women often know and recognize uses of power that we dislike and fear. Placed in settings where action has to be coordinated and leadership functions assumed, people often struggle to find other ways to use power than those they have observed. Several essays in this book illustrate the difficulty of struggling against patriarchal uses of power, though some of the individuals or groups described here achieve a degree of success in employing alternatives to status, dominance, or threat as bases of power.

Larson's study of reactions to victimization in the two Hellman plays reveals both extreme and moderate responses to being victimized by others' power. One character, Regina, becomes power-mad herself, while the maid, Addie, lacking in status or the power to force others to act, shows that she has more power of insight than her confused and self-absorbed white "masters." A third character, Alexandra, ends one of the plays appearing to have the capacity to conduct a purposeful search for equality, as her mother Regina has never done. Addie and Alexandra embody empowerment as an alternative form of power available to courageous and intelligent women.

Many of the groups described in this book attempt to change traditional power relationships or redefine power to mean empowerment for women rather than dominance by either women or men. Wyatt's study of the Weavers Guild is compatible with a traditional view of power in that it examines perceptions of leadership within the group. But Wyatt's results escape traditional categories of power or leadership.

She finds that leaders in the Weavers Guild are identified by members on the basis of a varied mix of personal qualities that aid the other members. Some of the identified leaders talk of efforts to moderate their influence within the group, by taking action intended to develop and support leadership behavior by other members. Though individual power is not denied, it is apparently not sought in this group, and greater value is given to the idea of empowering others in the development of their talent.

The Booth-Butterfields' study of the Jennies basketball team also reveals power as more acceptable if shared than if exercised as dominance by one person over another. The team combines athletic excellence in a highly competitive sport and a careful, even gentle style of interacting that the authors describe as "feminine." The authors suggest that the team offsets the intensity of their competition in the sport with a rather self-effacing style of talking about themselves and their peers. The pervasive concern to avoid interpersonal conflict within the team is a significant undercurrent in the talk of these young women. Individuals strive for personal excellence but are coached to seek team success rather than personal dominance on or off the court. Interviews suggest that the coach's power may lie in her ability to model self-control and dedication while limiting the team's exposure to distractions and the alien claim that power equals individual glory.

Strategic considerations are also involved in all of the research studies included in this book. Several of the studies give particular attention to the rhetorical choices women have to make in public and private situations. Williamson-Ige delineates the efforts of Shirley Chisholm to adapt her speeches to two different audiences of women. One of Chisholm's constraints is her own history as a black female politician who has faced opposition based on both sex and race. In contrast to other speakers who have urged black female audiences to affirm their race and avoid middle-class white feminism, Chisholm argues that all women share victimization in a sexist society, and all women can move toward equality through a philosophical and social revolution. The speaker's strategy of unification allows for differences in experience and symbols, but it ultimately portrays the sisterhood of all women.

Storytelling emerges as informal rhetoric in the research of Hall and Langellier. Their 10 storytelling strategies show how mothers and daughters can influence each other's inclusion or exclusion of certain story elements, often by means of responses as small as short phrases or single words. In the telling of family anecdotes the various forms of expansion, critique, and editing in the pairs of women emerge as rhetorical adaptations to the interview, as constructions of family history, and as enactments of the relationships between mothers and daughters.

Humor also involves strategic stories about behavior. White's study of feminist humor shows that feminists can act strategically to reverse patriarchal traditions and to create woman-to-woman bonds in moments of shared wit. When a student describes a male complaint about university health services for women as "pap smear envy," she has taken symbolic control of Freudian psychology, male-vs.-female competition, and medical tradition with three simple words. As revealed by White, feminist humor is a larger and more complex pleasure than the more patriarchal phenomenon of the "joke." Like the Aristotelian enthymeme, feminist humor develops interactively, calling on listeners to contribute their experience to the moment, and thus building a symbolic world in which feminists can overturn or reframe patriarchy for their delight and empowerment.

Implications of This Research

The material gathered in this volume supports strongly the claim that women communicating with each other try to nourish joint values and to pursue goals cooperatively. This result is more striking because the authors of individual chapters were not in contact with each other and were not urged to test particular theories. Many of them chose to work with the ideas of Cheris Kramarae and Carol Gilligan, with the result that much of the research reported here is sensitive to the muting of women's voices and the distinctive ways that women often construe situations and make decisions. Our results corroborate Gilligan's view that women's moral decision making centers on personal responsibility to actual people, based on attributing central value to caring human relationships. The research also confirms Kramarae's theoretical framework which treats women as rational speakers, examining alternatives for talk in environments which often mute their voices or ignore their words.

The theoretical and practical implications of the research in this volume are also reinforced by an unexpected source: researchers accustomed to studying not women, but American males and the values associated with a patriarchal system that has supported the paradigm of male dominance and female submission. Robert Bellah and his associates have recently described the 1970s and 1980s in America as an era during which individualism has become detached from its civic and religious roots. This process, Bellah reports, has left many people depending on only the personal accumulation of wealth or self-expression as basic sources of meaning. In *The Habits of the Heart* (1985) Bellah and his associates state the problem thus:

The question is whether an individualism in which the self has become the main form of reality can really be sustained. What is at issue is not simply whether self-contained individuals might withdraw from the public sphere to pursue purely private ends, but whether such individuals are capable of sustaining either a public OR a private life (143).

The women in *Women Communicating* make a clear response to this question. Working in many different settings, they affirm human connection while recognizing differences that emerge in the pursuit of common tasks. Conflicts between individuals arise on both small-scale and large-scale matters: mothers and daughters differ about what is appropriate to include in a family story; teacher-researchers debate about how much encouragement or pressure to give to new staff members; and filmmakers question how to credit appropriately the work done on a film. But conflict does not automatically become a reason to withdraw from social contact; nor does it lead the women involved to ignore issues of personal integrity.

Feminism in the latter half of the twentieth century has affirmed women as worthwhile individuals. At its best it has also affirmed images of community, as a context in which women—and men of good will— can accomplish more than any of us could do alone. But communities can only be built and sustained through humane communication. These studies demonstrate the intense work necessary to sustain community while people are trying at the same time to produce goods and services or attain other goals. Without awareness of others' views, shared commitment to process, and willingness to work for unity, participants drift away in fatigue or disgust. That so many of the efforts described here have not failed attests to the women's energy and to their depth of belief in joint human endeavor.

This volume demonstrates that the voices of women are varied and strong. We hope the book will further the revolution in thinking about the communicative experiences and contributions of American women.

References

Bate, B. (1988). *Communication and the sexes*. New York: Harper and Row.

Bellah, R. N., Madsen, R., Sullivan, W. M., Swidler, A., and Tipton, S. (1985). *Habits of the heart: Individualism and commitment in American life*. New York: Harper and Row/Perennial Library.

Burke, K. (1950). *A rhetoric of motives*. Berkeley: University of California Press.

Gilligan, C. (1982). *In a different voice: Psychological theory and women's development*. Cambridge, MA: Harvard University Press.

Johnson, F. (1986, April). Genders as cultures. Presented to the third Penn State conference on gender role and communication research, College Park, PA.

Kramarae, C. (1981) *Women and men speaking: Frameworks for analysis.* Rowley, MA: Newbury House.

Smythe, M. J. (In press). Analysis of the sex differences in communication research. In B. Dervin (ed.), *Progress in communication sciences.* Norwood, NJ: Ablex.

Author Index

Subject Index